Love and Hate

D1455128

Love and hate seem to be the dominant emotions that make the world go round and are a central theme in psychotherapy. *Love and Hate* seeks to answer some important questions about these all-consuming passions.

Many patients seeking psychotherapy feel unlovable or full of rage and hate. What is it that interferes with the capacity to experience love? This book explores the origins of love and hate from infancy and investigates how they develop through the life cycle. It brings together contemporary views about clinical practice on how psychotherapists and analysts work with and think about love and hate in transference and countertransference and explores how different schools of thought deal with the subject. An impressive array of international contributors present a broad spectrum of psychoanalytic perspectives, including Kleinian, Jungian Independent Group, and Lacanian psychotherapists, psychoanalysts and analytical psychologists.

With emphasis on clinical illustration throughout, the writers show how different psychoanalytic schools think about and clinically work with the experience and passions of love and hate. This book will be invaluable to practitioners and students of psychotherapy, psychoanalysis, analytical psychology and counselling.

David Mann is a psychoanalytic psychotherapist in private practice and in the NHS, where he is Principal Psychotherapist at the Tunbridge Wells Psychotherapy Service. His previous books include *Psychotherapy: An Erotic Relationship – Transference and Countertransference Passions* (1997) and *Erotic Transference and Countertransference: Clinical Practice in Psychotherapy* (1999).

Love and Hate

Psychoanalytic perspectives

Edited by David Mann

Routledge
Taylor & Francis Group

LONDON AND NEW YORK

First published 2002
by Routledge
27 Church Road, Hove, East Sussex BN3 2FA

Simultaneously published in the USA and Canada
by Routledge
270 Madison Ave, New York, NY 10016

Routledge is an imprint of the Taylor & Francis Group, an informa business

Reprinted 2007

© 2002 Edited by David Mann

Typeset in Times by Mayhew Typesetting, Rhayader, Powys
Printed and bound in Great Britain by MPG Books Ltd, Bodmin, Cornwall
Paperback cover design by Lisa Dynan

British Library Cataloguing in Publication Data
A catalogue record for this book is available from the British Library

Library of Congress Cataloging in Publication Data

Love and hate : psychoanalytic perspectives / edited by David Mann.
   p. cm
Includes bibliographical references and index.

    ISBN 1-58391-141-3 (hbk) - ISBN 1-58391-142-1 (pbk)
    1. Love-hate relationships. 2. Psychoanalysis. 1. Mann, David, 1954-

RC506 .L59 2002
616.89'17–dc21

                                             2002025440

ISBN 978-1-58391-141-9 (hbk)
ISBN 978-1-58391-142-6 (pbk)

Dedicated to my father and mother, George and Lilian Mann,
with love

Contents

Contributors

Kate Barrows is a training analyst with the British Psycho-Analytical Society. She is also a member of the Association of Child Psychotherapists. She works in private practice in Bristol and teaches, lectures and writes on a variety of psychoanalytic topics.

Francesco Bisagni was trained as a psychiatrist at the University of Milan where he worked for some years. Trained as an adult psychoanalytic psychotherapist in Milan and London, he is a member of Centro Italiano di Psicologia Analitica (CIPA) where he is a training analyst and teaches Infant Observation, Developmental Psychology and Theories of Psychotherapy. He is a member (psychoanalyst) in the US of the National Association for the Advancement of Psychoanalysis (NAAP) and has been teaching extensively in the US for many years. He was also trained as a child psychoanalytic psychotherapist in Italy according to the Tavistock Model and is now a Qualified Member of the Associazione Italiana di Psicoterapia Psicoanalitica Infantile (AIPPI). He currently lives in Milan where he works in private practice as a psychoanalyst and child psychotherapist.

Peter Geißler, DM DPhil., is a psychoanalyst, body psychotherapist, and founder of AKP (Arbeitskreis für analytische Körperpsychotherapie). His special interests include the integration of psychoanalytically oriented psychotherapy and bodily interventions, and on a theoretical level, integration of baby research in a new large theory. He has published various books on these topics.

Jackie Gerrard had a background in social work before training as a psychoanalytic psychotherapist in 1978. She is a full member, training therapist and supervisor at the London Centre for Psychotherapy and a full member of the Lincoln Centre. She works in private practice and also supervises at the Westminster Pastoral Foundation.

Sheila Gordon is a psychotherapist and an associate member of the London Centre for Psychotherapy, and has been in private practice in South

London since 1982. She previously read History at University College London followed by PGCE at the Institute of Education where she began to place her ideas about teaching and education in a psychodynamic context. She taught in a variety of schools over a period of 30 years before embarking on her second career as a therapist.

Sue Gottlieb is a psychoanalytic psychotherapist in private practice. She is a member of the London Centre for Psychotherapy and the Severnside Institute for Psychotherapy. She has a background in neurophysiology and has published numerous articles in professional journals.

Daphne Lambert is a Jungian analyst practising in Cambridge. She is a professional member of the Society of Analytical Psychology and is a Training Analyst for the Society. She has taken an active role in the growth of analytical psychology in Cambridge, which has become a flourishing centre for Jungian analysis. She has given a number of talks and workshops and also has a special interest in fairy tales.

David Mann is a psychoanalytic psychotherapist and a member of the London Centre for Psychotherapy. He is Principal Psychotherapist at the NHS Psychotherapy Service based in Tunbridge Wells, Kent. He is also in private practice as a psychotherapist and supervisor in Tunbridge Wells and South London. He previously trained as an art therapist and worked in a variety of psychiatric and therapeutic communities. He lectures, teaches and runs workshops around the UK and Europe and has extensively published in leading national and international journals. He is author of *Psychotherapy: An Erotic Relationship – Transference and Countertransference Passions* (Routledge 1997), which was also translated and published in Germany in 1999 by the Klett-Cotta Press, and he is the editor of *Erotic Transference and Countertransference: Clinical Practice in Psychotherapy* (Routledge 1999). e-mail: david.mann@being.freeserve.co.uk.

Richard Mizen is a professional member of the Society of Analytical Psychology. He worked for over twenty years in Health and Social Services and is now in full-time private practice as a Jungian analyst and as a supervisor in London and in Exeter. He is currently joint-editing a book on supervision which is to be published by Palgrave in the near future.

David Morgan is a psychoanalyst and a member of the British Psycho-Analytical Society and the British Association of Psychotherapists. He is also consultant clinical psychologist at the Portman Clinic and Chelsea and Westminster Hospital.

Lesley Murdin is a psychoanalytic psychotherapist in private practice in Cambridge. She runs the training courses in counselling and psychotherapy at WPF and has worked for many years for the UKCP, sitting on the Governing Board and chairing the Ethics Committee and Psychoanalytic Section. She teaches, supervises, has written various papers and recently a book: *How Much Is Enough*, on endings in psychotherapy, published by Routledge and edited *Values and Ethics in the Practice of Psychotherapy and Counselling* published by Open University Press.

Ingrid Pohl is a psychoanalyst in private practice in Stuttgart, Germany. Training and supervising psychoanalyst at the Psychoanalytic Institute of the 'Stuttgard Group' (Akademie für Tiefenpsychologie und analytische Psychotherapie). Extraordinary member of the German and the International Psychoanalytical Associations DPV/IPV.

Hester McFarland Solomon is a training therapist and supervisor for the Jungian section of the British Association of Psychotherapists. She is a Fellow and past Chair of the BAP and is currently Vice President of the International Association for Analytical Psychology. Author of numerous papers relating to Jungian and psychoanalytic topics, she lectures extensively in the UK and abroad. She is the co-editor of *Jungian Thought in the Modern World* (2000). To other co-edited books will appear in 2002: *Contemporary Jungian Clinical Practice* and *The Ethical Attitude in Analytical Practice*.

Martin Stanton is a psychoanalytic psychotherapist in private practice in Peckham, South London, a visiting Professor at the Middlesex University and a Consultant Staff Psychotherapist at University College London. He is author of numerous books, including *Outside the Dream* (1983), *Sandor Ferenczi: Reconsidering Active Intervention* (1991), *Out of Order: Clinical Work and Unconscious Process* (1997) and *Michael Balint: Psychotherapy as Primary Care* (forthcoming).

Paola Valerio graduated from Edinburgh University. She has completed postgraduate studies at various institutions, including Surrey and Canterbury universities and the Tavistock Clinic, and is currently involved in doctoral research looking at processes in groups for women who have been sexually abused. A member of the Jungian Section of the British Association of Psychotherapists, she has worked as an analytical psychotherapist at Invicta since 1997, providing individual and group analytic psychotherapy, supervision and assessment. She also works as a Jungian analyst in private practice in London, having previously worked as part of the Guy's and Maudsley NHS Trust between 1987 and 1997, based at the Bloomfield Clinic, Guy's Hospital. She has published book reviews and articles in various journals and retains an interest in the classical aspects of analytical psychology and in the politics of psychoanalysis.

Robert C. Ware, Drs theol. University of Nijmegen, the Netherlands, is a psychoanalytic psychotherapist and group psychotherapist. He is a native US American, married, settled and working in Germany in private practice since 1976. After completing psychoanalytic training at the CG Jung Institutes in Zurich (1976) and Stuttgart (1978), he did a six-year training course as a bioenergetic analyst in the school of Alexander Lowen. Co-founder of the Stuttgart Society for Bioenergetic Analysis. From 1988–98 he was on the editorial board for the periodical, *Korper und Seele* (Schwabe, Basel) of the Swiss Society for Bioenergetic Analysis and Therapy. Focal points of his work are the relationship between psychoanalysis and inter-active body psychotherapy, transference and countertransference, and interactive group analytical psychotherapy.

Acknowledgements

Michelle MacGrath has been my constant companion, mostly in love and occasionally in hate, my inspiration, critic, support and proof-reader, and her influence is felt in everything I do. I could not have done this book without her. I would also wish to thank our sons, Mark and Peter, who influence me in more ways than I can begin to describe.

In addition, I wish to thank various friends and colleagues for their feedback on my Introduction and my own two chapters: Liz Bonham, Carol Bunker, Maggie Cochrane, Tricia O'Dell, Kate Field, Jackie Gerrard, Celia Harding, Deborah Jones, Rob Leiper, Hilary Lester, Nick Riding, Boris Rumney, Rona Rumney and Paola Valerio. Whether I used their comments or not I found them interesting and helpful. However, the responsibilty for my final thoughts is mine. A special thanks to Celia Harding: if I had taken up all her ideas I could have filled several books!

Thanks are also due to Kate Hawes and Joanne Forshaw, Commissioning Editors at Brunner-Routledge, and to all the staff at Routledge for their assistance and support in producing this book.

Thanks as well to Jed Dmochowski and Ewa Sidorenko for their space and conversations; also to Gillian Walton for her insights.

The quotation of George and Ira Gershwin in Chapter 5 is reproduced with permission of International Music Publications Ltd. All Rights Reserved. The quotation of Doris Lessing from *Love, Again* in Chapter 15 is with the permission of HarperCollins Publishers.

Chapter 2 is a revised version of an article that first appeared in the *British Journal of Psychotherapy* 14 (3), 1998.

The desire for love and hate

(By way of a poetic polemic)

David Mann

in analytic psychotherapy too the reawakened passion, whether it is love or hate, invariably chooses as its object the figure of the doctor.

(Freud 1907)

Prologue

This book is about love and hate in psychoanalysis. Writing about such subjective passions seems more in the province of poetry than science. So in this introduction I am striving for a poetic rather than a scientific understanding about love and hate. In that regard, I have not attempted the usual introduction for a psychotherapy book which might contain an exhaustive literature review and an outline of all the chapters in the book. Rather, what I am trying to present is an account of love and hate from a deliberately subjective perspective which I hope is processed like poetry: passion converted into thought; reflection from the uniquely personal to the universal, that which turns specific passions into common themes of experience. A more scientific/rational approach runs the risk of desiccating the subject matter which, though sometimes legitimate, can be unfortunate. I would aspire to a more passionate engagement with love and hate. What follows are my reflections on a number of poetic (and occasional philosophic) images, which I hope pry open some of the themes of love and hate working from the personal to the collective and always with an eye on the significance for psychoanalysis. The various sections of this introduction are intended to expand areas of thinking about love and hate rather than to give a definitive analysis or any answers.

'Either you like somebody or you don't' (Mark, aged nine and a half)

When I began work on this book one of my children, then aged nine and a half, asked me what it was about. I said it was about why people either love or hate each other. He replied sagely, 'That's easy, either you like somebody or you don't.' Having read what some of the wisest minds in human history have said about love and hate, frankly, I have not been able to find a better definition than this to cover day-to-day relationships! In ordinary life it is as simple as that: you like somebody or you do not, and we use this criterion to try to spend more time with those that make us feel good while minimising contact with those that do not. We probably do not spend much time wondering why we like or dislike somebody, but, if pushed, some explanation can be found: 'I like her because she is funny', or 'I don't like him because he is arrogant', etc., etc. . . . .

The topic of love and hate becomes very much more complicated as soon as we try to look psychoanalytically behind our preferences and aversions. For example, we might ask does a sense of humour appeal because it allows us to sublimate hateful or aggressive feelings? Or do we not like arrogance because it reminds us of our father? At this point my son's definition begins to be less useful. It is complicated once we seek to find the unconscious motivations behind object choice, what transferences lie behind loving this person or hating that one? Where do love and hate come from: nature or nurture? This is a particular problem, especially as far as hate is concerned: are humans prewired to hate or is it a product of our interaction with the environment? If it is the latter, there is a possibility that society or individuals may one day transcend hate. If John Lennon was right when in 1967 he sung 'All You Need Is Love', then hate could be abolished. It is an idea that has motivated idealists and utopians the world over for thousands of years, and in so doing has produced a lot of hate as a consequence. In psychoanalysis, writers such as Freud and Kernberg emphasise the inherited predisposition to love and hate which the environment may influence but cannot stop; whereas Ferenczi and Suttie emphasise the environmental impact on the infant that leads to hate. There are others still who stand between these positions, linking environment and constitution. One way or another we all nail our colours to the mast on this topic; in my own case I am with Freud on this.

The origin of the idea for this book came from the concluding section of the previous book I edited on the erotic transference (Mann 1999: 173). There I noted that of the four women and six men contributors the women therapists more or less placed an emphasis on describing love to female patients while the men, more or less, wrote about sexual feelings to female patients. A personal question this left me pondering was why is it that male therapists – especially me – do not write much about love? This present book is, in part, my attempt to answer this question for myself and redress this imbalance.

In the plethora of psychoanalytic books, journals and articles about all aspects of the mind and clinical practice there is a noticeable scarcity of references to love and hate, especially to love. My impression is that these subjects give therapists no end of difficulties professionally because, as 'wounded healers' themselves, most analysts and therapists experience difficulties with love and hate in their personal lives. This is no surprise since such difficulties are most often the motivation for having a personal training analysis in the first place. To have problems with love also means having problems with hate, one of these affects cannot be in difficulty without problematising the experience of the other. In my view, problems with hate are essentially problems about love. Yet it seems that love is the difficult subject for analysts and therapists. I am in agreement when Lear writes: 'Analysts talk about sex and aggression with ease, but as soon as anyone starts to talk of love, from somewhere there instantly comes the response: But what about aggression? This would be reason enough for love to command our attention' (1990: 15), and 'Analysts tend to dismiss love as cosmological speculation for which Freud had a predilection but which goes beyond the bounds and concerns of psychoanalysis' (ibid.: 156). I would qualify this and say that the profession only talks about sex with ease so long as it is not discussed in terms of the erotic transference and countertransference (Mann 1997, 1999). However, as far as the rest of the quote is concerned there is little doubt: love is a problem on which analysts and psychotherapists have difficulty focusing.

The various chapters in this book all reveal the great stuggle that each author has in trying to describe the nature of love and/or hate. The role of unconscious transference emerges as the great determining factor. However, the nature of love and hate seems to reside more in the subjective than the objective, more in poetry than in science. My impression is that each author/chapter largely makes sense when read in isolation. There is considerable overlap between various ideas in different chapters, but there are also contradictions. Love and hate have been tricky subjects for psychoanalysis. We might wonder whether their very complexity has contributed to the relative neglect in psychoanalytic research: as therapists and writers we unconsciously opt for the relatively easy subjects where an examination does not reveal the author's vast personal ignorance. I praise the authors in this book for revealing the depth of what they know and experience, and in doing so highlight areas that require further exploration. As editor, I could not have hoped for more. I commend their honesty and courage in attempting to describe this difficult material.

This book is divided into two sections. The first concentrating on love, the second on hate, although most of the contributions discuss both and merely differ in their emphasis. It is of note that there are more chapters about hate than love (ten against seven), suggesting the former is the easier to grapple with. In my view, this would be consistant with the considerable defences that love evokes within psychoanalysis. There is also a sex divide between the men and the women writers. In Part I, only two out of the seven chapters are by men; in Part II, six of the ten chapters are by men. There is nothing scientific in this comparison, but if there is a conclusion to be drawn from the gender division of the contributors of this and, indeed, my previous book (Mann 1999) then we might be tempted to say that the men seem to find it easier to write about sex and hate (aggression) rather than love and the women seem to find it easier to write about love than sex and hate. Presumably the usual biological and cultural arguments apply here.

The intention of this book is to illustrate the complexity of love and hate in the psychoanalytic clinical setting. All the chapters are richly illustrated with clinical material to bring alive the issues of love and hate in the transference and countertransference. There is also an attempt to approach the subjects of love and hate from a variety of psychoanalytic perspectives. The various contributors represent the current diversity of psychoanalytic thinking. There are chapters from all the mainstream psychoanalytic schools: Kleinian, Freudian, Independent Group, Lacanian and Jungian. Sometimes the differences within these groups are greater than those between the schools themselves.

Written from these different perspectives the book illustrates some of the many complications and opportunities that therapists face when dealing with these passions in psychoanalysis. The aim is to at least act as a stimulus for thinking about love and hate in clinical practice.

A word about the title, 'The desire for love and hate'. It would be my contention, and I think that of many of the contributors in this book, that people have a desire for love and hate. There is a longing for both. The desire for love and hate reflects our need for different types of relationships, differing qualities of connection both within ourself and with others. I hope that what is meant by this becomes clearer as the Introduction and the chapters unfold.

> *'If any, so by love refined*
> *That he soul's language understood,*
> *And by good love were grown all mind'* – *John Donne*: The Ecstasy
> (Or an alternative subtitle might read:)
> *'Had we never lov'd sae blindly!'* – *Robert Burns*: Song

Does love lead to the deepest insights encouraging the mind to grow and understand the language of the soul, or is love totally blind with mystifying myopia? The answer apparently seems to be both. The lover feels he or she knows the heart of another, having an understanding unsurpassed in ordinary relationships. Although Freud had things to say about this narcissistic blindness (see below), he underestimates the demonstrable capacity for empathy that love sometimes brings. The paradox seems to revolve around the issue that, though we may have great insight into those we love, which is often self-evident to lover, beloved and spectator, and though we may also contain insight into why we love this or that person, love is never able to free itself from the unconscious. It would be impossible for love to save any of us completely from the unconscious and transference: even if we love and are loved do we still not have dreams? It is unlikely that even the most mature forms of adult love are ever totally free from transference. Our first unconscious love object, the mother, looms large here. Freud seems clear about the ultimate indissolubility of transference:

> This first object is later completed into the person of the child's mother, who not only nourishes it but also looks after it and thus arouses in it a number of other physical sensations, pleasurable and unpleasurable. By her care of the child's body she becomes its first seducer. In these two relations lie the root of the mother's importance, unique, without parallel, established unalterably for a whole lifetime as the first and the strongest love-object and as the prototype of all later love relations – for both sexes.
>
> (Freud 1938: 423)

So, there is, apparently, no escape from 'unalterable' unconscious transference even in mature love.

And is this any less true when dealing with hate? Are we any clearer when dealing with hate or are we just as blind? Hatred undoubtably can sometimes contain insight: we know our enemies' weaknesses and they know ours. The torturer, just like the lover, knows the secrets of the Other. Perhaps the only difference at the level of insight between love and hate is that with hate we seek to exploit the known weakness and vulnerability to cause harm and damage, whereas with love we might seek to protect or take care of the weakness and vulnerability. It would seem, therefore, that hate contains the same paradox as love: a fusion of insight and unconsciousness.

'It does not matter much what a man hates provided he hates something' (Samuel Butler)

Hate is not a respectable emotion. A number of programmes on the television and radio in recent years have discussed the subject. The conclusion generally drawn is that hate is a pretty bad thing. It is hard to hear anybody celebrate its joys. However, certain liberal 'hates' are excusable: to hate fascism, intolerance, racism, sexism is fine, even noble and a good thing. But these are abstract ideas. Nothing personal. In my view, that is sanitised hate. Real hate is less abstract and more personal. The racist's hate is not abstract: he hates the blacks because he fears they would take *his* job, scrounge from *his* taxes, rob *his* house, rape *his* woman or commit any other awful deed that would ruin *his* life. And every general of every army knows that war must always be personal: *you* kill that dehumanised invader/ defender or else *he* will kill *you*. We really hate that which will impinge on and threaten us personally.

Hate is rarely seen as a virtue. Take the Kleinian idea of hate: in the paranoid-schizoid position hate is an aspect of splitting, unrelentingly destructive in fantasy as it attacks the bad, frustrating breast. Hate is destructive and linked to the death instinct. However, hate in the depressive position may have a more positive connotation, as mentioned earlier, if what is hated and attacked leads to guilt and then reparation – the attempt to make good. Hate is positive if it makes us feel bad, thereby holding out the prospect of being turned into something else. There is a value judgement implicit in such a view: hate is bad unless turned to good. Within this framework there is no space for the idea that to hate and attack something or someone might well have a positive value in itself. Must we always make amends for hate to be acceptable? Elsewhere I have suggested (Mann 1993) that one of the functions of aggression to outsiders is to divert it away from important family relationships. For example, the father's rivalry with his son needs to be displaced elsewhere if the boy is to avoid being overwhelmed by the father's hostility and thereby preserve the family unit.

Because hate seems inevitable perhaps it also needs to be viewed in a more positive light. Children's games, at all stages of development, are replete with destructive aggression. Neubauer (1995) notes that the play of pre-Oedipal and Oedipal children reveals a subjective enemy, feared for personal reasons (the wicked witch, the lion under the bed, etc.) and representing the child's early fantasy life and displacement of the primary object by powerful symbolic images. By latency, the child no longer seeks a reason to destroy the enemy whether playing war scenes or cowboys and indians: the forces of good and bad are divided and the child seeks no further reason why he or she selects one or other particular enemy for destruction. The adolescent, in contrast, insists on the designation of who or what is right and who or what is wrong. Neubauer concludes: 'Thus it seems whether we examine our topic from a structural or object relational point of view, love and hate are part of the matrix of the human developmental condition' (1995: 154). Yet to think of hate as a good thing would seem to flout many moral, liberal, rational, enlightened and religious tenets. However, it would seem to me that hate, in certain circumstances, can be all these things. There are clearly circumstances when to eschew hate speaks more about repression of affects, reaction formation, foreclosure and general unconscious self-destructiveness and when, far from being enlightened, it is just plain madness.

Can hate be celebrated? Take an example of tribalism. When Arsenal Football Club play at home, at some point during the game, no matter who they are playing, the chant about their North London rivals will begin: 'Stand up if you hate Tottenham. Stand up if you hate Tottenham . . . [repeated again].' At this the entire stadium of 38,000 people (excluding the opposition supporters) will rise. I can assure the reader who has not been to an Arsenal home game that this is a most invigorating feeling! But can this be viewed as the thin end of a destructive wedge? What separates the tribal football chant from the killing fields of ethnic cleansing and 'final solutions'? Are these distinct kinds of hate or much the same thing merely distinguished by degree, intensity and ferocity? I would suggest that hate can be a satisfying and worthy emotion in its own right without being merely a feeling that leads to 'better' or more 'civilised' emotions such as concern or guilt. I hate Tottenham because I love Arsenal, and it is not necessary to feel guilt or concern towards them as every defeat and catastrophe that befalls them can be sumptuously enjoyed. Just as there is no light without shadows so it is hard to imagine love without hate.

Should love always be celebrated? For example, should we find the religious evangelist loving? A frequent sight on the posters outside churches is a picture depicting a landscape, a flower, a sunny sky or such like, but always devoid of anything human, presumably illustrating the love and peace of God. But is this an image of love or hatred? Devoid of the human environment, such an image is close to misanthropy, misogyny and androphobia. Is this love of God a reaction formation about the hate for anything to do with humanity or is it genuine love?

I do not underestimate the passion involved behind abstract ideals. What we love and hate are often closely linked. To illustrate with some personal examples, I would say that, along with all the usual liberal ideals, I would also use a word like 'love' to describe my passions for psychoanalysis, surrealist art, the music of Richard Thompson, Arsenal Football Club and quality neckties. All of these elicit wonderful feelings in me on virtually a daily basis, and I can get quite passionate about them. However, it follows that I hate unthought-out critics of psychoanalysis, unimaginative art, the need to explain (yet again) to somebody else who has not heard of 'Richard who?', Manchester United and Tottenham Hotspur football clubs and dull neckties! If I add to this list dog owners who do not clean up after their pet has fouled public footpaths this probably covers most of the ordinary loves and hates I am likely to feel in an average day. Yet, though these love/hates may impassion me on a frequent basis do they constitute real passion? They certainly cause excitement, are repeated and are enduring. But is this real love and hate? Though personal, they remain somewhat abstract. These cannot be the most significant loves and hates, my deepest passions. As Freud (1915) notes, love takes us into the pure pleasure relation of sexual objects both in the narrowest sense and sublimated forms. Serious loves are my family, some close friends, my work and my writing. I am also aware that the very things I love most may also momentarily elicit my hate.

My passionate hates, those devoid of ambivalence, are quite specific and are usually focused on individuals who have hurt me. I have not noticed any momentary love. Whereas love is usually mixed with ambivalence, it seems hate may be encountered more often in its pure form. But the passion of hate tends to burn itself out, either becomes cold or exhausts itself as life takes over. We move onto more profitable and beneficial relationships. Hate might even then turn to indifference as we advance into a more loving experience – that is until something else occurs to stimulate our hate once more. From there we begin the cycle again. The pendulum of love and hate never seems to stop. Perhaps love and hate are the only true perpetual motion.

'The mystery of love is greater than the mystery of death' (Oscar Wilde: *Salome*)

How much of a mystery is love? By and large I would imagine most people agree with Oscar Wilde, with the possible exception of the 'wise men' (Freud, see below) who think all love is a waste of time but who betray their preoccupations about love by their inability to ignore it. Does love become less of a mystery under psychoanalytic investigation? Consider the following:

Freud's views about love and hate, as in much of his thinking, evolved and changed over time and were not always, he knew full well, totally consistent. In 'Instincts and their vicissitudes' (1915) he linked love to pleasure: if the object becomes a source of pleasurable feelings a motor urge is set up that brings the object closer to the ego, where it is incorporated. We might then say we love the object. If the object is unpleasurable we feel 'repulsion' and hate it. The hate can be intensified with aggression, leading to an intention to destroy the object. But Freud knew that love and hate cannot be reduced to relations of instincts to their objects but 'are reserved for the relations of the *total ego* to objects' (Freud's italics). That is to say, instincts do not love objects, but the ego to its objects may love. In this case, Freud argues, love applies when there is a synthesis of all component instincts under the primacy of the genitals in the service of reproduction. The same would also be said of hate: 'The ego hates, abhors and pursues with intent to destroy all objects which are a source of unpleasurable feeling for it.' Hate, therefore, has no empirical connection to the sexual instinct but is derived from the 'ego's stuggle to preserve and maintain itself'.

In Freud's view, love and hate come from different sources and have separate development before pleasure and unpleasure make them opposites. Hate is seen as older than love and is in intimate relation to the self-preservation instinct. The early stages of love use incorporation and devouring and, in that sense, love is hardly distinguishable from hate in its attitude to the object. Not until the genital organisation is established does love become the opposite of hate. Ambivalence in love is a result of the early stages of loving which have not been wholly surmounted. In as far as hate contains a degree of ambivalence, it is of interest to wonder if this is due to a similar organisation at its early stages.

In a later work on group psychology (1921) he describes sensual love as easily extinguished once satisfied, though capable of becoming enduring when mixed with affectionate components which are inhibited in their aims. Affection, rather than sensual love, is more likely to produce lasting ties. I would link this idea to Freud's 1915 paper that unpleasure may not necessarily terminate in hate and destruction if mollified or softened by affection which lessens the hate and may even offer a context for understanding that which for the moment is frustrating. In this same paper Freud links love to narcissism and the 'overvaluation' and idealisation of the loved object: the object we love has qualities to which we aspire. The ego enriches itself with the properties of the object: 'The object has been put in the place of the ego ideal.'

By the time Freud writes 'Civilization and its discontents' (1930) he is ready to confront one of the paradoxes of love: given all the problems it causes, why does love remain popular? He notes that genital love affords the greatest satisfaction and provides the prototype for happiness. This might suggest that pursuing genital satisfaction is the way to find happiness but, as he realises, the danger is to become dependent on the external world, the chosen loved object, and, therefore, to be exposed to extreme suffering by rejection, unfaithfulness or death. He concludes: 'For that reason the wise men of every age have warned us most emphatically against this way of life; but in spite of this it has not lost its attraction for a great number of people.' Actually, I think Freud was wise enough to know, and I detect a glint in his eye as he wrote this, that these 'wise men' were just plain wrong – love with its infantile origins is not an option, simply how it is.

Klein's views about love were developed in her 1937 paper, 'Love, guilt and reparation'. She emphasised the constant interaction between love and hate. As far as the baby is concerned the mother is loved when satisfying (an integral part of the child's sexuality) and hated when his or her desires are not gratified; the hatred is harnessed to aggression and the wish to destroy the frustrating object. Yet this aggression is also felt to be destructive to the infant's own body. Since the mother is generally the first person to satisfy the child's self-preservative needs and sensual desires, and the first to give security, the part she plays in the mind is a lasting one. The mother is split in the child's mind between the good breast and the bad breast: the breast which satisfies and the breast which frustrates. The baby's impulses and feelings are accompanied by the primitive mental activity of 'fantasy-building'. Pleasant fantasies accompany actual satisfaction, while destructive, hateful phantasies are aroused by frustration. The important feature of the destructive phantasies is that for the baby, whatever is desired in phantasy has actually taken place, the bad breast has been destroyed. However, the fantasised destruction is liable to produce guilt because the good breast upon which the infant depends and which it loves is also damaged. Klein identifies the power of love with the forces that preserve life. As the infant becomes aware of the conflicts between love and hate, there arises the fear of losing the loved object. This inaugurates an important step in the psyche. Feelings of guilt and distress enter as components of love. The infant wants to mend the object that has been harmed by destructive phantasies. Identification with the object requires the capacity to disregard or sacrifice some of our own feelings and desires to be able to put the other person's feelings first. This results in reciprocal roles of taking the part of both the good parent and the good child with the loved person. In her later work Klein more fully described this changing relationship to the mother/breast as moving from a paranoid–schizoid position characterised by splitting love and hate, to a more developmentally advanced depressive position characterised by ambivalence.

Klein considers that a 'happy love relationship' implies a deep attachment, a capacity for mutual sacrifice, a sharing of grief as well as pleasure, and in common interests as well as in sexual enjoyment. Sexual satisfaction affords not only satisfaction but reassurance and support against feelings of guilt resulting from early sadistic wishes. This increases feelings of gratitude, tenderness and love. Problems in developing the capacity for love can arise in various circumstances, including if the mother expects nothing back from the child thus making the child selfish. Klein is often rightly criticised for underestimating the role of the actual parents, but she does recognise:

> The unconscious minds of children very often correspond to the mother's unconscious mind, and whether or not they make much use of this store of love prepared for them, they often gain great inner support and comfort through the knowledge that this love exists.
>
> (Klein 1937: 320)

Various problems may occur in developing the capacity to love: the child may not correspond to what the parents wished it to be; the parents may be overambitious; a fear of loving (which affects men and women) may disturb the relationship between the parents; love may be diminished by denial or suppression; an overdependence on love may be used as a defence against guilt and destructive fears. Unconscious death wishes to the mother may be carried over to her own child when she in turn becomes a mother.

Klein recognised that men often choose a woman who is like their mother and women choose a partner like their father, but these unconscious memories, feelings and fantasies are usually disguised. The new relationships must also contain 'fresh elements' in order to avoid a direct replication of the parent.

If the adult has a viable notion of him or herself as a loving and loved individual, positive feelings such as joy, appreciation of beauty and enrichment require the internalisation of a loving mother's breast and the father's creative penis, the symbols of generous and kind parents. The satisfaction of self-preservative needs and the gratification of our desire for love are 'forever linked because they are first derived from one and the same source' (ibid.: 336). Hate in ourselves may be so dreaded it may be dealt with by projection into others, whereby the frightening figures in our minds are externalised in other people with malevolent qualities. A person with a suspicous mind, for example, is likely to induce unpleasant thoughts and suspicion in others while a friendly, trusting attitude is likely to induce similar feelings in the way others deal with us. Good relations with ourselves are essential for the development of love:

> If we have become able, deep in our unconscious minds, to clear our feelings to some extent towards our parents of grievances and have forgiven them for the frustration we had to bear, then we can be at peace with ourselves and are able to love others in the true sense of the word.
>
> (Klein 1937: 343)

Just as Freud points to the importance of affection in lasting mature relationships, Kernberg (1995b) emphasises a number of qualites for mature sexual love. High on the list is the capacity for tenderness. Tenderness reflects the integration of the libidinal and aggressive self and object relations and the tolerance of ambivalence. As such, it represents the psyche pulled between the desire for fusion and 'consolidation of difference'. Also included are care, idealisation and empathy. Love is, therefore, frequently about the capacity for integration:

> This integrative function of intercourse and orgasm is also carried out in the polarity of love and hate because the capacity for fully experiencing concern for the loved person (which underlies an authentic, deep human relationship) presupposes the integration of love and hatred – that is, the tolerance of ambivalence. It seems to me that such ambivalence, which is characteristic of stable significant human relations, is activated in sexual intercourse when sexual and aggressive excitement are blended.
>
> (Kernberg 1995a: 38)

The obstacles which stop stable and gratifying relationships with the opposite sex are either pathological narcissism or an incapacity to resolve Oedipal conflicts with a full genital identification with the parental figure of the same gender. I might add that these problems may also inhibit stable and gratifying relationships with the same sex. The capacity to fall in love is the 'basic pillar' of the couple and requires the ability to link idealisation with erotic desire and the potentials for a relationship in depth, to recruit aggression in the service of love. The capacity for love is the facility for a sense of goodness in the self and the other in spite of the many risks when linking biology to the emotional world.

Finally, I wish to mention the work of Lear (1990). Freud had discovered that in the smells, feelings, secretions, inhibitions and fantasies of sexual life lay the developmental force of nature. Describing how Freud likens the mother's breast to the prototype for every loving relationship whereby the finding of an object is, in fact, a refinding of it, Lear emphasises how the breast is psychologically experienced by the infant. The breast is 'psychologically metabolised' which allows it to be subject to archaic and higher-level mental activity. This allows the possibility of every 'refinding' also being a discovery. The real world 'must in some sense be the world as it appears to us'. Because sexuality is so pervasive, the world must, therefore, be a world which is a fit object of sexual investment. Since love is historically minded it seeks its own past so love aims to restore a lost unity. Yet it also pulls in the opposite direction, fuelling higher and more complicated unities. Love, therefore, is not just a feeling or a discharge of energy but an emotional orientation to the world: 'It is via a certain type of erotic relation with the world that this development can take place' (p. 153). Love, then, runs through the world that we invest with our love. Citing Freud he makes the point that 'living means the same as being loved' (Freud 1923: 58). It is then possible to think of psychic structure as 'structured love' (Lear's italics). In a good enough world the infant's earliest identifications involve taking in a more organised love from the mother's loving responsiveness: the infant's

> Disorganised love, one might say, is doing more than seeking satisfaction or tending towards discharge. It is attacted to organised love which responds to its needs, it takes in that love by the fantasied act of identification and so becomes more organised.
>
> (Lear 1990: 169–70)

Love is more than a tendency to unification: love is active and works its way in and through the mind. It is not so much that humans make the world lovable by investing it with their love; rather it is because the world is lovable that people can develop into creatures capable of loving it. It is through the transactions of love that the individual comes to be. Lear concludes:

> Love cannot, then, stand outside love and see what it really is. The only objective perspective of love, Freud seems to suggest, is one that works its way through love. Psychoanalysis, which aims at an objective study of man, must itself be a manifestation of man's erotic attachment to the world.
>
> (Lear 1990: 181)

Lear does not have much to say about hate or aggression. He does, though, make the interesting point that he wished Freud had chosen hate or strife, and not the death instinct, as the opponent to love: love is a psychological force, death is not; death is a biological force with psychological consequences. Hate or strife would be more appropriate psychological forces to set against love. However, this incomplete account of hate leaves Lear's ideas only partially sketched. Clearly few, if any, individuals experience love in such a pure form as he describes. If we accept his description about love and the world, and I have no difficulty with that, we must also accept that the infant will experience the mother's ambivalence so that the identifications with love will also include the identifications with her hate. In addition, Lear has not allowed room for the individual's genetic disposition to rage and aggression, which will inevitably play a part in the experience of love.

Whatever the theoretical orientation of the writer, it seems that from the variety of psychoanalytic perspectives each has something useful to say about love and hate. Taking an overview it is possible to say that each contending theory has a mixture of sense and non-sense. Taken as a collective body of knowledge, psychoanalysis offers probably the greatest opportunity to understand the processes of love. Psychoanalysis is divided into factions and schools, each tending towards favouring their own self-confirming literature. In my view, this is unfortunate at the best of times but becomes especially so when trying to grapple with the truly big subjects: love and hate. The enclaves of the theories we feel comfortable with always help our understanding, but only by looking beyond our enclaves will we see the richer picture of the scope of love and hate. This may also mean looking outside psychoanalysis as well. There is a growing body of scientific research about love and hate. Within psychoanalytic writing there is a greater trend to academic objectivity. This is much needed. My only concern would be that we do not ignore art and literature. This may be particularly important regarding love and hate; such peak subjective experiences may need the best of our subjective methods to gain a full appreciation.

My overall impression about love from a psychoanalytic understanding is that it no more diminishes the mystery of love any more than looking through a telescope diminishes the mystery of the stars. Rather, the insights and knowledge lead to a greater fascination: we know more but find ourselves at a higher level of mystery. Knowledge reveals only more questions; there is always just one more poem to read; one more portrait to look at. Psychoanalysis pulls back some of the veils on love by showing the infantile origin. But in broadening the landscape of love and hate we are then confronted with the vast terrain of Passion's Empire. In my view, it is possible to love and hate these satisfying frustrations of Eros with reason and passion and yet the mystery remains.

'Love's mysteries in the souls do grow,
But yet the body is his book' – John Donne: *The Ecstasy*

John Donne draws our attention to the age-old link between the mind and the body, that love registers both in the psychological and the physical. There is little structural evidence in the brain to suggest we are hardwired for love or hate. However, the brain is hardwired for sex and aggression, pleasure and unpleasure. A rage centre is found in the brain, near the hypothalamic locus for sexual excitment. No such locus is yet known for hate or for love. The limbic system of the brain is the more primitive part of the structure that controls elemental feelings such as sexual arousal and rage. Specific neural circuits link this part of the brain with the frontal cortex which controls the rational processes and our ability to think. These two systems can be in conflict. The link is formed with neurotransmitters such as serotonin and dopamine which allow these two parts of the brain to communicate. There is some evidence suggesting that people, usually men, prone to explosive violence have either too little serotonin (which acts as an impulse inhibitor) and/or too much dopamine (which stimulates intense surges of elation). There are other studies that attempt to link rage to the presence of the hormone testosterone, which is about eleven times higher in men than in women, and it is suggested this might account for the greater amounts of aggression in men. There is also some evidence that sexual attraction is partly under the influence of chemicals produced by the body. For example, the presence of pheromones, detected by smell, heightens sexual attraction. How much such neuro-chemistry is biologically given or due to environmental impact is a matter of debate. For our purposes here it is sufficient to note that sexual excitement and rage are part of our biological inheritance and can be located organically and reside in the brain presumably for protection and survival adaptation. Love and hate, on the other hand, are affects most likely arising from these other primitive systems but, as far as we know, having no specific organic basis of their own. Blum (1995) would suggest that love and hate are secondary processes, requiring an object for their expression. Kernberg (1995a) considers the capacity for love and hate to be inborn, but requiring the environment to activate them. If they are inborn their location in the brain has yet to be discovered. However, there is a case to suggest that love and hate, like curiosity or pattern organising, are inherited potentials.

Looked at from the opposite perspective, there is increasing evidence concerning the effects of love on the physical body. Reviewing some of the literature on the impact of love and intimacy on survival of physical illness, Ornish (1998) concludes that they are powerful determinants of our health. For example, many studies have shown that married people live longer, with lower mortality for almost every major cause of death, than those who are single, separated, widowed or divorced. The percentage of people surviving at least five years after the diagnosis of cancer is greater for married than unmarried persons in almost every category of age, gender and stage of illness (Goodwin *et al.* 1987). Ornish writes:

> When you feel loved, nurtured, cared for, supported and intimate you are much more likely to be happier and healthier. You have a much lower risk of getting sick and, if you do, a much greater chance of surviving . . . While the evidence on the relationship of psychosocial factors to illness is controversial, most scientific studies have demonstrated the extraordinarily powerful role of love and relationships in determining health and illness.
>
> (Ornish 1998: 24–9)

From the infant's experience of pleasure and unpleasure develop the passionate connections to the object of love and hate. Infantile sexuality infuses the baby's experience with the mother, the mother's experience of the baby becomes instrumental to the child's sexual development. The polymorphous perversity, erotic desire with no fixed object, will become organised by the mother's ministrations to the infant's body. The mind originates and is organised through the body: the development of self is through the experience of the flesh and bodily fluids as the baby's limbs and physical needs intermix with those of the mother. In this way, the mind begins to be organised by the incestuous desires felt for each other by both the baby and the mother. The ego is thus, as Freud put it, essentially a body ego. Put another way: the ego is forged out of the fires of the body's incestuous pleasures and unpleasures. Because the body is essentially erotic in its experience with the other it would follow that the ego is therefore essentially erotic in character.

It is not only in our dreams that we are hostage to the erotic. The erotic suffuses waking life either directly or in sublimated form, whether in relation to the other or self. Despite either psychotic or perverse foreclosure of the body, the body is always there and will not go away just because it is denied · or disavowed. Psychoanalysis, with its ban on physical touch between analyst and analysand and its emphasis on 'the talking cure', seeks to emphasise the mind and the symbolic – though this can sometimes be at the expense of an awareness of the part played by the body, especially the body-erotic. The body is given symbolic and psychological significance but cannot be solely reduced to these: the body is a biological bedrock which may be influenced by psychological processes but is not governed by these alone. Yet how much does the ego remain a body ego as the psyche matures? Clearly there are circumstances where the mind will affect the body, for better or worse. But does the mind ever become independent from the body? If our brains make hostage of our dreams, can we escape, be free from biological influence? Certainly a strand of cultural determinism within psychoanalysis, coagulated around the French influence, comes close to foreclosing the biological facts of the body. The problem may be summarised by a story from the European Union. Some years ago the EU suggested standardising the size of condoms. It was the Italians who were reported to have raised objections that the proposed size was too big for them! This story may or may not be apocryphal, but that is not the issue; it does, however, highlight how biology and the mind, anatomy and culture intermix, especially in the arena of the erotic. While the erotic gives priority to fantasy and creations of the mind, it is worth noting that the content of erotic fantasy most frequently has the participation of bodies (or parts of bodies) as central to the excitement. With the exception of fetishism, most people are not excited by objects. The body, both as biological fact and object of fantasy construction, retains its status as the basis of erotic connection, pleasure and unpleasure.

'Eros sits on his throne, one of the great powers; Nought else can prevail against Invincible Aphrodite' (Sophocles: *Antigone*)

Freud opposes Eros with Thanatos. Accordingly, the psyche is dominated by two opposing drives: a life instinct and a death instinct. The importance of addressing the question of the death instinct is because this is where Freud located destruction and hatred. It cannot, therefore, easily be bypassed in a text about love and hate. Freud's hypothesis of a death instinct has been neither confirmed nor accepted by most psychoanalytic thinkers apart from the Kleinian school. Both sides in the argument have their reasons, but I do not intend to rehearse these discussions here. Rather than examinine the theories and evidence I intend to take a different approach by looking at Freud's use of metaphors and writing style. My choice of instrument here is determined by the poetic emphasis of this present thesis. If we look at Freud's metaphors we discover that Sophocles was right – nothing can prevail against invincible Eros, especially the theory of the death instinct – and that at heart, Freud probably agreed with the author of *Antigone*. (Incidentally, we might also note that when Freud nicknamed his daughter, Anna, 'Antigone' he thereby cast himself knowingly or unconsciously as her father, the blinded Oedipus. Such an identification with the characters in the master work of Sophocles might suggest Freud had a greater belief in the truth according to Sophocles rather than the truth according to himself, especially as far as his own theory of the death instinct was concerned.)

Listed below are the major metaphors Freud used to describe the life instinct, Eros (all italics are mine):

- 'the *clamour* of life proceeds for the most part from Eros' – *The Ego and the Id* (1923)

- 'Eros, which *holds together everything* in the world' – *Group Psychology and the Analysis of the Ego* (1921)
- 'the main purpose of Eros [is] that of *uniting and binding*' – *The Ego and the Id* (1923)
- 'Eros, the *preserver* of all things' – *Beyond the Pleasure Principle'* (1920)
- 'Eros alone, the *preserver* of all living things' – *Leonardo da Vinci and a Memory of his Childhood* (1910)
- 'Eros (or the love instinct)' – *An Outline of Psychoanalysis* (1938)
- '[the ego] becomes the representative of Eros and thenceforth desires to *live and be loved'* – *The Ego and the Id* (1923)
- 'Eros and Ananke [Love and Necessity] have become *the parents* of human civilisation' – *Civilisation and its Discontents* (1930)
- 'we suppose that Eros, by bringing about a more and more far reaching combination of the particles into which living substance is dispersed, aims at *complicating life* and at the same time, of course, *preserving* it' – *The Ego and the Id* (1923)
- 'Eros, the *mischief-maker'* – (ibid.)

We may note the descriptions: Eros clamours, holds together, unites, binds, preserves, lives, loves, is a parent, complicates and creates mischief.

The following are the major descriptions of the death instinct (except where stated all italics are mine):

- '*Self destructiveness* as an expression of a "death instinct"' – *Introductory Lectures on Psychoanalysis* (1916)
- 'the death instinct which is operative in the organism – *primal sadism* – is identified with *masochism*' – The Economic Problem of Masochism (1924)
- 'the aim of life is death' – *Beyond the Pleasure Principle* (1920)
- 'instinctual life as a whole serves to bring about death' (ibid.)
- '*death instinct* [Freud's italics], the task of which is to lead organic life back into the *inanimate state*' – *The Ego and the Id* (1923)
- 'the death instinct would thus seem to express itself – though probably only in part, as an instinct of *destruction*' – (ibid.)
- 'a representative of the *elusive* death instinct is the destruction, to which hate points the way' (ibid.)
- 'we are driven to conclude that the death instincts are by their nature *mute* and that the clamour of life proceeds for the most part from Eros' (ibid.)
- 'in melancholia the superego can become a kind of *gathering place* for the death instinct' (ibid.)
- 'death instinct, which desire to be at *peace*' (ibid.)

We may note these descriptions: Thanatos is self-destructiveness, primal sadism, masochism, inanimate state, destruction, elusive, mute, a gathering place, peace. What I find striking is that these images, apart from 'inanimate state', are hardly incompatible with the energised burst of life and vitality Freud attributes to Eros. Destruction, perversion, elusiveness and peacefulness are so easily compatible with the images of clamouring, uniting, binding, preserving, complicating and creating mischief we might as well ask what is the difference. And if the metaphors are so easily interchangeable what real distinction can be made of the theories? That is to say, is Freud's attempt to describe the death instinct really much different from his attempt to describe the life instincts? He would have us believe so, but his distinctions are not so clear cut. I will describe this more fully below, but it seems that the qualities Freud gives to the death instinct are even better understood as further qualities of the self-preservative life instincts.

I think we can also examine this instinct for inertia by what physics might tell us. The obvious comparison is with Newton's second law of thermodynamics: entropy ensures that in any irreversible closed system disorder always increases. This applies to the very building blocks of atoms, the fabric of the stars and the universe itself; that is to say, everything will eventually wear itself out. In effect this is a decay into inertia, but it hardly constitutes an instinct since entropy applies not only to organic but also inorganic matter. So there is no doubt that the ultimate result of life is entropy, peace and inertia from disorder and decay, but this is hardly an instinct to return to inorganic matter, which must also ultimately decay under the laws of entropy.

We could also take a religious perspective here and think of the instinct to be at peace as the Nirvana principle, as Freud thought of it: a dominant tendency to reduce internal tension due to stimulation which expresses the trend of the death instinct. Freud concedes that this gets its energy from the life instincts and in so saying virtually suffocates the existence of the very thing he is trying to breathe life into: the theory of the death instinct. I would add, in passing, that my understanding of the religious concept of Nirvana is that though this may transcend human desire, and therefore achieves peace free from bodily desire, this is far from an experience of disconnection. Indeed, the reverse seems to be the case, since what is experienced is connection with God, and, therefore, the universe. In other words, Nirvana is a proliferation of connections rather than disconnections.

But let us return to the idea that all the attributes Freud wishes to assign to the death instinct can, in fact, be more readily contained within Eros itself. Let us turn again from the truths of science and discourse and cast our light on the other source of truth: poetry. The image of Eros (or his Roman equivalent, Cupid) that has dominated Europe since the Renaissance is the soppy, Christianised cherubic baby/child. The Cupid most commonly seen on Valentine cards is a poor shadow of his former status and power. The original Cupid, pre-Renaissance, is altogether more powerful and demonic.

Hesiod, the ancient Greek contemporary of Homer, was writing nearly 3,000 years ago towards the end of the eight century BC. In Hesiod's *Theogony*, Eros is one of the three primal entities at the beginning of all things: in this creation myth first there is Chaos, then Gaia (Earth) then Eros (Love). All appear by spontaneous generation. It is tempting to think of these as baby (Chaos), mother (Mother Earth) and the pleasure bond between them, incestuous desire (Eros, Love). At any rate, the rest of creation cannot begin without Love. Eros must be present if gods and people and monsters are to come forth. It is also of note that such creation myths rarely, if ever, begin with the seeds of destruction in place. The ancient myth-makers, who intuitively understood so much of the unconscious, never suggest that in the beginning of creation there is a mythological equivalent suggestive of the death instinct. We might wonder why the myth-makers have not alluded to something so primal as an instinct towards inertia and death. But to return to my main point: Hesiod's description of Eros is of interest:

> . . . Love, most beautiful
> Of all the deathless gods. He makes men weak,
> He overpowers the clever mind, and tames
> The spirit in the breasts of men and gods.
>
> (Hesiod 1973: 27)

Eros both weakens and destroys yet also tames and civilises. Could 'tames' mean to make peaceful, to quell desire, reach a state of near Nirvana? The reader can no doubt see where I am heading here: the description of Eros seems to combine the very elements that Freud splits and allocates to the dual instincts of the forces of life and death. The point here is that, love and hate, civilisation and destruction are synonymous with a single entity: Eros.

Another illustration will underline my point. In his tale of Cupid and Psyche, Apuleius, the Roman poet writing in the second century AD, sees the former as a dangerous god:

> that most reckless of creatures, whose wicked behaviour flies in the face of public morals, who armed with torch and arrows roams by night through houses where he has no business, ruining marriages on every hand, committing heinous crimes with impunity, and never doing anything good.
>
> (Apuleius 1990: 43)

A little later, when the prophesy is made about whom Psyche will wed, Cupid is described thus:

No human son-in-law (hope not) is thine,
But something cruel and fierce and serpentine;
That plagues the world as, borne aloft on wings,
With fire and steel it persecutes all things.

(Apuleius 1990: 47)

In fact, in Apuleius' story Cupid is handsome, honest, caring and loving. What brings about his transformation is his love for Psyche and his deliberately wounding himself with his own arrow. The point worth stressing, therefore, is that the destructive, persecuting side of Cupid was well understood by the ancient thinkers; there is nothing incompatible between the god of Love and his wanton destructiveness. There was no need to hypothesis about two 'Cupids', one of love and one of destruction; there was no need for a Cupid and his brother, Thanatos. From the very beginning he was both. Love and hate unite in Cupid. However, let us abandon the Latin form and return to the original Greek and its Freudian connotations: love and hate unite in Eros.

Part of Freud's adherence to the death instinct was the need to understand the constant conflicts within the psyche. The mind is clearly in conflict, so what two opposing forces might account for it? For Freud, the dual poles of the life and death instincts conveniently describe the two antagonistic sides. But, as has often been pointed out by the critics of the death instinct, all the supposed evidence for Thanatos is just as easily accounted for by other explanations. One of the oddities of Freud's need to propose the idea of a death instinct to explain the conflict with the life instincts is that he does not seem to take full account of the ample opportunity for conflict within the life instinct itself. The struggle between love and hate, creativity and destruction within Eros would be conflict enough for most minds. Not only is aggression necessary for survival and preservation, it is often vital in the conquest of love itself. Even if aggression leads to the total destruction of an object this does not mean that disconnection or severance from the object is the goal; and even if destruction results in disconnection from an object it is often in the service of securing other connections, for example destroying a rival that threatens our relationship to a loved object. We also know from perversions, especially sadism and masochism, that this form of violent love/hate is still an attempt by the subject to stay united with his or her object. In that sense, sadism and masochism are concerned with maintaining a relationship at any price because any kind of relationship is preferable to disconnection and being alone in the universe. It would follow from this that all the attributes of the death instinct are better understood as qualities in the service of survival, self-preservation and the life instincts.

From the infant's experience of pleasure and unpleasure develop the passionate connection to the object: it is loved and hated. In this framework,

Freud's hypothesis about Thanatos can be viewed as redundant. Aggression, anger and hate are as easily understood as life instincts concerned with preservation of and relationship with the object. Hatred, including sadism, is concerned with preserving and uniting with the object in a destructive attack. It is paradoxical, but destructiveness should not be confused with either a need for peace (inertia) or severance. Even the obliteration of a hated object may be done to preserve a loved object (whether internal or external). At its core, hatred is concerned with establishing connections, not making disconnections. If anything both hatred and destructiveness, bristling with energy as they both are, are concerned more with vitality than inertia. Hatred is thus as much a part of Eros as love.

Before leaving Freud and his metaphors I wish to make one other literary comment on Freud's style. His main work accounting for the death and life instincts is his 1923 paper, *The Ego and the Id*. Throughout this paper Freud is fully aware, and reminds us, of the difficulty of finding evidence for the silent death instinct. Once he comes to the end of his exhausting journey to demonstrate his theory of duality he reaches his climax with the closing words of the paper:

> It would be possible to picture the id as under the domination of the mute but powerful death instincts, which desire to be at peace (prompted by the pleasure principle) to put *Eros, the mischief-maker*, to rest; *but perhaps that might be to undervalue the part played by Eros.*
>
> (1923: 401; my italics)

This last line is an extraordinary admission from Freud. Having laboured so hard to reach some certainty about the duality of the opposing life and death instincts he then, in the last line, completely undercuts his own argument and concedes that, after all, perhaps he has not fully taken into account the nature of Eros. He admits he has 'undervalued' Eros as a power. Of course, he may only be admitting to undervaluing the fact that Eros and the desire to be at peace are equally matched. But if they are of equal strength how could a death instinct hope to exert its influence more than 50 per cent of the time in an equal struggle? I might add that, if Freud is ready to concede he has not taken full account of the power of Eros, he might also have inadvertently given away Love's powers, depriving Eros of the hate and destruction that are some of its rightful characteristics. Eros, the unifier, is also capable of unifying love and hate, creation, preservation and destruction within a single concept of the powerful life instinct. But not only does Freud concede he has possibly underestimated Eros he also uses a striking metaphor here: Eros is a 'mischief-maker'. For sure, creating mischief is one of the classical characteristics of Eros, but nowhere else does Freud speak of Eros in this way. Why now is Eros suddenly a mischief-maker? Why has Eros gone from unifier, connector, preserver and force of love to creating mischief? I suspect that the mischief created is with Freud's theory itself. It is difficult to believe that Freud is totally unaware of the theoretical mess he has created by splitting Eros into two separate and opposing instincts. In his last line, Freud's doubts emerge: Eros has created mischief with Freud's attempt to hypothesise about a powerful and mute force in the psyche. Freud, who loved the work of Sophocles so much he identified himself with Oedipus and his daughter with Antigone, at least unconsciously knew, as is betrayed by his metaphors and last-line doubts, that Eros cannot be so easily conquered.

'One has no right to love or hate anything if one has not acquired a thorough knowledge of its nature' (Leonardo da Vinci)

The rest of this quotation from Leonardo is as follows: 'For in truth great love springs from great knowledge of the beloved object, and if you know it but little you will be able to love it only a little or not at all' (quoted in Freud 1910: 163).

When commenting on this quotation from Leonardo Freud (1910) makes the observation that such a response, though highly commendable, is not what usually happens in ordinary life and that, in fact, Leonardo is completely mistaken. If anything, humans love and hate impulsively from emotional motives which are sometimes weakened by reflection and consideration. Indeed, it is more often the case that love and hate thrive precisely on ignorance. Freud considered that Leonardo himself had led a life in which his affects were controlled and subjected to an instinct for research: he had converted his passion into a thirst for knowledge.

But, I wonder, what knowledge did Leonardo really have about love and hate? I was initially shocked when reading Green (2000) who describes him as a paedophile. To an extent this is to judge a historical figure by our present standards. However, Leonardo's sexual preference for young boys was not within the morals of his own times. Though they did not have the term, even in his own days Leonardo would have been judged a paedophile. So to return to the epigram, one of the world's greatest geniuses – artist, inventor and paedophile – tells us we have no right to love and hate unless we have knowledge. Given what we now know about perversions in general and paedophilia in particular, we might wonder if Leonardo knew anything at all about love or even how much he really understood about the nature of his hate. In the case of paedophilia love is really hate, but this hatefulness is what passes for love amongst the abused. Leonardo was a genius with a thirst for knowledge, yet we might wonder how much thorough knowledge he had about himself.

Of course none of us is perfect. I am not just trying to criticise a great man since, at some level, we all have feet of clay. Yet it is precisely this problematic feature to which I wish to draw attention. One of the problems Leonardo poses is: who can we trust as an authority to speak about love and hate? Who might we feel has more worthy insights about the nature of either? Might it be the geniuses, poets, Plato, religious leaders, politicians, agony aunts, Freud and psychoanalysis, psychologists, this writer, media celebrities or perhaps a stranger you meet at a party? They would all make a claim for our attention, but however worldly-wise they might appear one glance at their personal lives would usually convince us that (with possibly a few exceptions, if any) everyone generally seems to have much the same struggles with love and hate. After all the spillage of ink how much clearer are we? If I have any answer it is that there is no real alternative but the struggle. However limited or shallow the nature of insightful knowledge into love and hate, we must grapple with it in our own way. Of course, an individual choice (either with conscious preference or unconscious determination) might be to withdraw from loving or hating relationships altogether, but this in itself still requires the chooser to find his or her own way through the problems thrown up by love and hate. Whatever the solution, we seem to have no choice but to engage with the inherent issues that love and hate necessitate. There seems no alternative, no escape, we can only hope our survival strategies for dealing with both are good enough.

' "You must sit down," says Love, "and taste my meat." So I did sit and eat' (George Herbert: *Love III*)

How much of a choice do we have about love? Can we decline the invitation to taste the meat of love? Is love that optional, like deciding whether to have a meal or go on a diet? Up to a point it sometimes is: if in love the lover can sometimes deny his or her love or if we deny the evidence that somebody loves us. Alternatively, if love is recognised we may decide not to give it expression due to any number of reasons, such as inhibition, or a wish to preserve an otherwise stable relationship. So, in a way, there is some choice, at least for some adults.

But can we truly opt out of love? When Love told George Herbert to sit and eat was this a request or a command? The question can be looked at in various ways. As adults, how much choice do we have about love? Cupid, with his notorious blindfold, would suggest that we have little control over who we might or might not fall in love with. Why we fall for this person and not that one is usually a mixture of both conscious and unconscious factors, generally with the latter having the strongest input. Many individuals may have charmed us, appealed to the eye or mind, ignited our passion or unlocked our trust and affection, but we do not usually fall in love with them all. On the whole, there seems little free will about whom we give our heart to. Of course, falling in love is not the same as being satisfied in love. We may not be loved by the one we want who may either ignore or misuse our feelings. Unable to break their repetition compulsions, many people driven by a history of abusive relationships turn again and again to the same kind of destructive or perverse situations. Even if a more loving alternative is found it is not always taken with alacrity but rather can be experienced as boring and unexciting.

And this is not to mention the fundamental importance of transference and the residual nature of incestuous desire for the opposite-sex parent which permeates adult relationships. With this we have precious little choice. Originating in infantile sexuality, the infant's innate desire for pleasurable erotic experience begins to organise the polymorphous perversity of the infant's erotic drives: the first love and sexual objects are always the mother and/or father. This places incestuous desire right at the heart of unconscious processes and defines the prototypes of love and hate. The nature of the infant's attachments to the mother are through the experience of pleasure and unpleasure, love and hate. This experience cannot be avoided by the infant and the parent. Environmental impact may determine a good enough or less than good enough outcome for the infant, but the passions must be negotiated. In that sense, there is no opt-out clause from primitive love and hate: they have to be experienced in some way and, thereby, become either transformational or problematically inhibited. These infantile experiences of love and hate form the prototype and reside in varying degrees of influence in later adult expressions of love and hate. Love and hate, in one way or another, are inescapable. We may avoid expression of either or shun all relationships, thereby nullifying any sensation of passion, though, of course, this is itself an individual's catastrophic experience with love and hate: though avoided and suppressed, they still organise the inhibitions in the psyche.

I do not think there is much in the last few paragraphs with which most psychotherapists would disagree. I imagine the reader nodding in agreement with what I should think to most psychoanalytically minded folk would be a fairly obvious account of love in the developing psyche. I have laboured this point because I want to draw attention to something rather more unusual. It has been an extraordinary experience editing a clinical psychoanalytical book about love and hate. Truly a task of love and hate. During the early preparations of this book I thought this an interesting subject and I did not expect any problems finding contributors, or that anybody would be short of material about love and hate since, after all, this gets right to the heart of all therapeutic process. Let me assure the reader that this was a very naive assumption on my part. In fact, I was faced on quite a few occasions with replies from therapists and analysts along the lines of: 'I have no clinical experience of love or hate, no clinical material I could use. It [love and hate] has never been an issue in my clinical practice.' I found similar responses in conversation with other therapists who also seemed at a loss to think about love and hate in their clinical practice. This was all said in good faith. Do we believe this or not? I think we must at least believe they have not encountered love or hate in their clinical practice. To my mind this begs the question: have therapists not seen love and hate because it has not occurred in their practice or because they have resistance to its recognition? Either there are therapeutic cases in which love and hate are not central issues or we are talking about countertransference blind spots. Would it be cynical to suppose the latter is more likely? Then call me a cynic! I would ask how can love and hate not be present in psychoanalysis? I know from my previous work on erotic transference that many analysts and therapists have little experience of discussing this with their patients. Are we now to add love and hate to the list of the unspeakable? If therapists are not discussing love, hate and the erotic with their patients what on earth does that leave to talk about? And if we add humour (another psychoanalytically tabooed subject; cf. Lemma 2000) to the list of the unmentionable, then is there anything left that is important to humanity in general and patients in particular? If we strip love, hate, Eros, sexuality (and humour) from clinical practice how do therapists address anything of importance in the unconscious?

To an extent, the problem is understandable. There is a certain desiccation of passion when coining psychoanalytic theories and terms. For example, what passions are not being described when mothers and babies are thought of in terms of attachment (Bowlby), attunement (Stern) or reverie (Bion)? Are we really to believe that mothers and babies are not essentially about passion: do babies just attach (or not attach), or mothers just attune (or not attune)? When analysts use such descriptions what pleasures and unpleasures are not mentioned? Mothers and babies are like the rest of the population: they prefer to feel good rather than bad. If there are attachments, attunements and alpha functions it is because they are pleasurable to both mother and baby; failed attachments, misattunements and beta functions are unpleasurable. In other words, whatever it is that mothers and babies do it is motivated by the pleasure/unpleasure principle so vividly described by Freud. That is to say, love and hate; Eros, prevails. We might wonder, then, why love and hate have almost disappeared from psychoanalytic thinking; both are barely reported. Many therapists are not working explicitly with reference to love or hate. Some patients, quite a few of whom are training as therapists or analysts, never discuss love and hate as training patients. It is as though, in a world preoccupied with love, hate, sex and violence, psychoanalysis occupies a small area of the mind where they have little relevance. In my view, I cannot see how therapeutic practice is outside the realm of Eros, a point emphasised by Freud (1907): 'in analytic psychotherapy to the reawakened passion, whether it is love or hate, invariably chooses as its object the figure of the doctor'. Love and hate are omnipresent. Can we believe that love and hate no longer occur in psychoanalysis as they did in 1907? Have love and hate gone out of fashion since then? Are psychoanalytic patients these days presenting a set of problems where love and hate in childhood have not been significant issues? Has the human mind come so far since 1907 that love and hate have disappeared from life via some fast-track evolutionary natural selection? Have love and hate been displaced, have they ceded ground to other more fundamental and infinitely more significant emotions such as . . .? (If you have an answer to this question then please let me know!) Given the nature of the unconscious and the transference, it is very difficult to imagine that love and hate will not be present. We may have no influence over their existence, but what is more variable is the therapist's capacity to recognise their presence. Eros will be present, but what potential resistances in both the patient and the therapist will accompany it? I would suggest potentially rather a lot! To return to George Herbert's epigram: I do not think any of us, including therapists, have a choice but to sit and eat at the table of Love. However, on the whole, it is best to do so, as far as possible, with your eyes open.

I will conclude, as I began, with a quote from Freud on the inevitability and desirability of the passions. I think that on the subject of Eros Freud is a great stabiliser in the gales of tempestuous passions:

> The process of cure is accomplished in a relapse into love, if we combine all the many components of the sexual instinct under the term 'love'; and such a relapse is indispensable, for the symptoms on account of which the treatment has been undertaken are nothing other than precipitates of earlier struggles connected with repression or the return of the repressed, and they can only be resolved and washed away by a fresh high tide of the same passions.
>
> (Freud 1907: 113)

References

Apuleius (1990) *Cupid and Psyche*, Cambridge: Cambridge University Press, 1999.

Blum, H. P. (1995) Sanctified aggression, hate and the alteration of standards and values. In S. Akhtar and S. Kramer (eds) *The Birth of Hatred: Developmental, Clinical, and Technical Aspects of Intense Aggression*, Northvale, N.J. and London: Jason Aronson Inc.

Freud, S. (1907) Delusions and dreams in Jensen's 'Gradiva', Pelican Freud Library, vol. 14, Harmondsworth: Penguin Books, 1987.

Freud, S. (1910) Leonardo da Vinci and a memory of his childhood, Pelican Freud Library, vol. 14, Harmondsworth: Penguin Books, 1987.

Freud, S. (1915) Instincts and their vicissitudes, Pelican Freud Library, vol. 11, Harmondsworth: Penguin Books, 1985.

Freud, S. (1916) Introductory lectures on psychoanalysis, Pelican Freud Library, vol. 1, Harmondsworth: Penguin Books, 1979.

Freud, S. (1920) Beyond the pleasure principle, Pelican Freud Library, vol. 11, Harmondsworth: Penguin Books, 1983.

Freud, S. (1921) Group psychology and the analysis of the ego, Pelican Freud Library, vol. 12, Harmondsworth: Penguin Books, 1991.

Freud, S. (1923) The ego and the id, Pelican Freud Library, vol. 11, Harmondsworth: Penguin Books, 1983.

Freud, S. (1924) The economic problem of masochism, Pelican Freud Library, vol. 11, Harmondsworth: Penguin Books, 1983.

Freud, S. (1930) Civilisation and its discontents, Pelican Freud Library, vol. 12, Harmondsworth: Penguin Books, 1991.

Freud, S. (1938) An outline of psychoanalysis, Pelican Freud Library, vol. 15, Harmondsworth: Penguin Books, 1993.

Goodwin, J., Hunt, W., Key, C. and Samet, J. (1987) The effects of marital status on stage, treatment and survival of cancer patients, *Journal of the American Medical Association*, 3, 125–30.

Green, A. (2000) *Chains of Eros; The Sexual in Psychoanalysis*, London: Rebus Press.

Hesiod (1973) Theogony. In D. Wender (translator) *Hesiod and Theognis*, Harmondsworth: Penguin Books.

Kernberg, O. F. (1995a) Hatred as a core affect of aggression. In S. Akhtar and S. Kramer (eds) *The Birth of Hatred: Developmental, Clinical, and Technical Aspects of Intense Aggression*, Northvale, N.J. and London: Jason Aronson Inc.

Kernberg, O. F. (1995b) *Love Relations: Normality and Pathology*, New Haven, Conn., and London, Yale University Press.

Klein, M. (1937) Love, guilt and reparation. In *Love, Guilt and Reparation and Other Works*, London: Virago Press, 1988.

Lear, J. (1990) *Love and its Place in Nature: A Philosophical Intrepretation of Freudian Psychoanalysis*, New York: The Noonday Press.

Lemma, A. (2000) *Humour on the Couch: Exploring Humour in Psychotherapy and Everyday Life*, London and Philadelphia: Whurr Publishers.

Mann, D. (1993) The shadow over Oedipus: the father's rivalry with his son, *Free Associations* 4(1): 44–62.

Mann, D. (1997) *Psychotherapy: An Erotic Relationship – Transference and Countertransference Passions*, London: Routledge.

Mann, D. (1999) *Erotic Transference and Countertransference: Clinical Practice in Psychotherapy*, London: Routedge.

Neubauer, P. B. (1995) Hate and developmental sequences and group dynamics: concluding reflections. In S. Akhtar and S. Kramer (eds) *The Birth of Hatred: Developmental, Clinical, and Technical Aspects of Intense Aggression*, Northvale, N.J. and London: Jason Aronson Inc.

Ornish, D. (1998) *Love and Survival: The Scientific Basis for the Healing Power of Intimacy*, London: Vermilion.

Part I

More about love than hate

Chapter 1

In search of love and hate

David Mann

> Psychoanalysis is nothing if not a special emotional relationship between analyst and analysand.
>
> Lear (1990: 5)

Love and hate: 'Now you see it, now you don't'

In this chapter I wish to explore ideas about how much therapists love their patients and how much the therapeutic process is an act of love. To talk about love necessarily includes a consideration of hate which will also be addressed in this chapter.

Most therapists probably agree that love and hate are important in most therapies. After all it is a truism in psychoanalysis that most patients 'fall in love' to some extent with their therapists but, as time goes on, will experience some degree of hate as their wishes are frustrated. And inevitably every countertransference will be a mixture of positive (loving) and negative (hating) feelings. Winnicott (1954) saw love and hate built into the analytic setting itself: 'The analyst expressed love by the positive interest taken, and hate in the strict start and finish and in the matter of fees. Love and hate were honestly expressed, that is to say not denied by the analyst' (p. 285). Nevertheless, despite these assumptions about love and hate as inevitable transference and countertransference issues there is minimal discussion of either in the literature. As Gerrard (1996, 1999) notes, love in psychoanalytic work 'has been much neglected'; Blum (1997) makes a similar observation about hate. In fact, although love and hate can be inferred in much psychoanalytic writing, description and discussion is hardly ever couched in such terms. Love and hate are not generally thought of in those words – they are usually avoided. In psychoanalysis, love and hate are passions that do not easily find a thinker. There is clearly a tension here: while there is a general acknowledgement of the pervasiveness of love and hate in psychoanalysis there is a marked under-reporting of either in seminars, conferences or the literature. It is not my intention here to explore the reason behind this discrepancy, although I do wish to draw attention to the level of ambiguity that love and hate have within psychoanalytic theory and practice.

The qualities of love are not easy to define. Love seems to be used to describe a wide variety of situations. The ancient Greeks had different concepts to describe this profusion: *agape* = brotherly love, *eros* = sexual love, and *philein* = love of truth or knowledge. Fromm (1957) makes similar distinctions and lists a whole variety of loves: that between parents and child, brotherly love, motherly love, erotic love, self-love and love of god. Suttie (1935) equated it with feelings of tenderness. Menninger (1942) had seen love as 'experienced as a pleasure in proximity, a desire for fuller knowledge of one another, a yearning for mutual identification and personality fusion' (p. 272). Freud (1915a) largely conflated love and sex and used the terms interchangeably. Bergmann (1988) proposes that Freud had three distinct theories of love: it originates in infantile prototypes; with narcissism the self can be taken as a model for a love object, the ego ideal is projected onto the love object and love is reciprocated; in *Instincts and their Vicissitudes* (1915b) Freud tried to show how the sex drive becomes love after a synthesis of all the component instincts under the primacy of the genital and in the service of reproduction.

In previous publications (Mann 1997a, 1999) I have subsumed love under the general umbrella term of 'erotic'. The very word 'love' spans a range of emotions from strong liking, to a maternal care and protectiveness (which has a strong appeal in psychoanalytic circles), to lust or spiritual *agape* (a love that transcends the merely sexual). Love is truly amorphous and allusive and resists specific definition. Yet the irony is that, though it is difficult to define, most of us somehow feel we recognise it when we see it in others – whether it is between parent and child, adult lovers or loyal friends. We know it when we see it but would be hard pressed to say exactly what it is we see. Some people, as I will elaborate below, do have trouble recognising love in others, and this is often connected to pathological disturbances in their capacity to feel or experience love.

The loving therapist

Summarising some of the literature, Gerrard (1996, 1999) notes that the patient needs to experience 'the therapist as a loving mother' (1999: 30). Such loving feelings would include qualities identified by Coltart (1992) as patience, endurance, humour, kindness and courage. To this list is added containment and reverie (Bion 1970) and 'extreme tenderness' (suggested by Suttie 1935). Gerrard emphasises that these loving feelings must emanate from the therapist's authentic self. In emphasising this she wishes to avoid the suggestion of a sentimental idea about love. In my view, though, such a description of love devoid of incestuous and sensual pleasure, not to mention the conspicuous absence of hate, does not easily succeed in escaping the alluring idealisation of sentimentality. Winnicott (1947) draws attention to the function of the inevitable hate that a loving mother feels towards her child. What is absent from this description of a 'loving mother' is a mother with passions and desires. I would also add, and perhaps this is a particular objection that a male therapist would make, that it seems unhelpful to me to set the therapist up as a single parent. If there is love in the analytic setting it will surely also touch issues about 'a loving father' (to adapt Gerrard's phrase), and would these feelings be any different from those ascribed to the 'loving mother'? If a loving father and a loving mother are different, what distinction do we wish to make about such parental love? What we could say about this psychoanalytic construction of 'the loving mother' is that she is modelled on what psychoanalysis would consider to be the ideal analyst (I shall take up this point again in the discussion section, pp. 42–6). It seems to me that fortunately for most infants the ordinary, good enough, loving mother is not like the psycho-analytic construction but will have a more passionate relationship with her children. A mother, like everybody else, has an unconscious so therefore experiences a mix of erotic loving and hating feelings and fantasies. In my view, if psychoanalysis is going to take the mother and baby unit as its template then it needs to acknowledge the passions that both participants feel for each other.

The British object relations tradition (Klein, Fairbairn and Winnicott and their followers) has usually tended to take fright and flight from the Freudian concept of Eros. Freud is quite clear on this point: erotic attraction is the active ingredient in analysis and in the psychological development of the child. So, while Gerrard's description of the loving mother usefully opens up the discussion about love in psychotherapy she does not avoid the pitfalls of a sanitised, sentimental love as a consequence of severing love from Eros. I would, therefore, broaden and build upon Gerrard's description by reintroducing Eros. I would say the patient needs to experience the therapist as a loving mother *and* father who, in addition to possessing patience, endurance, humour, kindness, courage, reverie, con-tainment and extreme tenderness will also allow for a full experience of the necessary life-enhancing passions and desires of love and hate. This is no prescription, nor simply an application of technique. Along with Gerrard, I would agree this must be authentically experienced as love and hate.

The depressive position

Gabbard (1996: 20–1) notes that Kleinian theory tends to overvalue the love in the depressive position, with the emphasis on integrating, guilt and concern. He points out that the love in the paranoid–schizoid position can have a distinctly creative quality: 'what is integrated in the depressive position is broken up and created anew in the paranoid–schizoid position

. . . The fragmentation inherent in paranoid–schizoid functioning springs from the lover's reaction to momentary passions. With respect to staying in love, the stability of the relationship is informed, negated, and preserved by its spontaneity.' Gabbard sees the rhythm between these alternating states as essential to love that does not stagnate: feelings of buoyant merger and intolerance of separation fuel love as much as guilt and concern.

If we stop to consider what ordinary loving mothers are like with their infants it does not take us long to see that they are not all patience, tenderness and thoughtfulness: mothers as well as infants move between paranoid–schizoid and depressive positions. At times, they will hate their babies; at other times the love is so intense they wish to gobble the infant up – and in fact pretending to do this is very pleasurable to both. But when the mother is angry and hates the infant what then? The infant must gradually come to realise that when the mother hates him or her it is not forever, nor is it hating everything about the child; also that the mother's hatred does not lead her to annihilate the baby but that the excess of negative feelings will be contained and restrained. Essentially, the infant must come to realise that the momentary hate will be limited and does not overwhelm the mother's love. In suggesting this, I am expanding the Kleinian view of the depressive position to contain not just the child's awareness of ambivalence towards the parent but also the child's awareness of the parent's ambivalence to him or her. This ambivalence is not just a 50/50 split between love and hate. Rather, with the ordinary mother the positive loving feelings overwhelmingly dominate the hate, which enables both the mother and child to survive and thrive. Loving must always contain some ambivalent hate, but the love exceeds the hate. The child can come to feel secure in his or her mother's love when her hate is experienced as managed and love-dominated. In this way, the movement from the paranoid–schizoid position to the depressive position is an intersubjective development – that is to say, a realisation of the relational connection between our mind and that of the other. Not only does the infant realise that the person that is hated is the same as the one that is loved but also that the mother who he or she has experienced as hating him or her is the same as the one they know loves them. I think this reformulates the depressive position in a more complete way by allowing inter-psychic as well as intra-psychic development; that is to say, the depressive position is essentially relational. And all the while, both the mother and child move back and forth from paranoid–schizoid to depressive loving and hating, integrating, disrupting, creating and stabilising love and hate anew.

The patient, the analyst and love

Why do patients usually seek psychotherapy? Now this is clearly a complex question and no general explanation applies to all. It is not true for all patients, but is probably true for most, that generally a person seeks psychotherapy because they experience problems in their intimate relationships and are having difficulties with loving and/or feeling lovable (Mann 1997a). In this respect, most psychotherapy is usually concerned with developing the relational capacity for intimacy and love. Again, Freud is quite explicit here: 'Every psychoanalytic treatment is an attempt at liberating repressed love which has found a meagre outlet in the compromise of a symptom' (1907: 90). Generally, when beginning therapy patients (and quite a number of therapists) do not feel lovable. They may feel either that they are empty, with no love inside them, or that their relationships are false, or, alternatively, they may feel full of negative experiences and badness (hate). Other patients might have a notion of love but find it difficult to express it. Of course, this inarticulation or inhibition is itself the habitual way the patient expresses their love. Predictably the patient's problems with love find expression in the transference. Love and hate come to dominate the transference in all their manifestations, including erotic expression (Mann 1989, 1994, 1995, 1997a, 1997b, 1999, 2001; Green 1997). If it is a truism that patients fall in love with their therapists then the difficulties with love will emerge in how they love the therapist. In the same passage just cited Freud goes on to write: 'that in the analytic psychotherapy too the re-awakened passion, whether it is love or hate, invariably chooses as its object the figure of the doctor'. But the therapy is also an opportunity for a new transformational object (Mann 1997a) so the repetition is never an exact replica of the past but becomes infused with the therapist's capacity to be different.

Love can seem a risky business. Fairbairn (1940) makes the point that love can feel too threatening. Love can close down psychological distance between individuals and, therefore, can be experienced as a threat to a fragile sense of self. Hate, on the other hand, creates more distance and erects barriers against the potentially destructive nature of intimate contact with the other. I would elaborate this further and say that hate also enables the individual to maintain contact with others since it still maintains a passionate connection. However, the advantage of creating distance is that this enables a connection, a relationship, that does not threaten to smother the self. Schizoid traits in the personality may leave the individual feeling more comfortable inducing hate rather than love in libidinal objects. Dealing with hatred and aggression can, in this sense, be much safer than the intimacy of love. Describing sexual passion, Kernberg (1995) also points to a significant feature of mature love: that it implies an act of hope in our own goodness and the goodness of the other, that giving and receiving love will not do harm either to ourselves or the other. We trust that if somebody is inside us they will not do harm and that if we are inside them they will neither harm us nor be harmed. Love implies a mastery of ambivalence: that tenderness and concern will contain and detoxify aggression. This hope in the goodness of ourselves and the other will need to survive the vulnerable position that love places us in: when in love the individual runs the risk of severe hurt as the loved object may be lost, may die or reject us. Love thus forces the individual to face his or her dependency on the object that is needed. This has been poetically put by Shakespeare in *Venus and Adonis*: 'If I love thee I thy death should fear.' For these reasons love is a much more difficult emotion to tolerate and manage than hate. The ability to give and receive mature love requires sufficient ego strength and a capacity to not be threatened by emotional proximity and distance, and a trust that tender intimacy will not result in aggression. A therapeutic issue from this is that most patients on entering psychotherapy do not have a trust in the hope that they and the therapist will survive the expected mutual aggression, that the intimacy of therapy could be loving rather than aggressively hateful. For therapy to achieve its optimal efficacy both the patient and the therapist will gradually need to acquire a sense that the other will not harm them.

Just because the patient experiences him or herself as unloving and unlovable this does not, of course, mean they are unlovable. Any individual can subjectively feel they are unlovable or unintelligent or unattractive or lacking a sense of humour whereas an observer might realistically perceive that individual to be quite lovable, bright, attractive or humorous. The point is that others might not experience us as we experience ourselves. On the other hand, though, if we do feel unlovable the repetitions of the transference in our relationships will often bring about enactment in the other leaving them feeling we are intrinsically unlovable, which then confirms our subjective experience of ourselves. Characteristically, what the patient initially brings in the transference is their dysfunctional way of loving (and hating). In that sense, the transference is how the patient loves the therapist. That is to say, they will love and hate the therapist the way they have loved and hated significant others from the past. This is the problem posed by the transference when somebody who feels themselves to be unlovable or unloving seeks therapy. The transference will often make it difficult for the therapist to have an authentic loving feeling towards them. In that sense, the patient makes him or herself unlovable and, through enactments, the therapist is likely to experience the patient in that way, thereby confirming the patient's worst fears. The picture is further complicated when we introduce the therapist into the equation. As Gabbard notes:

> However, the other person in the room, the analyst, also brings characteristic patterns of loving into the relationship. The love that each of them feels is in part a reaction to the specific nature of the other's individuality so that the 'love' experienced by both patient and analyst is jointly constructed to some extent.
>
> (Gabbard 1996: 110)

Though this chapter is essentially about love this cannot be addressed without reference to hate. There are plenty of thoroughly reasonable grounds why it is possible to hate somebody in a healthy way; indeed where hating *is* the only healthy response (see Chapter 9). In psychotherapy, just as a patient (and therapist) will bring a dysfunctional form of loving with varying degrees of incapacity to love, so too will they bring a more pathological, dysfunctional hate which disturbs this relationship. The importance of hate is that, like love, it is a passionate connection to an object and, therefore, locates the patient and therapist in intimate issues of aggression concerning fusion and differentiation: how each may destructively get inside the other or fight to remain separate. To establish a relationship with what is unlovable (hateful) in the patient might be the first stage in the therapist making authentic contact with him or her. Being aware of what the patient does to make us hate them or what it is about our own erotic subjectivity that makes people/the patient hateful to us means (1) we establish an authentic emotional link with the patient and (2) we are reminded that we have a wish to be therapeutic. The wish to be therapeutic regarding hate and unlovability exemplifies the therapist's love. In this process the therapist and patient need to find a way of hating and loving each other that is less fantastical and that has a more realistic relation to love and hate.

The nature of the therapeutic action relies on the unconscious passionate engagement that psychotherapy provides. Here two individuals, each with an unconscious full of loving and hating fantasies and feelings, incestuous and murderous desires, come together expressly to work out and understand the intermixing of unconscious experience and why it is they passionately hate and love one another or what sort of obstacles they both experience that inhibit genuine love and hate. In as far as they do this more or less successfully we could understand this as the triumph of love over hate. In as much as the therapist and patient fail, hate has got the better of the relationship. The patient, we know, is looking to be loved by the therapist and in the transference will want to make the therapist an unrealistically lovable (or hateful) person. Just like the ordinary loving mother who keenly waits for the baby's smile of pleasure and recognition, the therapist has, I believe, a similar experience of wanting to be loved and may also unconsciously and unrealistically make the patient either lovable or hateful. Since this is unconscious, both participants are likely to experience resistance concerning the recognition of the fantastical nature of their love and hate. Levine (1994) has described the transference and countertransference as a continual 'stream of jointly created events'. In that respect, we keep in mind that analysis is always a two-person enterprise. Both the patient and the therapist are evoking and repeating their habitual patterns of love (and hate). However, these patterns are a result of mutual influence: the erotic subjectivity of each is influenced and modified by the erotic subjectivity of the other. The transference is never an exact replica from the past but is subject to variation, depending on the mix with each object. This presents both of the analytic participants with not only a chance to repeat their old pattern of love and hate but also allows the possibility to love and hate in a different way from the past.

Clinical

I wish to use the following clinical material to illustrate my themes.

Mr C is in his mid-forties. He came to therapy because he has a fantastic life that others would envy; but he was not happy. He quickly told me he hated his mother, all his siblings felt the same way and they would compete for who hated her the most. He assured me it was him. Mother was all bad: 'she could torture for England at the Olympics' was his experience of her. He seemed locked into a cycle of hatred, violence and revenge for his now dead mother. He recalled two lads who had killed their parents on the island of Jersey a few years earlier. He understood them. He felt he would like to kill his mother but was cheated by her death. He thought that revenge was the only way of satisfying his hate. For a while during the therapy he was obsessed with killing and torturing his mother. He realised the torture he wanted to inflict was quite specific: he wanted to tie her up and force her to listen as he told her again and again all the wrong she did to everybody and what he felt about her. In this way he was both identifying with the aggressor's wish to do what was done to him, while the psychic violence of the revenge fantasy also entrenched his self-criticism, thus perpetuating what was felt as his mother's torture of him. He was therefore continuing the violence against himself that his mother had begun. This was gradually relinquished as he realised that his hatred kept him too passionately connected to his mother. He suddenly remembered the emotions he always felt most acutely when Mum was ignoring him for days on end. When she at last spoke, even if only to utter a criticism, he felt happy to have her attention again. Thus his mother's hatred formed a connection, was the currency of contact: being nasty was at least a relationship, the alternative was an unbearable emptiness and disconnection.

Having so much mutual hatred made separation and mourning difficult. In fact, he had never fully separated. His marriage had degenerated into a replay of his childhood at the birth of their first child. From then on he experienced his wife as his mother and, in many respects, his wife then responded with mutual retaliation. Only by gradually relinquishing the hateful attachment to his mother could he then improve his marriage and begin significant psychological shifts away from his mother. His wife noticed the difference and their relationship improved.

In the transference he tried to resist the conscious recognition of his experience of me as his negative mother. At different times he felt I was 'staring him out' or deliberately withholding my thoughts. At other times, he thought I was bountiful in generosity in the way I shared my thoughts.

But at this stage, having relinquished some of the hate, he had nothing to fill the emptiness. This emptiness reminded him of his mother's sulking silence. Emptiness felt annihilatory. It could feel dead, terrifying. It was often tempting to slip back into the revenge fantasies to fill himself up with a feeling that at least seemed vitalised. What was lacking was anything as an alternative to hate as a form of intimate connection.

Up until this stage I had felt nothing special about this therapy. It had progressed well because I had been technically good enough: 'all in a day's work' as I have come to think about non-authentic involvement. I do not mean this in a pejorative manner, but to indicate those aspects of clinical practice when the therapist uses the conscious resources at his or her disposal. Empathy and theoretical understanding, both of which lubricate the analytic process, establish rapport but are not necessarily where the important work is done. The transformational material resides in unconscious operations. During one session my mind wandered to a memory of the previous weekend when I played with a dog that was jumping up and licking me, much to our mutual pleasure. I am used to what appears to be random thoughts popping into my mind but I could not see this memory of the dog in any way as a piece of useful countertransference material so I dismissed it from my mind. A few minutes later Mr C then summarised what he had been saying by concluding, 'You *can* teach an old dog new tricks and I am sure I *can* be different.' The imagery startled me as, being canine, we had just both shared what had seemed to be a positive feeling about dogs. Of course, this might just have been a chance encounter between our thoughts but it was my impression that one was linked to the other. These had appeared as two separate thoughts but they were unconsciously connected. It made me realise that what Mr C was wanting was a loving mother, not just a different mother to the one he had experienced as a child but also one different from me: that we should enjoy each other (as I had with the dog) and learn (as he wished).

A slip of the tongue during a session betrayed his desire. He said he had read a book called, *Women are from Mars and Men are from Venus* [sic]. I commented on his incorrect recall of the title, suggesting he was not only locating all the Mars/warlike aggression with his mother/women rather than with men but that the Venus/love was with men and him. I thought he was trying to tell me he was trying to locate an image of himself as lovable despite his experiences with his mother and was wondering, perhaps, whether we could be a loving couple. I think I needed to appreciate that experience. In fact, I had been more aware of the mild irritation he stimulated in me concerning everything from his periods of smug complacency to my conscious envy of his material circumstances, or to what I took to be his doubtful praises about my therapeutic efficacy. What I had given less attention to were the likeable and lovable sides of him that were trying really hard to emerge, not just in the therapy but in his marriage and with his children. I think what was being re-enacted was an overemphasis on his faults as had happened with his mother and wife, at the expense of all that was lovable about him. The fact of my having located the capacity for a strong positive feeling towards him seemed to have beneficial effects in his marriage. Over the next few weeks he reported a definite change in their relationship. His wife now reported that the most significant difference she had noticed was that he was now listening to her. My understanding is that he had not previously listened to her because the transferential hate had got in the way. Once I was able to recognise something in him that was not hatable, but was more deserving of love, so he was able to relate to his wife in a more loving way.

I will describe a second patient to illustrate the issues of love and hate in a different aspect. Mrs W described herself as filled with anxiety and anger, which she located as a sensation just below the ribs as though somebody was constantly hitting her. She had had a poor relationship with her mother, especially once her father had left home when she was ten. Her adult life had been lived in a manner persecuted by all and sundry; she was estranged from her ex-husband and children. She thought she had failed at everything, including as a mother. Her mother had always wanted a boy, so Mrs W had felt a disappointment from birth. In my view, she also poorly mothered herself.

The whole of life was experienced by her as a continuous impingement on her well-being. Rather like the narcissistic misanthropes I describe in Chapter 9, she hated the world and wanted to be free from people. She felt as if she had no skin. She wished to be cared for 24 hours a day, like a baby, and bitterly resented all those, including me, who did not provide her with this.

We spent a long time in her therapy trying to make connections between her past and present, but it had little meaning for her. She hated herself and thought others would have the same feelings about her as she did towards herself. She believed other people would think she would be better off dead, and was convinced that I, too, would prefer her dead. She had always associated violence as belonging to others, but came to realise not only her own violence in wishing to destroy other people but also towards herself. She readily felt this expressed her masochistic tendencies. She said she did not like the kind of non-directive therapy I practised; that it was less helpful than a previous period of CBT with a psychologist. Since I did not give her answers she could not use what I did say, which she generally felt compounded her sense of helplessness.

Though there was much that was very positive about Mrs W, her capacity to indulge in self-pity was strongly repellent. Though I never said as much, my feelings about her led me to be particularly challenging, though falling short of the outright attacks that would have played into her masochism. Consciously, I knew I was anxious to avoid an enactment whereby my aggressive dislike, which certainly felt like hate, might make me sadistically too challenging. It slowly dawned on me that my conscious attempts to avoid one form of enactment meant I was unconsciously falling into a different sort of enactment. In this case, feeling inhibited about my possible aggression actually stopped me from recognising the vitality and liveliness of some of her more difficult sessions. Though I did not wish her dead, there were times when she appeared dead, lifeless and inert. We were most engaged, most connected, at precisely those times we were both, for different reasons, anxious with each other: her expecting to be attacked, me worried I would attack her. At these times we both found the therapy difficult. At this level of mutually inhibited sado-masochistic aggression I came to think that this connection is what passed for love in Mrs W's life; that she was not just repeating a hateful kind of relating but that this was a kind of loving, as intimate as she could get. Whatever the quality of relationship, we were definitely psychically inside each other at an unconscious level. For her, love was a frightening business. Realising that I had been in the grip of a countertransference inhibition that was affecting what I could feel, think and say freed me from fearing both my aggression and her masochism. I saw that these were both aspects of her way of loving.

Having understood this, I now began to address my interpretations to this transferential hating-love of hers. I could sense these interpretations were neither spoken by me with aggression nor received by her with masochism. We connected at a place different from our previous mutually inhibited positions. For example, in reply to my comment about her anxiety that I could be inside her in a new way, a way unlike the masochistic relating that was familiarly comfortable, she said, 'No matter how much you are loved you are always alone when you die.' I took this to mean she could not allow something loving inside her since it could not weaken or lessen the hate. She hated the idea of dying because 'even in Heaven you must share God with others'. What she wanted was an exclusive relationship. She felt she could only be understood if somebody was right inside her, and she in them in the way she was used to. This was a fusional fantasy leading to a trauma because she could not come to terms with the difference between herself and another.

During this process she came to realise that her hate for me was her form of loving, that she used this to establish intimacy and a connection. The hate meant she could consciously keep me at a distance but unconsciously keep us passionately and closely bonded. She talked about it being a crime for her to allow a good experience. She felt her crime was to be born a human, and to escape punishment she had to divest herself of human feelings, particularly love, aggression and her sexual-self. What she gradually came to realise was that she was human after all and that was all right. She felt less persecuted by my interpretations. Much to her surprise, in her life outside therapy, she started a relationship.

A series of dreams illustrate this psychic change. She had had a recurrent nightmare for many years of being in a house that is menacing. Though there were variations on this theme the 'story' remained the same. The first dream upon starting therapy was in this vein: 'I am in a house alone. I know there is something bad in the house but I cannot see it.' She thought the house must represent her or her life. At this stage she is aware of hate, bad objects and aggression but cannot identify the source and certainly does not recognise it as her own. By the middle of her therapy I had begun to see her hating as her form of loving, so our connection to each other had begun to change. With this her dream also began to change: 'I am in a house made of cardboard, it is raining and the sides are collapsing but I just sit there frightened.' She thought the falling-down house was a breakdown of her old self and defensive walls, that the therapy might be getting through to her. The prospect of this change left her vulnerable and anxious. Towards the end of the therapy the dream changed again, a split emerging: 'I am still in a house that feels threatening but now there is part of the house that feels good but I can't get into it.' Next there were two houses, one threatening and one lovely. She was in the former but felt she might just cross over to the lovely one. I think these dreams represented staging posts along our journey from therapeutic hate to love. First she needed to recognise her hate; then she saw the hate as her kind of loving; and finally she came to a different kind of positive love. We could say that, initially, it was easier for her to hate me than to love me. However, I think the more accurate reading is that hating me was her love, and it was only by both of us enduring this sadistic/masochistic love that could she find there might be another way of loving, a more loving love not dependent on destructive hating to form a relationship.

What I have tried to illustrate in the two examples of Mr C and Mrs W is the passionate engagement between the analyst and analysand at a deeply unconscious level. Each will become intimately inside the other and will reproduce their habitual patterns of loving and hating. In both examples I saw this indicating first a repetition of old modes of passionate relating that then moved onto a different kind of connection. In my view this process was best understood as a movement from dysfunctional loving full of hate towards a more functional form of loving where intimate contact could be made without fear of destruction.

Discussion

Neutrality as a defence against passionate intimacy

Developments in the psychoanalytic understanding of countertransference have advanced considerably since the 1980s. There is now widespread agreement, at least amongst those who write about the subject if not the greater part of the non-writing profession, that patients and analysts are likely to share similar affects and experiences with the same degree; love, hate, sexual feelings, along with other affects, can be more openly discussed and acknowledged within the profession.

Yet psychoanalytic understanding develops in an uneven manner: areas of advance alongside areas of stasis. Some aspects of psychoanalytic theory progress rapidly while some of the older assumptions still linger even though they do not easily fit with new developments. Of course, this might indicate eternal verities, but is as likely to point to defence and resistance either to the new ideas or to abandoning old and comfortable theories. It would seem to me that the prevailing ideas about the 'therapist's neutrality' do not sit comfortably with what we now know about countertransference. In the context of this chapter, psychoanalysis seems to have a preference for theories about the therapist's neutrality and rules of anonymity. To talk about the therapist as having loving feelings towards the patient conflicts with many analytic ego ideals, such as the therapist having an evenly hovering attention, or therapeutic objectivity, or working 'without memory and desire' (Bion 1970). The therapist's ability to remain detached from the patient's issues, or his or her capacity to remain outside any attachments or involvement with the therapeutic passions, has always been seen as the most worthy of analytic positions, a triumph of the rational over the irrational, of secondary over the primary processes, of consciousness over the unconscious, the analysed dream over the unanalysed dream. The therapeutic expectation is that, even if such an analytic ideal is impossible to attain, it should at least be aspired to.

However, advances in the psychoanalytic understanding of countertransference include a wide variety of emotional states that leave the therapist affected: enactments, counterenactments, role responsiveness and projective identification all locate the therapist in a position where for some or much of the time (and it could be argued *all* of the time) he or she will be unconscious of their own processes and, therefore, far from the analytic ego ideal. Even though we now know how inevitable and often how useful the countertransference is, as analysts we cannot escape a feeling that it is not quite acceptable until analysed, and even then it leaves us feeling at least a little uneasy about our experience with the patient. It is as though the analytic ego ideal becomes a persecuting superego that keeps the countertransference from not being quite respectable or, at least, untrustworthy. Despite the tremendous advances in our understanding of countertransference it is as though the analytic ego ideal of the therapist being uninvolved in the unconscious processes has the counter-productive effect of inhibiting a full appreciation of the therapist's subjectivity and unconscious psychic states. This observation has also been made by Coen (1994) where he considers that the analytic ideal encourages 'constriction and discomfort' for a full range of feelings, especially those of the more passionate variety: loving and hating. He argues that whatever restricts the analyst's access to all his or her feelings and wishes, including loving and hating, will interfere with the patient's change and growth. He would have us focus on those persistent feelings and attitudes between the therapist and patient that 'serve as barriers to fully loving and hating one another'. In particular, he considers that in the analytic setting such barriers are protecting against varied dangers associated with allowing oneself to be vulnerable to loving and wanting to be loved. On the whole, Coen's view is that antagonisms and fighting remain safer than loving feelings for the analytic couple; that negative feelings 'block access' to more intense loving and hating.

There is now a substantial body of psychoanalytic writing that critiques the idea of the therapist's neutrality (cf. Balint and Balint 1939, Gitelson 1952, Klauber 1986, Greenberg 1996, to name but a few). To do an extensive review of this literature would be interesting but it would draw me away from the focus of this chapter. Instead, I wish to indicate how the theory of neutrality is problematic when working with love and hate and acts as a form of resistance to experience. In the view that I am taking in this chapter, the idea of the analytic ego ideal whereby the therapist somehow stands outside the passions that afflict the patient and the ordinary person, the ideal that the therapist is neutral constricts and discomforts actual clinical practice because the analytic ideal can rarely be more than yet another counter-transference position. The idea that, for example, to have no memory or desire is *not* a dispassionate relationship to the patient or various aspects of his or her psyche. In my view to have no memory or desire is to take up a particular countertransference position to both the patient's material and agencies in his or her psyche while also determining a countertransference response that the analyst has to his or her own processes, to his or her own memory and desire, to his or her own unconscious. Therefore, the wish to have no memory or desire is a countertransference manifestation to both memory and desire of analyst and patient. What I want to suggest is that the analytic ego ideal of what makes a good analysis or analyst is inherently a subjective position that influences how the therapist will experience both the patient's and the therapist's unconscious. It is for this reason that I consider that the idea of neutrality as an analytic ideal bears the hallmarks of an idealisation and is therefore primarily defensive in purpose. The analytic 'neutrality' is continuously subverted and breached intra-psychically by (1) the unconscious (which is always unconscious until *after* the event, e.g. as witnessed with enactments) and (2) by our growing understanding of inter-psychic experience as related by the intersubjectivity exchange. 'Neutrality' thus becomes compromised time and again owing to the activity of both the patient's and the therapist's unconscious. Such instability in 'neutrality' should lead us to question whether neutrality can, in fact, be neutral. Like a sieve, neutrality leaks the unconscious and is, therefore, unable to act as a container of our ideas about what the therapist is actually doing. If this proposition is accepted it is but a little step to see that our current concept of neutrality is both weak (as an intellectual concept) and virtually useless in clinical practice. In clinical practice neutrality is at best merely useless and, at worst, a repressor and inhibitor to awareness of full emotional engagement and the progression of insight this creates. Lest I am misunderstood here I am not suggesting we abandon 'neutrality' for the sake of the 'real' relationship between the patient and therapist. Both participants use transference and see the other through their own erotic subjectivity.

The opposite of love is not hate but indifference. Love and hate both passionately bind the subject to the object. This is not true of indifference which is the absence of connection, or even the absence of a wish for connection. Genuine neutrality stands closer to and has more in common with indifference than it does with the intimate passions. In my opinion, indifference or genuine neutrality are not options in psychoanalysis: the therapist and patient are engaged in a passionate, intersubjective connection of love and hate whether they like it or not.

The particular countertransference that clusters around the analytic ego ideal is a general apprehension of any, especially prolonged, loving or hating feelings in the therapist. Defined here as countertransference, the analytic ideal of neutrality is not neutral but a neutered position in relation to the passions of love and hate. Gabbard (1996: 65) gives a lovely metaphor: 'The analyst who can only talk about passions but cannot experience them is reminiscent of the anecdote about the music critic who could read the notes on the page but couldn't play the keyboard.' The poet and philosopher Kahlil Gibran (1926) also depicts what I am trying to describe:

> Your soul is oftentimes a battlefield, upon which your reason and your judgement wage war against your passion and your appetite.
>
> Your reason and your passion are the rudder and the sails of your seafaring soul;
>
> If either your sails or your rudder be broken, you can but toss and drift, or else be held at a standstill in mid-seas.
>
> For reason, ruling alone, is a force confining; and passion, unattended, is a flame that burns to its own destruction.
>
> Therefore let your soul exalt your reason to the height of passion, that it may sing;
>
> And let it direct your passion with reason, that your passion may live through its own daily resurrection, and like the phoenix rise above its own ashes.
>
> (Gibran 1926: 59–60)

I personally have doubts about introducing 'the soul' into this thought but otherwise I think Gibran describes the analytic dilemma quite well.

The alternative to neutrality is to accept the analyst's involvement and participation at the level of the unconscious. The most primitive passions are stirred in psychoanalysis for both participants. Rather than take flight or repress these passions the therapy is better served for both participants if the feelings can be experienced but contained and then understood.

I should emphasise that I am not advocating a tactical abandonment of silence or encouraging countertransference disclosure à la Karen Maroda (1991). Discussion with my analytic colleagues leads me to assume I probably consciously reveal less and speak less than most therapists I know. If anything, I would wish to intensify the therapist's silence in order for him or her to pay closer attention to their lack of neutrality; that is to say, where the love and the hate is situated and what might be the present inhibitor (resistance) to their recognition. But I would not equate the therapist's silence with the classical idea of blank screen or the view that just because we do not speak we are therefore not communicating. Just because the therapist says nothing it does not stop the unconscious from expression, a communication that the patient's unconscious scanning will undoubtedly detect.

What I am advocating is the need to redefine the obstacles that inhibit awareness and experience of the major points of connection and disconnection with the patient; in other words, that which prohibits the full appreciation of how much they love and hate each other, that which connects with all that is both lovable and unlovable (hateful) in each other.

Transformative passion

There has been a long debate in psychoanalysis about the curative power of analysis: catharsis versus insight. In my view, neither are quite right. It seems generally understood that therapy needs more than just a spillage of feeling: once unloaded it is seldom enough and, ultimately, mere catharsis usually leads to little substantial and sustainable psychic change because, apart from achieving riddance of an emotion, nothing much else has happened. On the other hand, over-intellectualisation and an idealisation of insight offers a different problem. I think most experienced therapists are familiar with patients coming for their second (or third) therapy where it seems the problem in the previous therapy was that, while they might have been intellectually challenging or have gained interesting insights, they have not really got to the 'guts' of their problem and have not fully engaged with the more powerful emotional content of the psyche. Szasz (1963) suggests that the emphasis on transference interpretation protects the therapist from having to feel the passions generated in analysis. I do not agree with him that this is always the case, but I do agree that transference interpretations can sometimes be used this way. Such 'insight'-based therapies often reach an impasse, particularly when the therapist has personal difficulties forming intimate relationships due to either schizoid or narcissistic factors in his or her personality which lead to an avoidance of intimate emotional contact and overemphasis on intellectualisation. In such an instance the therapist's inhibition collides with the patient's inhibition, which might then result in a defensive impasse. Insight is not enough unless coupled to emotional connection and then change. Having insight into why we feel unlovable is not usually enough to make us feel lovable; though patients generally experience great relief, and sometimes happiness, at feeling deeply understood by the therapist, being understood is not the same as feeling loved or lovable.

It seems to me that what is created in analysis is a situation that the patient has probably not experienced before, not only an expansion of their emotional repertoire but also an experience of self and a connection to another that transcends all the previous self-ideas about falseness, emptiness or badness. I am not advocating an earlier concept of 'corrective emotional experience', although I consider that the idea of a corrective emotional experience is much maligned and there is more merit in this idea than the critics would have us believe. However, what I am suggesting is not so much that the therapist gives a better experience than the original parents (the original meaning of 'corrective') in that I do not think they are necessarily more loving, kind or caring than the patient's actual parents (though given some of the histories our patients bring, a therapist with a modicum of ego integration is often a substantial improvement on the patient's previous relationships). The essential feature I would emphasise is the therapist's willingness to seek, along with the patient, to find what is lovable and to explore what are the obstacles that stop them both from loving and hating each other more fully. It is from this that the patient has a new experience with the therapist. The patient develops a new sense of self. We could perhaps describe this as the patient realising they are not so awful and they are actually lovable. What is re-worked and internalised is the internal model of relationships which now makes loving (and more realistically hating) possible. Lear (1990: 213) sees the very act of therapy as creating the possibility of love: 'A good enough interpretation must, at its core, manifest a loving acknowledgement of the drives . . . But a good enough interpretation is more that a secondary-process conceptualisation. It is a conceptualisation that is lovingly directed towards and in touch with its "object". A good enough interpretation is thus structured like an emotion. For the interpretation is itself a sublimation.' A therapy full of vibrant loving and hating not only allows these feelings but will endeavour to find an understanding of the conflicts and inhibitions that possibly prevented the patient and therapist from previously experiencing these feelings.

Both the analyst and analysand will reproduce their habitual pattern of loving and hating. But because each analytic pair has its own character, how these two erotic subjectivities interact will be the key factor. The resulting 'stew' from the intermixed unconscious subjectivities of different individuals means it is never quite the same repetition. In other words, the habitual patterns of loving and hating are never quite repeated in identical fashion. How these repetitions mix creates a different experience for both participants at the point of overlap between their erotic subjectivities. Herein is the opportunity for both patient and therapist to then transform their old experience into something new.

I believe this kind of process is well accounted for in the psychoanalytic literature. Describing the interplay between the separate realities of the mother and baby Winnicott (1971) thought of this as a transitional space, created by both participants, mutually owned yet also different to them both. Ogden (1994) coins the term 'analytic third' to describe this process in therapy: the subjectivities of the two participants jointly create something new, another subjective experience, a new subject: the analytic third. The analyst's erotic subjectivity introduces a new element to the re-creation of the patient's past; the same applies with the patient introducing something new in the re-creation of the analyst's past.

The real difference between love and hate in the analytic setting compared to any other situation is not so much about the relative degree of which is more real or more or less infantile and transferential. The significant difference lies in what the therapist does with this love. Unlike any other situation where love and hate may be found, except perhaps between parent and child, the therapist seeks to find meaning in the experience. It is not so much that the therapist is dispassionate and objective, rather it is more that the passionate engagement that the transference and counter-transference entails is hand in hand with a love of curiosity, exploration and insight. It is also in this process that love is stronger than hate for the analytic pair. Modell (1991) describes the asymmetrical nature of the analytic encounter not as an asymmetry of desire but of the communication of desire. That is to say, the therapist uses their desire not just to reciprocate but to aid understanding. Put another way, Lear (1990: 13) writes: 'For one thing, love is not something that can be appreciated from the outside. The very activity of coming to understand love is itself a development, a unification, an act of love.'

To return to the problem of 'neutrality'. Generally, I am not convinced that therapists neither love nor hate their patients. Fortunately for most psychotherapy patients their therapists are not so neutral, and this would be despite what therapists might say to themselves and, perhaps more importantly, what they are prepared to make public to colleagues. By and large, I have the impression that most psychoanalytic practice is better than the psychoanalytic theories. What we do is superior to what we think we do.

I should say I am not attempting to de-throne the importance of interpretation – far from it since I think this is the most important of all the therapeutic tools. I would, though, like to scale down the idealisation of the interpretation technique and place it in a more relational context. What I mean is this: the interpretation does not rest on some assumption of neutrality or dispassionate hypothesis-come-suggestion-come-statement that provides insight and is, therefore, the most objectively important thing a therapist does. Rather, in addition to providing insight, I would locate the interpretation as also demonstrating the therapist's love, or at least his or her willingness to let love be stronger than hate. An interpretation, therefore, is also a commentary on the nature of the relationship between the therapist and the patient. It is an expression of trying to find understanding, which we all agree is a good thing, amongst the hate, badness and emptiness of the patient's lovelessness and unlovableness. The mutual resistances and pathologies between patient and therapist could lead one or the other of them to repulse each other. I would see such a destructive outcome as symptomatic of the dominance of hate: an unwillingness to explore and find an intimate loving connection. However, when a transformative experience is possible, this will happen if the therapy is good enough. The interpretation then brings the patient and therapist into relation to each other, defining their relationship as a mutual search for goodness amongst the mess, love in the midst of hate. Insight is connected to and becomes an expression of love.

Actually, what I am saying here needs to be unpacked a little further. It would be my view that both love and hate bring the individual into an intimate proximity and relationship to each other: the quality may be different but the binds are just as strong. With love the intimacy usually is progressive and towards a creative experience; with hate the intimacy is a drive for a more destructive experience but is equally concerned with making connections. More precisely, what I mean is this: the therapeutic couple are connected by love and hate. Which of the two is dominant will determine the nature of the insight. Here I would invoke Bion's ideas of knowledge (K) and minus knowledge (−K). A connection dominated by love leads to insights which enhance, inform, transform: K. A connection dominated by hate produces a knowledge that destructively leads away from the truth, a false knowledge or an absence of knowledge, −K, that can only lead to impasse or therapeutic breakdown.

I am of the view that the extent of the passionate engagement between the analyst and analysand is substantially connected to the level of psychological pathology in the patient. With the more neurotic disorders it would seem the degree of passionate involvement in the transference and countertransference does not seem great, though I would argue it is still present. With the more severe pathology, such as the so-called personality disorders and borderline conditions, both the transference and countertransference is more intense with a concomitant increase in the feelings of love and hate. It is almost axiomatic that patients with severe pathology stir tremendous feelings of passion in the transference and countertransference. Even with less severe presentations love and hate (and their various permutations and gradations) will still be the major issues for most patients and, therefore, for most therapists. Given the power of more destructive emotions (for example, envy, pathological hate and aggression, abuse, perversion, and so on) we might wonder what emotion that either the analysand or analyst could possess that could possibly de-toxify and hold back the negative, keeping hope in the therapeutic venture aflame through deep impasse or negative transference and countertransference? What emotion has the capacity to make hate bearable and malleable? What emotion can possibly attempt to convert pathological hate and destructive aggression into something more developmentally advanced so the patient (and therapist) might be able to have more real, positive and loving relationships? I will concede there might be various answers to these questions but I would seriously doubt whether any answer does not in essence boil down to the capacity of love. Both the therapist and the patient need some sense that behind the unconscious fantasies of the transference and countertransference, there must be a feeling of goodness that can survive the bad, otherwise neither party can proceed with hope. Nor is it possible to imagine how pathological passions (both transference and countertransference love and hate) can be turned into realistic positive emotions if love does not play a part.

As I stated at the beginning of this chapter, love and hate need to be comprehended within the concept of Eros, the connecting principle. Eros forges connections between people or breaks some links in order to form others. In that sense, Eros both combines or separates in order to recon-figure the psyche and the internal and external relationships. As such, Eros will bring the analyst and analysand into a bond, initially of pathological transferential and countertransferential love and hate. With the sufficient working through of the kind described in this chapter the bond becomes less transferential and more realistic, but no less loving despite the de-toxification of projected elements.

In order to present my case in this chapter I have perhaps laid the emphasis down a little stronger than I am comfortable with. Clearly love, with or without hate, is not going to be enough on its own to bring about therapeutic change. On the other hand, it seems equally clear that analysis is hard put to go beyond an intellectual activity without it. Therapy needs more than love and hate, but it is very difficult to proceed without them.

The goal of therapy is not to abolish the patient's passions. It would be hoped that a good-enough therapy means that love has a greater influence in the patient's life than previously under the domination of feelings of lovelessness or hatefulness. By this I mean that by the termination stage the patient has a greater sense of their capacity to be loved and loving and will have a less pathological experience of hate. With the conclusion of therapy it is not that the patient will be full of insight and free from hate. Rather, the pathological constituents of love and hate will have been de-toxified. After this, hopefully, what remains is a more realistic appreciation and experience of healthy love and hate.

References

Balint, A. and Balint, M. (1939) On transference and countertransference, *International Journal of Psycho-Analysis*, 20: 225–30.

Bergmann, M. S. (1988) Freud's three theories of love in the light of later developments, *Journal of the American Psychoanalytic Association*, 36: 653–72.

Bion, W. R. (1970) *Attention and Interpretation*, London: Maresfield Reprints, 1988.

Blum, H. (1997) Clinical and developmental dimensions of hate, *Journal of the American Psychoanalytic Association*, 45(2): 359–75.

Coen, S. J. (1994) Barriers to love between patient and analyst, *Journal of the American Psychoanalytic Association*, 42(4): 1107–35.

Coltart, N. (1992) What does it mean: 'love is not enough'? In *Slouching Towards Bethlehem*, London: Free Association Press.

Fairbairn, W. R. (1940) Schizoid factors in the personality. In *Psychoanalytic Studies of the Personality*, London: Routledge and Kegan Paul, 1986.

Freud, S. (1907) Delusions and dreams in Jensen's *Gradiva*. In *Standard Edition* 9: 1–95.

Freud, S. (1915a) Observations on transference love. In *Standard Edition* 12: 157–73.

Freud, S. (1915b) Instincts and their vicissitudes. In *Standard Edition* 14: 109–40.

Fromm, E. (1957) *The Art of Loving*, London: Unwin Paperbacks, 1984.

Gabbard, G. O. (1996) *Love and Hate in the Analytic Setting*, Northvale, N.J.: Jason Aronson Inc.

Gerrard, J. (1996) Love in the time of psychotherapy, *British Journal of Psychotherapy*, 13(2): 163–73.

Gerrard, J. (1999) Love in the time of psychotherapy. In D. Mann (ed.) *Erotic Transference and Countertransference: Clinical Practice in Psychotherapy*, London: Routledge.

Gibran, K. (1926) *The Prophet*, London: William Heinemann Ltd, 1980.

Gitelson, M. (1952) The emotional position of the therapist in the psychoanalytic situation, *International Journal of Psycho-Analysis*, 33: 1–10.

Green, A. (1997) *Chains of Eros: The Sexual in Psychoanalysis*, London: Rebus Press, 2000.

Greenberg, J. (1996) Psychoanalytic words and psychoanalytic acts, *Contemporary Psychoanalysis*, 32: 195–203.

Kernberg, O. F. (1995) *Love Relations: Normality and Pathology*, New Haven, Conn.: Yale University Press.

Klauber, J. (1986) *Difficulties in the Analytic Encounter*, London: Free Association Books.

Lear, J. (1990) *Love and its Place in Nature: A Philosophical Intrepretation of Freudian Psychoanalysis*, New York: The Noonday Press.

Levine, H. (1994) The analyst's participation in the analytic process, *International Journal of Psycho-Analysis*, 66: 665–76.

Mann, D. (1989) Incest: the father and the male therapist, *British Journal of Psychotherapy*, 6: 143–53.

Mann, D. (1994) The psychotherapist's erotic subjectivity, *British Journal of Psychotherapy*, 10(3): 344–54.

Mann, D. (1995) Transference and countertransference issues with sexual abused patients, *Psychodynamic Counselling*, 1(4): 542–59.

Mann, D. (1997a) *Psychotherapy: An Erotic Relationship – Transference and Countertransference Passions*, London: Routledge.

Mann, D. (1997b) Masturbation and painting. In K. Killick and J. Schaverien (eds) *Art, Psychotherapy and Psychosis*, London: Routledge.

Mann, D. (1999) *Erotic Transference and Countertransference: Clinical Practice in Psychotherapy*, London: Routledge.

Mann, D. (2001) Erotics and ethics: the passionate dilemmas of the therapeutic couple. In L. Murdin and F. Palmer-Barnes (eds) *Values and Ethics in Psychotherapy*, Cambridge: Cambridge University Press.

Maroda, K. (1991) *The Power of Countertransference: Innovations in Analytic Technique*, Chichester: John Wiley and Sons.

Menninger, K. (1942) *Love Against Hate*, New York: Harvest, Harcourt, Brace and World.

Modell, A. (1991) The therapeutic relationship as a paradoxical experience, *Psychoanalytic Dialogues*, 1: 13–28.

Ogden, T. H. (1994) *Subjects of Analysis*, Northvale, N.J.: Jason Aronson.

Suttie, I. (1935) *The Origins of Love and Hate*, London: Free Association Press.

Szasz, T. (1963) The concept of transference, *International Journal of Psycho-Analysis*, 44: 432–43.

Winnicott, D. W. (1947) Hate in the countertransference. In *Through Paediatrics to Psychoanalysis*, London: Hogarth Press, 1987.

Winnicott, D. W. (1954) Metapsychological and clinical aspects of regression within the psychoanalytic set-up. In *Through Paediatrics to Psychoanalysis*, London: Hogarth Press, 1987.

Winnicott, D. W. (1971) *Playing and Reality*, Harmondsworth: Penguin Books, 1985.

Chapter 2

Love

Paradox of self and other

Hester McFarland Solomon

Unlike fictional literature, analytic literature contains relatively little about love. Of course, there are exceptions,[1] but by and large analytical attention has addressed other, often negative, emotional states much more consistently and systematically. Perhaps it is truer to say it has given them a higher profile, as if they were, for the clinician, more pressing, more interesting, more exciting or perhaps more easily thought about. Attention to hatred, envy, jealousy, perverse and violent feelings, anxieties, depressions and psychotic states and various forms of attacks on and retreats from the possibility of psychological transformation, has ensured that much of our analytic thinking remains focused on negative states of mind. And yet states of loving are nothing less than the driving emotive force underpinning much of the physical development of the self and propelling much of the self's psychological development from birth until death. Love is certainly one of the primary emotions at the core of object relating, and this has deep implications for the impact of love on the relationship between patient and therapist. However, the fairly copious use of the term 'erotic' (for example, the 'erotic transference', and the far less frequently described 'erotic countertransference') is often a signal that the state, attitude, or feeling being designated is considered to be pathological. Hence, we see little in the analytic literature about the love that a patient might feel for their therapist, or the therapist for their patient, or indeed about the love that might be shared between them.

It would be tempting to broach an object relations account of love by making a series of theoretically accessible and easily identifiable distinctions: between erotic and passionate love on the one hand and agapaic and compassionate love on the other; between love experienced and expressed

This chapter is based on a paper presented to the Annual Conference of the Institute for Psychotherapy and Counselling, held at Fitzwilliam College in Cambridge in July 1997. The title of the Conference was: 'What is this Thing Called Love: Should Psychotherapists Love Their Patients?' A version of it appeared in the *British Journal of Psychotherapy* (1998, vol. 14, no. 3).

from within the paranoid–schizoid position or from within the depressive position; between the evocation of the rule of abstinence which forbids any form of abuse of the patient and an equally professional stance which may seek to formulate interventions, however carefully fashioned, designed to penetrate or at least soften the most hardened defences as a necessary prelude to change; or again, between the analytically familiar notions of idealisation and denigration and their apparent correlates in loving and hatred; and, not least, between forms of love and forms of hate or of indifference.

The problem in seeking to delineate a pattern in the dynamic of what is called 'love' is that love can take a multitude of forms and meanings, each one with its own different feeling state, developmental stage, mode of enactment, and yet each identifiable by the one who feels it as a state of loving. There is, for example:

- love between mother and child, father and child, and siblings
- love of a spouse
- love of a friend
- love of a pet
- erotic love
- altruistic love
- love of God
- love of one's country or a principle
- love of a work of art, or a natural landscape
- love of a patient for his/her therapist
- love of a therapist for his/her patient

A person who seeks to communicate any of the above states may use the word 'love' to designate their feelings, but the actual experience of love in these modes will vary enormously – from passionate involvement of the self, body and soul, through to a feeling akin to altruistic sacrifice of the self. And, of course, feelings of love are almost always found in combination with other emotions such as possessiveness, jealousy, resentment, tenderness, pride, loyalty, longing, admiration, desire, and so on. Furthermore, in love, paradoxes and contradictions abound: the role of narcissism in love ineluctably links love of self with the love of the other, thereby enhancing the self at the very moment of the self's surrender to and mingling with the other; equally, love is ambivalent, and the couple that live only for each other must soon find ways of creating distance and space between them.

Love has many contexts, but the principle that links all of them is of the self in relation to another, a not-self – in Jungian terms, the self in *coniunctio*. It may be helpful to define these terms briefly. On the one hand, Jung provided us with a view of the self as an integrating and organising principle, underpinning identity from the earliest moments of existence (what contemporary Jungians might call the primary integrate) to the fullest individuation one may achieve, and notwithstanding the self's ubiquitous capacities to be divided within and against itself, to have sub-selves or sub-personalities. At the same time we think of the self as possessing the capacity for a coming together, a union, or relating with another, where 'another' need not necessarily be another person but may include elements interior or exterior to the self: the *coniunctio* of inner and/or outer elements, of parts or wholes, of conscious or unconscious – what we might call internal and external object relations. It is the *quality* of the coming together that is important and takes up so much of what is experienced and explored in the consulting room (for a fuller discussion see Solomon, 1997: 383).

A major principle that permeates Jung's psychotherapeutic approach, and therefore the theoretical concepts that underpin it, is the teleological principle. A teleological understanding of the self offers the view that psychological events and states have purpose and meaning and may, under the right conditions, provide the means by which the self achieves not only the best available solution to date to problems confronting it, but also how it may develop and grow. This concerns the nature of change, and, in particular, the grounds on which the self attains its fullest possible actualisation. The teleological principle in turn underpins Jung's concept of the transcendent function, which provides us with a way of thinking about how the self may access the inner sources of its own creativity and maturation through the struggle and conflict between dialectical opposites and their union, when a synthesis and integration in a third thing, the *tertium quid non datur*, may be achieved. This may happen internally, and it may also happen between the self and another. It is an archetypal situation, a pro-tophenomenon, whereby the self reaches out to bridge what is experienced as a gap between self and not-self, thereby creating a new situation (Solomon, 1994). These are the conditions in which any universal human affect, including love, may be experienced and expressed.

Of course, where there is the possibility of a coming together, there is also the possibility of a sundering. The self's capacity to be in states of *coniunctio*, but equally to be divided against itself and against others, has a correlate in the Jungian distinction between the symbolic function and the forces of the diabolic shadow. The shadow is that aspect of the self that it seeks to disavow and project outside itself. It is an aspect of the self felt to be 'diabolic' in the sense that its Greek derivation, *dia-ballein*, suggests (to throw or tear apart), in contrast with 'symbolic' which derives from *sym-ballein* (to throw together). The diabolic aspect of the psyche is essentially anti-relational, it eschews loving states of mind, and divests the symbolic function of its value and human quality. It is, instead, intent on its own triumph over the other through destruction, deprecation, dismemberment, mayhem or death (Kalsched, 1996) – the opposite of love. In contrast, the symbolic capacity signifies the possibility for integration and the symbolic life through the holding together of opposites and the creation thereby of a third thing, the fruits of particular acts of *coniunctio*. We may think of the symbol, therefore, as the manifestation of the potential for loving in its ability to unite both concrete presence and intangible meaning. In this sense, love in its different manifestations underlies the Jungian notion of the transcendent function.

Having set out the conceptual matrix into which I would like to locate my thoughts about love in this chapter, I propose to attempt to think about the earliest love situations in order to search for an understanding of the bases of love, which I assume are the primordial links to an understanding of what happens in later life, including in the consulting room. The view of love I wish to explore here is based on what we can say about the earliest affects experienced by the infant. The assumption is that the manifestations of transference and countertransference that we encounter in the consulting room contain direct links to these earliest affective sources. Inevitably, we will have to address those preverbal exchanges that happen between the first couple in love – the first loving couple: the mother and her infant, and the infant and its mother – which form the basis of all later exchanges. In other words, the examination of the origins of love begins at the preverbal level and is part of the self/other interpenetration that occurs at that time and thereafter. Can there be any evidence of earlier forms of loving than this primordial pair?

Infant observation *in utero*

Although we are well aware of the dangers of extrapolating from infant observation studies to adult psychological functioning, nevertheless the wealth of theoretical and clinical conceptualisation derived from this new method of enquiry has already reaped a rich harvest and will no doubt continue to do so. The following is an extract from an unusual sort of infant observation, that of an *in utero* observation made via ultrasound scan, of twins, one male, one female, therefore dizygotic like the vast majority of twins (that is, separated in the womb by a fine and very pliable membrane). The observation was made by Tavistock-trained Dr Alessandra Piontelli (1992) in Italy. I think the extract touches directly on the issues raised above about the primary nature and uniqueness of the self, about innate differences in character, despite the same uterine environment, about early relations between self and other, and about early manifestations of a capacity for what we could identify as expressions of loving.[2]

This extract is taken from an observation at twenty weeks *in utero*, some four and a half months after conception. The little girl, Alice, was always the quieter one, more sleepy, apparently pleased to be contained by the womb environment, whereas the little boy, Luca, was always the more active of the two, initiating movement, searching out and exploring the boundaries of his uterine environment. The twins were very much wanted and accepted by the parents, who were both excited and curious about the character of each.

> The little boy [Luca] seemed much more active than the girl. He kept turning and kicking and changing position and stretching his legs against the uterine wall . . . As his mother remarked, 'Oh, my God! . . . look at him . . . he is so small and he already seems fed up with being in there . . .' From time to time Luca would interrupt his motor activities and seemed to turn his attention towards his sister. He reached out with his hands and through the dividing membrane he touched her face gently, and when she responded by turning her face towards him, he engaged with her for a while in a gentle, stroking, cheek-to-cheek motion. From then on we nicknamed them 'the kind twins'. His sister, Alice, seemed much more sluggish. Most of the time she seemed asleep, or moved her head and hands slowly, almost imperceptibly, but each time she responded to his gentle stimulation. Once he went back to his turning, stretching, and so on, however, she seemed to plunge back into her state of passivity and/or sleep.
>
> (Piontelli, 1992: 129–30)

And then again a small extract from the 24th week:

> *Dr. S*: And this is the other twin . . . they are very close . . . their heads are in contact . . . they seem to be hugging each other . . . they still have some space at this stage . . . but they seem to like each other's contact . . . they are really very close . . . they are not Siamese though . . . they are almost certainly a boy and a girl . . . and divided by a membrane . . . nor could they become Siamese at this stage . . . they simply like each other's company . . . last time too they were hugging each other . . . look how this one keeps its hand close to the other . . .
> *Dr. F*: It is just moving its face . . . sort of stroking each other's face . . . cheek to cheek . . .
>
> (ibid.: 130–3)

And again at 36 weeks:

> *Dr. F*: Look what the boy is doing! . . . he keeps banging his head against the cervix . . . he wants to get out! . . . he is rather independent this one! . . . his sister is much more quiet . . . he is also doing something with his legs . . . sort of touching his sister with them . . . rubbing his feet against hers . . . he is not kicking her though . . . they always seem to like stroking each other . . .
>
> (ibid: 135)

These twins continued their very close relationship throughout their childhood, yet each child retained the dominant features of their personalities as observed *in utero*: the little boy bright, precocious, seeking freedom to grow but still very attached and loving towards his sister, and the little girl, slower, more passive, more dependent, but nevertheless related to and loving and responsive towards her brother. Throughout, the parents demonstrated their continuing capacity to relish and hold in mind the differences in their personalities, and they went on to provide the home and school environments that suited each one.

The extracts show that from at least five months after conception there is a capacity for repeated exchanges between the twins, *in utero*, that appear to be loving, tender and that demonstrate an attachment to each other that is confirmed post-partum. Equally demonstrated are the very different temperaments of each, such that we might say that a compensatory relationship developed between them, as if they had somehow found a kind of partnership between the thrusting, seeking, more extroverted aspects and the more introverted, quiet, passive aspects of a combined personality. The twins began their uterine development with different but compensatory temperaments, and at the same time they were sensitive to each other, regularly seeking each other out with tender demonstrations of physical contact. *They were two separate selves within one relationship.* During foetal gestation, the attitude of the parents towards their infants and between themselves was reflective of the quality of the relationship between the infants *in utero* and post-partum. A regular and consistent pattern of being and behaving developed *in utero* differently for each twin, but at certain and regular moments they would join in a mutual exchange.

Lest we are tempted to think of the situation *in utero* in idealised terms via the example of the 'kind twins', Piontelli also provides ultrasound observation of other sets of twins with much more problematic *in utero* relationships, including fighting, parasitism, and other kinds of aggressive power struggles or depressive withdrawals, negative modes of relating that are seen to carry on subsequently post-partum between the twins and within their families, in large measure reflective of the emotional climate pertaining in the extra-uterine environment. We might conjecture along with Piontelli that the primordial bases of those human emotions and responses that later develop into states that can be identified as loving and hating might find their roots in these earliest emotional climates in the intra- and extra-uterine environment.

Fordham (1988) has described a model of the self that might explain the dynamic pattern in the twinship observed by Piontelli between tender, shared relatedness on the one hand or separate individual behaviour on the other. In Fordham's model, the self oscillates rhythmically between states of deintegration and reintegration, a dynamic pattern observable from infancy throughout life. He writes:

In essence, deintegration and reintegration describe a fluctuating state of learning in which the infant opens itself to new experiences and then withdraws in order to reintegrate and consolidate those experiences. During a deintegrative activity, the infant maintains continuity with the main body of the self (or its centre), while venturing into the external world to accumulate experience in motor and sensory stimulation . . .

(Fordham, 1988: 64)

Astor (1995) describes the process as follows:

Fordham called the dynamic of the self deintegration and reintegration since the self was an integrate. Deintegration was the term used when referring to the energy going outwards towards objects and reintegration when the energy was returning to the self.

(Astor, 1995: 237)

The observation cited above suggests that this pattern is already well established *in utero*, such that the self, from within its own self, at certain moments ceases being in a state of interiority on its own and reaches out for, finds, and exchanges something with another entity, a not-self, eventually returning back to itself. This searching/finding/exchanging/returning-to-self protophenomenon constructs patterns of being and behaving, and is an innate, archetypal, deep structural capacity from the start. If the baby is a singleton, it can be observed *in utero* to be responsive and related to aspects of its uterine environment, both through its own behaviour, movement, patterns of sleeping and waking, as well as through the sensory stimulation coming from within and outside the mother's body, and also through the provisions unique to each intrauterine milieu – the umbilical cord, placenta, amniotic fluid, and the various sources of extra-uterine stimulation – sounds, vibrations, movement and changes in the composition of the uterine environment during the nine months of gestation. The view of this early situation that I am offering here is of a primary self and, at the same time, a primary capacity for relatedness from the earliest weeks after conception. Furthermore, and of particular interest to us, there is evidence of affectional states, including loving states, from very early on – in fact from as early as it is possible to observe *in utero*.

This *in utero* responsiveness to, and capacity to reach out towards, another, a kind of primordial mutual containment, attachment and attunement, may account for the often stunning evidence we glean from our patients whereby, despite their own experiences of deprivations and deficits in the early caring environment, and despite inevitable difficulties, they are sometimes able to muster capacities for loving or enhancing relationships in later life that could not have been predicted from their remembered histories.

Further evidence from studies of neonates show that the foundation of shared affects and emotions is located very early, and certainly preverbally. The work of Stern (1985), Brazelton *et al.* (1973), Trevarthen (1980), Gaddini (1992), and many others whose theories were developed from the pioneering work of Klein, Winnicott, Bick, Tustin and Fordham in the treatment of and theorising about early infant development, attest to the fundamental and universal propensity for the young infant to experience, and for its mother to share in, profoundly felt affective states that are registered, exchanged, recalled and modified between them. Especially interesting in this respect is the increasing body of psychoneurobiological evidence demonstrating that, as the infant's brain is only partially developed at birth, the maturation of the corticolimbic system that occurs during the first one to two years of life is dependent on the quality of the relationship between the infant and its mother, or other care givers (Schore, 1996). In other words, there is now experimental evidence from the new field of psychoneurobiology that shows that the future development of those right hemisphere structures that regulate attachment and other emotional and cognitive behaviours is deter-mined by the quality of the mother–infant interaction in the first weeks and months post-partum, in which the infant is an active – and proactive – participant. In this sense we may say that the infant actively participates in the development of the very corticolimbic systems that underpin the quality of their cognitive and affective behaviour, including loving behaviour (Solomon, 2000).

The *in utero* observations of the 'kind twins' provide strong evidence of a primary impulse to love that is nourished by proximity, physical contact, responsiveness from the other and by the containment of the parents who relate to and enjoy the growing foetuses. The twins experienced from the start a three-dimensional world in which there was space and time to be in their different states of self and to be in relation to the other twin. In Fordham's terms, this resembles the rhythmic deintegrations and reintegra-tions that mark the periodic movement of the self from within itself to outside itself and back again, via contact with a not-self, imaged in our example *in utero* by the periodic exchanges of physical contact, of caressing, across the fine differentiating membrane that separates them. Here is a tender preverbal and previsual object relationship, where, without the stimuli of language or sight, a mutuality exists and develops, and carries on consistently over time, to create the particular quality of relationship that the twins continued to share after birth. Even though the little girl seemed inactive by nature, she responded to her brother's affectionate overtures in kind.

But what if the object is not satisfactorily available to maintain contact, containment and mutual exchange? In Stern's language, attunement may be unavailable; in Bowlby's (1969) model, there may be no reliable presence with whom to form an attachment. What if there had been a responsive object, however bizarre, but once available for love, who then became lost, absent, vacant, empty, or crazy? What happens, then, to love? We know that when the self has not experienced satisfactory containment within a consistently loving relationship, an enormous deficit occurs. A massive narcissistic wounding follows after the first unmet deintegrations, and the self, in order to survive, has then to seek out, or possibly even to create, its own substitute for containment and a semblance of loving mutuality.

When a loving relationship with a present object is not available, a loving attachment to an absent object may develop as a substitute in order to provide a phantasy of a presence, albeit a present absence (Bion, 1962). Later on, this may evolve into an addiction to absent objects, as it becomes increasingly impossible to achieve a satisfactory loving relationship with a present object. Sometimes, a perverse object choice is made in an attempt to find a better solution than the attachment to an absent object, the inevitable failure of which then provides the self with further evidence that love is simply too risky a business and must be foresworn. Anger or hatred towards the absent object is equally unavailable, for strong negative emotion also runs the risk of piercing the unconscious delusion that has been created of an attachment to an absent or perverse object. In the example that follows, far from engendering negative affects such as anger, rage or hatred in the face of real loss, the loving attachment to an absent object which arose from the original narcissistic wound developed into a characteristically confused, fazed and perplexed state of mind that was also experienced for certain periods in the transference/countertransference relationship.

Clinical example

Fay was seven months *in utero* before her mother realised she was pregnant with her. As a baby, she was maintained in a quasi-sterile environment for no medical reason – her mother, along with a succession of nurses who were employed to look after her, wore surgical face masks when they fed and tended her, and when she slept her cot was covered by mosquito netting, although the family lived in a major Western city. Some time after her birth, a subsequent pregnancy was aborted. Her mother developed a serious psychiatric disorder when Fay was about four years old, from which she never fully recovered; she was hospitalised for the next fifteen years. She was discharged when Fay was in her late teens, after a bitter divorce from her father, but she was not properly rehabilitated and continued to live a limited and often bizarre life until her death, shortly before Fay entered into a second analysis with me. Her father was generally well meaning towards Fay but uninvolved in her day-to-day care, leaving an increasingly unwell wife and a series of nurses to get on with things while he pursued amorous relationships which he then required Fay to evaluate as potential partners for him. Once Fay started school, her father set high standards of achievement, employing, as substitutes for the nurses, a series of tutors and professionals to provide lessons in sports, elocution, dance, and other skills. She felt that she invariably performed below the standard set by her father and his delegates, the professionals. Conversations with him were like legal debates, and to negotiate an increase in pocket money, or permission to go out with friends, she was obliged to present her case as if she were a little lawyer.

Fay always felt herself to be profoundly alone. She has sad memories of banging on the locked door of her mother's study while her mother remained out of touch and unresponsive behind it, wrapped in her own activities. She felt defeated in her attempts to achieve the skills that a growing child usually acquires by playing with and imitating adults and other children. Instead, there were nannies, nurses, coaches, tutors and doctors, all treating her as an object they were paid to care for. It was difficult for Fay to feel that she received safe and therefore truly loving care, sustained over time, and personally related to her. To compensate, she would use concrete objects as symbolic equivalents for the relationships she longed for, especially with her mother. She would wrap herself up in her mother's fur coat, enjoying sensuous and sexualised feelings, and was fascinated by her mother's feminine accoutrements – she would play for hours with hairnets, jewellery, lipsticks, mascara, cigarette holders, clothes, shoes, gloves. She created breast-like enclosures from pillows and cushions which she would place at the bottom of the stairs so that she would be near anyone who came by. She kept with her, in her bed, dozens of stuffed and several real animals when she slept.

By the time Fay's mother became crazy, hospitalised and perpetually absent, the material objects that Fay had used as symbolic equivalents for a loved but bizarre and inconsistently available mother became spoiled and hateful for her. Bits of tobacco in coat pockets and at the bottom of satin bags, hair pieces that resembled rats' tails, disgusting old tubes of lipstick and mascara brushes, all became emblematic of the crazy mother that she could not possibly internalise and identify with for fear of risking or compromising her own sanity thereby. Fay developed allergies and other physical symptoms that ensured that she remained in a fuzzy, woolly world where a clear and cogent sense of her self in relation to others was unavailable. She moved awkwardly, as if in a daze and unsure of her footing. As an adult, she moved next to a prominent landmark as a point of orientation in an otherwise featureless (i.e. loveless) internal world.

Fay had little experience of being loved for the person who she was. Her mother was unable to hold on to reality, let alone hold on to a realistic perception of her daughter, which might have helped Fay to negotiate the hurdles of the developmental stages and the mental passage back and forth between the paranoid–schizoid and depressive positions, and her father was unable to provide an adequate substitute for the experience of a benevolent combined parental presence. This meant that Fay's attempts to reach out for love, containment, and attunement were repeatedly thwarted and responded to only intermittently and in a limited way.

However, at the same time, Fay did not fail to thrive. She developed social skills that ensured that she had constant companionship from friends, and she developed psychosexually, albeit her choice of partners inevitably reflected a certain absent and/or bizarre quality imparted by her earliest object relations. She successfully bore and reared a child to whom she was able to demonstrate more or less consistently the love and thoughtful commitment she felt she had not received herself. Her educational achievements were solid and impressive, she became an expert in a particular field, and she lived an active and interesting life. However, there was a lack of consistency in loving object relations. When Fay chose her lovers, they were usually absent in an important way, either emotionally or concretely; if present, the archetypal qualities of their personalities were so unmitigated that they tended to be abusive and/or sadistic.

When, in phantasy, the loved other can only be absent, a pattern of trauma is laid down that will remain difficult to change, being reinforced in a repetitively compulsive way by object choices that lead to further subsequent failures (Covington, 1996). This is particularly so if the original defence occurred at a very early stage in the development of the self, since to dismantle the defence, for example through analysis, is tantamount to jettisoning the only place of safety in an otherwise overwhelmingly chaotic and unstable inner world. In such circumstances, overwhelming negative feelings, such as hatred, may be unavailable because they are too threatening to the defensive structure. The opposite of love in such circumstances may be experienced in the analytic relationship not as hatred but as bewilderment, disorientation, and a profound sense of loss, as if wandering in a fog. In these cases, hatred can be an achievement, when the fantasised attachment to the absent object is allowed to be relinquished.

As a substitute for a satisfactory *coniunctio* that might have provided a context in which a fulfilling and creative life could be lived, Fay would instead continuously have to indulge in a semblance of creative activity, 'generating hypotheses' as she called it, about herself, the world, and the motivations of others, thereby convincing herself that an intercourse had occurred which had led to the creation of interesting, and lovable, mental babies that would attract the appreciative attention of her mother, father, and thereafter her parental substitutes. The illusion belied deep feelings of powerlessness, emptiness, and isolation, filled as she was by phantasies of absent objects, the only sources able to evoke in her inner world access to the memory of loving experiences. Fay's attachments to absent objects represented her repeated attempts to keep present the only kind of object that she could love safely; that is, an absent one. If she did attempt to keep an object present, she was hampered by the archetypal nature of her internal object relations such that she would seek either to devour them with stifling acts, particularly of anxious overfeeding and sexual voraciousness that mimicked loving attachment, or else she would choose objects who were potentially dangerous and violent towards her.

Fay was terrified of discovering either that she loved me or that I loved her, or else that one of us was crazy. Our earliest encounter provided a snapshot of the internal object relationships that we would only understand in depth much later. Fay attended an initial consultation in the summer term, when we agreed to begin analysis four sessions per week directly after the summer break. There was a letter awaiting my return in September, informing me that she had decided not to embark on treatment. A year later, Fay approached me again, out of the need she felt, and we agreed to begin, this time building up from one to four sessions weekly over the course of a year. Later, Fay explained that, between the first consultation and her decision to abort the therapy in September, I had been transformed from an accessible, containing and thoughtful analyst with whom she looked forward to working, into a monstrous, crazy witch figure, of whom she was deeply terrified.

Love entered the consulting room slowly, hesitantly. At first, Fay seemed to be very wary of me and would express this by her vague and distant demeanour. In turn, I would feel dislocated from her and noticed that I could not keep details of, in particular, her psychosexual history clearly in my mind. I had a singular difficulty in recalling whether her ex-husband was now dead or alive, an uncomfortable feeling in the countertransference of which I did not relieve myself by asking clarifying questions, as I thought that my discomfort must be related to Fay's own feeling about, so it turned out, her mother after she was ensconced in the mental hospital, not literally dead but not alive or available to Fay.

However, over time, a warm and gently loving atmosphere began to grow between us. Fay explained how extremely important my constant, reliable and accepting presence was to her, particularly the repeated vision she had of me as I opened the door to her in the same way each time. She seemed to marvel at my constancy. And she had a particular way of responding appreciatively to my comments, observations and interpretations that evoked loving feelings in me. We were embarked on a joint meaning-making project in the face of her tremendous inner struggle to keep value and a sense of relating to me accessible in her inner world. I think we created, in Ken Wright's (1991) felicitous description of the earliest infant–mother exchanges, a 'positively amplifying circuit, mutually affirming both partners'. Schore (1996) calls it the 'system of reciprocal mutual influences'. This I would identify as a state of loving, akin to Piontelli's *in utero* observation of the 'kind twins'.

Discussion

I have attempted to show that love is the element that links the two most important areas of psychological enquiry; that is, (1) the primary self and its growth and development, and (2) the self in relation to another. The evidence from infant observation *in utero* shows that, from its very beginnings, the self can be identified by consistent modes of being and behaving that include a capacity for loving exchanges. This means that there is, at the same time, both a primary self and a primary capacity for relating and loving that are contiguous.

This view is underpinned by exciting developments in psychoneurobiological research that demonstrate that the earliest exchanges between the infant and its mother or care givers shape the postnatal maturation of the structural connections within the cortical and subcortical limbic areas of the right hemisphere that come to mediate socioaffective functions as the self matures (Schore, 1996). Thus, the 'positively amplifying circuit that mutually affirms both partners' directly determines the growth of the neonate's brain in its capacity for emotional and relational attachments, at the same time as the mother is captured by and devoted to her infant.

In Fay's case, repeated attachments to absent objects, evoking objects that can be safely loved because they are absent, suggest that the psyche is propelled to reach out from within the self and find an object to love, even if it must be an absent one. Indeed, for Fay, attempting to love an available object represented an early situation that was dangerous to her self. In the face of the danger that might have led her to create, through internalisation, an inner world populated by overwhelmingly crazy and/or persecuting internal objects, Fay responded by repeatedly accessing her potential for loving and for relatedness through her unerring attachment to absent but safely lovable objects. In so doing, powerful negative emotions such as rage and hatred were eschewed in order to keep her internal world intact.

It is the linking function of loving that deepens and widens our inner worlds, from our earliest moments of being and throughout the rest of our lives. The first loving link is the prototype for all subsequent mental linking, whether reaching out towards another, or indeed towards any ideas or pursuits that, through reintegration, allow the psyche to grow. Winnicott said (1964: 191) 'A child is lucky if "conceived of" as well as being the result of physical conception.' I take this to mean that an act of love between man and woman that results in a real conception and that includes the mental conception of a potential child is for that couple and for that child a very great expression of humanity and human potential. Fay had to keep on 'generating hypotheses' in her repeated attempts to restore and transform internally her own unconceived conception. She eventually allowed herself to re-enter analysis, thus providing an opportunity for an intimate and intense relationship as a means of helping her to achieve this restoration.

Conclusion

The experience of paradox derives from the basic paradigm of simultaneous contradiction and inclusion. This has to do with the nature of being human, where being a self and the knowledge of self co-exist. The self cannot know itself, nor achieve its fullest expression in individuation, except in relation to another. The self first knows itself through another, and the earliest pair in primary mutual preoccupation is, of course, mother and infant.

The paradox of love is that, at the very moment that the self searches out and finds another with whom it is possible to relate, it enhances and enriches itself. Analytic literature is full of discussion about the vicissitudes and difficulties of unloving states that pre-empt the conditions upon which love can be most fully lived. Paradoxes, however enriching, can also be deeply uncomfortable to experience; so too, love. Love that encompasses self and other may be uncomfortable and difficult to achieve at times, but it thereby carries the deepest potential for the realisation of what it means to be human. This is the capacity of the self to realise itself in relation to another.

Notes

1 There are a number of Jungian contributions on love (as distinct from the erotic transference or countertransference) which include Jung (1926), Spielrein ([1912] 1994), Kast (1986), and Colman (1994). From the psychoanalytic literature, Gerrard has provided a useful bibliography and literature review in her account of 'Love in the time of therapy' (1996: 163).
2 I am grateful to Elizabeth Urban for drawing my attention to this text.

References

Astor, J. (1995) *Michael Fordham: Innovations In Analytical Psychology*, London: Routledge.

Bion, W. (1962) 'A theory of thinking', *International Journal of Psycho-Analysis*, 43.

Bowlby, J. (1969) *Attachment*, London: Hogarth Press.

Brazelton, T.B., Tronick, E., Anderson, L.H. & Weise, S. (1973) 'Early mother-in-law reciprocity', in *Parent–Infant Interaction*, Ciba Foundation Symposium 33, Amsterdam: Elsevier.

Colman, W. (1994) 'Love, desire and infatuation: encountering the erotic spirit', *Journal of Analytical Psychology*, 39, 4.

Covington, C. (1996) 'Learning How to Forget – Repeating the Past as a Defence Against the Present'. Paper presented at a Conference entitled 'On Memory', organised by The British Association of Psychotherapists, October.

Fordham, M. (1988) 'Principles of child analysis', in M. Sidoli and M. Davies (eds), *Jungian Child Psychotherapy*, London: Karnac.

Gaddini, E. (1992) *A Psychoanalytic Theory of Infantile Experience: Conceptual and Clinical Reflections*, London: Routledge.

Gerrard, J. (1996) 'Love in the time of psychotherapy', *British Journal of Psychotherapy*, 13, 2.

Jung, C.G. (1926) 'Marriage as a psychological relationship', *Collected Works*, 17.

Kalsched, D.E. (1996) *Mercurius Duplex: Archetypal Defence Against Early Trauma*, New York: Association for Analytical Psychology.

Kast, V. (1986) *The Nature of Loving: Patterns of Human Relationship*, Wilmette, Ill.: Chiron.

Piontelli, A. (1992) *From Fetus to Child: An Observational and Psychoanalytic Study*, London and New York: Tavistock/Routledge.

Schore, A. (1996) 'The experience-dependent maturation of a regulatory system in the orbital prefrontal cortex and the origin of developmental psychopathology', *Development and Psychopathology*, 8.

Solomon, H.M. (1994) 'The transcendent function and Hegel's dialectical vision', *Journal of Analytical Psychology*, 39, 77–100.

—— (1997) 'The not-so-silent couple in the individual', *Journal of Analytical Psychology*, 42, 3.

—— (2000) 'Recent developments in the neurosciences', in E. Christopher and H. Solomon, *Jungian Thought in the Modern World*, London: Free Association Books.

Spielrein, S. ([1912] 1994) 'Destruction as the cause of coming into being', *Journal of Analytical Psychology*, 39, 2.

Stern, D. (1985) *The Interpersonal World of the Infant*, New York: Basic Books.

Trevarthen, C. (1980) 'The foundations of intersubjectivity: development of interpersonal and cooperative understanding in infants', in D.R. Olson (ed.) *The Social Foundations of Language and Thought*, Toronto: Norton.

Winnicott, D.W. (1964) 'This feminism', in C. Winnicott, R. Shepherd and M. Davis (eds) *Home is Where We Start From: Essays by a Psychoanalyst*, London: Penguin Books, 1986.

Wright, K. (1991) *Vision and Separation: Between Mother and Baby*, London: Free Association Books.

Chapter 3

The capacity for love

Sue Gottlieb

Our desire to love, and be loved, faces us with a profound dilemma. It is a fact of psychic reality that we need to become attached to a loved and loving person; for the infant this is certainly a matter of biological survival, but even when physical survival is no longer at issue we seek to transcend our essential separateness and aloneness by forming intimate relationships with significant figures, who we come to love and depend upon. One of the many paradoxes of love is that we can *only* develop emotionally, and become fully individuated selves, within an intimate relationship.

This primary, innate seeking of attachment is seemingly driven, on the one hand, by a fear of non-attachment, in the sense that awareness of our separateness arouses intense anxiety because it is connected with a sense of vulnerability and helplessness. But perhaps, even from the beginning of life there is a more joyful search for *relationship* too – a hopeful reaching for a satisfying object, that will lead to love and concern. If we are seen as being emotionally linked to our objects by love, hate and curiosity, then the desire for love may be understood as a kind of 'life instinct': a basic, irreducible force that exists in its own right and motivates our active search for nourishment and relationship from the beginning of life.

The desire for love is therefore our deepest emotional need, as essential to our psychological well-being as food is for our physical survival; yet to experience love for our objects also brings us intense pain and frustration. The problem with love, one might say, is that it necessarily stirs up hate too. To love someone is to need them and to be dependent upon them, and therefore to hate them when they frustrate us, as they inevitably do, and to hate the fact of our dependence. Our narcissism asserts that such pain is better avoided. Our dilemma, then, takes the form of a conflict between our narcissism and our love of life: whether to try to be fully related, which means tolerating this ambivalence and overcoming the depression it inevitably brings by learning to temper our hate with our love; or to try to avoid the pain and frustration by throwing away our object in search of a better one who will not frustrate us, or cynically giving up on relationships altogether as a bad lot.

Hackneyed though it may have become, Tennyson's conviction following the death of his beloved friend Arthur Hallam that "'tis better to have loved and lost / Than never to have loved' (Tennyson, 1850) is the hard-won product of what might be called 'successful' mourning. Despite the pain and frustration of his loss, he has in the end been able to retain his love for his lost object and, by extension, he considers that he was better for having been in a loving relationship, even though he lost it, than if he had not had it – though not to have had it, so the internal narcissistic logic goes, would have saved him the pain of loss.

But we also have to go through the same mourning process to *achieve* a mature capacity to love. In order to love, we are not only taking the risk that the loved one might die, or leave us, but we also have to face the deeper difficulty in coming to terms with the fact that our loved object, to be a 'true object' (Caper, 1999) rather than a narcissistic extension of ourselves, is essentially separate from us and beyond our control. The aim of love is union with another, but how that aim is achieved depends upon the extent to which we can come to accommodate, through a process of mourning, the fact of separateness. Narcissistic love is based on the premise that the pain of loss *is* too great to risk being fully related, and so it seeks to achieve that aim through appropriating and possessing the other, with the defensive aim of *denying* the fact of separateness and need; whereas mature, non-narcissistic love – which I shall call 'object-love' in the sense that it relates to a 'true' object – is based upon Tennyson's conviction and so it seeks to achieve that aim through making a *relationship* with the other which takes full account of our separateness and need. This is the distinction between love in the paranoid–schizoid position and love in the depressive position.

In this chapter, therefore, I shall consider the nature of narcissistic love and of mature object-love, and the relationship between them. While narcissism is certainly opposed to object-love, and also to genuine self-love, I suggest that narcissistic 'love' may be usefully understood, clinically, as a protective defence against object-love and I shall illustrate the beginnings of a capacity for object-love as it emerges in a therapy.

Narcissism and object-love

Mature object-love is based upon the appreciative love of the object that has contained, nourished or protected the self. It is underpinned by depressive concern, and this gives it certain and particular qualities of deeply felt gratitude, reparativeness, affection and tenderness. Gerrard has aptly called it a feeling of 'extreme tenderness' (Gerrard, 1996), and in the same vein Robert Louis Stevenson emphasised that 'the essence of love is kindness; and indeed it may best be defined as passionate kindness' (Meltzer, 1988: 40–41). Gerrard also points out that genuine love is not 'idealisation, worship, clinging or a defence against hatred', although they may all be misconstrued as love. In essence, mature object-love is based upon 'the sane awareness of the need for nourishment from an external object that cannot be controlled by the self' (Segal and Bell, 1991). Mature love has a fundamental respect for reality, in the sense that it observes the psychological 'facts of life' (Money-Kyrle, 1971), which means tolerating, even celebrating, the fact of difference, doubt and imperfection and above all else the reality of personal dependence and need. The object of this kind of love is a more or less realistically perceived 'good-enough' whole object, who is perceived as *other* and remains independent of the self.

Narcissistic love is, in many ways, the opposite: it is based instead on the denial of the reality of dependence, in favour of a seeming state of self-sufficiency. The idea that what is needed lies outside the self is intolerable. The belief that it is better not to risk love – object-love – is the propaganda of the narcissistic self, which will, to some extent, advertise this state of absence of need as being superior to a normal state of dependence, which is perceived as contemptibly weak and dangerous (Rosenfeld, 1971). Difference, uncertainty, imperfection and the 'facts of life' are hated, because they point to the reality of our need for others and our vulnerability and, ultimately, a belief in the ideal is maintained at the cost of the real.

Narcissism is a self-idealisation at the expense of the object, achieved by simultaneously appropriating what is regarded as good in an external object and expelling into that object what is regarded as bad in the self. By these means the individual in a narcissistic frame of mind feels that everything that is valuable is either part of him, or external to him but under his omnipotent control, so creating an illusion of self-sufficiency.

The object of narcissistic love is an idealised part of the self, projected into an object (just as the object of narcissistic hate is a denigrated part of the self located in an object), although subjectively it will not be perceived as such – Narcissus claimed to be in love with an external object and did not realise that his 'object' was his own idealised reflection. Because of these extensive projections, of the self into the object, people cannot be seen for who they really are. This aspect of the narcissistic choice of object was described by Freud in his study of Leonardo da Vinci, in his observation that the relationship to the *real* external object is denied and the self is taken as a model in whose likeness objects of love are chosen (Freud, 1910). Objects chosen on this basis cannot be treated with depressive concern in terms of their *own* needs; instead the object is treated as an extension of the self. The essence of narcissistic relating is a determination to control the ideal object, to make it feel like a part of the self, and when it cannot be controlled the idealised sense of fusion and grandiosity gives way to feelings of alienation and persecution.

Narcissistic and true object relationships are associated with very different states of mind and also with different senses of identity and intimacy. Because object-love is based upon a sense of separateness it allows for genuine (depressive) intimacy, based on the reality that the other is known only from the outside, by a process of getting to know them emotionally. It has a particular quality of humility, uncertainty and doubt and respect for the other's privacy (Fisher, 1993). A couple linked in this mutually autonomous way may be receptive to one another's projections without feeling their individual identities to have been destroyed by being invaded, swallowed up or taken over. By contrast, when in narcissistic relating the needed object is incorporated, such that one *becomes* the breast, rather than be aware of one's separateness *from* it and need *for* it, the resulting sense of identity is a grandiose pseudo-maturity. In so far as separateness is denied, a state of fusion will be conflated with true intimacy. Pseudo-intimacy is a rather excited and idealised sense of being the same as the ideal object, and knowing it perfectly. The resultant relationship has no room for conflict, difference, ambivalence, or, for that matter, true desire for the object, and it brings with it a claustrophobic fear of being taken over.

These distinctions are necessarily schematic and in practice, of course, any subjective feeling of love will contain narcissistic and non-narcissistic elements in varying proportions. One might say that only object-love can properly be called 'real' love, to mean a relationship with an object which, while positive, does not idealise it and does not lead to an identification with it, but the same word is used for these two quite different psychic phenomena. Perhaps this is because, subjectively, both feel 'real' and 'true' (Bishop, 1998). The narcissist will certainly hold *his* love to be the 'real thing', quite real enough to die for, if not a superior thing to object-love, which he will perceive contemptuously as being too mundane and unexciting. But, on further analysis, experiences which the narcissist considers to be deeply loving turn out to be methods of avoiding real love associated with dependence. Because death is romantically misperceived, from the narcissistic perspective, as a state of perfect consummation – an eternal union with the ideal object, rather than a loss – death is often preferred to the recognition that this form of love might be, in reality, unsustaining. After all, in the original myth,

> Narcissus is trapped, gazing at something that he subjectively believes is a lost loved object but that objectively is the idealized aspect of his own self. He believes himself to be in love. He dies of starvation, however, because he cannot turn away toward a real object from whom he might have been able to get what he really needed.
>
> (Segal and Bell, 1991: 172).

Why the need for narcissism?

One might ask, then, why Narcissus could not tear himself away from his idealised reflection and find the life-giving object he needed. Narcissism is called upon, universally, as a defence against the awareness of separateness and the anxieties associated with it. Our anxiety lies in the fact that the loved object is both needed and beyond our control. In considering the 'sensation of hunger that is associated with . . . a breast that does not satisfy but is of a kind that is needed', Bion starkly states that: 'This needed object is a bad object. All objects that are needed are bad objects. They are needed because they are not possessed in fact; if they were possessed there would be no lack' (Bion, 1962: 83–84). The needed object is loved and valued, but therein lies its badness too: as soon as the good object frustrates the infant, as it inevitably does, it is recognised as being separate from the self, and able to deprive the infant of what it really needs and depends upon. The fact of its separateness from the self evokes feelings of helplessness and dependence. The object is therefore hated for being good, needed and yet *not* a part of the self. A sense of dependence necessarily stirs painful feelings of envy too; envy being a resentment of the fact that the object has the capacity to give him what he cannot provide for himself (Rosenfeld, 1964). The object is therefore hated and envied (as well as loved) precisely at the point when it is recognised as being valuable and able to provide relief, because it evokes the pain of dependency.

Put very schematically, there are two ways for the personality to deal with the hatred and anxiety associated with need: it can either come to be *accepted*, through the developmental process of mourning; or it can be *denied* by instituting a more defensive fantasy of possessing or becoming the needed object. Identifying projectively with the needed object is the narcissistic solution to the problem of need. Thus, as Rosenfeld says, 'the omnipotent narcissistic object relations therefore obviate both the aggressive feelings caused by frustration and any awareness of envy. When the infant omnipotently possesses the mother's breast, the breast cannot frustrate him or arouse his envy' (Rosenfeld, 1964: 171). When an object is possessed in this omnipotent way, it is no longer experienced as being external to the self (and therefore able to evoke feelings of need); rather, it is equated with the self and the boundaries between self and other are confused. By becoming the object one has everything and needs nothing. There are in fact two simultaneous steps in this defensive procedure: at the same time as appropriating the ideal qualities of the needed object, feelings of vulnerability and need are projected (Joseph, 1959). Thus, by denying (or preventing) the autonomy of his objects, the individual is able to maintain a belief in self-sufficiency and an illusion of having achieved it. Of course, to some extent we all adopt both solutions – denial and acceptance – so that one speaks of a narcissistic and a non-narcissistic part of the self, which are inevitably in conflict with one another.

Object relations are necessarily narcissistic for the individual in a paranoid–schizoid state of mind: because a good internal object is lacking, pain and distress are emotional experiences which cannot be digested, so anxiety is overcome by splitting off disturbing aspects of both the self, and the object, and projecting them into other people. An ideal self is thereby created, in a relationship with an ideal object. Love for the object, and the self, is conditional upon it being ideal. Love in the paranoid–schizoid position is based upon the phantasy (or narcissistic illusion) of having exclusive access to, and possession of, the primary ideal object.

The paranoid–schizoid position is of course a normal state of mind in a young infant, because a good internal object has not yet been secured and dependency on the mother's life-saving presence is absolute. The infantile form of love, as it evolves in the 'normal' paranoid–schizoid position, necessarily has a narcissistic flavour in the sense that the infant seeks a relationship with an ideal breast only and will, to some extent, deny a sense of separateness by drawing upon an illusion of possessing it. Anxiety about separation is usually dealt with by becoming bossy or controlling – a product of the illusion that one can omnipotently control the comings and goings of the much-needed object upon whom one depends. Evidence that the other is an independent object with his or her own mind is experienced in a persecuting way as a betrayal and an infidelity. To some extent this possessiveness is indulged by the parent, who anyway strives to protect the infant from being overwhelmed by experiences of frustration, and recognises that it may be a temporary way of dealing with the anxiety of feeling vulnerable and small until a sufficient sense of agency has built up through the experience of being emotionally contained. In the ordinary course of development, the normal infantile omnipotent phantasy of owning, or being, the ideal object may then be relinquished, painfully, to allow mature object-love to develop. This process of relinquishment (to which I shall return) is the symbolic aspect of *weaning*. Hitherto projected parts of the self are recovered and owned as part of the self, allowing a more realistic perception of self and object to emerge. Weaning is about the irrevocable physical loss of the breast, but in a wider sense it is about the move into the depressive position: 'a life-long developmental process of giving up omnipotent illusions' and, through mourning, coming to terms with one's real condition (Fisher, 2000). Upon this is based the capacity for object-love.

But the degree of omnipotence involved in these narcissistic object relations is crucial. The narcissistic defence used in a powerfully omnipotent and systematic way, perhaps to counter excessive hatred of need, will create for the individual a pathological paranoid–schizoid position – a rigidly structured 'narcissistic organisation' which functions as a kind of permanent refuge from the pain of separateness and need. When ordinary human need is so hated, the two-dimensionality of the paranoid–schizoid position means that the part of the self capable of feeling need is regarded as having an inferior status, while the needed object – the person who is capable of satisfying the need – is perceived as being superior because they are imagined to have no needs themselves. Certainly the needed object will be experienced as feeling smugly superior and cruelly wishing to lord it over the humiliated, inferior, needy subject. In this situation one acquires superiority by turning the tables and becoming the needed object. Now, the person feeling in possession of his ideal object will feel superior to those into whom the inferior state of not-being-in-possession has been projected. In such an organisation, it is the omnipotent infantile phantasy of possessing the breast which, rather than being relinquished, gets idealised and is regarded as the best and truest form of love – a superior thing indeed. This gives rise to a particular type of love relationship: the fixed omnipotent identification with the nourishing (superior) object precludes the possibility of being nourished and restricts the capacity to love. The object is loved narcissistically and 'needed' in a strictly limited sense: as a receptacle for the unwanted, denigrated infant part of the self, and the apparent concern for his welfare is undermined by contempt for his perceived weakness. Situations which require this part of the self to be re-owned – such as a loving relationship – are avoided.

Example of narcissism

I shall now give a brief illustration of this sort of narcissistic organisation as one meets it in ordinary clinical practice. (I am focusing on the elements of narcissism in the personality rather than drawing a rounded picture of a whole person.) Mr A was a middle-aged unmarried man, and while consciously longing to find the 'right woman' with whom to live, and even at times aware of feeling deeply lonely, at another level he was really quite uninterested in sustaining a close relationship. Although he looked like a man dying for love – as indeed he was, like Narcissus – he was unable to put himself in the position of really needing love, either in the analytic relationship or in his external relationships.

In the therapy, Mr A would be briefly aware of feelings of real need for my help and understanding. But because his vulnerability and feelings of need were intensely humiliating for him, and he perceived himself as being weak and inferior, he would quickly re-establish a more comfortable position in which he was protected from the emotional turbulence of *really* needing me. Ashamed of feeling small, vulnerable and exposed, he turned himself into an omnipotent character who did not really *need* therapy, beyond having me give him a 'pointer in the right direction' from time to time.

He had many love affairs with women which followed a particular pattern. Although initially very keen he would withdraw as he got close or there was a possibility of commitment. He would remain friendly and apparently interested, but, essentially, he had gone 'cold' inside. Sometimes he was aware that something about her, such as a physical imperfection, would be increasingly off-putting but more often his feelings of interest would 'just' disappear as if his appetite had faded away. At this point he was actually quite comfortable, and content to let the relationship remain as it was, but feelings of persecution would build up as the woman, reasonably enough, wanted to develop the relationship and had been led by him to believe that he did too. Although at first she had seemed ideal, and particularly caring in a maternal way, now she would seem increasingly demanding and 'pushy' and he would speak about her infantile demand-ingness in a very denigrating way. Then he would be aware of another woman he felt passionate about and 'really' wanted.

In the therapy, I could see that Mr A's *appearance* of interest and concern was actually very convincing, because it operated at the level of self-deception. He did, of course, have genuine feelings of curiosity, but much of the time he was playing the part of a grateful well-motivated patient needing therapy, and his dreams about slick con-men indicated his unconscious recognition of this aspect of himself. I came to realise that his life was arranged in such a way that he would never have to expose himself to the pain of separateness, need and real dependency on a feeding object, and that his 'comfortable position' was a rigid narcissistic organisation.

As I came to understand it, these love affairs, which were invariably with younger women in a state of great vulnerability, were the means by which he located his needy self in his objects. Once freed of his feelings of need and appetite, which were essentially unbearable for him beause they exposed him to too much anxiety, he lost interest in the woman as she was, along with his capacity to love. He had lost too much of a vital part of his personality to be able to sustain a relationship. He was, however, reluctant to lose her com-pletely because *she* now contained this part of him. This situation was relatively stable, and comfortable for him, until she asked for more.

Mr A very much enjoyed his 'comfortable position' and found it an ideal state of mind. He assumed that I would enjoy it as much as he did and feel equally satisfied, but I found the atmosphere claustrophobic. He was in a rather too comfortable – if not complacent – state of mind and he seemed to be occupying an overly benign Garden of Eden sort of world from which all negativity and difficulty had apparently been removed. What he offered me was a mutually idealising relationship, in which we could adore one another and never be apart, and exist in a state of total agreement. It would be what Meltzer has described as a 'doll's house marriage': a narcissistic (pseudo-intimate) collusion where 'a sort of continual honeymoon exists and love is wonderful – I love me and you love me' (Meltzer, 1971). Mr A was actually very effective at pulling people into this world – most of his friendships seemed to operate as mutual admiration societies, for example – but it took me a while to understand how he did this. He would introduce a dream, for example, as being particularly 'fascinating'. The dream would indeed be fascinating but he would get too fascinated and pleased with himself, and rather than treat it with genuine curiosity as a way of helping him understand something about himself, the dream would become an art exhibit to be admired. When I found myself worrying that my 'ordinary' basic interpretations were not sufficiently sophisticated or 'clever', I realised that this was his unconscious way of trying to pull me into the narcissistic world too. If, by appealing to my narcissism, he could get me similarly fascinated in him and his dreams then we could jointly overlook the actual meaning of the dream and admire one another instead. The interpretation that I was being pressurised to overlook was, of course, the one addressing his sense of need and vulnerability.

In fact, a considerable degree of manipulation and even bullying went into the maintenance of his overly agreeable attitude. He put me under great pressure to fit in with him and keep frustration (and evidence of separateness) out of our relationship, such as by readjusting break times so that we could be on holiday at the same time, and telling him where I was going when I went away. He reacted to evidence of reality (his need for me) with absolute outrage and made me feel that I was being extremely cruel and unreasonable not to go along with him, and I had to be clear within myself about the difference between cruelty on the one hand and kind firmness on the other. This was easier to do when I was able to glimpse that, hidden underneath his narcissistic defence (the outraged bully accusing me of injustice), was an infant in an absolute panic about losing me.

If I suggested things might not be as perfect for him as he claimed, he regarded me as being a bit of a misery, spoiling the mood. Following the pattern of his external relationships, he now experienced me as wanting more from him (as indeed I was, in a sense) and attacking the equilibrium of his comfortable position. What he 'really' wanted, he said, was not the frustrating, inferior analytic (feeding) relationship that I was offering him, but 'another kind' of relationship that he claimed would be more exciting and enjoyable for us both. I understood this longed-for 'other relationship' to be the comfortable position reinstated in a pure form elsewhere. He mistook it for an adult sexual relationship but actually it had a very infantile quality. His daydream of an infinite and infinitely satisfying intercourse where he could keep me in a permanent state of pleasure was, I think, an omnipotent infantile phantasy of total, exclusive possession of the breast (not even a whole mother) with absolutely no separation. This phantasy generated enormous excitement for him: he was cast as a superman (actually a super-infant) omnipotently able to maintain the breast in a youthful state of eternal and plentiful lactation (a super-breast perhaps), essentially under his complete control. This sort of love – actually an omnipotent infantile phantasy – was highly idealised by him, and consciously held as the greatest form of love.

Mr A's comfortable position was created by a two-step process of simultaneously appropriating my idealised qualities and projecting into me his hated infant self (Joseph, 1959; Rosenfeld, 1964, 1971). By projecting himself into me, perceived as a totally ideal breast, and then identifying omnipotently with me, the fact of our separate identities was thereby denied, so obviating any feelings of dependency. By claiming my idealised functions for himself he had no real need of me as a separate object. My true function for him as a feeding (thinking) mother was thereby reduced, and this belittling process was represented graphically in his many dreams of me as being very small, often through an ingenious miniaturising (shrinking!) process.

In simultaneously projecting into me his unwanted feelings of need and vulnerability, Mr A freed himself of such feelings and perceived *me* as being in a state of need. He spoke to me in a 'loving' way that I found hollow and unmoving, just as I found his expressions of gratitude to be rather over-done and sentimental. He was extremely alert to any signs of physical or emotional vulnerability in me, and quickly constructed rescue fantasies around them. There were of course some genuinely reparative elements in his attitude to me, linked to his remorse and concern for his depressed internal mother, but, overall, his concern had an exaggerated, patronising quality which suggested that he was mostly exploiting my perceived neediness and vulnerability to bolster his own sense of self-righteous superiority. His concern for me was patronising inasmuch as it was for an unwanted part of himself located in me.

The net effect of these two steps was to produce his feeling of blissful complacency. He was now an ideal breast, rather grandiosely nourishing the world, in a superior state of self-sufficiency, and I was reduced to being in an inferior state of need. Mr A was extremely concerned to be punctual and pay me on time, saying how much he hated to keep me waiting. I came to realise that his alarm about being late and having to rush to the session (often at dangerous speeds which made me worry for his safety) was not because *he* might miss something, but because, in his mind, *I* would be dying for a feed from him, as if he was a kind of peripatetic breast. In effect, he kept me in this denigrated position, in his mind, so as not to be aware of *his* need for *me* and he tended to construe my interpretations which addressed his vulnerability as my infantilising attempt to reverse this situation, and make *him* the scorned infant feeling helplessly dependent on me.

A narcissistic organisation of this kind clearly creates a developmental impasse: the individual is defended against psychosis, but restricted in his capacity to move fully into the depressive position and develop a capacity for mature object-love; a truly borderline position. Yet it is only resorted to in an attempt to protect the individual from what are felt to be intolerable realities of relatedness. If narcissism is a universal defensive response to frustration then it follows that the greater the degree of deprivation the more omnipotent the narcissistic defence will be. I think it is significant that

Mr A experienced the women he projected into as 'pushy', indicating his projected need to 'push into' an emotionally unavailable internal mother. It was clear, both from his history and from my experience of him, that Mr A had in fact had far too much real exposure to insecurity. Dependency for him had been an experience he would wish never to repeat. His idealisation was essentially of an object that his sane self regarded as bad: an impenetrable mother who could not take in her infant's projections and know about the extent of his suffering.

Idealisation in narcissistic and object-love

I think it is crucial to distinguish this kind of rigid defensive idealisation from the more 'normal' splitting and idealisation in the service of development. There has been a certain tendency, in Kleinian thinking, to regard *all* idealisation as being pathologically defensive in nature, although Likierman has delineated clearly how Klein herself, in her thinking about early object-love, did explore two kinds of primitive ideal experience without explicitly differentiating them; one 'the product of a primitive mode of appreciation' and the other a 'defensive exaggeration' (Likierman, 1993).

In practice the distinction, in both the transference and the counter-transference, is fairly clear: the narcissistic identification with an idealised object, which produces Mr A's feelings of superiority, grandiosity and a mood of unshakeable complacency, evokes a corresponding counter-transference hatred. My infuriation with the omnipotent part of him were mixed with deep concern and sorrow for the despairing infant part of him, walled-off underneath the narcissistic grandiosity.

Our capacity to be in a sufficiently balanced state of mind to be both open to projections and analytic about them, at any one time, depends upon the state of integration of our love and hate for the patient. There was a real risk that, in my hatred of his bullying omnipotence, I would retaliate by rubbing Mr A's nose in his underlying feelings of smallness and inferiority. Highly narcissistic patients such as Mr A are very testing of our capacity, as therapists, to contain properly our own hatred; neither denying it in a sentimental collusion (by joining him in the overly comfortable Garden of Eden) nor being taken over by it (and thereby losing touch with, and any loving concern for, the desperate infant behind the playground bully). Caper (1994) points out that when we find ourselves needing to cure the patient, rather than analyse him, it is because our anxieties about our own destructive impulses are uncontained, and we are searching for reassurance that our own love (expressed as creativity and reparativeness) has not fallen victim to our destructiveness. My hatred for Mr A was specifically evoked, from time to time, by a sense of being tricked by the con-man in him but, painful as it was at the time, it was only when I was fully in touch with the depth of my hatred that I could once again be properly and sympathetically in touch with the hurt person walled-off underneath the narcissistic persona, and able to address his inflated picture of himself in a non-condemning way (Gottlieb, 1994).

In contrast, the state of idealisation arising from the necessary identification with a *good* object creates a very different mood. For example:

Miss B described a weekend walking in countryside near her old home. She gave me a long, joyful description of the setting, and memories of walking with her father in a carpet of beech leaves, scuffing them like cornflakes. A little dog was 'lost' in them. She remembered a dream about being pregnant, which stood in marked contrast to her more usual feeling of barrenness.

She told me about this experience in a particular way – turning to me – and in response I felt pleasure, in the way that the observer of an infant contentedly at the breast, provided he or she has had a similarly good experience to draw on, will feel a sense of pleasure in an empathic identification with the baby. (The observer who has not internalised such an experience will feel murderous.) The beautiful trees, the forest of cornflakes flooded in milk – so deep the little dog (the baby) can get lost in them – all sound like an infant feeding at the breast being appropriately hungry and excited. The pregnancy indicated her hope that she might have a new beginning with me, in the transference; a proper mother with plenty of milk, undaunted by a really hungry baby. This is a 'normal' idealisation of the feeding breast, imbued with loving excitement: a sense of inexhaustibility and abundance. Feelings such as these, of love and gratitude, 'arise directly and spontaneously in the baby in response to the love and care of his mother' (Klein, 1937: 311). Because they arise as part of the paranoid–schizoid position, where good and bad experience are so split, the loved breast is then subjectively experienced as a boundless, ideal source of mental sustenance, and the corresponding love for the good feeding mother is experienced as a state of 'complete gratification' (Klein, 1952). It is nonetheless an aspect of healthy primitive experience and different from the manic state of omnipotence that is the result of a narcissistic type of identification with an idealised object.

It is significant that my feelings of interest, and love, were evoked by Miss B turning to me. Gerrard points out that loving feelings are engendered above all else by the effort to make contact: 'genuineness, a wish for connectedness and a capacity for work and play in the patient are the principal ingredients which will engender loving feelings in the therapist' (Gerrard, 1996). This raises the question: how are such feelings of love expressed in the analytic relationship? In asking what a mother does with her infant when she loves it, Bion suggests that 'leaving aside the physical channels of communication . . . her love is expressed by reverie' (Bion, 1962: 35–36). In the analytic relationship mature love is expressed not through 'physical channels' but, similarly, I suggest, through reverie – a wish to know the patient emotionally, through being open to projections and thinking about them.

Mourning

The developmental function of the paranoid–schizoid position is to build up and take into the self, by a steady process of introjection rather than omnipotent incorporation, enough of this sort of experience of goodness to allow the narcissistic phantasy of possessing or being the ideal object to be relinquished, and to allow hate to begin to be safely experienced in conflict with love, rather than entirely split off from it. This constitutes the first step into the depressive position, and the beginnings of a capacity for mature object-love.

As the omnipotent infantile phantasies are given up, their loss must be mourned. This is the 'work' of the depressive position – a highly complex psychological task which is exactly the same as that facing the bereaved person in mourning (Steiner, 1993). What it requires (and what makes it so difficult) is a readjustment to reality. Essentially, what is being relinquished is an illusory omnipotent belief that an object can be, and indeed was, controlled and possessed in a perfect Garden of Eden sort of world. Of course, the infant never did, in reality, have uninterrupted possession of the breast. Now love and hate are increasingly felt at the same time and towards the same person, with all the attendant guilt and remorse one feels as a result of hating the person one loves and needs, and regards as good – 'good' because they have been open to us, and containing. If these uniquely painful feelings can be borne without reverting to the narcissistic position, then guilt and concern emerge, and the possibility of reparation and being able to feel *for* the object. As projections are withdrawn, we can perceive ourselves and our objects in a less distorted way, as more real and human. With the survival of the object, and our love for the object, in the face of our hatred, we feel profound relief and gratitude; in other words, mature (depressive) object-love. One might, indeed, define emotional maturation in exactly these terms, as the growth of an 'internal capacity for marriage' (Waddell, 1998); a gradually evolving process of relinquishing the narcissistic mode of relating in favour of the depressive mode, and a new-found capacity for object-love.

Illustration of a moment of emergence

Mr A was slightly late for his session, and he told me in a genuinely anxious and troubled way about his hectic schedule and his feelings of being rushed. In particular he was trying to accommodate a new evening class, which he felt ashamed to admit was for beginners. He said, in a touching way, that he felt like a highly tuned engine that was being over-revved and in danger of blowing up. I understood this in terms of the new (less inflated) picture of himself he was trying, like a beginner, to accommodate: although he was under consider-able internal pressure to manage his dangerously over-busy schedule in his usual omnipotent (highly tuned) way, actually by projecting his vulnerability into others, he was seeing himself, far more realistically, as far from omni-potent and near to breakdown. It was clear that he felt supported by my sympathetic recognition of his vulnerability and he was relieved by it rather than humiliated.

He then explained that he had been late because he had stayed at home to read a letter, when he should have been on his way to the session. The letter was a reference he had been waiting for, and he had hoped that it would be glowing and say marvellous (actually idealising) things about him. It did, which was nice, but it made him late to see me and, now, that seemed a silly risk to have taken. It was clear that, on this occasion, he felt this lateness to be his loss, rather than mine, and he became very tearful, although he did not understand why it should make him so upset.

I think his tears were the mark of a complex internal shift. He was experi-encing acutely painful depressive feelings as he emerged from the comfort of his narcissistic position. He found the narcissistic picture of himself, as reflected in the letter, terribly appealing, but ultimately worthless in terms of his own development and self-esteem. His tears were about his recog-nition of me as someone of genuine value to him: not colluding with him in giving him a glowing reference but wishing to know about, and support him in, his vulnerability rather than condemning it as a weakness, and not hitting him back for his belittling of me. For the moment, he was able to bear his feelings of separateness, dependency and envy without having to jump back into the comfortable position, although he could recognise the lure of the position, in the form of the idealising reference. He was glimpsing, with remorse and sorrow, the harm of this position: both the harm he did me, in his mind, by belittling me but also, and more import-antly, the harm it did *him*. He clearly recognised the dangerous position his omnipotence put him in, emotionally and physically. In staying to read the letter he was being Narcissus sticking to his narcissistic reflection and depriving himself of the help he really needed from me.

Mr A was just at the beginning of the depressive conflict: trying to bring his love and hate closer together and develop some trust in his own capacity for loving reparation rather than magical pseudo-repair. But at least, in that moment, he had undone the comfortable narcissistic position by retrieving the hated infant part of himself that he had located in me and returning to me the qualities of mine he had appropriated. He could therefore recognise us as separate and see more clearly what belonged to him and what belonged to me. He was experiencing proper concern for himself and his needs, and because he was seeing his own vulnerability in a less self-condemning light he was less driven to project it scornfully into me. By the same token, he was now experiencing genuine love for me as a helpful person with a mind of my own, rather than a narcissistic love for me as an ideal object under his control: our relationship could be a marriage of minds rather than a state of narcissistic identification.

Failure of mourning

Such moments of emergence from a narcissistic retreat into a more depressive mode of relating are inevitably shortlived because it is so difficult to reverse the earlier trend towards possessing the object. Over the course of a therapy a pattern evolves of emergence followed by retreat, although, if all goes well, another small piece of (internal) ground is gained with each emergence. In the face of frustration we cling tenaciously to the belief that somewhere else, or with someone else, there is access to a unique, uncomplicated and blissful experience – such as a state of pristine wholeness in which separateness, need and vulnerability are not experienced. In Plato's *Symposium* on the nature of love, for example, Aristophanes recounts the myth that men are merely halves of original wholes, bisected by Zeus as a punishment for their 'overweening pride' (Plato, 1951). One wonders whether the 'overweening pride' was narcissistic omnipotence, and whether Zeus was, perhaps cruelly, reminding man that narcissistic self-sufficiency was indeed an omnipotent delusion. To some extent this is a fantasy we all fall back on, especially when frustration is particularly hard to bear. Relinquishing it again is part of the lifelong process of mourning, and the cycle of losing and recovering one's objects and capacity to love. But for some the belief may not be relinquishable, except with the greatest of difficulty. As I came to understand it, Mr A's particular difficulty in this respect was to do with the fact that he did not have enough trust in his own love to be able to tolerate the ambivalence that integration would imply. He feared that his hatred was responsible for the depression of his internal mother, and he doubted that his love was strong enough to mitigate the effects of his hatred. In these circumstances, the 'other place' or 'other relationship', where we adamantly believe such a blissful experience to be attainable, become idealised and the frustrations of reality are bitterly resented rather than accepted. This is the basis of Mr A's search for the 'right woman' and the 'other relationship'.

Britton (1992) has suggested that the Oedipal illusion may be a way of reinstating and preserving the ideal of one's sole possession of the desired parent. The illusion is preserved by splitting it off into a special area of thinking protected from reality, like a reservation. I think the hardened narcissistic organisation functions as a similar kind of reservation, like a daydream or masturbatory fantasy, where reality can be treated with contempt and the phantasy of exclusive possession of the ideal object can continue to be enjoyed. Mr A's reservation of distorted reality – his inflated picture of himself and his phantasy of the 'other relationship' – was not only clung to but ruthlessly protected. He dreamed, for example, *of lying in a coffin, alive, on top of two dead bodies. He felt a little claustrophobic, and worried about being trapped, but his misgivings were overshadowed by the celebratory mood of the occasion which was very grand, like an East End gangster funeral.* The dream makes clear, I think, the usual position of his object, firmly *beneath* him, and also his feeling that he would rather kill his object (the two dead breasts), and risk dying himself, than admit the reality of his neediness and the unattainability, in the real world, of his longed-for 'other relationship'. His sane misgivings about this narcissistic position received short shrift in the dream, in which the death of his needed object is largely celebrated and turned into a grand occasion.

Successful mourning

We are, on the other hand, assisted in the struggle to give up our infantile omnipotence, in favour of object-love, by the fact that there is so much to be gained by doing so. Any relationship based on omnipotent narcissistic identification (even an idealising one) creates a number of problems from the point of view of the individual. A phantasy of taking over the object always has, as its converse, a fear of being taken over *by* it; euphoric, even God-like superiority turns instead into a feeling of terror. When he was in a state of intrusive identification with me, Mr A was excited by the sense of fusion – his take-over of my mind leading him to believe that he knew what I was thinking, with no room for doubt – but it also left him with no room for ordinary criticism, or discrimination. Consequently, he felt he would have to agree with (actually swallow compliantly) all my interpretations, which made him feel trapped and without a voice. The individual in a paranoid–schizoid state of mind, who loves his objects narcissistically (on the basis of projecting his unwanted needy self into them), will therefore feel that love is a dangerous thing, liable to deplete and confuse rather than enrich him, and he will also fear that his objects stay not through choice but because they are controlled by him.

When this kind of narcissistic identification gives way to a depressive mode of relating, painful though it is, there is also potentially a feeling of relief and sanity. One no longer fears being taken over by the object, or depleted by loving. Rather, loving is experienced as an enrichment of the self. Alarming as it was for Mr A to let us be separate rather than fused, it liberated him from his claustrophobia and gave him the freedom to explore my mind and his own mind – to develop a K link. Furthermore, a sense of truth is established by experiencing both love and hate for our object. Referring to the 'common emotional view', Bion says that a sense of truth is experienced if the view of an object which is hated can be conjoined to a view of the same object when it is loved and the conjunction confirms that the object experienced by different emotions is the same object. A correlation is established.

(Bion, 1967: 119)

Knowing the truth, and knowing that one's love for the object survives one's hatred for it, brings a deep sense of worthiness, security and self-esteem, none of which are achieved through self-idealisation.

Conclusion

Our narcissism is always in conflict with our desire for object-love, because with love also comes the anxiety, guilt and grief associated with dependency. Our narcissism dictates that we are better off trying to avoid pain of this sort by turning away from a full relationship, or from any relationship. Mature love, in contrast, is based on the conviction that the profound enrichment of loving and being loved outweighs the pain of dependency. I have suggested that particularly omnipotent narcissistic object relations are set up as a defence against object-love when the anxieties associated with object-love are felt to be intolerable. When these anxieties can be understood and worked through, the balance may be tipped in favour of object-love, and the capacity for love strengthened.

References

Bion, W.R. (1962) *Learning from Experience*. London: Karnac Books.

Bion, W.R (1967) A theory of thinking. In *Second Thoughts*. London: Karnac Books, 110–119.

Bishop, B. (1998) Processes of love and separation in Jane Austen's mature work. *British Journal of Psychotherapy*, 15, 80–89.

Britton, R. (1992) The Oedipus situation and the depressive position. In R. Anderson (ed.), *Clinical Lectures on Klein and Bion*. London: Routledge, 34–45.

Caper, R. (1994) Does psychoanalysis heal? A contribution to the theory of psychoanalytic technique. *International Journal of Psycho-Analysis*, 73, 283–292.

Caper, R. (1999) Internal objects. In *A Mind of One's Own*. London: Routledge, 95–110.

Fisher, J.V. (1993) The impenetrable other: ambivalence and the Oedipal conflict in work with couples. In S. Ruszczynski (ed.), *Psychotherapy with Couples*. London: Karnac, 142–166.

Fisher, J.V. (2000) A father's abdication: Lear's retreat from 'aesthetic conflict'. *International Journal of Psycho-Analysis*, 81, 963–982.

Freud, S. (1910) Leonardo Da Vinci and a memory of his childhood. *SE* 7, 3–122.

Gerrard, J. (1996) Love in the time of psychotherapy. *British Journal of Psychotherapy*, 13, 163–173.

Gottlieb, S. (1994) Hateful relationships. *British Journal of Psychotherapy*, 11, 8–19.

Joseph, B. (1959) An aspect of the repetition compulsion. In *Psychic Equilibrium and Psychic Change*. London: Routledge, 1989, 16–33.

Klein, M. (1937) Love, guilt and reparation. In *Love, Guilt and Reparation and Other Works*. London: Hogarth Press, 1975, 306–343.

Klein, M. (1952) Some theoretical conclusions regarding the emotional life of the infant. In *Envy and Gratitude and Other Works*. London: Hogarth Press, 1975, 61–93.

Likierman, M. (1993) Primitive object love in Melanie Klein's thinking; early theoretical influences. *International Journal of Psycho-Analysis*, 74, 241–254.

Meltzer, D. (1971) Sincerity: a study in the atmosphere of human relations. In A. Hahn (ed.), *Sincerity and Other Works: Collected Papers of Donald Meltzer*. London: Karnac, 1994, 185–284.

Meltzer, D. (1988) *The Apprehension of Beauty*. Strath Tay, Perthshire: Clunie Press.

Money-Kyrle, R. (1971) The aim of psychoanalysis. In *The Collected Papers of Roger Money-Kyrle*. Strath Tay, Perthshire: Clunie Press, 1978, 442–449.

Plato (1951) *The Symposium* (Walter Hamilton, trans.). London: Penguin Classics.

Rosenfeld, H.A. (1964) On the psychopathology of narcissism: a clinical approach. In *Psychotic States*. London: Karnac Books, 169–179.

Rosenfeld, H.A. (1971) A clinical approach to the psychoanalytic theory of the life and death instincts: an investigation into the aggressive aspects of narcissism. In E. Bott Spillius (ed.), *Melanie Klein Today, Volume 1: Mainly Theory*, London: Routledge, 1988, 239–255.

Segal, H. and Bell, D. (1991) The theory of narcissism in the work of Freud and Klein. In J. Sandler, E. Spector Person and P. Fonagy (eds), *Freud's 'On Narcissism': An Introduction*. London: Yale University Press, 149–174.

Steiner, J. (1993) The recovery of parts of the self lost through projective identification: the role of mourning. In *Psychic Retreats*. London: Routledge, 54–63.

Tennyson, Alfred Lord (1850) *In Memoriam A.H.H.* In *The Collected Poems of Alfred Lord Tennyson*, Hertfordshire: Wordsworth Editions, 1994, 285–365.

Waddell, M. (1998) Late adolescence: fictional lives. In *Inside Lives: Psychoanalysis and the Development of the Personality*. London: Duckworth, 157–174.

Chapter 4

Love and hate in the analytic encounter with a woman therapist

Lesley Murdin

The gender of the therapist should make no difference to the analytic work that is done. All patients coming for psychoanalytic therapy will present the father and mother transferences and we will be able to accept and respond to them with appropriate countertransference. This is the received wisdom given in training and implied by the therapeutic technique of those who use transference. Interpretations imply that we think in terms of father and mother, brother and sister and we assume that the unconscious makes no distinctions between male and female. Perhaps it does not, but I should like, in this chapter, to consider the ways in which the subjective gender and sexuality of the therapist meeting those of the patient will affect the kind of analytic therapy that evolves. Even if the strong distinctions are made only in the conscious mind, these alone will affect the use to which any given therapist can be put, especially in the areas where love and hate are powerful.

A majority of those coming forward to train as psychoanalytic psycho-therapists and psychodynamic counsellors are women. Candidates for training in psychoanalysis are also increasingly likely to be women. This is a generalisation based on informal enquiries, not hard statistics. I do not know whether this situation is cause or effect, but perhaps it is connected to the predominant metaphor in psychoanalytic theory throughout the second half of the twentieth century: the mother–infant relationship. If this is the case, we need to pay attention to the effect on both men and women when they come for therapy. There is often not a great deal of choice and most people will go to a woman therapist. My experience with allocation of clients to psychotherapy at WPF Counselling and Psychotherapy's clinic is that where a specific gender is requested, it is more often a woman than a man. Perhaps, from past experiences, there is anxiety about working with a man. A woman therapist fits more easily with a non-threatening nurturing image. The request may well be defensive of course, and may indicate the fear of confronting the father and the challenge that he may represent.

As a result of this, the woman therapist has a particular responsibility to understand and continually analyse her own response to her sexuality and the effect that she is having on any patient because it is easier to allow it to remain unconscious. O'Connor and Ryan (1993), for example, have made clear the importance of the discourse in which the therapist situates him or herself and that gender and sexuality in particular are constructs which may not be finally understood once and for all within the limits of Oedipal theory. The mother/Madonna/whore splits explored by Welldon (2001) emphasise the cultural imagos that the woman herself will have internalised, as will her male patient. The virgin mother icon underlies some of the female ideal in our culture and may create difficulties for the woman who needs to function analytically and allow the patient to express love and hate in the oral or anal areas, and to maintain her stance when the passion is at the more genital level. Theories emphasising intersubjectivity – for example, Goldberg (1994), Ogden (1994), Schlesinger (1994) – make clear the extent to which the therapist's experience must contribute to the quality of the relationship.

Transference love, according to Freud, comes about in any therapy when the patient is able to show the therapist what he or she is like when in love. This is not a problem if the therapist merely does what Freud suggests, showing the patient the image of what he or she is like when in love. Freud speaks about the patient as female

> For the doctor, ethical motives unite with the technical ones to restrain him from giving the patient his love. The aim he has to keep in view is that this woman, whose capacity for love is impaired by infantile fixations, should gain free command over a function which is of such inestimable importance to her; that she should not, however, dissipate it in the treatment but keep it ready for the time when, after her treatment the demands of real life make themselves felt.
>
> (Freud 1915: 169)

He goes on to say that the therapist should not throw a single sausage in the way in the manner of the man who spoilt a dog race by throwing one sausage which distracted the dogs from completing the race for which the prize was to be a whole garland of sausages.

The prize envisaged for the woman may well be a whole garland of sausages, but the theory also encompasses the process that a man might need to undergo. A man could also show what he is like when he is in love and might demonstrate the way in which his infantile impairments interfere with this adult functioning in a relationship. Is a man more likely to find it difficult to reveal to a woman what his love and hate are like when they are in the infantile pre-Oedipal area? For both sexes therapy will bring out regressive longing and dependency needs. Love will be difficult to distinguish from hate when it is expressed in terms of the oral desire to bite, chew and consume or the anal desire to damage, wipe out, drown. In my view, men may find these manifestations of love and hate difficult to express to a woman, particularly when the hate is felt to be indistinguishable from the love as it is in early states dominated by ingestion and excretion.

Love and hate are affects constantly seeking expression through the vast metaphorical attachments and elaborations that cultures have provided. Often the task of therapy begins by finding metaphors to express in some way the changes in the nervous system and in the associated physiology of the individual who is experiencing love or hate. The rule for most of the talking therapies is that pretty much anything is under greater control if it can be expressed in words, and this is the task of therapy. For most of the analytic therapies, acting out of loving feelings is limited and in all the psychotherapies it will certainly not be expressed in genital sexuality. In many cases, love is so diffuse and variable a concept that one could hardly catch it enough to legislate against it. No one is sure what love means at all, never mind what it means in the analytic encounter. Being *in love* is to suffer from an encapsulated temporary psychosis. As Theseus puts it in Act V, Scene 1 of *A Midsummer Night's Dream*:

> The lunatic, the lover, and the poet
> Are of imagination all compact.

All see with a temporarily distorted vision or, like Cupid, are completely blind. If a patient falls in love with a therapist he is for that time not himself. The therapist owes a particular duty of responsibility to someone who is in this state. This is a question of ethics as well as of clinical technique. A symptom that someone might bring to therapy in the first place might be summarised as 'I don't know what love means' or 'I don't know whether I love him or her or not.' Love both as presenting problem and as therapeutic encounter may imply eroticism, affection, tenderness, hate, violence. It must imply, in Levinas's terms, responsibility for the other (e.g. 1985). In so far as it needs the attention of a therapist it will lack something of mature interdependence.

These contrasts arise because of the enormous weight of meaning and significance carried by the word *love*. Concentrating on the object will give some idea of what love means in a given context: I love my child, I like my friend. What it means to the subject, the exact quality of feeling that any individual is going to accord the status of love as opposed to liking or friendship, is much more problematic. It can be defined as a problem in so far as it crystallises the difficulty that an individual has with achieving the balance of sexuality and erotic gratification against concern, gratitude and the feelings that are associated with caring for and preserving the object. Stoller (1979) defines erotic desire by the elements of hostility, secrecy and the forbidden that it contains. All of these will be in opposition to the warmth, affection and goodwill of agapaic love. Sexual love could be manifested as oral gratification as opposed to mature interdependency: I could eat you up as opposed to I like to be with you. As love is a relational concept it always implies that the therapist may love as much and as destructively as the patient.

Nevertheless, love in its passionate, obsessional manifestation must be the legitimate concern of a therapeutic relationship and cannot be helped from a developmental or hermeneutic perspective unless it can be seen. The therapist must see how the patient loves, but she cannot then stay out of the picture. If you accept that an aim of long-term therapy may be that the patient achieves the capacity for mature interdependent love, you must also accept that resolution cannot be achieved within the transference relationship. The abstinence that is required of the therapist is that of the parent who steadfastly declares: 'No, you cannot marry me. Go out and find a man/woman of your own.' There is no alternative to the therapist modelling abstinence and self-restraint, no matter what his or her feelings and desires may be. The therapist must resist the siren call of his or her own bodily and emotional response and in addition avoid the counter-obsession so subtly described by Ian McEwan in his novel *Enduring Love*. In it McEwan demonstrates the difference between love and obsession. The main character is pursued by a man who may or may not exist but who becomes the obsession of the man pursued. The obsession threatens to destroy the real enduring everyday love that is available in the partner. Avoiding such an obsessional response does not mean, however, that the therapist can remain detached. Later in this chapter I shall discuss the situation of the female therapist in relation to the erotic material of male patients. One of the skills of therapists in general must be expertise in distinguishing between varieties of love. When might we be entering into dangerous therapy, for example where a disrupted attachment history combines with an obsessional personality? When might it be appropriate to put up a bar and when might it be counter-productive or stifling to development?

Lester (1985, 1990) made some important points about the relevance of the analyst's gender to the development of specific areas of transference. Analytic work leads to the most tempting opportunities for therapists to express narcissistic needs by encouraging and basking in the patient's pre-Oedipal or Oedipal love. Lester (1990) suggests that in the cases of sexual abuse of patients that she had seen in Canada, the reason for the male analyst's transgression was that he mistook the female patient's demand for 'love' for a sexual demand when it should have been seen as pre-Oedipal and should have met with an appropriate response at that level. A related but opposite problem occurs when a male patient is working with a female therapist. Lester suggests that his fear of the powerful mother makes it impossible for him to risk giving expression to Oedipal longings for her, and his fear of castration keeps him in the pre-Oedipal sphere. Thus we would expect complaints from patients with acting-out therapists to focus on sexual enactment for male therapists and inability to accept sexuality for female therapists. In practice, of course, complaints can centre on either the enactment of sexual wishes or the mishandling of the refusal to enact.

Women analysts may be less inclined to enact sexual desire, but not a great deal of information is available, with the exception of a few papers such as that of Lester (1985) suggesting that men find it difficult to make an erotic transference to a woman therapist – not only because of the fear of their own internal castrating object but also because of the fear of their superior physical strength and ability to force themselves on a woman. The power imbalance between the one who is in the position of analysing the other is also inhibiting. An acknowledgement of the dependent pre-Oedipal wishes to a woman might threaten a man's sense of his masculinity because they bring him back to the original dependence on a woman.

For the feelings that belong to Oedipal desire and rivalry, he is aware that in terms of his physical strength he is often the more powerful of the two and would be able to overcome the therapist if he chose to do so. For this reason it may be difficult for a man to acknowledge his feelings of love or hate for his woman therapist, since he will be afraid that either could be acted out if he let himself respond spontaneously. In her turn, the woman therapist is facing her own fear that mentioning sex will be heard as a seduction: she was asking for it. She may have her own desires, going as far as her own rape fantasies to deal with. Both of these anxieties may reinforce each other or may break down into the feared action. For this reason, a woman therapist has the obligation to ensure that the therapeutic situation is safe for her so that it will be safe for her patient. Seeing male patients with a history of poor impulse control is obviously not a good idea unless the environment provides support in an emergency. In addition to the practical management issues of ensuring this kind of basic security for both, the therapist has to ensure that she is willing and able to deal with the more frightening or difficult aspects of the man's transference.

Such preparatory care is essential but may in itself lead a woman therapist to expect love from her male patients. A straw poll on a radio programme in August 1999 found a majority of the public in favour of the proposition that therapy creates more problems than it solves. In other words it creates a transference neurosis. Patients are encouraged to express their thoughts and feelings about the therapist, or perhaps to *have* such thoughts and feelings. Women are given strong social imperatives not to show encouragement to a man in any situation, let alone one in which there is privacy and maximum opportunity for intimacy. The therapy situation may well amount to having a relationship where none existed before. Moreover, it is, or should be, a relationship which is never more than a tease. Love me, but I won't love you back we say, or at least I won't love you as much as you love me. Ernest Gellner is among those who have written critically of this effect:

But when in distress they seek their shepherd, they are instructed to abandon all semantic restraint, and display not only their intimate and shameful secrets, but also the total and deplorable chaos of their mental content, which otherwise they must strive to hide. They must 'free associate'; then it would seem they develop feelings for the person in front of whom they have so abased themselves. The intensity of the feeling so generated appears to confirm the validity both of the theoretical and the specific insights attained in the course of the therapeutic sessions, thus producing that characteristic blend of strong feeling and sense of cognitive and liberating illumination which defines mystical experience.

(Gellner 1992: 52)

It may be true that to some extent we create the effects that we then happily analyse, but this is not necessarily a bad thing. The constructive use of the transference neurosis can be for the ultimate benefit of the person who comes. In any case, it is not possible to make someone fall in love. Therapists are not as powerful as that. Power is always an issue, however. The woman therapist is likely to find herself in a position where she has to deal with the power imbalance in which she is the more powerful person in the therapeutic relationship. If she is culturally and emotionally predisposed to be seductive in a way that is subtle and indirect, she may behave with her male patients in a way that they will find confusing. If her own training analysis or therapy has been with a woman, will she be sufficiently able to recognise her own mode of seductiveness with a man? She may be afraid that interpretations will seem seductive if she mentions the patient's loving feelings for her. Alternatively, she may not notice that her interpretations are in fact seductive.

This sort of seduction within therapy can lead to total breakdown of the therapeutic relationship. Valentine (1996) wrote an unusual paper on therapeutic failure in which she referred to the arbitrary authoritarian interpretations made by some analysts and related this to the nature of the power relationship in psychoanalytic work. Analysts who listen only to a transference subtext and ignore entirely the patient's reality are likely to bring about an ending which will certainly feel like a failure to the patient, even though the analyst might well be able to contend that there is benefit in the continued blows to the patient's narcissism that such interpretations have administered. Her examples are all of same sex partnerships between two women or two men. When the member of the therapeutic couple with most power is the woman, the kind of power that is exercised will of course vary depending on the model being applied and the nature of the woman and her transference to the patient. Nevertheless, there are bound to be implications in the kind of power relationship that develops for the ways in which love and hate can be revealed and demonstrated by the patient.

In an attempt to avoid the whore in herself and in the countertrans-ference, the woman therapist will look to theory to provide other meta-phors. Writing from a Jungian perspective, Solomon, at a Conference of the Foundation for Psychotherapy and Counselling (1998), spoke of the need for love to be the motive force in seeking out another to whom to relate. Her theoretical perspective is that the self can develop only in relating to another and that therefore in the therapeutic relationship the expression and management of the loving relationship will be of the utmost import-ance. She returns to the infantile metaphor: 'The self first knows itself through another, and the earliest pair in primary mutual pre-occupation is, of course, mother and infant' (1998: 282).

Since the female therapist's defence is likely to be to ignore material that relates to erotic love more than violent or aggressive feelings which will not permit themselves to be ignored, she will be inclined to interpret in the maternal area but leave out the passionate aspect of the transference which Winnicott called the relationship to the 'object mother' (1963: 76). Women therapists have been encouraged by the predominant theoretical orientation of the second half of the twentieth century in the humanistic therapies, as well as in the psychoanalytic, to emphasise the provision of reliable care as maternal. Such words as *care*, *holding*, *nurturing* crystallise the acceptable face of transference interpretation. Clearly the problem with this theoretical stance, particularly when it is defensively employed, is that it prevents a man from acknowledging and working with the destructive elements of his love and hate. Because acknowledgment is potentially destructive, therap-ists are wise to wait until the erotic is clearly manifest and seen to be so by a supervisor or consultant as well as by the therapist him or herself. Tech-nically, the work will be immensely difficult because the therapist who acknowledges the erotic within and on top of the maternal will run the risk of being seen as seductive. The erotic is, of course, not the only part of the transference that is avoided but it is an aspect of love that cannot be relegated to other relationships and left out of the therapeutic.

In the mother–infant metaphor lies the preoccupation that enables many women therapists to work comfortably with their male patients. They see the maternal transference and are able to deal very well with that. They can link the difficulties of the man to the difficulties of the baby or small child and feel safe enough. Problems of love and hate lead to the bedrock of the body and can be approached either through the metaphor of the mouth and the nipple or the anus and the faeces. Most dangerously, the therapist can acknowledge feelings connected with penis and vagina. These metaphors of course do not say all there is to be said about either love or hate. There is a kind of love that has nothing to do with fit and nothing to do with mutual satisfaction. This is the general good will or *agape* that can be felt for any other person. Such love may of course be lacking in a very narcissistic person and may be a part of what is sought in the therapy, but the love that is problematic and needs to be brought for therapy is much more often the passion related to what fits where and how we can allow a close enough approach for fitting together to be possible.

The man may also feel safe in the mother–infant area in that it is certainly familiar and he knows the feelings that it arouses in him. It may in some cases be sufficient to work in this area, and through such interpretations much useful work can be done. The difficulty here is that once the infantile behaviour is recognised and becomes a matter of choice, either the therapy must end or it may continue with the risk that the issues that relate more specifically to adult sexuality will have to be left untouched. If the therapist is not unduly preoccupied with her own image as mother, madonna or whore, she can leave the patient to bring whatever needs to be understood. Sometimes the most intimate feelings need to remain private. Melzer's (1973) theoretical approach to this difficulty is to define all problems with sexuality as infantile. As soon as sexuality becomes adult, by definition it is no longer a problem.

Women therapists can do a great deal of good for their patients by their maternal caring, by being what Winnicott calls the environment mother (1963), but must not forget the effect of the absence of a father to mediate and make safe the exclusive possession of the patient by the female analyst, who will most obviously and easily evoke the maternal transference at the level of dominating mother. When working with children the woman therapist could give some scope to her maternal feelings and might have a great deal to offer.

Dorothy Davidson (1973) illustrates the woman analyst working with a boy, raising questions similar to those in Melanie Klein's well-known work with, for example, Richard. The presenting difficulty was related to the hatred of the mother who was seen represented in the transference in which the patient would shout and hurl back all interpretation. The paper implies that what enabled the boy to change was the continuity of maternal care from the analyst. His hate was related to love, of course, but the love was difficult to access or even to remember, both for him and for the therapist. What is noticeable is the emphasis on the maternal transference to the exclusion of any consideration of how the lack of a father may have affected the child. There was no father to make the mother safe and therefore he continued to scream and try to use any apparently masculine weapon that he could find, however difficult that might have been for both of them.

So far I have concentrated on the female analytic therapist and her role in working with the male patient. The man himself brings the images of love and hate that will form the content of the therapy. A man may bring an image of sexuality which implies, paradoxically, that he can be the complete provider of all that is needed. This implies that the woman must be provided for, and therefore submissive and dominated. The projection will be unpleasant, as it will imply that the therapist wants to dominate too, and the result will be a struggle for dominion versus enslavement. The man who is caught up in this phantasy will be worshipping a powerful phallus and will project this into the therapist, who becomes a powerful phallic woman capable of giving him what he longs for. This situation prevents any possibility of intercourse where he must submit to being taken in and understood rather than being given further illusions of phallic power. The woman therapist, however, can neither abdicate from the transference role nor treat the man as a child. She must survive the phallic projections and still be available to try to understand the deeper need for female receptivity.

The experience in therapy of one man will illustrate both the power of the therapist and the therapy and the area where she (in this case) was not powerful enough. The therapist needed to take responsibility because the patient was not himself. P came to see me because he was suffering from a kind of blockage in his life and his career. He formed an attachment with me which was obsessional and controlling and masked his need both for mothering and fathering and for a truly genital adult love. He had married a younger woman and she was just about to have their first child. He had an interest in acting and had just been offered a part in the first production of a local drama group but was terrified that he would not be able to come up to his own and others' expectations of him. He had a job as a nurse which he despised because he thought his status was low, and he sabotaged any possibility of promotion or advancement and then complained that no one appreciated him.

His family background was evidently bleak. His mother was still alive, having separated from his father when he was eleven. She had lived with his stepfather ever since and the two of them lived a life which he described as a 'barren suburban-semi' sort of life. His father was much more exotic and had a successful career as an actor but had always been scornful of P who had heard him once tell his mother that 'the boy is too effeminate'. His earliest memory was of standing in his cot, shaking the bars and trying to get out but being kept in there while the rest of life went on downstairs. He had two older brothers who had successful and much-envied careers.

P wished to use therapy to help him in his relationship with his wife, which was in difficulties. He volunteered that she did not want sex with him and would not respond when he caressed her. As the therapist I found him unthreatening. He spoke fluently and continuously, and when he spoke about sex there was somehow a lack of danger or excitement about him that seemed to me to indicate that his desire for sex was theoretical. I was not in any way aroused by his talking about sex. The only relationship in fact that seemed not to be theoretical was with the baby when he was born. P passionately loved his baby who represented all the hope and longing that he did not seem to be able to feel in and for himself. He made himself, or tried to make himself, into a better mother to the baby than his wife could be. He wished to stay in the time warp of the mother–son relationship, and that prevented him from moving on to a genital relationship to a woman. His wife was apparently co-operating in this impasse, and so did I.

He told me a dream which represents his difficulty and mine. He was in a room with a beautiful grand piano but he did not know how to play it. He found himself floating up towards the ceiling, and could not get down again. He was just below the ceiling, with his neck uncomfortably stiff and bent, when he found himself defecating on the room below and even on the beautiful grand piano.

This dream itself illustrates his need to be a perfect patient. He knew very well how much he was offering me in terms of symbolic meaning that I could enjoy interpreting. I was tempted to wonder just how much it was inspired by his reading of psychoanalytical textbooks (which he did a great deal). I had to take account both of the dream itself and of the fact that he chose to tell it to me, because the actual content seemed to me to be very strained, however freely he described the shit as falling. Sessions with P felt rather like his dream in the sense that we both floated way above the surface and it was impossible to make contact with each other or with the ground. The resulting sensation reproduced for me his insecurity and lack of connection, which was hidden beneath a constant articulate and perceptive exterior. He talked with wit and irony about the current scene in literature, art, philosophy and film in a way that I thoroughly enjoyed but which effectively prevented either of us from addressing what was going on inside him or between us. When I drew his attention to his skill in seducing me in this way, he would respond angrily that he knew he was a hopeless patient and there was no reason why I should understand or appreciate him any more than his wife did. He returned immediately to complaining about his wife. These complaints about his wife centred on her lack of care for the children. She did not clean the house to a hygienic standard, she did not make them wash their hands, etc.

At the time I saw the problem as related to the anal stage in developmental terms and tried to interpret his control in relation to me as an anal withholding in retaliation against the mother's failure to clean and care for him. This was inadequate. In some ways he was only too free in what he gave me. He resisted all my attempts to enable him to think about the way in which he prevented me from having the real treasure of his inmost thoughts. We were very bogged down in this view of mine. He had to walk out of his marriage and then suffer a depressive breakdown before I finally began to see that I was avoiding the essential erotic nature of what he was telling me. Some of the problem was my failure to take responsibility for the whole of his communication, not just the part that I was willing to hear.

When I was able to recognise my fear of what he might be like if he became a mature man with sexual longings as well as parent–child love, I was able to say that I could understand his wish to stay floating on the ceiling but that he had many times told me of his wife's failure to respond to him sexually. I said that I thought that I had presented him with a problem in that he could not be open with me in case I was frightened or angered by his desire. He responded with a whole succession of dreams and erotic fantasies about me which I found very difficult to hear, but I had to recognise that I had offered myself for this role. I said that I was willing to hear what he needed to tell me but that I might find that there were limits to what I could accept and in that case I would take the responsibility of telling him so. He seemed relieved by this boundary setting.

His fantasies, such as tying me up and masturbating me or watching me having intercourse with another man, became gradually less sadistic and more mutual as the therapy progressed. When his fantasies changed, his relationship with his wife also began to change.

The progress of this therapy illustrates the difficulty that arises when a woman therapist encounters love that is initially in the area of the infantile omnipotent phantasy. The man tries in this situation to hold the therapy unmoving by preventing the therapist from having any role at all either maternal or genital. The motivation of the patient is strongly to remain in the dominating but fruitless position of control that he has assumed. The motivation of the therapist is unfortunately similar in that she may well fear the change to a more mature functioning. Interpretations also will be feared by both as the possible source of further development. They will also be felt to risk the approach of the thinking function of the father and thus to threaten the continued existence of the counter-productive but relatively safe relationship with the mother.

Their response to their male patients carries for women some of the weight of their own searches and researches. Since so many psychotherapists are women, this can be a very important question. If Lacan had arrived at a truth when he said that the woman is seeking to find an answer to the question 'what is a woman?' through the study of what men find to desire in other women, then we must be on the lookout for the woman therapist who keeps a stalemate, a situation in which the man's desire is held transfixed and cannot move forward. If she does this and holds him in the pre-Oedipal arena because she needs to see his desire in relation to another woman, not herself, she will not be able to help him to move towards bringing desire and love together. P's desire for his wife was limited to the kind of caressing that he gave to his baby. He did not venture into more adult love because his mother could not allow it and barred the way.

Alternatively, the love that in P's case was held in check by both patient and therapist might be given free rein, as it sometimes is, with disastrous results. For example, I have been involved with cases of complaints where a therapist has panicked when she realised that a male patient had fallen in love with her and was pursuing her as a narcissistic love object. When this happens, the gifts, flowers, declarations that will be showered on the therapist will be felt as pledges from the patient which must not be rejected. If the inevitable rejection is not done sufficiently firmly from the beginning there may be a sudden breaking off of therapy by the therapist, which will be felt by the patient to be a terrible blow to his self-love and of course it is a blow to his belief in his ability to be loved.

When therapy breaks down in this way, everyone panics – particularly the therapist, who is at once afraid of complaints and even legal action. Suppose we tried a different approach and offered an opportunity to meet for conciliation sessions with an experienced couples therapist? Might it not be possible for the therapy then to continue or, if not, to arrange for a better ending and a referral to another therapist?

In the case that I have described, the female therapist tried to stay outside the danger zone of the erotic aspect of love. In this sense she barred the way. My point is that by taking responsibility for the therapeutic enterprise, the woman therapist must enable the man to find his own sexuality and his own ability to love without going to the opposite extreme of taking up the position of the woman who needs him to pursue her in order for her to delineate her own sexuality.

References

Davidson, D. (1973) 'Invasion and separation', in *Analytical Psychology: a new science*, London: Analytic Press, 1980.

Freud, S. (1915) 'On transference love', in 'Papers on Technique', *Standard Edition* 14, London: Hogarth Press, 1958.

Gellner, E. (1992) 'Psychoanalysis, social role and testability', in W. Dryden and C. Feltham (eds) *Psychotherapy and its Discontents*, Buckingham: Open University Press.

Goldberg, A. (1994) 'The analytical third, working with intersubjective clinical facts', *International Journal of Psycho-Analysis*, 75(3).

Lester, E. (1985) 'The female analyst and the erotised transference', *International Journal of Psycho-Analysis*, 66.

Lester, E. (1990) 'Gender and identity issues in the analytic process', *International Journal of Psycho-Analysis*, 71.

Levinas, E. (1996) *Emmanuel Levinas: Basic Philosophical Writings (Studies in Continental Thought)*, Indiana: Indiana University Press.

McEwan, I. (1997) *Enduring Love*, London: Jonathan Cape.

Meltzer, D. (1973) *Sexual States of Mind*, Strath Tay, Perthshire: Clunie Press.

O'Connor, N. and Ryan, J. (1993) *Wild Desires and Mistaken Identities*, London: Virago.

Ogden, T. (1994) 'Farewell to the objective analyst', *Internaional Journal of Psycho-Analysis*, 75.

Schlesinger, H. (1994) 'How the analyst listens; the pre-stages of interpretation', *International Journal of Psycho-Analysis*, 75.

Shakespeare, W. (1600) *A Midsummer Night's Dream*, Cambridge: Cambridge University Press, 1969.

Solomon, H. (1998) 'Love: Paradox of self and other', *British Journal of Psychotherapy*, 14(3).

Stoller, R. (1979) *Sexual Excitement*, New York: Pantheon.

Valentine, M. (1996) 'The abuse of power within the analytic setting', *British Journal of Psychotherapy*, 13(2).

Welldon, E. (2001) *Mother, Madonna, Whore*, London: Olnes Press.

Winnicott, D.W. (1963) 'The development of the capacity for concern', in *Maturational Processes and the Facilitating Environment*, London: Hogarth, 1985.

Chapter 5

'The way you wear your hat'. Love, hate and personality

Kate Barrows

> Failure to eat, drink or breathe properly has disastrous consequences for life itself. Failure to use the emotional experience produces a comparable disaster in the development of the personality.
>
> (Bion, 1962: 42)

Behind a wide range of apparently unrelated symptoms which bring people to psychoanalysis there often lies a common complaint. The patient is suffering from not being able to be his or her self, from feeling that he or she has no personality. To give some brief examples: one young woman felt that she just happened to be on this earth, but had nothing individual about her. It was a turning-point in her analysis when, after three years, she said that she was at last beginning to realise that she had a personality of her own. Another patient felt that she was just there to be used by others: they walked over her and she was a doormat for them to tread on but she did not exist in her own right. A young man sought analysis because he felt unable to develop his own life, internal or external. He could work at a routine job but felt that all that he could manage was the routine: he was there to fit in and nothing more. These patients describe themselves as being like cogs, ciphers or shadows. They feel impoverished in contrast to other people whom they see as having full lives and distinct personalities. They feel that they cannot 'use the emotional experience' of life and they have great difficulty in using the experience of psychoanalysis.

In this chapter I shall attempt to show how the feeling of lacking a personality can be traced back to an underlying conflict between love and hate, and how the successful resolution of this conflict requires the recognition of the object's individual personality.

Since the early days of psychoanalysis, the conflict between love and hate has been seen to be central to mental illness. Freud found that this conflict was at the root of the Rat Man's obsessional neurosis, and of other forms of neurosis. 'For we must remember that in every neurosis we come upon the same suppressed instincts behind the symptoms. After all, hatred, kept suppressed in the unconscious by love, plays a great part in the patho-genesis of hysteria and paranoia' (Freud, 1909: 240).

Klein went on to describe how, in order to internalise the good object which in her view comes to form the core of the ego, the infant has to come to terms with realising that he hates as well as loves the people upon whom he depends. He feels that his hatred damages his loved ones and estab-lishing them within his psyche is achieved through symbolic reparation of the damage that is felt to be done by his negative feelings. She contended that 'the child goes through states of mind comparable to the mourning of the adult, or rather, that this early mourning is revived whenever grief is experienced in later life' (Klein, 1940: 344). She placed this early experience of mourning firmly at the centre of human development:

> The poignancy of the actual loss of a loved person is, in my view, greatly increased by the mourner's unconscious phantasies of having lost his *internal* good objects as well. He then feels that his internal 'bad' objects predominate and his inner world is in danger of disruption.
>
> (1940: 344)

She accounted for this feeling of inner catastrophe in terms of the mour-ner's ambivalence towards the lost person, and the phantasy that his hatred has caused their death, or that his triumph about surviving has caused damage or led to retaliation, so that the loved person has become damaged or dangerous. To be able to establish the absent or lost person internally and securely, ambivalence has to be worked through and loving feelings gain the day.

Klein stressed that secure internalisation is accompanied by recognition of the mother's separate existence. I would like to emphasise that this acknowledgement includes awareness of – and ambivalence towards – the mother as a personality. It is not just that the mother feeds, holds and understands her baby, it is also that she does this *in her own way*. She has her own characteristic smell, touch, tone of voice, way of understanding and responding, good qualities and failings, her own ambience; in other words, she has her own personality. The care that she gives is mediated through her personality. When she is missed and remembered, it is not only for her caring functions but also for her unique and to some extent indefinable personality. The individual features that are remembered are evocative of the personality of which they are an expression.

The capacity to remember the uniqueness of the absent person has been delightfully expressed by George and Ira Gershwin in their memorable song, 'They Can't Take That Away From Me':

> The way you wear your hat,
> The way you sip your tea,

The mem'ry of all that,
No, no! They can't take that away from me.

The way your smile just beams,
The way you sing off key,
The way you haunt my dreams,
No, no! They can't take that away from me!

We may never, never meet again
On the bumpy road to love,
Still I'll always, always keep
The mem'ry of . . .

The way you hold your knife,
The way we danced 'till three,
The way you've changed my life,
No, no! They can't take that away from me.

It is the particular way that the loved person does things which stays etched in the memory and which evokes affection and love. Each verse moves from individual, evocative details to the way in which the loved personality has become part of the singer, through memory, through dreams and through change. The song suggests that 'the way you changed my life' has to do with the particularity of the person who is loved by the singer and the unforgettable impression which he has made upon her. The personality of the other has been internalised in such a way that the singer will never be quite the same as she was before they met. We are changed by the individuality of those whom we love, and appreciating the uniqueness of the other is an intrinsic aspect of internalisation. The whimsical 'they can't take that away from me' may suggest not only others who have taken away the loved person but also aspects of the self which might try to erode good memories.

However, one of the most poignant and painful things about the process of reinstating the lost object in the ego is that it brings home to us the fact that the uniqueness of the mourned personality can never be fully internalised or remembered. The internalised 'good object' will never correspond entirely to the external one: the loss is real.

Patients who suffer from feeling as though they lack an individual personality seem to have been unable to negotiate the pain as well as the joy of recognising the unique qualities of the central people in their lives. This uniqueness will of course include the hateful as well as the lovable aspects of their objects. Unable to bear the anxiety that their hatred may have damaged the people upon whom they depend as well as their own capacity to love, they void themselves of personality and feel themselves to be merely ciphers. They feel that others have all the personality and they have none – they barely exist as individuals in their own right.

The patients I have in mind sometimes attempt to disguise or compensate for this lack by defining themselves as 'bad characters' – better a bad character than none at all. The idea of being hateful can also give an illusion of superiority and invulnerability. However, their apparent hardness may also conceal an underlying hypersensitivity to damage, and the fact that they have hardened their hearts to avoid persecution, despair or the fear of loss. This may have been in response to early trauma, such as separation or illness or lack of maternal containment, or due to constitutional factors. The balance of these different elements may take a long time to emerge and indeed may never be finally elucidated.

Clinical material

Mrs Z came to analysis with a particular symptom which masked many others. Despite her respectable background, to her surprise she had found herself stealing from a shop one day and had had a panic attack as she approached the door. There was no financial need for her to steal, so the problem seemed symbolic, both of her inner poverty and of her terror of being caught. It turned out that her life was highly restricted: she had stopped working because of anxiety about making mistakes, although in reality what mistakes she made were minor.

She looked after her family, but bitterly described herself as a 'doormat' for her husband and children. The choice of this term seemed telling, as it was indicative of her state of being perpetually on the threshold. Others walked through the doorway, went in and out, but she was neither in nor out, paralysed with fear and grievance and unable either to show or to conceal what she had inside her. She felt that she lacked personality, she was there for others to use, and her bitterness was what defined her. She avoided entering into relationships with others if she could, and she was scornful of social life, regarding it as petty and stupid. She was particularly afraid of showing herself as having anything good to offer and would dress down or dumb herself down in order to avoid provoking envy or any possible accusations that she might be showing off.

Occasional dreams broke through her restricted emotionality, however. These dreams usually emerged as if out of an arid wasteland of negativity. She did not have associations to them, but in themselves they contained evocative and poignant images. Early in her analysis there was a dream *that a little bird had fallen out of its nest. It did not have feathers yet so it could not fly. It was in the middle of a big empty space, perhaps a road, and it was lost and frightened. It could not remember how to get back to its nest and no mother or father bird was coming to look for it.* The image of the little bird often came back to my mind, and I felt that Mrs Z needed me to keep looking for her, in particular for the lost and defenceless aspect of her which could feel dropped out of the nest too soon.

This dream was strikingly in contrast to her conscious and prevailing attitude to her analysis: she asserted that it had nothing to offer her and that she could get nothing from it. The virulence of her scorn was shocking and intimidating. She soon started saying that we were just going over the same old things and that it wasn't getting anywhere, that maybe she should stop. As well as feeling like the fledgling bird that might be dropped too soon, I felt treated like a doormat, and that I was struggling against the odds to keep the analysis alive. A dream from the second year of the treatment threw some light on this situation. *She was in a boat like a punt stuck in a long narrow gully with her husband, who was pushing the boat along with a pole. Her young daughter was lying looking as though she might die in the bottom of the boat and there were three serpents twining themselves around the little girl as if to squeeze the life out of her. There was freezing cold water washing over the boat. Her husband said, 'One more push and we'll get through.'* She had no associations to this dream and said that she felt stuck. After some time I wondered aloud whether the dream had anything to do with birth. She then remembered that she had been told that she nearly died when she was born, as the umbilical cord was tightly twined three times round her neck. Icy cold water had been washed over her in the effort to enable her to be born alive.

I was struck by the way in which this dream emerged out of an ongoing atmosphere in the analysis in which I felt at times strangulated, that freezing contempt was poured on my efforts and that the analysis might die, while at other times I had to carry the optimism, like her husband. After she told me the dream, and that she was stuck, I felt that I had to give 'one more push' by suggesting that the dream had something to do with birth. On this occasion she seemed able to make use of me to propel things forward so that she could think about the dream and the dangerous situation which it represented in the analysis, as well as the connection to what she knew about her birth. The analysis seemed like the difficult birth in her dream and it was uncertain whether we would 'get through' to safety or to a degree of confidence about being able to keep the vulnerable part of Mrs Z alive.

There were other images which illustrated the way in which new developments would instantly be seized on and destroyed. For instance, there was an image of tadpoles in a pond, which as soon as they began to flicker were spotted and devoured by the fish which live in the pond. Later on in the analysis when more progress had been made, Mrs Z described how a group of refugee children had been rescued from a merciless regime, but when they were left unguarded for a moment the enemy police came and took them to their deaths. So even though I was felt to have rescued her, we were never safe from a murderous representative of a totalitarian regime which could swoop at any moment. It often did. Instant attacks would take place, in particular upon emerging personal qualities in Mrs Z: there would be a flickering of a refreshingly new quality in a session – humour, warmth or some other form of positive feeling – only for it to be wiped out by ruthless scorn.

Bion has described a situation which he calls 'minus container/contained':

> The most important characteristic is its hatred of any new development in the personality as if the new development were a rival to be destroyed. The emergence therefore of any tendency to search for the truth, to establish contact with reality and in short to be scientific in no matter how rudimentary a fashion is met by destructive attacks on the tendency and the reassertion of the 'moral' superiority.
>
> (Bion, 1962: 98)

This describes very accurately the fluctuations in Mrs Z's analysis. Her oscillations between wanting to understand (K) and 'minus container/contained' seemed to occur when her hatred got the better of her loving feelings, killing off the possibility of insight as if it were a rival to her scornful state of morally superior negativity.

There were several factors in Mrs Z's life which contributed to this constellation. There was her dangerous birth and an early separation from her mother when she was a few months old. There was the fact of her being an older child with enormous resentment towards her younger sister. There was also the fact of her parents having escaped the ravages of a totalitarian regime, but having passed on something very harsh and condemning to their children. Her father was portrayed as scathing in the extreme, while she saw her mother as unable to stand up for herself or for the children. Mrs Z had introjected the cruelty and the passivity as well as the guilt about having anything valuable, especially valuable internal objects and aspects of her personality. She saw her mother as being a doormat rather than able to assert her own personality. This also meant that she was downtrodden by Mrs Z and her sister and perhaps unable to contain feelings of hatred or to recognise the loving feelings that could be so easily jettisoned.

Elsewhere I have discussed the aspect of a patient's experience that relates to their parents' unassimilated internal ghosts. 'The child comes to identify not with his parent, but with his parent's unmourned internal ghost. This prevents him from developing a life and personality of his own' (Barrows, 2000: 70). There was evidence that my patient's father's savage scorn was connected to retaliatory and punitive internal figures of his own, exacerbated by the cruelty of an extreme political situation. The parents' survival of a tyrannical regime seems to have to have left them dominated by hateful unassimilated internal figures, which in turn made a mark upon the personalities of their own children.

Mrs Z gradually became more aware of the annihilating effects of her dismissiveness and scorn. She called it 'putting the mockers on' and nothing could survive her mockery without becoming in her mind an object of contempt. She described herself as knowing the price of everything and the value of nothing. She defined herself as being harsh and unfeeling and I often felt that the more sensitive aspect of her personality that was attacked by this harshness was projected into me for safekeeping. I also felt that she was testing out the strength of my personality to see if she could make me give up hope. There were times when she did make me feel like giving up, and it seemed important that her anxieties about the debilitating effect she could have on me and the analysis were taken seriously.

However, after a few years of analysis the quality of Mrs Z's life had changed greatly for the better, so that she became able to resume work, her family and social relationships improved and her appearance became livelier and more attractive. Although she could say that she felt this to be due to her analysis, she still often felt it to be pointless and useless. Something in her was still stuck and she wanted me to know it, and not to be too encouraged by the changes in her life. She had a dream that *she had a contraceptive stuck inside her and her husband and someone else were trying to pull it out*. There certainly seemed to be something inside her mind which prevented conception, and which made emotional intercourse feel fruitless.

It was much easier for her to see herself as destructive and harsh than to risk good feelings. She also preferred to feel badly treated and to fill her mind and her life with people who let her down and behaved hatefully towards her rather than with people whom she could respect or rely on. She complained endlessly about staff who were unreliable, but she was unwilling to look for people on whom she could depend. Similarly, she seemed more comfortable with feeling that her analysis was not delivering the goods than with feeling that her analyst was reliable enough. It was easier to be scornful and angrily disappointed. In fact, she was unreliable herself and missed many sessions. She would often leave before the start of the holidays and return after me. I felt that she was dealing with breaks by projecting her feelings of being dropped and unwanted, not worth making a priority, and I often wondered whether I would see her again.

However, depressive concerns gradually began to emerge: she spoke one day of a family friend who was dying of multiple sclerosis, describing him with real respect as a good and interesting person who had spent his childhood in poverty and had grown up with a real and generous commitment to change. Mrs Z described him as 'a lovely personality', with a good marriage and very likeable children. She also liked his wife, who was lively and optimistic despite her challenging work with deprived women. I pointed out how much she seemed to respect this man and his family; she agreed, and said that it didn't seem fair for someone like him to die. She talked about not having suffered immediate losses and how she felt that she wouldn't be able to bear it. She then went on to talk about people who die from self-destruction, for instance from alcoholism. As she talked, her tone gradually became somewhat monotonous and repetitive, like that of an alcoholic. I said that she might be afraid that she can kill off her capacity for respect, for recognition of good qualities and of liking someone's personality, including mine. Perhaps she felt that I was committed to change and remained optimistic even though I was working with her feelings of deprivation. I added that she would rather feel that she kills things off inside herself than risk holding onto her appreciative feelings and the fear of a loss that she might not be able to bear. She agreed that this does happen, and added that she wants to be able to do her analysis all by herself. I talked of her wish not to need anyone or anything else, including me and her analysis. She then said that she didn't want to need me because she would then want the analysis to go on forever, and she might not be able to do without it.

It was practically unheard of for Mrs Z to describe anyone in really appreciative terms, particularly in terms of their personality. She might talk about people's possessions or skills, but not their personalities. It was striking that she thought in this more rounded, appreciative way about someone who was dying, and that thinking about her friend or her analyst in this way seemed connected to fears of loss. Perhaps the loss which she feared was not just that of her friend or her analyst as a valued personality, but also that of the emerging personality in herself, the likeable patient of an appreciated analyst rather than the characterless patient of a deprecated analyst.

During this period in her analysis, aspects of her own personality began to emerge of which there had previously been only small glimpses. These aspects were to do with her appreciation and enjoyment of others and her capacity for care and concern – in particular, concern about whether she was doing the right thing by her children. Before a holiday she expressed her worry that she might not be giving her daughter, who had learning difficulties, a chance to work for her exams. She explained how this daughter, in particular, was easily distracted and needed help in settling to her work. (This was in contrast to her other daughter who was well-motivated and did not need special help in getting down to her studies.) Mrs Z was planning to fill up the house with visitors and activity and felt that it might be hard for her daughter to concentrate. I wondered whether she felt guilty about not protecting her daughter. She replied in an off-hand manner that she didn't know whether it made any difference. I pointed out that she might be worried both about her daughter and about whether she was leaving any space for herself to do emotional work in the holiday: she was planning to fill up her mind in order not to have time to be in touch with her feelings or to think about them. I suggested that she then threw doubt upon whether it made any difference because she was afraid of the responsibility if it did. She replied that she had just realised that she had made plans which entailed her missing the last session before the holiday 'without any thought whatsoever'.

This sequence gives some idea of the difficulties that Mrs Z faced in terms of beginning to take responsibility, both for her daughter and for her own personality, before a separation. She could see that her daughter needed a secure setting but could not bring herself to provide it. Similarly, she sabotaged the secure setting of the analysis by cutting out the last session before the holiday. She found it hard to hold onto the value of her loving feelings, either for her daughter or for herself and her analysis. Freud memorably stated: 'A man who doubts his own love may, or rather *must*, doubt every lesser thing' (1909: 241). In the case of Mrs Z, she seemed to retreat to doubt in the face of the difficulties of looking after her loving feelings and those whom she loves. To be aware of loving aspects of her personality made her more anxious than her familiar doubt and cynicism.

A subsequent session further demonstrated how her reparative wishes could be jeopardised by an omnipotent, controlling part of her. She talked about a lovely old building in need of restoration, describing its unique character in some detail. She said that 'ruthless' council planners were refusing planning permission to have it restored in the way that she wanted because of a tree that was in the way. She was angry at not being allowed to cut down the tree to make parking space. She described how the planners are not sensitive or thoughtful people; they are 'don't care professionals'. I pointed out that she was angry at not having total control, at the planners or the tree for getting in the way, like a father who imposes unwelcome limits. Her attacks on me for setting the boundaries of the analysis also turned me into a 'don't care professional'. She projected onto her analyst and the planners a ruthless aspect of her personality. This ruthlessness also sabotaged a sensitive and thoughtful aspect of herself that was capable of appreciating the character of her object. She wanted to have control and to do the reparative work and the work of the analysis on her own terms. When this wish was thwarted, the resulting feelings of anger and grievance threatened to undermine the progress which had been made to far and to interfere with further developments.

The fact that she was concerned with an historic building is also significant, in that coming to terms with her history, both in terms of its damaged and damaging aspects and the good things which it had given her, was vital to Mrs Z's capacity to feel at home with her personality. The historic building may also have contained a reference to her analysis as having a history, and analysis itself having a history before either of our lifetimes. Mrs Z began to express a real interest in the process of her analysis, wanting to know how it worked and surprised that it did seem to work. She also wanted to know in what ways it could help her and the nature of its limitations. Perhaps her interest in the nature of analysis was analogous to her interest in the personality of her friend: she was interested in the character of analysis.

There were by this stage in her analysis many occasions when Mrs Z would make a sensitive observation or raise a real concern, only to dismiss it. She had often told me how she did not like babies until they were competent, and I had understood this partly in terms of her sibling rivalry and partly in terms of her attitude to her own vulnerable self, liable to be overwhelmed by feelings. I was surprised one day when she told me how she and her husband were worried about a baby, a niece who seemed to be unusually withdrawn and unresponsive, and not able to enjoy relating to people. She described the baby's personality sensitively and then dismissed her concerns, saying that she was probably imagining it. I pointed out that she found it hard to trust her own judgement, both about the baby and perhaps about a withdrawn part of herself that found it hard to enjoy relating to people, including her analyst. The dismissal seemed a derivative of the virulent hatred that dominated the earlier part of her analysis: an off-hand dismissiveness could still threaten her developing emotional and observational capacities and personality.

As she gradually became able to use her capacity for observation and to relate to the personalities around her, including that of her analyst, she began to get in touch with aspects of her own personality which had not been able to develop, hampered as they were by conflicts of love and hatred and fears of retaliation, damage and loss. A more loving and thoughtful side of her began to emerge and to develop the capacity to be aware of and to stand up to her hatred. She began to enjoy life.

Discussion

Freud described the pathological identification which can take place due to unacknowledged hatred of the object. He wrote of 'an *identification* of the ego with the abandoned object. Thus the shadow of the object fell upon the ego . . . In this way, an object-loss was transformed into an ego-loss' (Freud, 1917: 149). I would add that the ego-loss can also imply a loss of personality because the subject's personality becomes confused with that of the lost object. Stultification of both subject and object ensues. Mrs Z's identity as a doormat was confused with that of her downtrodden internal mother. Similarly, her attacks on herself for being a doormat seemed to emanate from a part of her which identified with a ruthless aspect of her father, so her original complaints against herself also represented attacks by her internal father on her internal mother. This constellation often served as a highly effective form of contraceptive, preventing the conception of new emotional experiences or insights. It dominated the transference so that I felt undermined and bullied, or in turn felt like being scathing towards Mrs Z for her negativity. At times I felt like throwing her out of the nest or not bothering to go and look for her. It seemed important that I took seriously her fear that this might be the case and her anxiety that she might have played too far upon my patience and provoked an intolerant aspect of my personality. I also felt invited to ignore the glimpses of positive feelings that gradually appeared on the scene, as there seemed to be safety in negativity which threatened to prevent new hope or insights from being taken seriously.

Mrs Z gradually became more able to perceive the positive as well as the negative aspects of the central personalities in her life, including her analyst, and this seemed to lead to greater differentiation and freedom of movement between herself and her objects. She and they could now retain more of the individual characteristics which defined their personalities. This seemed to have been what was happening during the period when Mrs Z simultaneously acknowledged her admiration of her friend and his family and began to develop a wider range of emotional capacities of her own. She also began to be able to see her parents in their own right, with some compassion and appreciation and less bitterness. On one occasion she wondered whether her mother had been so consistent that she had taken her for granted. She recognised that she took my consistency for granted in similar fashion.

To attempt to maintain loving feelings, the appreciation of other personalities, and to allow her own personality to develop exposed her to enormous risks. She feared that her ambivalence might prevent her from being able to look after those she loved within her psyche, and that if she allowed herself to love them more fully, they might not be able to stand her ambivalence and this would lead to their loss. For change to take place it seemed important that I should be aware of the pressure to be drawn into a hateful relationship and to ignore the loving aspects of Mrs Z. Being able to help her to see the relationship between her love and her hatred was central to the work of her analysis, so that she could gradually come to see what she was doing to her own capacities as well as to mine and those of analysis.

Patients who feel that they lack a personality seem to have experienced their hatred, or that of their object, as too devastating for them to survive with their personality intact. However, as Bion wrote, 'hate would not exist if love were not present' (Bion, 1962: 10), and in a successful analysis these patients gradually gain an awareness of the conflict that has led to the splitting off of their loving feelings. Integral to this new awareness, as I hope to have shown, is the capacity to recognise the individual personality of the object and hence their own unique identity.

This might, at first sight, appear to present analysts and therapists with a paradoxical situation, in so far as in the analytic relationship they aim not to intrude their own personality. Yet the analytic work is inevitably mediated through the analyst's personality, which is communicated in many ways, through tone of voice, movement, appearance and, last but not least, unconscious communication. It is through their acceptance and use of their own individual countertransference responses, coupled with their ability to take seriously the patients' observations about them, that the analyst provides the patient with the experience of someone who is able to make use of his own mind and personality. The internalisation of this capacity in turn paves the way for the patient to get more in touch with their own feelings and to develop a sense of having a personality of their own.

References

Barrows, K. (2000) Shadow Lives: a Discussion of *Reading in the Dark*, a Novel by Seamus Deane. In J. Symington (ed.) *Imprisoned Pain and its Transformation. A Festschrift for H. Sydney Klein*. London and New York, Karnac Books.

Bion, W. (1962) *Learning From Experience*. Reprinted in *Seven Servants*. New York, Jason Aronson, 1977.

Freud, S. (1909) *Notes Upon a Case of Obsessional Neurosis*. SE 10. London, The Hogarth Press and The Institute of Psycho-Analysis, 1955.

Freud, S. (1917) *Mourning and Melancholia*. SE 14, 1957.

Klein, M. (1940) Mourning and Its Relation to Manic-Depressive States. In *Love, Guilt and Reparation and Other Works, 1921–1945*. London, The Hogarth Press and The Institute of Psycho-Analysis.

Chapter 6

The Origins of Love and Hate revisited

Sheila Gordon

Like all psychotherapists I have had plenty of opportunity to observe love and hate in the clinical setting – in myself, in my patients, and in the relationship between us. I have struggled to distinguish between the many guises of love and hate and to try and understand how they arise, how they relate to one another, and what their uses are.

Much of my early thinking about all this was rooted in Ian Suttie's *Origins of Love and Hate*, a book published in 1935, recommended to me many years before I thought of becoming a psychotherapist by my tutor at the Institute of Education. Reading it was a powerful and formative experience.

Suttie's ideas

Ian Dishart Suttie MD was a Scottish psychiatrist born in Glasgow in 1889. During his posting to Mesopotamia in 1918 with the RAMC he became interested in the role played in mental illness by social and cultural factors. He was influenced by the anthropological thinking of his time, with its emphasis on the mother–child bond in primitive social organisations. He was also impressed by Sandor Ferenczi's contribution to psychoanalytic thought, with its emphasis on the importance of 'real sincere sympathy and maternal friendliness' in the psychoanalytic process (Ferenczi 1955: 160). He went on to develop, through his work in Scottish mental hospitals and later at the Tavistock, his own independent and highly original thought on psychopathology and the function and technique of psychotherapy.

Origins of Love and Hate, his only complete book, embodies his theory and was a significant challenge to the Freudian tradition of psychoanalysis.

Suttie could not accept Freud's account of the origins of human emotions. He regarded Freud's long-elaborated view that the instinctual drive to maintain constancy and to reduce sexual tension is the mainspring of later development (Freud 1895, 1905) as reductionist and inaccurate.

As Greenberg and Mitchell conclude in their account of the drive/ structure model 'the thrust throughout Freud's writing indicates that a relationship to an external object is achieved developmentally' (Greenberg and Mitchell 1983: 40). Suttie, on the other hand, believed that the 'infant mind was dominated from the beginning by the need to retain the mother, and that this innate need was the motivation which powered all future growth' (Suttie [1935] 1988: 15). He appears to assume that the infant has both a capacity and a desire to relate to the mother as a whole object from the beginning.

Suttie made a further radical break from Freud with his view of the mother's role in child rearing. His anthropological interests as well as his experience had led him to believe that the mother rather than the father was of primary importance in the early years. He believed that all later successful social relationships are both a result of and a compensation for that early secure period of mother/infant pleasure. Moreover, he was quite clear that the capacity for that early bond is there from birth, is the direct result of 'biological need for nurture', and that this relationship between mother and child 'to the infant mind has the quality of tenderness from the beginning' (Suttie [1935] 1988: 4,31). Suttie's concept of infantile love therefore seems to be wholly benign, and in favourable circumstances capable of straightforward growth into mature relationships. This firmly differentiated him from Freud, who, of course, believed that the development of mature human love demanded a gradual and difficult reconciliation between the opposing forces of 'affection' and 'sensuality' (Freud 1905: 248).

In a complete reversal of Freudian theory Suttie claimed that it was aggression and hate towards an object that were developmentally based – the consequences of impaired relationships and thwarted love (Suttie [1935] 1988: 31). He could not endorse Freud's view that aggression was a primal element of the psyche and an independent energy source in its own right (Freud 1920). The therapist's task was therefore not primarily to analyse the patient in a detached and impersonal way but to provide an environment of care and concern, and a committed *relationship* which would enable the patient to recover from early disappointment and separation anxiety and would be a corrective for previous maternal failures (Suttie [1935] 1988: 213).

As an education student in the early 1950s I found the book deeply satisfactory and inspiriting. I liked Suttie's optimism, his clarity and his courage. I was heartened by his belief in the essential naturalness of loving human relationships as I was by my tutor's own firm emphasis on the importance of good relationships in classroom teaching. All this came as a breath of fresh air into an educational world where I found that children were still often regarded as unpromising and recalcitrant material to be 'knocked into shape'.

I was already used to a psychodynamic perspective on human development because in the preceding year, although officially a history student, I had been discovering psychoanalysis – as yet at a theoretical rather than an experiential level – and I had been delving haphazardly and with great relish into Freud's writing.

Although I found such completely unfamiliar perspectives exciting, not to say heady, Freud's view of the human psyche was a lot to take on board at the age of 22. My own life was opening up, and I was savouring the pleasure of being young in a London that was coming alive again after the war. None of that co-existed very well with Freud's unremitting insights into reality and a world-view that set its sights on 'common unhappiness' as a desirable goal (Freud 1895: 393).

As I confronted the difficulties of teaching pupils who were often reluctant, sometimes hostile, it was a relief to turn to Suttie's more hopeful account of the roots of human behaviour. If he was right that 'the germ of goodness or of love is in the individual (of every species which has evolved a nurtured infancy) from the very beginning' (Suttie [1935] 1988: 52), and that aggression and hostility arise only when that innate predisposition is frustrated, then perhaps even the most intractable classroom stand-off could be improved by a positive approach and an emphasis on a pleasurable teacher/pupil relationship.

And, on the whole, so it proved to be, although I have to say – and this is important for the ensuing discussion of Suttie's stance – the establishing of good and pleasurable relationship with the pupils was dependent on very firm boundaries and a clearly understood authority. The later Lacanian concept of 'the name of the father' was at that time well represented (Lacan 1977: ch. 6)!

When I began to train as a psychotherapist many years later I was surprised to find that Suttie's book did not appear on any reading list or feature in any seminar, although object relations theory by that time was very much in vogue. It seemed odd to ignore a man who already in 1935 was writing, 'We can reject therefore once and for all the notion of the infant mind being a bundle of co-operating or competing instincts, and suppose instead that it is dominated from the beginning by the need to retain the mother' (Suttie [1935] 1988: 15). Surely this was a foreshadowing of the work of Winnicott, Fairbairn and Guntripp, and yet I searched in vain for any attribution in their texts, or acknowledgement by their exponents.

I also noticed that although Winnicott's work on the importance of play between mother and child was constantly emphasised, Suttie's work was again never mentioned in any of his writing. And yet in 1935 several years before Winnicott published *Why Children Play*, Suttie was stoutly claiming: 'Play is a necessity not merely to develop the bodily and mental faculties, but to give to the individual that reassuring contact with his fellows which he has lost when the mother's nurtural services are no longer required or offered' (Suttie [1935] 1988: 18). So we see that not only did Suttie develop his theories before Winnicott but that he had reached an elaboration that Winnicott took some time to evolve (Winnicott 1942, 1971). Suttie was quite clear at the outset, just as Winnicott was later to be, that the 'primal attachment to mother' and jointly pleasurable relationship that follows are gradually replaced by the growing child's successful relationship with other individuals and with the 'whole social environment' (Suttie [1935] 1988: 16).

Re-reading his book at that time, thirty years after my original encounter, I was constantly puzzled by the general neglect of such an original thinker – one who after all had 'published first'. The trouble was, as Bowlby points out in his introductory essay to the 1988 edition of *Origins*, Suttie died just after the book was published – a serious misfortune for an author! What's more he had somewhat alienated the psychoanalytical establishment of the day by presenting his ideas as a challenge to Freud's work rather than as a development from it. Suttie's robustly polemical style meant that his medicine did not slip down easily! So as his occasional apologist I got used, at best, to a polite but uninformed acknowledgement, and, at worst, to a tendency to confuse him with a well-known television puppet! I was delighted when the 1988 edition of *Origins* was published with John Bowlby's appreciative Foreword.

Knowing that the book to which I am now contributing was going to be about issues of love and hate in the clinical setting, it seemed logical to offer a contribution on a book that was specifically focused on this early contribution to our understanding of object relations. I felt that I owed a debt to Ian Suttie and decided that I would now, after twenty years as a psychotherapist, be interested to discover how far his ideas were borne out by my everyday practice. I must say that I have been surprised to discover the extent of my present theoretical separation from him and the radical changes that twenty years as a psychotherapist have made to my views, which were originally so close to his.

Love and psychotherapy

Certainly it is still clear to me, as it was to him, that the mutually respectful, increasingly pleasurable alliance between patient and therapist provides the environment where growth and insight can flourish. The analytic setting does seem to work to some extent as the favourable maternal environment that Suttie believed was essential to the development of the infant's capacity to love. I know that any disturbances to that environment – premature interpretations, wandering attention, cancelled sessions – can by the same token produce the anxiety, terror and rage that Suttie identified as the result of deficient mothering. If the work goes reasonably well I do find that the setting itself does some of the work – anxiety is diminished and the patient becomes more hopeful. In Suttie's words a 'basis of companionship' is little by little discovered and the patient is restored 'to a feeling-interest integration with other minds' (Suttie [1935] 1988: 213). I still find this aspect of his work to be valid, just as I earlier found that good and enjoyable relationships in the classroom were essential for real education to happen. I can see that the provision of such a reliable and attuned setting can be regarded as an expression of the therapist's 'love'. I have already put forward elsewhere my belief that the mutual rapport and bond that is ultimately reached by therapist and patient is a mature form of intimacy (Gordon 1999).

I am interested to find, however, that I am now less convinced that it is a primary drive to attachment that brings my patients into therapy, and I am correspondingly less convinced that the baby innately 'knows' that relationship with an object is its comforting and nourishing destiny. Patients come to us just as babies come into the world in states that are distressing, uncomfortable, and sometimes unbearable. What they want above all is an easing of their stress and diminution of anxiety. In my countertransference I can certainly feel a drive to help that may parallel a parental response. However, I do get the impression at the outset of the therapy that the patient experiences me as a potentially useful agent rather than as a nurturing whole person who is available for relationship.

Usually at the very beginning of the therapy, even at the first session, patients start to experience a sense of relief as the built-up tension that led them to come is gradually discharged. I surmise that it is only *after* that first experience of satisfaction and relief that they begin to perceive me as some kind of satisfactory object, which is worth struggling towards. I do not find it fanciful to see some similarity in this to the state of the newborn infant. The neonate is, after all, unprotected at the moment of birth from all the consequent pains, discomforts and stress of the new world into which it has been ejected. In both circumstances I can well imagine that it is the discharge in tension and the feeling of relief and comfort that leads both the baby (and the patient) to a drive *towards* the source of his comfort and sustenance. Therefore it does now appear to me to be the experience of discharge, as Freud stated, that is the primary motivation towards the gradual building of the relationship with an object. I now think that Suttie's suspicion of what he saw as Freud's reductionism led him into a split with Freudian theory that now seems over-extreme and unnecessary.

Suttie himself stated that there was no clear-cut answer to the question of whether 'the attachment-to-mother was merely the sum of the infantile bodily needs and satisfactions which refer to her, or whether the need for a mother is primarily presented to the child's mind as a need for company and as a discomfort in isolation' (Suttie [1935] 1988: 16). He, of course, plumped for the inborn drive for comfort (a term that inevitably implies innate knowledge of an object). I get the impression in re-reading the book that the concept of an innate capacity to love was for him a psychological, indeed almost a theological, necessity.

For myself I now find no difficulty in believing that the drive towards a relationship with the object grows in infinitesimal stages only as the object comes to be associated with the relief of tension and the experience of satisfaction. It is a developmental process dependent on repeated satisfactory experiences, as Freudian drive theory suggests. As Freud said, 'Repeated experiences of satisfaction have created an object out of the mother' (Freud 1926: 170).

An account of a patient will, I hope, clarify further this present theoretical difference from Suttie and illustrate my contention that the desire for relationship with the therapist/object is not there from the beginning but is gradually derived from the efficacy of the therapeutic setting. A young woman of 25, whom I shall call C, came to see me having been referred by her GP. She looked as though the hounds of hell were at her heels – thin, taut with tension and with heavy dark circles under her eyes. Her presenting symptom was a propensity to intense panic attacks over the last six years, apparently occasioned by her work as a trainer which involved her in making presentations to an audience of around fifty people. Immediately before the presentation she would be overcome with physical symptoms – breathlessness, rapid heart rate, numbness and pins and needles in her limbs. She knew intellectually she must be 'too frightened to breathe' but at the time was only aware of being 'in a bubble' of total confusion and panic.

The story she told was one of constant but unrecognised anxiety and a feeling of complete isolation. There seemed to have been no opportunity for her as she was growing up to communicate any difficult or painful feelings to anyone. Her father had left home when she was seven, and C had been left with her mother who, though loving, was consumed with her own unbearable feelings of abandonment. They were short of money, their home was sparsely furnished and uncomfortable, and the fridge was always empty. The only way that C's buried feelings could safely be expressed was by frequent rows with her mother. Any disclosure of her own depression and sense of impoverishment was too overwhelming for her mother to be safely contained; the only safe way out was an exchange of aggression. Moreover, her appreciation of her mother's essential affection for her and an understanding of the difficulty of her situation stiffened C's resistance to any validation, let alone discharge, of her own powerful emotions.

During the first three sessions, as I listened to her story, I was able to make some interpolations that allowed her to understand and even experience some of the true depth of her pain and the difficulty of *her* situation as well as her mother's. The experience of being understood resulted in visible relaxation, and even after the first session she was able to get a good night's sleep for the first time for many months. However, not surprisingly she missed the fourth session and three or four days went by without any message from her. I normally write a brief note to patients who have failed to turn up, just noting the fact and confirming that I will keep their next scheduled appointment for them unless I hear anything to the contrary. I found myself in this instance not sending the usual note and decided to let whatever was happening between us play itself out. I could see that as the therapy progressed she was indeed going to need courage and strong motivation to stay with the process, bearing in mind the transference fears she was likely to have. After four days she left an agitated message on my voice mail, apologising for the missed session which was on account of a train cancellation and explaining that she could not telephone me because she had lost my address and telephone number! In the end she had telephoned the GP who had originally referred her to me, and got my number from him. I was aware that I felt immensely pleased that she had struggled through the resistances to find me at the end of it all. The next session was certainly marked by a new energy and what I can only describe as a feeling of celebration.

As I experienced the sessions and noted the growing commitment to the work it seemed clear that this was an incremental and gradual development as Freudian theory had postulated. I could readily believe that it was because of the initial usefulness of the sessions in helping to relieve some of her tension and provide constancy that the drive to find *me* as a desirable object had become strong enough to enable her to continue the work.

Nevertheless despite this theoretical distance from Suttie's work that I now discover, I still endorse his plea that the therapist should not be afraid to show the humane concern and responsiveness that he called 'love'; and I still agree with him that it is fundamental to therapeutic success. I think, for example, that my patient C persevered in her struggle to come back, not only because she had experienced a relief from anxiety but also because she sensed that there was a real 'someone' to find.

Psychotherapy and hate

For Suttie the infant's love of mother was the primal emotion. He regarded hate, on the other hand, 'not as a primal independent instinct but as a development or intensification of separation-anxiety which in turn is *roused* by a threat against love' (Suttie [1935] 1988: 31). He acknowledged that there is a 'potential disposition to react with anger and fear' but he appears to believe that these are only used by the infant, in order to get the mother's love. As he sees it, 'Anger is then aimed not at the direct removal of frustration, or attainment of the goal of the moment, still less at her destruction, but at *inducing the mother to accomplish those wishes for the child*.' 'Hatred', he therefore claims, 'is just a standing reproach to the hated person, and owes all its meaning to a demand for love' (Suttie [1935] 1988: 23).

It follows, then, that according to Suttie, if the mother or analogously the therapist is successful in providing the essential rapport, hatred and aggression can be discarded. They are not in his view inevitable. (Klein and Winnicott would have agreed, of course, that the favourable maternal environment greatly mitigates the baby's experience of rage – neither of them could have agreed with him that aggression would be thereby dispensed with: see Klein [1930] 1975: 296ff., and Winnicott [1958] 1965.)

Certainly I find that in line with the thinking of all three of them the extreme states of rage that patients often bring are lessened and made more manageable as the therapy proceeds and the reliability of the setting does its work. I fully agree that the provision of such an environment is part of our job. I further agree with him that total deprivation of such an environment by the mother, and, by implication, by a culture, will result in pathological expressions of hatred and rage (Suttie [1935] 1988: 50).

As I write these lines I am poignantly reminded of the fate of the ten-year-old Nigerian boy who was attacked and left to bleed to death in a Peckham Street. I remember the voice of the Peckham teenager interviewed on the radio about her own reactions to the killing and to the area in which she lived. I remember her matter of fact statement, 'Sometimes I carry a knife for protection; sometimes I carry one because I am so angry with life I want to kill someone!' Suttie no doubt would have seen her rage and anger entirely as an 'insistent demand upon the help of others' and an expression of her deep anxiety and sense of isolation.

Nowadays, of course, we have plenty of empirical evidence to show that there is indeed a connection between deprivation and the development of aggressive and violent responses. Suttie, however, in his chapter 'The Origin and Nature of Society' seems to go much further. He acknowledges 'that the abiding problem and central task of mankind has been maturation and the harmonisation of his love-needs with his appetite-needs and the attaining of maximal satisfaction in both' (Suttie [1935] 1988: 125). He goes on to imply that this is no easy task and that 'some suppression by the group' as well as by the individual may be necessary. However, he thinks of this as a 'negative solution' and appears to imply that some sort of ideal accommodation is ultimately possible in the wider social setting as well as the therapeutic one. It does seem that his interest in challenging Freud's theory of innate aggression led him to what for me now seems a utopian standpoint. I can agree that aggression can be mitigated by certain favourable environments, but I doubt very much that it can be eliminated – nor do I think that this would be an entirely desirable outcome. (It is interesting to note that by the time *Origins of Love and Hate* was published Melanie Klein had been working and writing in London for several years, and she had already published work putting forward her concepts of innate infantile destructiveness) (Klein [1930 1975]. Yet Suttie makes no reference to her whatsoever.)

I myself now lean much more to the idea that the capacity for rage and anger is not only innate but has an essential and valuable part to play in the safe survival of the psyche in its journey towards independence and maturity. Human beings need to hate and to be angry from time to time so that they can bear to stand alone and fight for themselves and their own protection – even when the adversary is someone they love.

This was not a position that Suttie could have entertained. He saw hate and aggression as pathological symptoms of a failure of relationship. Such emotions would be made unnecessary as the rapport with the therapist is established. 'The discovery is made by the patient that there is no real occasion for anxiety and hatred' (Suttie [1935] 1988: 217).

My own belief that hatred and aggression are not only inevitable but also potentially useful leads me to an entirely different conclusion about the purposes of therapy. I now see that one of the functions of therapy is to enable patients to become conscious of the nature and force of their human capacity for anger and hate, to contain both emotions safely and to use them constructively when the occasion arises.

I further believe with Winnicott that therapists need the freedom to feel hatred in its many forms. This must be so if the patient's hatred is to be successfully worked with. As Winnicott says, 'It seems to me doubtful whether a human child as he develops is capable of tolerating the full extent of his own hate in a sentimental environment. He needs hate to hate' (Winnicott [1947] 1982, [1958] 1965: 202).

I would add that both therapist and patient need to feel safe with the whole complexity of feelings that come up in the transference and countertransference. Otherwise whole areas of potentially useful material remain unexplored. Moreover the genuineness of what is happening in the session becomes weakened, and boredom threatens! As I made clear in my paper 'Bringing Up Eros' it is my view that negative feelings must be accepted and genuine disagreements must be faced if the therapist and patient are to achieve an energetic and creative working alliance (Gordon 1999).

A young woman whom I will call R came to see me. She was large, vigorous, intelligent and explosive. She came from a comfortable, middle-class, intellectual background and her parents were indisputably generous and well meaning. She was, however, full of rage and contempt for them. She resented the closeness of their relationship, which she saw as dominated by the father, and she was convinced that they showed more affection to her two siblings than they did to her. Although she had gone to university she worked in a relatively low-paid job, where she found other members of her team similarly unsatisfactory. She was often overtly critical of them and from time to time treated them to the explosions of rage with which her parents were very familiar.

The early sessions were marked by constant doubts about the therapy as I took on the transferential role of the inevitably disappointing and ineffectual object who was not really strong enough to give her what she wanted. However, as we went on working she got used to the safe, reliable setting and began to take and value the nourishment it provided. She also began to enjoy the exchange of ideas and thoughts with me so that as the positive transference was established so was a more mature alliance. So far I think Suttie's ideas can be said to be validated – the anger at the early failure of the transferential mother was softened by a reasonably satisfactory experience – and the capacity for relationship was strengthened. It should be noted, however, that although her anger with me was diminished, her fury with other individuals, including her parents, persisted, albeit at a diminished level.

After several months it seemed that I again became enveloped in a negative transference, this time not as a disappointing figure but as a deliberately frustrating and withholding one. The rage was mainly focused on my adherence to time boundaries and fees. After all if I really cared about her I would give her 'what she needed'. This time the hatred was clear to see and feel, although I did not find it in any way disturbing. I could feel in the countertransference a determination to resist her spoken and unspoken demands, and a determination to look after myself. I went on in the usual way trying to stay with her feelings of primitive rage and anxiety and helping her to explore her wish to have me under her omnipotent control. Things came to a head one evening when she was so angered by the end of the session that she announced her determination to stay on! I found this somewhat daunting as well as infuriating. I had another patient due in half an hour and there was no way in which I could physically dislodge this large infantile adult. I pointed out that there was a reality, which had to be accepted, and that I had other patients to see. However, I acknowledged her difficulty at that moment and told her that I myself would leave the consulting room. I asked her to find her own way out sometime within the next quarter of an hour. I was very relieved to hear her leave quite soon with only a moderately slammed door.

I wondered during the interval what the next session would be like, but had no real doubt that there would be one. Sure enough R appeared on time looking quite composed and interested in telling me about her subsequent feelings. Apparently she had left my house full of hatred 'not just for me but for the world'. She had gone to the bus stop where fortunately there was no one else waiting and had kicked the iron base of the bus stop until it got too painful! She reported that she felt much better after that and indeed had managed to see how absurd it all was. I am sure that this was able to happen because I had not tried to be sympathetic, but had concentrated on looking after my own part in the relationship and my own justified interest in securing an empty room for the next patient. It turned out that this was exactly the experience she had missed as her determinedly 'loving' parents had gone on masochistically trying to 'cure' her of her anger by patience and kindliness. The 'love' she had actually needed was a more realistic, less idealised love, which would have been based on a more accurately empathic response to her own needs – and also to the needs of the parents.

The uses of hate

Suttie certainly acknowledges that hate and anger deriving from unsatisfactory early experience will be brought by the patient and eventually expressed to the therapist. However he clearly identifies this as negative transference of feelings from past frustrations and disappointments. It is Suttie's view that these negative feelings are to be interpreted to the patient entirely as an understandable 'protest against love-privation' (Suttie [1935] 1988: 252). They would certainly not be interpreted in Kleinian terms – as a feature of the patient's own innate destructiveness; cf. Klein [1930] 1975.

There is consequently no place in his theory for the therapist's own aggressive feelings, let alone any thought that such feelings could be useful to the patient. Rather, the therapist's role is ideally 'very like that of Christ, serene without being aloof, sympathetic without being disturbed' (Suttie [1935] 1988: 217).

Experiences over the years with patients like R now lead me to very different conclusions.

For example, although I can accept that R's extreme expressions of anger might well have been to some degree mitigated by a different parental response, I see no reason to doubt that it was essentially an innate part of *her*. Moreover, I see nothing pathological in her basic annoyance with me. It seems quite likely to me that human beings are born with the natural tendency to rage against the frustrations that reality imposes and that this capacity in us all for temper tantrums remains a constant component of the psyche and is perhaps a useful source of energy.

Children's earliest experiences of their impotence in the face of an uncooperative reality, and their consequent rage, are focused on the parents – who inevitably withhold for various reasons the gratification that the infants demand. It was this kind of fury that R had been able to experience with me. Because I had refused to 'feed' her until *she* allowed me to stop, and had 'closed a door' which separated her from my relationship with the next patient, she had been taken over by a massive temper tantrum on both pre-Oedipal and Oedipal levels.

When she found that neither of us was destroyed by her anger, her anxiety and the destructive spiral of despairing rage that it provoked were considerably lessened. She also found that feeling angrily separate from me had not resulted in the end of the world and that indeed the situation could be repaired. I further believe with Winnicott that her hatred of me was useful because it enabled her to destroy me as a nurturing commodity and enabled her to come to terms with me as a 'whole object', a real flesh and blood person with a boundaried shape (Winnicott 1968: 218–27). A much more profoundly interesting and satisfying exchange between us could now begin.

In this context another patient, L comes to mind. She had grown up in a family where although gentleness and politeness were highly valued her younger sibling had freely expressed her anger and bad temper. The family's response had been to calm her down and placate her, and L had differentiated herself from this younger troublesome sister by becoming the 'good child'.

She came over as an essentially likeable and friendly woman who took her therapy seriously. However, during most of our meetings she would at some point slip into an over deferential and self-denigrating stance. Remarks like, 'You can't want to hear about this . . . I'm probably just making a fuss about nothing' seemed to appear out of nowhere – and I kept wanting to shake her out of these sudden relapses into inauthenticity.

One day she began the session by telling me that she thought that I had been 'irritated' with her at our last meeting. I admitted that this was so, but also suggested that she might also have been irritated with me. I said that I thought that during this somewhat difficult stage in our work it was possible that she experienced me as a nagging dissatisfied parent because I was continually pointing out the strength of her defences. She accepted all this quite readily and told me that to her surprise the mutual irritation 'hadn't seemed to matter very much'. She had not felt at all cast down by our being rather 'at odds' but had, to her surprise, felt quite relaxed about it. She went on to tell me that in a dispute at work a few days before she had not sought to placate everyone during a disagreement about holiday arrangements but had stood her ground. She found she no longer felt impelled to protect herself and everyone else from any possibility of conflict.

R had been able to hate me and yet survive; L had been able to feel 'fed up' with me and go forward. I believe that this clash with the object usefully propelled them both into a state of *bearable isolation,* a concept that I suspect that Suttie would have seen as a contradiction in terms (cf. Winnicott [1958] 1965).

I believe that human beings need to be aware of their separateness and to bear it however uncomfortable and even painful that sometimes is. Only then can they ever achieve real intimacy (Gordon 1999). Moreover, they must be able to protect themselves against objects that threaten their psychological survival, whether that object be a parent, a friend, an organisation or a therapist. If the desire for relationship overrides all others they are trapped, imprisoned by the fear of loss and unwilling to take any steps that may lead to separation. There has to be some willingness to risk conflict and aloneness on the way to maturity. So it looks to me as if man does well to keep in touch with that primary narcissistic relationship with the self that Freud postulated and Suttie so passionately disputed.

Conclusion

From many years hindsight I can see that Suttie lost much in his polemical view of Freud and regressed into some serious oversimplifications of Freudian theory. Certainly Dorothy Heard implies in her introduction to the 1988 edition of the *Origins of Love and Hate* that it was its extreme stance that led Fairbairn to distance himself from Suttie. This would explain the lack of any attribution from him or from the later writers whose ideas so often echoed his own (Suttie [1935] 1988: Introduction).

Suttie did admit that even 'the reductive method of analysis' practised by Freud and his followers could convey 'a responsiveness, which is unweary-ing, tolerant and even appreciative, insighted and alert' (Suttie [1935] 1988: 211). Although he greatly disliked Freud's interpretation of his patient's love as transferential rather than real, he acknowledged that Freud's own attitude to his patients was essentially loving (Suttie [1935] 1988: 253). He did not, however, appear to have any appreciation that the painstaking interpretation of the patients' unconscious blocks and their rescue from the elaborate persecution of their super ego are in themselves a very practical form of love. His view of the therapist's role now sounds to me over-idealised, and insufficiently appreciative of the transformation that pains-takingly acquired insight, worked through, can bring.

His unwillingness to accept that hatred as well as love was a primary emotion led him, I now believe, into further theoretical difficulties and at times almost into sentimentality. He seems on occasion to describe rela-tionships – whether between mother and child or between therapist and patient – as they *should* be rather than as they uncomfortably are.

And yet with all these provisos born of hindsight, I still marvel at his courage. He was writing at a time when Freud still dominated the psycho-analytical world, and when many of Freud's own more modified ideas were still to be developed. It was a time when the strictures of the authoritarian paediatrician Frederick Truby King dominated the upbringing of most middle-class children and when the treatment of infants was, as a result, often withholding and undemonstrative in the extreme (King 1923; Mander 1996).

Suttie was prepared to challenge that patriarchy and to make his plea for loving and affectionate attitudes. I still believe that he helped to give legitimacy to the humane and compassionate aspects of psychoanalytical psychotherapy that had been so often left unacknowledged in the pursuit of scientific respectability.

I still enjoy his originality and his passion as I did when I first discovered his book, and I am thankful for the influence that he has had on my own work. It was a good place to start from.

References

Ferenczi, S. (1955) *Final Contributions to the Problems and Methods of Psycho-Analysis*, London: Hogarth Press.

Freud, S. (1905) Three Essays on the Theory of Sexuality, *Standard Edition*, London: Hogarth Press.

—— (1920) Beyond the Pleasure Principle, *Standard Edition*, London: Hogarth Press.

—— (1926) Inhibitions, Symptoms and Anxiety, *Standard Edition*, London: Hogarth Press.

Freud, S. with Joseph Breuer (1895) Studies of Hysteria, *Standard Edition*, London: Hogarth Press.

Gordon, S. (1999) Bringing Up Eros, in David Mann (ed.) *Erotic Transference and Countertransference*, London: Routledge.

Greenberg, R. and Mitchell, S.A. (1983) *Object Relations and Psychoanalytic Theory*, Cambridge, Mass. and London: Harvard University Press.

King, Sir Frederick Truby (1923) *Feeding and Care of Baby*, London: Macmillan.

Klein, M. ([1930] 1975) The Importance of Symbol Formation in the Development of the Ego, in *Love, Guilt and Reparation*, London: Hogarth Press.

—— ([1936] 1975) Weaning, in *Love, Guilt and Reparation*, London: Hogarth Press.

Lacan, J. (1977) *Ecrits. A Selection*, London: The Hogarth Press and The Institute of Psychoanalysis.

Mander, G. (1996) The Stifled Cry of Truby King, *British Journal of Psychotherapy*, Vol. 13, No. 1.

Suttie, D. ([1935] 1988) *The Origins of Love and Hate*, London: Free Association Books.

Winnicott, D. (1942) Why Children Play, *New Era in Home and School*, 23: 1–12.

—— ([1958] 1965) The Capacity to be Alone, in *The Maturational Processes and the Facilitating Environment*, London: The Hogarth Press.

—— (1968) The Use of an Object and Relating Through Identifications, in D. Winnicott, C. Bollas, M. Davis and R. Shepherd (eds) *Psychoanalytic Explorations*, London: Karnac Books.

—— (1971) Playing: A Theoretical Statement, in *Playing and Reality*, London: Tavistock.

—— ([1947] 1982) Hate in the Countertransference, in *Through Paediatrics to Psycho-Analysis*, London: Hogarth Press.

Chapter 7

Freeing Eros in the playroom of therapy. The interface of hate and love

Sexualisation, abstinence and 'celibate' countertransference[1]

Robert C. Ware

In the language of mortals Psyche's child is called Pleasure. But in the language of heaven . . . this child is the mystical joy which among all peoples is described as the fruit of the highest mystical union. It is 'Joy indeed, but surpassing sensuality.'
(Neumann 1971: 140, citing Tejobindu Upanishad 8 in Denssen 1897, p. 665)

Introduction

Starting from the conception of a metaphoric erotic–sexual 'playroom' in the analytic hour I shall reflect on working through eroticism and sexuality in a psychoanalytic, body-psychotherapeutic therapy with a 40-year-old married woman.[2] Narrating my own experience in this analysis I follow the Ariadne thread of a highly charged, eroticised countertransference. My contention is that the induced sexualisation of the therapeutic relationship, originating in a latent incestuous, sadomasochistic father fixation and in a delusional idealisation of an absent mother, represents the *interface of hate and love* in transference/countertransference. Scenic enactment of these inner object relationships within and outside therapy constituted the pre-eminent form of (unconscious) communication within the therapeutic dialogue, and symbolic physical activity at times assumed the mutative function of classical analytical interpretation.

Hinshelwood (1994: 39) remarks about play therapy with children that interpretations 'attempt to put into conscious words those ideas, emotions . . . and relationships that are hidden, or part-hidden; in effect, to speak the unspoken to the child. With children there is much more of a sense of doing something together with the patient (or even *to* him or her); this contrasts with adult psychoanalysis, where there is a tendency to speak *about* things, [though] in latter years . . . there has been a realization that adult psychoanalysis is also a "doing something" together with the patient.' In body-oriented analytical therapy with adults this 'doing something' together with the patient is extended to sensumotoric interaction which can be both *response* in the sense of 'vivid, direct and imaginative play' (ibid.: 44) and, on occasion, non-verbal *interpretation* that expresses, reflects and makes conscious unspoken ideas, emotions and relationships in an experiential way – 'speaking / the unspeakable / in the unspoken' (a haiku verse).

In the mutuality of the analytical relationship 'speaking about the erotic feelings one has towards the other person already constellates intimacy with them' (Pfannschmidt 1998: 367). When in the course of this chapter I narrate a relational, action-symbolic and body-therapeutic approach I do not argue in exclusion of any other approach, but hope to illustrate an alternative, which I have found to be highly effective and which I consider every bit as psychoanalytic as so-called classical technique. I shall concentrate less on the defensive aspects of the eroticisation than on its progressive, developmental potential. With Worm (2000: 88) I distinguish between 'eroticised [sexualised] transferences, which correspond to a surrogate or a defensive need, as opposed to erotic transferences, in which an integrated sexuality wants to be developed'. Although with my patient we were apparently dealing throughout with sexualised transference and induced countertransference, in the course of time and as perhaps the most important achievement in this therapy there arose a genuinely erotic relatedness.

As in the therapy my reflection culminates in the analogous conception of a 'celibate' countertransference – refraining from overt or subliminal sexual acting out for the sake of a more esteemed value. This proved to be a fundamental precondition for the interactive and interpersonal working through the defensive sadomasochistic eroticisation of the therapy relationship and fostered the achievement of an encompassing, mature experience of erotic drive and erotic imagination in their various (archetypal) manifestations as sexual drive, psychic life principle and spiritual reality. Diligent restraint applies also to the subtle hazards of the therapist's narcissistic gratification while working with erotic and sexual transferences. The crucial question of how a therapist accesses his own unconscious process in the course of scenic enactment and interactivity will hopefully become clearer as we go along. Suffice to say, this is the core of countertransference analysis, which must use the scene itself with all its emotional, cognitive and bodily resonances as a mirror of the goings-on in the 'mutual unconsciousness' (Jung) of the therapy couple.

Underlying the interplay of sexualisation and abstinence in the interface of hate and love in eroticised (sexualised) and erotic (love-based) transference and countertransference is a conception of sadomasochism adopted from Jessica Benjamin (1988: 51–84) which I would paraphrase as hatred searching for a love object. *Hate* [Old English *hete, hatian*] is defined in my dictionary as 'intensely hostile aversion, compounded of anger and fear, and centered on a real or supposed cause of injury'. *Hatred* is specified as 'the *passion* of hate [hate + *red*, OE *roeden*, condition]'. *Love* [OE *lufu*], by contrast, is 'a powerful emotion felt for another person manifesting itself in deep affection, devotion or sexual desire; the object of this emotion; God's regard for his creatures; charity (the virtue); a great liking, fondness.' I purposely begin with schoolish definitions to underscore how playing with words is a favoured pastime of creative imagination. We shall be pursuing the development of the *red hate* of sadomasochistic object relationship as it slowly transmutes into its apparent opposite, a passionate or *red* love. The prime object of our research will be to explore possibilities of dealing with sexual and erotic passions within a therapeutic relationship.

In effect, I shall be narrating a story of 'retelling a life' (Schafer's 1992 description of therapeutic process). The story I wish to reflect upon is that of a 40-year-old married mother and her search for passion and loving relationship. It began as a highly fragmented incestuous and sadomasochistic entanglement of inner and outer object relationships. Disentangling the passionately felt, feared and acted-out love, hate and desire moulded the process of erotic and sexual enactment so characteristic of this therapy. The story (therapy) begins at the hate end of the continuum where, as Britton remarked, eroticisation represents 'hatred for the real object world' (Doctor 1999: 93). In fact, throughout this therapy we dealt extensively in transference/countertransference dialogue with deeply confusing, in part idealised, but especially sadomasochistic and highly charged eroticised (sexualised) parental introjects. These inner objects mirrored her experiences with a highly gifted but extremely narcissistic, latent incestuous and sadistically acting-out father. They appeared in therapy in projections, projective identifications and unconscious enactments, both with the therapist and with an extramarital lover, whose virtual presence as third person helped generate the triangular space needed for therapeutic growth. As we worked through the meandering, often conflicting and tortuous paths of her process 'Kathleen' (as I shall call her) came eventually to integrate the fractured aspects resultant upon lifelong cumulative traumatisation into a consistent and meaningful life history. Thus genuinely erotic impulses – encompassing sexual drive, mind, psyche and even religious-spiritual strivings – took shape and gave direction and gestalt to her life, where previously there had been only traumatic suffering and chaotic experience.

Eros and sexuality generally appear in therapy in conjunction with comprehensive relationship disturbances. In countertransference reactions one not infrequently encounters sexual phantasies, feelings, wishes and impulses. Often they are experienced as unwelcome distractions and even distressing intrusions in the work of analysis. When erotic and sexual phenomena occupy centre court in the therapeutic interaction, they can embroil even the most experienced psychotherapist in a maelstrom of contradictory feelings, drive impulses and ethical conflicts.[3] Although love and sexual feelings are presumably unavoidable in countertransference and possibly even essential to productive analytical work (Hirsch 1988), they are still today seldom discussed in professional discourse. Experiential clinical case material is even more rare. Eros and sexuality are without doubt among the most unspoken of psychoanalytical topics and are subject to enormous professional resistance.

Erotic, as used here, comprises all physical and mental expressions of love to the extent that a measure of sexual attraction and sensual pleasure are included. Sexual refers in a more restricted sense to genital drive impulses: excitement, pleasure, stimulation, phantasies, behaviour. The combination erotic–sexual indicates that both aspects are intended equally. Erotic and sexual refer to somatopsychic phenomena that possess a complex and highly *symbolic* character. They are frequently metaphors for other conflicts, disturbances and developmental issues in the life of a person. Nonetheless, '*sexuality has to be present for its symbolic meaning to be interpreted*' (Samuels 1985: 207, italics in the original). Whatever their ultimate (symbolic) significance may prove to be in the course of analysis, the initial compelling concreteness within the transference/countertransference relationship should warrant extensive study. Erotic–sexual phenomena at times exhibit an agonising craving for immediate gratification and they possess catastrophic potential for abuse of the patient.[4] Instead of defensive reticence, both professional ethics and technical prowess demand open discussion.

The erotic–sexual 'playroom' of therapy

In an article on 'The Use of Pleasures in the Analytic Hour', Pfannschmidt (1998) postulates a psychoanalytic approach to erotic and sexual feelings, phantasies and impulses in the therapeutic relationship that fosters developmental growth. To this goal he proposes the metaphor of an '*erotic–sexual playroom*'. With direct reference to Winnicott's transitional space as the psychic realm of creative imagination this interactive playroom comprises the therapeutic couple and their experience of erotic and sexual feelings. In appropriate instances, and without sacrificing the asymmetry of the therapeutic relationship, Pfannschmidt advocates that patient *and* therapist speak openly of their erotic and sexual feelings and phantasies, 'enjoy' them when possible, and work through them analytically (ibid.: 368). At times, of course, erotic desire and sexual fantasies can produce extreme anxiety, even horror (Kumin 1985), and are not pleasurable in the least. These too should be explicated and worked through. Similarly, impulses on the therapist's part to seductive teasing, subliminal narcissistic or covert sexual gratification must be convincingly worked through in the analysis of the transference/countertransference interaction. As with the case material I present here, they are not infrequently an essential element of the scenic enactment itself. Abstinence is maintained, in my view, as long as the therapist is not pursuing his own drive gratification but rather the analysis of the relational interaction in transference and countertransference. In an imaginative, 'playful' manner fostering experiential exploration analyst and patient engage themselves in resolving the conflicts issuing from the fears and inhibitions regarding sexual enjoyment and erotic pleasure.

Already in 1946 Jung envisioned this transitional space in the transference/countertransference relationship when he wrote of the 'mutual unconsciousness' of doctor and patient (§ 364, 367). Jung was all too aware of the dramatic (and even traumatic) potential of what transpires in this energy field. Without using the terminology he graphically describes the phenomenon of projective identification when he writes of unconscious 'infections' occurring in transference/countertransference (§ 358 fn 17; § 365). This 'infection' (a medical metaphor) is part and parcel of what Christopher Bollas (1987: 248ff.) calls 'countertransference capacity' as a receptacle for unconscious communications from the patient, whereby at times 'by virtue of the analysand's object usage of us in the transference . . . our analytic mind becom[es] distressed or deformed' (ibid.: 249). Thea Bauriedl emphasises a further aspect of the phenomenon:

> The analytic relationship is an interlock of transference and counter-transference on the part of both participants . . . Transference signifies perception and behaviour in one's own previous relational system, countertransference signifies perception and behaviour in the relational system of the relationship partner. What takes place in the analytic relationship is in this view an *'unconscious enactment of a mutual scene'*.
>
> (Bauriedl 1998: 354; my italics)

Pfannschmidt makes two statements about the 'use of pleasures' in the erotic–sexual playroom of the analytic hour which I find to have programmatic significance.

1 'The understanding that erotic and sexual phantasies . . . will not be physically acted out with the attendant social consequences but rather under the safeguard of the [therapeutic] setting . . . playfully expressed, makes it possible to experience and enjoy them, and thereby within the interaction itself to change and work through them, in order to integrate them anew in one's own body experience (the self).'

2 'This playful experience in the erotic space, where the analyst . . . guarantees the protected playspace, while at the same time allowing himself as partner in play to be affected erotically and does not deny being affected, is the presupposition for changing and developing erotic experience and for integrating anxiety-ridden, unknown, split-off, repressed sexual impulses and feelings.'

(Pfannschmidt 1998: 368–369)

To the extent that we consider any interaction between analysand and analyst, including the feelings, phantasies, impulses and actions of both, as the unconscious enactment of a mutual scene, the countertransference becomes the single most important receiving organ for the frequent unconscious communications of the patient. The condition for a *lege artis* 'use of pleasures' is then a conscientious examination and informed analysis of the countertransference – in any event the keystone of every relational, interpersonal psychoanalysis. Whether it be question of erotic–sexual, aggressive, envious or joyful, motherly, fatherly or whatever reactions, one must consistently investigate according to the principles of the psychoanalytic art, what in a given situation is being 'played' or enacted in the mutual scene.

The second condition for the use of pleasures in the therapeutic relationship is an explicit and irretractable understanding that neither the erotic–sexual nor the aggressive drive impulses will be acted out in harmful physical activity against the person of the other (analysand or analyst) respectively against his/her personal integrity. The foremost obligation of the therapist is at all times to respect, protect and foster his patient's *and* his own personal integrity and inviolability. Every compromise in this area, e.g. a therapist gratifying his own erotic fantasy by revealing it, or self-revelation that is not in the interest or even against the express wish of his patient, is detrimental to the therapeutic relationship as sole ground for a meaningful collaboration. *Acting out* is used here as a technical term for destructive resistance and is distinguished from *enacting* in the sense of an unconscious communicative *mise-en-scène* (cf. Ellman and Moskowitz 1998; Streeck 2000). This is of particular significance for the assessment of interactive (for example body-oriented psychotherapy, bioenergetic analysis, psychodrama, gestalt therapy) and other applied forms of analytical psychotherapy methods, where a plethora of direct physical and active imaginative techniques make possible the conscious scenic enactment of aggressive and even erotic–sexual feelings, phantasies and impulses, occasionally even in concrete physical confrontation with the therapist. Modified bodily aggression and erotic–sexual forms of expression can thus be transformed and dealt with without impairment to persons or objects. This regularly produces an intensification and deepening of emotional experience and efficacy in the therapeutic interaction (cf. Heisterkamp 2001).

Increasingly over the years I have come to the conviction that the deepest therapeutic work is done in and on the multiple disturbances of relational intimacy within the transference/countertransference relationship, providing our patients with good enough 'potential space' in our countertransference capacity (Ware 2000: 6–9). Providing space means setting boundaries, first of all the boundaries of my own tolerances, including of course the limitations of my own narcissistic, perverse or abusive tendencies. Giving room means as well ongoing development and integration of one's own sexuality, emotionality and gender identity. In this respect our patients are at times our best teachers.

As an illustration of interactive, body-therapeutic, psychoanalytical therapy I shall now describe in some detail a therapy which moved from hate to love by means of a sadomasochistic relational style that proved to be progressive and positive in its developmental thrust. That is to say, it embodied and was able to realise in the course of therapy 'both the desire for independence and the desire for recognition' (Benjamin 1988: 52). 'Kathleen' – my pseudonym for the patient – exemplifies the at times extreme mental, emotional and instinctual oscillations in an erotic–sexual process of knowing and understanding in the 'playroom' of the analytic hour. The therapy with Kathleen took place towards the end of my sixth decade after more than twenty years' experience with body-oriented analytical psychotherapy. It placed enormous demands on my therapeutic knowledge and ability and was often a challenge to my ethical principles.

An erotic–sexual process of knowing

At the time of therapy Kathleen was 40 years old, a gifted and quite attractive working mother of two children in their late teens. Need for therapy was occasioned by intense depressive periods, agitated distress and insecurity, marriage conflicts, sexual disinterest towards her husband and inner withdrawal from him. Early on in the therapy relationship deeply confusing, in part idealised, but particularly sadomasochistic and highly charged sexualised father-introjects were constellated in the transference and, even more intensely, in the countertransference. In the first year of therapy Kathleen lived out these father-introjects in a passionate extra-marital relationship. The affair increasingly developed sadomasochistic features with alternating roles. From the beginning I had the phantasy that Kathleen acted out her sexual drives outside the therapy so that she would not overburden and endanger the therapeutic relationship. Later on she confirmed this.

Still, the therapy relationship was not at all free of eroticism and sexuality. From the beginning I experienced strong sexual feelings and wishes towards Kathleen. For a time I experienced as well a jealous rage towards her lover. The unusual strength of these affects – much more than I had previously experienced in therapies – led me to see them as 'induced' countertransference reactions (Downing 1996: 316–336), specifically, projective identifications of an envious, extremely jealous and 'latent incestuous' father (Hirsch 1994: 198–213). They were at once tormenting and tempting, at times difficult to contain and, had they in any way been acted upon, would surely have destroyed the therapeutic bond and constituted a 'soul murder' of the patient. Of this I was painfully aware. Initially I endeavoured to acknowledge the presence and importance of these feelings in the countertransference and to work them through alone with the help of occasional supervisory reflection. Kathleen came once a week for a double session. After about a year's time she gradually came to recognise the incestuous sadomasochistic repetition pattern in her affair with a married man and father of a large family. In despair she began, as she expressed it, to 'wean' herself from him. In a state of existential desperation she telephoned one day and literally implored: '*Can you be mother to me for a time?*' Her apparent anguish touched me. I don't recall having said anything specific other than to signal my availability.

Up until this point in therapy Kathleen's mother had been conspicuously absent, except for occasional mention as an idealised angelic creature, whom an envious spouse had assiduously kept apart from Kathleen and her siblings. Kathleen's idealisation of her mother served to defend against her very early loss of mother and the resultant existential abandonment anxiety, which now for the first time could be experienced in therapy. To better understand the following scene it is important to know that Kathleen was separated immediately after birth for several weeks from her mother, who had suffered an acute appendicitis after giving birth. Kathleen's unusually passionate extramarital affair, throwing caution to the winds, seemingly reproduced the sadomasochistic enmeshment of her incestuous father relationship. However, as now became apparent, in the love affair she sought the early symbiotic fusion with the lost mother on a deeper level with unrelenting intensity.

In the first therapy session some days after her telephone request Kathleen experienced extreme anxiety, terror and panic, extensive coughing fits and agonising abdominal cramps. Only towards the end of the 90-minute session did it become apparent that she had regressed to affective depths which corresponded to her earliest, postnatal mother abandonment. Insight into this circumstance came in conjunction with a recollection on my part of the '3-month-colics' of my infant daughter nearly twenty years previous. Before the recollection occurred (and I related it to Kathleen) I had simply held Kathleen very firmly for sometime – as I had my infant daughter – while she writhed and screamed in intense pain. In the grips of such tormenting somatopsychic affects Kathleen needed physical holding and containment – so my spontaneous decision at the time in accordance with my own style of body-oriented analytical therapy. In this extreme situation to let her suffer without concrete, physical assistance would have subjected her to needless repetition of the early trauma of existential abandonment. Instead of therapeutic reliving with the possibility of working through, we would have risked renewed, therapy-induced retraumatisation.

Psychodynamically we can assume that in the face of early maternal deprivation Kathleen sought shelter and solace in a pseudo-hysterical, precocious Oedipal recourse to her narcissistically disturbed father. However, instead of finding support and containment, the child was subjected to almost daily beatings, verbal shaming and narcissistic abuse. Later on as a teenager and as an adult she went alone with him to the basement sauna where he regularly entrusted her with matters he 'couldn't discuss with his wife'; not infrequently he 'touched [her] immodestly'. In this respect Kathleen had suffered all her life a second traumatising abandonment at the hands of a much-loved father who showed no respect for the self-boundaries of his daughter. Now in the current separation from her lover Kathleen incurred yet a third abandonment crisis, which in effect recapitulated the earlier traumata. Despite continuous 'professions of love' for Kathleen her real lover (in her inner world he was an essential father/mother self-object) could not or would not leave his wife and children. Thus Kathleen's 'weaning' from her friend constellated deep-rooted abandonment anxieties which manifested in the somatic 'language' of the infant. In her therapist Kathleen sought an early father/mother self-object as a saving anchor and safety net both for the torment of the revived murderous incest wound but also, and especially now, against the disproportionately more threatening *nameless* anxiety of postnatal maternal abandonment.

Kathleen's somatic enactment resulted from a complex transference dynamic, in which positive and negative aspects of father and mother all played a role. Here I shall simply take up a single dimension following the thread of the countertransference. Although consciously attempting to be 'mother', as she had desired, I felt throughout the session, as the memory of my infant daughter indicates, much more like a father. This bodily feeling I take to be a syntonic countertransference experience of 'father's body' (Ware 1996–97). In it I find evidence of a decisive inner movement by Kathleen from her precocious Oedipal fixation on the negative incest father towards an earlier pre-Oedipal positive father representation. Kathleen sought the missing positive mother and found in her stead the saving third in the early (pre-Oedipal) father. In effect she experienced me as a good selfobject, as it were father and mother in one.[5] By means of verbal encouragement and empathic physical support I sought to enable her to better survive the revival of postnatal traumatic abandonment and, as the scene developed, to find meaningful connections in the throes of over-powering affects. Thus occurred, in the face of renewed acute breakdown of postnatal maternal support, a retroactive reparation of earliest triangulation with an empathic father figure. In this way triangular developmental space emerged that had originally been foreclosed both by the loss of mother and later by the 'devouring' aspects of a severely jealous and latent incestuous father. In the course of therapy these sadistic incestuous developments also found more satisfactory resolution. Relived trauma sequelae thus received a coherent 'place' within a personal developmental story, became part of a lived history and could be integrated into a meaningful 'personal myth' (Jung).

The use of pleasure and desire

In the following months Kathleen's lurching and careening in and outside the therapy continued overtly much as before. However, she increasingly sought to counteract the recurring 'insane panic' of early abandonment anxiety by claiming on 'father's body' in the transference/countertransference relationship the protection and solace denied her as an infant. More and more she could assimilate for gradually longer periods of time the soothing experience as she sat before me on the carpet and allowed me to hold her in my arms 'like a child on papa's lap' – how we both experienced the scenic enactment in this phase. (Later she 'outgrew' this compensatory need and discontinued it of her own volition.) A deeply religious yearning for wholeness and 'spheric experience' came to light. Experiences of yearning for symbiotic fusion with the early mother often changed almost imperceptibly to yearning for passionate sexual fusion with her lover. And the transference/countertransference relationship became increasingly – as I one day spontaneously blurted out in response to a remark of hers – '*a very sexual relationship!*'

This most peculiar statement was at once an interpretative declaration and a throwing off of the putative yoke of stringently ascetic analytical 'abstinence'. It was as if I had said: 'From now on let's just call the child by its proper name.' In retrospect it was, I believe, a decisive step towards working through the resistance in the transference as opposed to working *on* it (Körner 1989). For Kathleen sexualisation was much less threatening and anxiety producing than the early abandonment she parried with it. Openly addressing this defensive sexualisation made it possible to work with it, identify its purpose and realise its potential as a search for a loving object 'surpassing sensuality' (cf. epigraph, p. 125). Continuing attempts to resolve the charged eroticisation of the therapeutic relationship by working exclusively on my own on the countertransference reactions would only have resulted in more avoidance, denial and exacerbation of the relational problem they produced. Up until this point in the therapy it seemed detrimental to address and confront the issue openly.

Speaking to her now of the erotic and sexual feelings I experienced towards her generated in time a new and genuinely erotic intimacy between us, where eroticism and sexual feelings, phantasies and impulses could be experienced, explicitly shared and subjected to analytical reflection. Speaking to her *about* the feelings sustained a crucial reflective distance to the feeling experience itself; in this self-reflective space a new intimacy arose, which I hold to be something quite different from the shared feeling intimacy of actual lovers. I hesitate to say, with Pfannschmidt, that we 'enjoyed' these feelings or even this sharing – it was mostly hard and often self-denying work – but there was also a deeper joy in the new sincerity in our relationship. It created an intimate space in which new growth and further transformation took place, for Kathleen and for me. Now that her conventional defence was acknowledged and valued as a potential space for growth and intimacy it ceased to be solely defensive. Eroticism and sexuality became a new 'idiom', a language of intimacy, in which wholly new levels of meaning were discovered and explored.

The freeing of Eros in the analytical dialogue

Kathleen's husband had been her first and, until the beginning of therapy and her extramarital 'friendship' her only sexual partner. In marital sex she had felt 'from the very beginning' that she had to 'nurse' (German *stillen*, to breastfeed, but also to satisfy or still) her husband like an infant. Presumably as a result of her own early traumatic deficit she adopted a maternal feeding position in the sexual relationship in order to project and gratify vicariously her own oral needs. However, over time she felt ever less satisfied as a woman with adult sexual needs and gender desires for recognition and esteem. The initial oral fixation of Kathleen's sexuality was further contaminated by the massive brunt of sadistic-incestuous cathexis in the powerful father/adoring daughter constellation. For more than twenty years Kathleen had effectively defended against this latent incestuous and oral conflict dynamic with an overcompensating 'nursing' in marital sexuality. The price she paid for her denial was an increasingly intolerable renunciation of adult sexual gratification and erotic fulfilment.

Within the imaginal playroom of our therapy relationship, in its own way no less intensively informed by sexual Eros, there occurred a developmentally necessary innerpsychic 'incest'. This *symbolic* (archetypal) incest is for Jung the 'specific content' of the transference as an instinctive process. As instinct it is, together with its phantasy contents, partly concrete, partly symbolical or '*unreal*', i.e. not a proper instinct, but a symbol containing 'the spiritual meaning of the natural instinct' (Jung 1946: § 362). Such unconscious and chaotic contents, writes Jung, exert great fascination on the patient and can have a similar inductive effect on the unconscious of the therapist. They isolate the patient in 'a spiritual loneliness' neither he nor anyone else can understand, though in the 'mutual unconsciousness' (§ 364) of transference/countertransference the therapist partakes of them as well. In this context Jung remarks further that the unconscious psychic 'infection' of the doctor bears as well 'the therapeutic possibility' (§ 363–365).

About this time in her therapy Kathleen read Erich Neumann's (1971) commentary on Apuleius' Roman fairytale of Amor and Psyche. With explicit reference to Neumann Kathleen determined at this juncture in her therapy that *her* issue was not a backwards-directed family incest but a forward-looking 'freeing of Eros'. This reorientation, puzzling at first but pregnant with meaning, proved to be a most helpful specification of the therapeutic task and the goal of treatment. According to Neumann, in order to free Eros, 'hitherto held captive in an incestuous relationship', the son-beloved of the Great Mother Aphrodite 'must become a human lover' (ibid.: 91). 'Eros must be freed from his status as a son–lover before he can enter into a free and independent relation with Psyche' (ibid.: 105). Only in this way can Psyche realise the fullness of her feminine identity. 'Here again the solution to the problem consists not in [heroic] struggle but in the creation of a fruitful contact between feminine and masculine' (ibid.: 102).

More and more Kathleen sought – as she said frequently in a later phase of therapy – not only, not even primarily, a full and satisfying adult sexuality but a mature feminine identity fully capable of relationship and adult love. As did Psyche in the Roman tale, so too Kathleen pursued a path from sadistic sexualisation (hate seeking a loving relationship) to sexual eroticism and mature capacity for erotic relationship and com-mitment. The ongoing drama enacted on the stage of the therapy relation-ship continued to be perplexing, often bewildering, at times agonising. Yet the transference/countertransference proved to be an alchemical vessel, in which the revived pathogenic relationship dynamic could be melted down, purified and transformed, and from which a new feminine identity could issue as from an interpersonal cauldron. So, too, 'with each of her labors she apprehend[ed] – without knowing it – a new category of his [Eros'] reality' (ibid.: 107).

'Erotic knowing': 'celibate countertransference'

In this final section I want to concentrate on a pecularity of the trans-ference/countertransference which I call 'chaste' or, preferably, 'celibate' countertransference. I ask the reader to lay aside the usual clichés about clerical celibacy and to focus on the relational developments in the therapy process. In the Prologue to his autobiographical *Memories, Dreams, Reflections* (1961: 3) Jung writes about a *'personal myth'* (in German: 'the myth of my life') and elsewhere (1921: § 9) about a 'psychological personal equation'. As a former Roman Catholic priest, celibacy and the vow of chastity are an integral part of my own history and personal myth, sig-nificantly a part whose deeper meaning I only came to appreciate experi-entially in my work as psychoanalyst. In the gestalt of psychotherapeutic abstinence this 'chasteness' commends itself as well to the personal equation of my professional identity. This circumstance now played a decisive role in the further progress of the erotic–sexual process with Kathleen.

I want to postulate an analogy between the ideal of priestly chasteness and the precept of therapeutic abstinence. The sexual abstinence of the psychotherapist is a purposive professional 'partial celibacy', which is most effective when the therapist as private person enjoys a loving, passionate and pleasurable sex life.[6] In this respect therapeutic abstinence is essentially different from the prescribed celibacy of the Roman Catholic clergy (cf.

Drewermann 1989). But for psychotherapists and clerics alike the return of the repressed (whether Eros, sexus, power, greed or overweening ambition) constitutes the gravest threat to the success of the work. 'Celibate' (Lat: 'unmarried') abstinence comprises renunciation of or refraining from living a sexual relationship (*a fortiori* from 'having sex') in the sense of gratifying instinctual sexual desire. Renunciation, however, is not the heart of the matter, but doing so *for the sake of a higher value*. Analogous to the ideal of the celibacy of the Catholic priest, the chasteness and abstinence of the psychotherapist serves the goal of psychic healing, personal transformation and the realisation of the self in his patient as in himself. In the 'bride chamber' (Jung 1946: § 503) of erotic–sexual transference and counter-transference the figure of the celibate priest transforms the occurrence beyond a merely 'secular' renunciation and places it in a sacral context. The deeper insight into the erotic relational nature of refraining from sexual acting out for the sake of a higher value occurs in therapy ideally against the backdrop of a gratifying sexual relationship and is a constitutive condition for an interactive and interpersonal working through of defensive sexualisation.

We are still within the bounds of the erotic–sexual 'playroom'. As ever-new dimensions of Kathleen's personal myth and pursuit of Eros came to light this playroom continually expanded. In the midst of a very turbulent late phase of her therapy Kathleen telephoned one day and cancelled her session on very short notice. Her father-in-law had died, her husband needed her support, and her friend–lover had informed her of a new relationship with a younger woman. She had not eaten for three days and under these circumstances did not feel safe driving a car. (Kathleen lived more than an hour's drive from my practice.) Besides, the past night she had *dreamed: 'I slept with you . . . It was only half an act, a kind of impotence.* [An attempted coitus, I asked; she confirmed.] *. . . I told you about (her lover); you were very unhappy with me and came towards me . . . You turned away from me and didn't want to have anything more to do with me.'* End of dream and of the brief telephone conversation. As had often happened at crucial junctures in therapy Kathleen's primal mistrust veered again into abandonment anxiety. For the first time she reported a transference dream with sexual content. That she told me the dream on the telephone testifies to her inner confusion, fear and ambivalence about the dream content. She fears, the dream suggests, that the therapeutic bond could also prove to be as 'impotent' as the real love affair, 'only half an act', a kind of therapeutic coitus interruptus. Will I now abandon her as her lover and her father-in-law have done? In the three days not eating there is a recurrence of the early loss of her mother. The early abandonment conflict revives in full force. In the dream she attempts (unsuccessfully) – one final time, as it turns out – to defend against her catastrophic anxiety by sexualising the relationship to me.

A week later Kathleen came as usual and opened the session with an extremely unusual request. She wished, she said, to have me recite '*the Our Father in Latin*' and to '*stroke or caress*' her! Leaving aside defensive aspects of this interaction I should like to stress a prospective-final aspect which emerges at this point. In retrospect I think Kathleen wished to have my therapeutic fatherhood grounded 'in heaven', so that she might ground all the more firmly in my earthly 'father-body' – concretely in the phantasy of being held and caressed without 'confusion of tongues' (Ferenczi [1933] 1972), which is to say, *without sexualisation*. By contrast to the latent incestuous sexualisation she had incurred in the 'vernacular' of her real father, she now sought a 'lingua sacra', a sacred idiom, in which to elaborate, cherish and esteem the deeper reality of her erotic–sexual womanhood without the contempt and violation she had suffered all her life. Finally, in the recitation of the 'Our Father' a transcendent Third is introduced into our relationship, making possible a deeper living triangulation such as Kathleen had never experienced with her parents.

Kathleen now defined *her* 'transference': she needed me, she said, 'not as father, nor as therapist, nor as man, but as *priest*, who prays for me and over me.' Kathleen knew that I am a former Roman Catholic priest. She herself had been raised 'agnostic', with no religious affiliation. With the 'Our Father' (in Latin) and the priest request Kathleen swore, as I heard it, herself and me to the sacral character and sacred space of *the therapeutic bond*. She had often exhibited a very sensitive spiritual aspect, that also wanted to be realised in her life. Now she appealed to the priest as mediator of a primal wholeness in the 'great round' of a heavenly, ultimately feminine-maternal being. In this context the priest is a total self-object, mirroring and idealised in one and holding out the prospect of attaining the wholeness of one's own self. We might say with Jung that at this focal point of therapeutic transformation a priest-*archetype* constellates. In the priest-archetype, Jung writes in a treatise on the transformation symbolism in the Mass, there occurs the manifestation of an order outside time in which transformation of substances (transsubstantiation) takes place as a true and real '*miracle*', 'the revelation of something existing in eternity' transpiring symbolically here and now in the ritual of the Mass ([1942] 1954: § 307; emphasis in the original).

Now, having arrived at the deepest point of her own abandonment and despair Kathleen hopes against hope for just such a 'miracle' of archetypal transmutation. In the light of 'Our Father' and the priest-transference her wish to be stroked and caressed embodies a profound need for a healing laying on of hands and priestly–fatherly blessing. Kathleen's need to be touched is both action language and action symbolism. It embodies her deep need for personal awareness and the realisation of understanding closeness and empathic acceptance against the terrifying threats of early abandonment. Thus she entrusts to me for safekeeping (German: *zu treuen*

Händen, lit. to loyal hands) her innermost 'true self' like a newborn child in the gestalt of an adult woman. At the same time the adult woman, too, needed to be seen and 'held', so that the split-off and maimed earliest self-representation might be integrated into the adult personality.

In the work with Kathleen sexual eroticism was a constant dimension of the therapeutic relationship, in which I too sought increasingly to be as open and transparent as possible. As time progressed and when it seemed therapeutically appropriate I began, cautiously at first, then ever more directly, to reflect upon and 'analyse out loud' my perceptions and cognitive associations and also the erotic–sexual feelings and impulses aroused in me. I had come to see them as aspects of therapeutic relationship which mirrored in my sexual feeling and erotic desire Kathleen's erotic self. In contrast to the ambivalence and the latent incestuous advances of her father, which had only produced enormous psychic confusion in her search for feminine identity, my clearly bounded openness seemed an effective antidote. Kathleen needed to hear concretely and honestly what I was feeling as therapist–father unobtrusively owning his own feelings and at appropriate moments expressing them sincerely and forthrightly. She often perceived quite accurately what I was feeling and increasingly did not hesitate to ask specifically. In this way she, too, initiated and fostered a dialogic form of relational analysis. Had I entrenched myself behind rigid rules of abstinence or other interpretative strategies it would have meant to Kathleen that I was no different than her father, pursuing a surreptitious agenda of my own contrary to her healing and growth interests.

In the course of this body-oriented analytical psychotherapy there were a great many spontaneous physical interactions bringing about physical contact, touching the patient and allowing myself to be touched by her, physically, emotionally, mentally, body-and-soul. With respect to the 'use of pleasure and desire', however, two parameters seem in retrospect to have been essential. One was the explicit refraining, in favour of dialogical verbal analysis of transference and countertransference, from any physical intervention which might be construed as even latently sexualising. Whenever I touch a patient I always make explicitly clear that the sole justification for doing so is to foster their healing process. How the patient responds to my touch, verbally *and* non-verbally, is of the utmost importance, and that too I make quite explicit. Secondly, with Kathleen I persistently took pains on occasions of bodily interventions and in general to realize a good enough and genuinely erotic (as opposed to eroticised) fatherly recognition, affection, appreciation and respect – also in a bodily way – for her awakening and her adult erotic–sexual feminine identity and relatedness. To illustrate: it became customary after a time working intimately together in some very deep regressive situations, to terminate sessions with a brief but heartfelt stand-up embrace. This everyday leave-taking gesture (in Germany) between two adults becomes in the therapy context a mutative interpretation without words. It reflects a therapeutic attitude and intervention that Andrew Samuels has called 'erotic playback' (1985; 1993: 149–164; cf. Ware 1996: 268–271). Playback is indeed a highly significant and potent therapeutic gesture of respect, esteem, affection and acknowledgement of the person, and I frequently and consciously 'use' it – normally it just happens spontaneously – to reaffirm and anchor in the adult person what has been elaborated and acquired in deep regressive work.

Conclusion

At the end of her extremely intensive analytical psychotherapy Kathleen herself summarised the process in which she had found her 'midpoint, master and *daimon* in passionate abandon'. In the approximately two and a half years of her therapy much remained unfinished. Yet Kathleen was successful in penetrating to the previously split off, early abandonment issues and affects in connection with the postnatal loss of her mother. This primordial trauma was the ground on which the later incestuous-sadistic abuse by her father took place, which constituted the second focus of this therapy. In the work with Kathleen it was possible to resolve early splitting mechanisms, to mitigate the sadomasochistic entanglements in object relationships and to integrate the cumulative traumatisation into a meaningful life-story – 'to bring meaning into what seemed meaningless' (Neumann 1971: 98). Out of traumatic suffering and chaotic inner and outer experience came a life pregnant with meaning. In particular, *erotic* growth impulses – sexual, psychic and mental, even religous-spiritual erotic impulses – were discovered and confirmed, and these shall surely give direction to the further course of Kathleen's life. So it came about at the conclusion of her therapy that she could summarise its achievement in three heartfelt, passionate words: '*I have loved!*'

The new edition and re-enactment of old drive and role conflicts with the therapist now cast in the role of father restores lost developmental passages and provides opportunities for new beginnings. That means, in effect, the therapist inevitably becomes 'part of the act' (the induced enactment) and participates temporarily in the patient's regressive state. Presumably the analyst cannot avoid enmeshing himself at least for a time in the transference enactments of his patient's pathological object relationships. Quite the contrary, it is his way of entering into the old systemic behavioural and feeling patterns, so that they can be 'analysed' (Greek: 'dissolved') as it were from within, and new relational patterns developed. In analytical process the crux of the matter is 'not only the interpretation of old experiential patterns but the generation of a new and prior to now never experienced form of relationship, in which a great deal of the reality of the analyst is involved' (Mertens 2000: 78). In this respect, my story of Kathleen has been a very personal love-story about the metamorphosis of hate pursuing a love-object in search of loving relationship.

Notes

1 Originally a paper presented in German at the 2nd Vienna Symposium on Psychoanalysis and the Body in October 2000 at the University of Vienna, Austria. The English translation by the author has been extensively revised and rewritten.
2 In contrast to Germany, where in the past decade considerable literature exists concerning psychoanalytic body-psychotherapy and the use of interactivity, movement, physical contact and touching in analytic therapies (e.g. Downing 1996; Heisterkamp 1999; 2001; Moser 2001), to my knowledge little at all has been written in English (cf. Ware 1996–97). There is, however, increasing psychoanalytic interest in 'enactment' (cf. Ehrenberg 1992; Ellman and Moskowitz 1998) and a body of related literature by Bioenergetic Analytic authors (Alexander Lowen *et al.*) on working with the body in psychotherapy.
3 Irvin Yalom (1996) elaborates this material in experiential fashion within a fictional therapy setting. Although not set in the context of a therapeutic relationship, André Brink's novel, *The Rights of Desire* (Brink 2000) develops with utmost sensitivity the selfsame conflicts of sexual desire and erotic concern of an older man (a positive paternal self-object) for a younger woman who flouts his desire through her own acting out. It is a most moving testimony to the development of what I shall later refer to as 'father's body' in an erotic (initially eroticised) 'countertransference' situation.
4 'When a therapist engages in sex with a patient, he or she is engaging in potentially homicidal activity' (Kenneth Pope, cited in Anonyma 1994: 1; cf. Ware 1995).
5 More precisely defined, 'a selfobject is neither self nor object, but the *subjective* aspect of a self-sustaining function performed by a relationship of self to objects who by their presence or activity evoke and maintain the self and the experience of selfhood' (Wolf 1988: 184).
6 Where this optimal condition is lacking, the therapist must be all the more firmly grounded in his own sexual identity and ethical conviction.

References

Anonyma (1994): Anonyma über Anonyma, *Psyche* 48: 1–29.
Bauriedl, T. (1998): Ohne Abstinenz stirbt die Psychoanalyse. Über die Unvereinbarkeit von Psychoanalyse und Körpertherapie, *Forum Psychoanal.* 14: 342–363.
Benjamin, J. (1988): *The Bonds of Love. Psychoanalysis, Feminism and the Problem of Domination*, Pantheon Books, New York.
Bollas, C. (1987): *The Shadow of the Object. Psychoanalysis of the Unthought Known*, Columbia Univ. Press, New York.
Brink, A. (2000): *The Rights of Desire*. A Novel, Secker & Warburg/Random House, London.
Deussen, P. (translator) (1897): *Sechzig Upanishad's des Veda*, Leipzig.

Doctor, R. (1999): Understanding the erotic and eroticised transference and countertransference. In: D. Mann (ed.) *Erotic Transference and Countertransference: clinical practice in psychotherapy*, Routledge, London, pp. 89–98.

Downing, G. (1996): *Körper und Wort in der Psychotherapie. Leitlinien für die Praxis*, Kösel, München.

Drewermann, E. (1989): *Kleriker. Psychogramm eines Ideals*, Walter, Olten & Freiburg.

Ehrenberg, D.B. (1992): *The Intimate Edge. Extending the Reach of Psychoanalytic Interaction*, Norton, New York/London.

Ellman, S.J. and Moskowitz, M. (eds) (1998): *Enactment: Toward a New Approach to the Therapeutic Relationship*. (Library of Clinical Psychoanalysis), Jason Aronson, Northvale, N.J./London.

Ferenczi, S. ([1933] 1972): *Sprachverwirrung zwischen den Erwachsenen und dem Kind* (1933). *Schriften zur Psychoanalyse II*. S. Fischer, Frankfurt am Main (1972), S.303–313.

Heisterkamp, G. (1999): *Heilsame Berührungen. Praxis leibfundierter analytischer Psychotherapie. 2 Auflage*, Pfeiffer, München.

Heisterkamp, G. (2001): Mittelbares und unmittelbares Verstehen im psychotherapeutischen Handlungsdialog. In: W. Milch and H.J. Wirth (eds) *Psychosomatik und Kleinkindforschung. Ein Fachbuch zu Ehren von Prof. Dr. Hans Müller-Braunschweig*, Psychosozial-Verlag, Gießen.

Hinshelwood, R.D. (1994): *Clinical Klein*, Free Association Books, London.

Hirsch, I. (1988): Mature Love in the Countertransference. In: J.F. Lasky and H.W. Silverman (eds) *Love: Psychoanalytical Perspectives*, New York Univ. Press, New York, pp. 200–212.

Hirsch, M. (1994): *Realer Inzest. Psychodynamik des sexuellen Mißbrauchs in der Familie. 3 Auflage. Überarbeitete und aktualisierte Auflage*, Berlin/Heidelberg/New York, Springer.

Jung, C.G. *Collected Works*, 20 Volumes, Routledge & Kegan Paul, London [Abbrev.: *CW*].

Jung, C.G. (1921): Psychological Types, *CW* 6.

Jung, C.G. ([1942] 1954): Transformation Symbolism in the Mass, in *CW* 11.

Jung, C.G. (1946): The Psychology of the Transference, in *CW* 16.

Jung, C.G. (1961): *Memories, Dreams, Reflections*, Vintage Books, New York.

Körner, J. (1989): Arbeit *an* der Übertragung? Arbeit *in* der Übertragung!, *Forum Psychoanal*. 5: 209–223.

Kumin, I. (1985): Erotic horror: desire and resistance in the psychoanalytic setting, *Intl. J. of Psychoanalytic Psychotherapy* 11: 3–20.

Mann, D. (1997): *Psychotherapy: An Erotic Relationship. Transference and Countertransference Passions*, Routledge, London/New York.

Mertens, W. (2000): The Psychoanalytic Quarterly, *Psyche* 54: 73–89.

Moser, T. (2001): *Berührung auf der Couch*, Suhrkamp, Frankfurt am Main.

Neumann, E. (1971): *Amor and Psyche. The Psychic Development of the Feminine. A Commentary on the Tale by Apuleius*, Bollinger Series LIV, Princeton Univ. Press, New York.

Pfannschmidt, H. (1998): Der 'Gebrauch der Lüste' in der Analysestunde. Oder: Warum es so schwer zu sein scheint, Psychoanalyse und Erotik unter einen Hut zu bekommen, *Forum Psychoanal*. 14: 364–383.

Samuels, A. (1985): Symbolic Dimensions of Eros in Transference-Countertransference: Some Clinical Uses of Jung's Alchemical Metaphor, *Intl. Rev. Psycho-Anal.* 12: 199–214.

Samuels, A. (1993): *The Political Psyche*, Routledge, London.

Schafer, R. (1992): *Retelling a Life: Narration and Dialogue in Psychoanalysis*, Basic Books, New York.

Streeck, U. (ed.) (2000): *Erinnern, Agieren und Inszenieren. Enactments und szenische Darstellungen im therapeutischen Prozess*, Vandenhoeck & Ruprecht: Göttingen.

Ware, R.C. (1995): Scylla und Charybdis. Sexual abuse or 'false memory syndrome'? Therapy-induced 'memories' of sexual abuse, *Journal of Analytical Psychology* 40: 5–22.

Ware, R.C. (1996): 'Vaterkörper' – Der Dritte in der Triangulierung am Beispiel männlicher Identitätsfindung, *Analytische Psychologie* 27: 258–277.

Ware, R.C. (1996/97): On Finding One's Male Identity in 'Father's Body', *Quadrant. Journal of the C.G. Jung Foundation for Analytical Psychology* 27(1), pp. 61–77.

Ware, R.C. (2000): Interaktive körpertherapeutische Gruppentherapie und Gegenübertragung, *Analytische Psychologie* 31: 1–25.

Wolf, E.S. (1988): *Treating the Self. Elements of Clinical Self Psychology*, Guilford Press, New York/London.

Worm, G. (2000): Liebe oder Missbrauch – zum Umgang mit erotischen Übertragungen. In: T. Ehrensperger (ed.), *Bioenergetik im Spannungsfeld der Geschlechter, Liebe, Erotik, Sexualität in der Körperpsychotherapie*, Schwabe, Basel, pp. 83–96.

Yalom, I. (1996): *Lying on the Couch*, HarperCollins, New York.

Part II

More about hate than love

Chapter 8

The importance of being able to be hated as a prerequisite for love

David Morgan

One view of psychoanalysis is that it should provide a way of deeply understanding psychic disturbance and that achieving this involves a setting that allows for the elucidation of unconscious fantasy as it arises in the here and now of the consulting room.

My emphasis in this chapter is on the important role of interpretation, as a direct response to the clinical phenomena of extreme hate and love and how it manifests itself in the consulting room. There are no short cuts to getting this sort of help, and all clinicians are tempted to avoid these extremes by manipulating the environment in some way so that the danger of real help is avoided. Analytical technique can be altered, indeed famous papers describing the necessity of shouting at patients have been written.

As Segal states:

> projecting aspects of oneself or one's internal objects into an analyst who doesn't identify with them nor react to them, but who can really think about them is a corrective experience. It helps the patient become aware of themselves and be able to distinguish phantasy from reality. Techniques which involve the analyst in becoming a good object for the patient are often not therapeutic as they collude with splitting processes which alienate the patient from himself. In addition, such techniques may make the patient feel that the analyst cannot tolerate being a bad hated object and this is an important consideration. Psychoanalysts can choose our profession at least partly out of wishes to repair damaged internal objects (which has to be distinguished from the determination to control them). It is important however that the analyst can tolerate the presence of an object that cannot be repaired, and allow himself to be perceived as bad and hated without sinking into despair or retaliating whether with hostility or too much therapeutic zeal. Manoeuvres to secure a positive transference clearly evade this struggle.
>
> (Segal 2000)

To assume that there has been any experience of real thinking prior to coming for help is an assumption on our part; whether there have been minds that have been attacked and their contents destroyed, or whether there has actually been a real absence, is in someway less important than the experience of an analyst in the here and now who is able to think about them. I have often had the image in some cases of lost souls who both fear and desire to break the spirit of all those who get close; this can be seen as a profound destructive attack on the object, an expression of the most primitive hatred, but also an exploration of whether the object has anything in their repertoire to deal with the unbearable experience being put into them, a representation of a part of the patient's experience of hopelessness in the face of extreme feelings.

I have been impressed in the long, once weekly, treatment of a now ex-drug addicted patient, of how certain she was of my depression, and my need for the sort of fix analysts need from their patients to get their highs. It seemed to help her a lot that instead of hating her for failing to provide me with this I was able to explore her fantasy of an object that required her to act as an anti-depressant. It can be seen by this that what is being explored at that moment is an object that can or cannot bear managing without drugs. The need to accept this projection so that its reality can be explored, in much the same way as maybe a child explored their original object. If I can accept this negative view of myself so that my reality can be explored then the possibility of an object that can think rather than identify or evacuate what has been projected may be established. It was clear that this patient had felt she had acted as an anti-depressant for her objects all her life, whether this was a true experience of her early life or a manic defence that involved using others to carry unwanted parts of herself whilst she blew her own mind, had to be explored with someone who could bear to be seen in such an unattractive manner.

In this way analysts have the opportunity to help traumatised patients by struggling to put into words the unspeakable and perhaps begin to symbolise the very concrete nature of some of their experiences, attempting to bring thought into worlds that can be dominated by psychic pain. These psychically indigestible experiences are the result of profound failures of containment that lead to destructive hateful attacks on life, both on the self and on others, a wish to kill off and deaden the very thing that threatens to make the pain knowable through evacuation into the other. The only alternative to these attacks can be a terrifying emptiness that often appears in dreams or hallucinations as a terror of falling forever, vertigo and feeling suspended over a void filled with what Bion described as nameless dread (1967a). This is a struggle to put into words the unspeakable, to try and symbolise often very concrete experiences. In particularly aggressive forms of pathological projective identification, as in the perversions and psychosis, this need to evacuate into the other is paramount.

They are means by which unbearable frightening feelings can be located in the minds and bodies of other people, or even into things. This activity is often compulsive because the action of expelling into objects is never accomplished. It is clearly a delusion to think that we can rid of parts of the self. I remember a famous case of a violent man being driven mad by a persistent auditory hallucination of beautiful music from radiators in the rooms that he found himself in. A poignant description of an attempt to rid oneself of all humanity, yet the music of this man's soul persecuted him with loving gentle music to melt the hardest heart.

This attack on their own minds and others', although in the main an evacuation rather than communication, is therefore still at least some form of communication looking for containment. Another gross example of this projective identification was from a violent man who was convinced that I had only got a job so that I could target patients because I myself had been abused and was seeking vengeance in this manner. It was extremely important for this patient to explore the realities of my wish to use my position to abuse him. Thus the psychotic part of him was equated with me. He became fascinated by what it was in my mind that didn't capitalise on the experience of being in a powerful position in relation to him. Thus he was beginning to study a mind, if not his own, that might not just be one that reacts abusively. This object, i.e. me, is at least hopefully more able to think than the gangster's radiator or the children this man targeted. These communications are so concrete to begin with because abstract and symbolic thinking has completely broken down. As Segal (1950) states in her paper on schizophrenia, the symbolic becomes the equivalent of the original object. Thus a psychotic patient I saw on one occasion responded to a pair of black shoes I hadn't worn before by saying, 'Hello daddy'; they had reminded her of her father. She immediately became very anxious that I was going to attack her – that I would retaliate by forcing the madness back into her. By asserting my own sanity it was I who was mad and therefore capable of depriving her of her sanity by forcing my experience of my reality, that I was not her father, back into her. It is not enough in these situations of intense pathological projective identification for the analyst to be passive, silent or inactive (I think this is true for all patients, not just psychotic or borderline cases), or expect the patient to be able to explore what they are putting into others with their own minds. In these complex situations the analyst has to be prepared to enter into an intense experience but also to retain their capacity to put experience into words.

I remember very clearly a young woman who had been abused when she was a child. Her life seemed to have been dominated ever since by getting involved with abusive men. It was essential for her to be allowed to explore the relationship to the original abuser, confused as it was, with her own aggressive feelings and the pain over her abuse in a relationship with someone that could contain them rather than enact without becoming the abuser or becoming abused; that is, someone who knew the difference between taking care of her and abusing her. The attraction to the abusive men was that they at least contained the confused projection of her own aggression in their sadism and through a constant re-enactment there was some hope that they would help her rather than repeat the abuse. It was after some time of exploring this very concrete experience of me as potentially someone who might abuse her that she dreamt that she found a cat belonging to me and cut it to pieces, leaving it for me to find on my return. The attack on the cat, her association, and the cat belonging to me was the beginning of her recognising some of her own aggressive feelings – feelings that she needed to know about and I needed to be able to bear if she was not going to remain a victim of a need to re-enact all her life. This detailed exploration of what is put into the analyst is an invitation to explore the realities of concrete projections in the analyst's mind or thoughts. It is an invitation to be known, and in this exploration lies, I believe, the beginnings of the potential for symbolic thinking to develop. It contains the knowledge that it is possible to evacuate into something that might have the cognitive capacity to think rather than act or obliterate.

Premature interpretations that confront the patient are dangerous. If we expel these proto-thoughts back into our patients too soon it can lead to enactment. This can be seen as an expression of hatred towards the patient and is the reason why so many difficult patients are passed from one hospital or clinician to another, eventually leading to enactments of a violent retaliation on the minds or bodies of others in a reversal of their experience of rejection. For example, a young nurse in a supervision group presented a potentially dangerous patient that she was seeing. The patient was from Nigeria and had been sent to this country to train as a solicitor so that she could send money to her family back home. Unfortunately, with so much expectation riding on her passing her finals, she failed and had apparently been rejected and abandoned by her African family and now felt trapped in this country. She developed the delusion that everyone she met was a member of her family (like a child in a children's home who described the staff as his parents on the first day). She would make a nuisance of herself by going up to everyone in the street and greeting them like long-lost relatives, thus putting her own loss, confusion and anxiety about her own predicament into everyone else. It was the other who was in a state of confusion and she, by greeting them, was enacting the reparation with the family she was denied. When she was hospitalised, she continued this behaviour on the ward. We explored this in the supervision group and helped the nurse at the time to think about the patient's over-familiarity as defence against her loneliness and abandonment at the hands of her family – an unsuccessful attempt to deal with her loss by making everyone into her lost relatives. Unfortunately, the nurse took this on board and immediately communicated this to the patient (the dangers of group supervision). The patient accepted this insight and seemed to be helped by this understanding of her use of projective identification. However, that same evening she broke into a flat adjoining the hospital of someone unknown to her. The owner woke up to find a woman standing over her in a menacing manner. Nothing else happened but it was clear that what this woman was communicating was her own experience of being suddenly made aware of something that she was not prepared for. This feeling was then transferred into the poor victim who was unprepared for the frightening experience of someone invading her home and privacy. I feel, therefore, that the most difficult aspect of this in treatment is containing an often very violent countertransference and a consequent wish to put it back into the patient unprocessed, or to circumvent aggressive feelings in some other way.

My most important experience of this was with Dr L. She was a patient with a long history of hospital admission. I began seeing her as an outpatient. Her main symptom was a desire to kill herself in response to a persistent hallucination of her mother who was telling her that she was evil. This began in her medical training when she was an SHO working on an obstetrics and gynaecology unit where, instead of helping with the births, she found herself performing abortions. It was this mortal sin (she was Catholic) that voices began to accuse her of, telling her that she was evil and should die. When I began seeing her she had been in and out of hospital for the previous six years. She had been treated with ECT, and this was her first experience of psychotherapy following admission to the unit. At this time I had been seeing her for two years and she had stabilised long enough to see me outside the hospital on a three times a week basis. However, she became pregnant and was assailed by destructive impulses towards the child inside her; the feelings were very strong, but another part of her resisted them. The experience of being with her in this struggle was unbearable for me – to feel responsible for an adult was one thing, but for a child as well was too difficult in an outpatient setting. This wish to kill herself, and consequently the baby inside her, was uppermost in her mind and was accompanied by a feeling that this would be what her mother would want. Thus in her mind a mother was wanting to punish her own child with death and get her to kill her own baby. At the time I was overwhelmed with the pain and fear that this situation engendered, and I didn't know what to say. I was just aware of an enormous pressure to collude with her view of herself as unbearable and a wish to get rid of her. There was a great deal of pressure to become a cruel punishing object that wanted to abort her therapy because of the unbearable anxiety she was creating in the session with me. As a result of the hospital back-up, and the feeling that she was helping me, I was able to understand this as an intense projection of herself into her baby in particular – the unwanted, sick, broken-down bits, the inhuman parts that she felt she didn't want to own – and I explored with her the feeling that she thought of herself as someone who was so unbearable to me that, rather than think about her, I would write her off as totally useless and ultimately killable. She felt helped by this thought, an expression of my possible murderousness to her, that she might be unbearable to me. In the next session she brought a dream, the first she had ever remembered in the therapy; she is a doctor on the ward and is looking for a murderer who is killing all the patients. The murders occur in a particular sort of way; by firing arrows up the patients' bottoms. The arrows are tipped with poison and take all the nourishment out of the food so that the patients gradually starve to death, but don't know why. I was aware that one interpretation of this dream could be her view of my interpretations as abusive penetrations that robbed her of precious nourishment. It was also possible that her inner contents might not be so precious and my interpretations not so cruel, being an attempt to help her rather than an effort to bugger her up. At this point the persecutory feelings abated and I felt I was in a more usual transference situation. The question became who was murdering who. She was able to tell me that she had been extremely anxious that I might have preferred it if I had never taken her on, and she was convinced I was waiting for a chance to get rid of her. Thus it was that it became possible to begin to explore with her her experience of me as someone who resented having to think about and look after her. The baby was born normally and she reported that she had been surprised at how human he looked. She felt she had been enabled to do this because she felt her baby was able to relate to her as a whole person not just as a bloody nipple. It was a feature over the next nine years with this patient as she moved out of the hospital, her last admission being five years ago, that in the nine years I saw her for three-times-weekly psychotherapy, that she was helped in the main by an invitation to explore my reality as someone who might be able to bear her. When she was allowed to do this it seemed to help and seemed to discover me afresh each time as someone who could think about her rather than use her to evacuate my own madness into her. I think this is why I am not really in agreement with the approach that involves addressing the parts of the patient's mind as if they are almost separate entities – that the analyst's voice is somehow distinguishable from the persecutory ones and is right or benign. I feel this is an assumption and does not invite an exploration of the analyst's reality. I feel in doing this we are in danger of forcing the projections back into the patient in a premature way. I feel at these moments one's own hold on life is being tested to the full, and it is questionable, at least to our patients, whether we are capable of taking in their communications or that they will be expelled. I would suggest that some patients' experiences are so painful that they have to get into our bones before they can be thought about. Unless these profoundly traumatic experiences can be taken up in the transference, an un-analysable psychotic transference occurs whereby there is a partial re-enactment of the traumatic events rather than any real modification. This involves the therapist in what I feel are close-to-the-bone experiences that compel us through our interpretative work to find words to encourage thinking rather than succumbing helplessly to the experience.

Searles (1963) states that a patient's hatred of reality may also express a very justified hatred of his first object relations, which can be characterised by a profound failure of containment. The person feels, rightly or wrongly, that there has been a profound failure to bear anxiety, and they are returned to the child in a concrete form. Like with Dr L, there is an understandable horror at the experience of performing an abortion, and this leaves her in a world persecuted by cruel voices clamouring for her death – that she should be aborted. It was not surprising therefore, for me to discover over the last few years with her, as she became more stable, that Dr L's own mother was the youngest survivor of seven children, barring the eldest, who had all died in childbirth. The eldest had then died in the war. I gradually realised that it had been possible, without any knowledge of this history despite volumes of psychiatric notes and files, through the transference gradually to experience this traumatised mother who, like me, felt unable to face the awful experience of the possibility of dead patients or dead babies, my inability to help this woman, a mother's inability to give life to her children, unequipped to deal with her own child's murderousness, which then erupted in my patient when she had to perform abortions as part of her training which she had naively thought would all be about birth. This then left her in a world accused of the original crime and probably her mother's own unbearable guilt at being a survivor. Dr L's conviction about her own culpability was an example of her attacks on a mother who, due to her own pain and guilt, was felt unable to detoxify them and returned them back into her baby in an extremely persecutory way. In enacting the abortion she was doing in fantasy presumably what her mother as the only survivor in her family had felt: you are a murderous bad person who kills off other children and you deserve to die for your attacks on life. It was only very gradually, through a process of discovering whether I actually corresponded to this projection – that is, that I hated her for what she had done and wished she would die because she made me so aware of my own inadequacies – that the beginning of some other form of object other than one who just wanted to evacuate into her began to develop.

As Bion has written about in *Attacks on Linking* (Bion 1967a), a patient like this in therapy resorts to pathological projective identification as if it was a mechanism of which she had never been able to avail herself of sufficiently. It is essential for the analyst, therefore, to be able to bear to hold onto these communications long enough for their reality to be explored. In this way it is, I feel, possible for symbolic thinking to begin to occur – as Bion has described, the move from beta to alpha thinking.

It is true that some environments are felt to be so saturated by so much action that no mind is felt to exist that is capable of thought at all, so they are incapable of thinking about the other as someone other than someone who will act upon them; indeed, this is how the analyst can at first appear. There is, as in all projective identification, even those aimed at total destruction of the other, some accompanying wish that these communications, however aggressive, be understood by a mind that is hopefully capable of receiving them. Even the children who murdered Jamie Bulger were communicating in an awful way their own experience; that is, the psychological or physical abuse and death of a child far away from anyone who can help.

But as in this case, the mode by which they are communicated often ensures that understanding is unlikely to be found. This is particularly powerful in perverse patients. The exhibitionist deals with his own confused sexuality by shocking and sexualising innocent victims in unprovoked assaults, causing them great distress and anxiety. The voyeur, through a process of reversal, deals with persecutory paranoid anxieties by secretly watching other people and triumphing over them. The paedophile tends to select and abuse neglected children who are felt to lack adequate internal or external parents to whom they might turn. The murderer, as Chris Bollas (1991) has said, deals with his own experience of having an annihilated self by only feeling alive when he is annihilating other selves; that is, putting his deadness into them. Clearly, the most effective container to use, if evacuating the unwanted parts into someone, is an object that is not in a position to return them – one that resembles the projected parts (that is, the most successful projections are into objects that correspond to them). I would like to devote the rest of the chapter to a discussion of a patient with perverse defences, who used projective identification to attack his objects hatefully and how this hatred was managed in his treatment, with particular emphasis on his discovery of someone who might manage this hatred and help think about it. It led, I feel, to a better awareness of the worth of his objects and a nascent capacity to love.

My main interest is to explore how these issues arise in the transference and how the accompanying fear of a descent into psychosis, and the disintegration that accompanies their treatment, can be managed with interpretative work that invites the patient to explore my reality so as to discover an object that might be able to think rather than aggressively act upon him. This is of importance because it is often difficult for patients to distinguish between interpretation and aggressive intrusion. They evacuate, so consequently they will be evacuated into. This therefore becomes a cycle of fear where the patient's own active forcing of something into people, to use, empty and dominate them, recurs as a fear of being subjected to the same treatment (Hinshelwood 1989) – a particularly cruel version of talion law (Brenman 1988), a kill or be killed world, where I have to get you or you will get me. It is my view that it is only through the use of analyst-centred interpretations (Steiner 1992) that this cruelty can be addressed. Ultimately it is the analyst's capacity to keep alive loving objects in their own experience that then allows them to engage at this level.

Mr D is 30 years old. He has now been in analysis with me for five years. He came into treatment because of feeling confused and depressed because his wife refused to continue to participate in his transvestite fantasies and was threatening him with separation. He gave the impression she was being unreasonable and was attacking him. Another aspect of his life that he felt was unsatisfactory was that he wanted to follow a career as a writer, but in fact did nothing apart from writing articles for women's magazines that were always rejected. He lived on nothing but a substantial trust fund left to him by his mother's father, and in a house that had been purchased for him. He also used this money to pay for his analysis.

He was aware of how depressed and lethargic he felt, as if all the energy was in everyone else. This is a factor in massive projective identification. As the analysis progressed, I gleaned that Mr D had felt that his early childhood had been a lonely one. He told me that his earliest memory of his childhood was a rubber sheet that he used to turn to as a baby and kept as a child. I feel now that this could be seen as his defensive retreat to a reliable object over which he could exert power and comfort himself.

Mr D is the eldest of three children. He has a brother and sister, two years and four years younger than him respectively. His father abandoned the family when the patient was three. Mr D never saw his father again until last year when, as a result of his analysis, he decided to find him and confront him.

At the beginning of treatment, his mother appeared to be a cold and distant woman. However, more recently, she appears as more caring, though she seems to have become very depressed and unavailable before and after the time the marriage broke up. Mr D appears to have become very involved with caring for his mother at this time, as well as feeling it was his responsibility to put away childish things and set an example to his siblings. He can still remember the feelings of responsibility that he felt on the one hand, and feelings of sitting in his room feeling numb and desperately trying to hold onto reality on the other hand.

He found the experience of the putting on and taking of his mother's clothes extremely gratifying, providing him with relief from his feelings of confusion. His mother remarried when he was fourteen, to a man he respects but who was experienced as a disciplinarian. He got a lot of encouragement from his step-father to study at school, and felt his energy penetrated his lethargy enough to help him get to university. However, he soon found the work dense and difficult and barely got his degree. He felt more and more lethargic and decided to try and do a postgraduate degree, but instead he would tend to attract younger students to him and became something of a guru in the students' union. He dropped out of this course eventually as he was beginning to get migraines and felt he was unable to think. He married one of the students he had met and she became very dependent on him. She had been sexually abused by her father when she was five. Within this relationship they regressed to an internal world inside his house, living on his trust fund. He inculcated her into his transvestite activities where he would dress himself up as a woman. He felt this gave him power over her, which he found comforting. In this we could see that he projects into her his own needy infantile self whilst he becomes the breast. His wife's subsequent refusal to participate in his cosy arrangement led him to feel enormously distressed. His fragile world was collapsing. He described feeling almost catatonic with depression, only raising himself from this torpor to eat or evacuate.

He began his analysis as a rather overweight young man with a large beard. The beard is often a feature of the transvestite men that I have seen and seems to offer, amongst other things, the reassurance of these patients not being totally immersed in their objects. He told me that he spent a great deal of time at home trying to write articles for women's magazines. A concrete form, perhaps, of getting parts of his mind into women. However, they were always rejected. He would take out his frustration about his rejected work by berating his wife, often violently, for being stupid and lazy. He was able to do this partly because she was still a student, as equally stuck as he was. She was kept by him financially and he would often threaten her with eviction. They had hardly had any sexual relationship since they married other than the transvestite activity. She seemed at first willing to play the voyeur to his exhibitionism and was presumably re-enacting her own abuse by her father.

This need to withdraw from the object and control has been alluded to in the writings of Henri Rey (1989) and Mervyn Glasser (1989) as 'the claustro-agoraphobic dilemma' and 'the core complex', respectively. There is a need to control the object so that the fear of being overwhelmed by closeness of abandonment is avoided. In this situation with Mr D and his wife we can see that he uses her to carry his own projected infantile self. She has to be kept in this position lest she threatens him with any awareness of his own needs, whilst he retains the power to look after her or abandon her. Thus his own experiences are reversed and projected into his wife who was always frightened that he would leave. As we can see, the damaged or absent maternal object is replaced almost entirely in fantasy by the subject so that he feels he is in control; other people, like his wife, are reduced to the role of accomplices. I am reminded, somewhat cruelly, of the television personality Edna Everidge and her side-kick Madge. Madge, the real woman, is an impoverished old bag and triumphed over and humiliated by the pretend one. I have been disturbed by how many accomplices of seriously trans-vestite men have had early hysterectomies and have speculated how much this is the result of destructive assaults on their real female qualities, the original container that cannot be imitated but can be destroyed.

Thus earlier experiences of deprivation can be reversed through putting them physically and psychologically into the body and mind of the other. The main aim of the projection here is to evacuate into the other in such a way as the communicative aspect of the projections are unlikely to be recognised. Clearly his wife's experience of abuse made her an available recipient of his unwanted parts. She seemed trapped for her own reasons in an abusive relationship that used her as a projection bucket akin to a toilet mother. In the analysis with me Mr D quickly brought these matters to the fore. The dominant theme of the first year was his increasing fear about this needy self becoming conscious within the analysis.

After the first six months he was enormously anxious about becoming addicted to his analysis, which he said was an arrangement that would rob him of all of his autonomy, and that the whole of analysis was in some way a technical seduction designed to seduce him into a relationship with me so that I would be able to use him entirely for my own ends without a thought for him. He was convinced as to the accuracy of his perceptions and totally unaware of the irony they contained – a mirror image of how he used his wife. I was able to interpret these anxieties by saying that what he feared was really a rather empty analyst whose own life was so devoid of any real substance that I derived my only comfort by creating seductive situations by which I gained control of my patients, who then provided me with feelings of power that my own impoverished life lacked. He was interested in these observations and curious at my willingness to be explored as such an unattractive figure. It seemed to help him feel less anxious and explore what realities these accusations might have. I was thus taking up his projective identification of an extremely frightening part of himself and encouraging him to think about it as a possible part of me (which of course it could easily be) so as to discover whether his fears were authentic or not. As I have said, I think this invitation to analyse the analyst (Steiner 1992) is an extremely important element in work with all patients, but in particular in the case of the perverse and psychotic patient who needs an object into whom to evacuate for long enough before an accurate perception of the object can be discerned, rather than defensively perverting the setting as a pre-emptive strike to ward off the threat of the analyst's undoubted cruelty and perverseness.

However, the great difficulty with the aggressive patient is, of course, their capacity to act out. This was particularly disturbing with Mr D around the breaks. As his growing unease at his awareness with me developed his annoyance and fury with his wife increased. After a Bank Holiday weekend break he told me that she was a bloodsucker and he felt enraged with her. It was as if she was a parasite and he had felt as if he wanted to kill to protect himself. He responded to this by comforting himself through masturbation. Thus, he simultaneously projected his own emerging dependency into his wife whilst he, in fantasy, becomes the mother. He would then feel ambivalent about returning to his analysis and wanting to stay in bed rather than attend sessions. I told him at these times how I was the abandoning father living alone with his wife/mother into whom he has projected all his own needs. Thus he can avoid needing me, not only by owning all the source of his own gratification but also by getting rid of all his neediness by putting it into his wife. He fears my return because the analysis will put him in touch with his own needy self and a vengeful me who feels robbed by a 'him' who has taken over all my qualities and put his wife in the position of the patient. I was also able to connect this ambivalence and fear to his mother's second husband who pushed him out of the nest.

As I encouraged him to think about these things, rather than enact them, he became very critical of what sort of analyst he had. This was accompanied by further attempts to take his feelings outside the analysis and dump them into his wife. However, he felt less able to believe in what he was doing to her and she seemed more able not to take it. This led to furious attacks on me and an absolute certainty about my perverse aims. 'Wasn't Freud a charlatan anyway?' He voraciously devoured negative reports in the papers that were prevalent at this time and became an authority on Masson, whose texts he quoted at me. He was also at these times fond of calling me 'a complete cunt'. I was eventually able to take this up as his anxiety about how unreal he feared me to be. I was a man dressed up in the clothing of psychoanalysis, a discredited theory used as a way to control him. He responded by attacking his wife again. She was infuriating and driving him mad with 'his' incessant demands. He was unaware of this slip and I said to him that although he located this needy baby self in his wife, he was also aware that these feelings really belonged to him and that he feared his need for me would drive me away (like his father), so as a result he took them and put them into his wife where he could control them. What I think was happening at this time was that in the breaks I was becoming the abandoning object, the father, or the earlier mother that left him for her depression; he then projects into the depressed mother or wife all his own needs through an omnipotent fantasy of possessing the breast. After these times I would say he was searching for a mind into which he could evacuate his own experience of abandonment and loss, but in a way that might make it understandable to him rather than becoming identified with it as his mother and wife were felt to have become, or rejecting him and walking out like his father.

I believe this was a factor in his wife staying with him, and it is interesting that she applied to go into therapy at this time. After the third year there was an important development: his need to project the unwanted aspects of himself into his wife, who was becoming stronger abated. It was accompanied by a terror that he was going to slip into a massive depression. He dreamt of falling, losing his grip, being lost at sea and a lighthouse in the distance, also of losing himself in the underground. These dreams seem to contain the original fears of disintegration, of the overwhelming mother and the distant unavailable father that might have been able to throw light on his predicament and save him. His fears of being engulfed by a void at this time felt palpable, and he and I were confronted by the potential that he might break down. I was mindful of the attacks that he might make on his wife. I feared she may become the recipient of his breaking-down self. This emerged as a powerful wish to impregnate her. He thought that this would provide relief from his own experience. This was at complete odds with his wife's wishes. I was able to tell him that this was his wish to get rid of his own childlike feelings in his analysis with me by putting them physically into his wife, impregnating her with his own split-off self, an enactment of the transvestite wish to occupy the mother.

The original capacity to evacuate this part of himself into the mother/wife was contained in the transference with me, rather than being enacted, leading to a possible real child.

At this time he had a dream that confirmed this feeling about his own baby-like feelings beginning to emerge and his wish to be rid of them. He is living in a flat on the set of Eldorado, the soap opera that flopped. He is with his wife. He thinks it is wonderful but is then terrified to see a child looking into the window of the flat, feeling terrified that the child will get in and take over. It does get inside and the flat is then totally taken over by lots of children, and he and his wife are overwhelmed. I said that his dependency with me was very frightening for him because of his anxiety that I might not be able to cope. A week later he reported a second dream. He is again in a flat in Eldorado with his wife but this time he is aware of how frightening it is. In fact, the whole set is on fire. He realises this is just a superficial film set, and just as it is about to collapse, he and his wife are rescued by the Prince of Wales. As soon as they are out of danger, the Prince (a reference to my Welshness or baldness) is taken up by two small children. I said that although Mr D felt rescued by me from the dangerous illusion that he lives in with his wife and mother, I quickly abandon him, like his father, for people I deem to be more interesting than him. He feels aware that he needs his father's help to leave the fantasy world that he has been living in with his mother but, like his father, I will just leave him for other children. This was around the time that he found out where his father lived and, amidst great pain and sadness, discovered him to be remarried with two other children. As a result of this meeting with his father and the gradual strengthening of his wife and me in his mind, the terror of his own neediness returned. He dreamt that his wife was a vampire. She bites him and he in turn becomes a vampire too. The source of evil he feels is now in them both. I feel this vampire is a perverse image of the bloodsucking baby. They are then in the jungle searching for the true source of evil to try and save themselves. They see a huge statue of Orson Welles made of stone, the outside shell crumbles and it comes alive. They are now aware that this is the source of all evil. In the dream he attacks it and cuts it to pieces.

I feel this dream illustrates the dilemma for this man. Like Dr L, he desperately needs an object into whom he can project the cannibalistic parts of himself but fears that they will then hunt him down and kill him. The possibility of his projections being anything other than an evacuation which will then be evacuated back to him has not come about. I said to him that he feels frightened when I leave him and he becomes confused by his relationship with his wife as he did with his mother when they both felt like very needy children. He is aware of how much they need a third person, like the 'Third Man' (hence Orson Welles) to help them. However, rather than feeling me to be a helpful person that can think about this with him I become full of the cruelty that he fears so much, so I can then be justifiably destroyed. I would speculate that this image confirms that as a child he, in fantasy, took care of his mother, simultaneously trying to alleviate his own neediness and anxiety by getting inside of her. He seems to have recreated this situation with his wife. It was at this time – three years into his analysis – that he decided to get a job. This change seemed to involve an awareness of another providing some structure that made his fears of being engulfed and taken over more bearable, in that I might be able to think about his needs rather than be overwhelmed or rejecting him.

The previous groundwork of whether I had perverse aims or not helped this exploration to the point where he could explore the realities of his projections in his analyst, rather than put them into an object which could not help him understand, like his wife or mother. However, Mr D continued to explain to me very carefully that the papers were full of accounts of those who purport to care for others but in fact abuse them. Something I acknowledged would be important for him to analyse in me, what were my motives? This was also clear in his reference to the 'Third Man', who was someone making money out of selling drugs for sick children on the black market. This question of whether the patient has an analyst who understands the difference between caring for him and abusing him is crucial.

Following a weekend break he had berated his wife again, but he also told me a dream. He is on a working holiday in the USA. He is in the desert and he is worried that he has not got enough money. It all becomes rather like a 'Mad Max' movie. Then his mother appears and, as if by magic, gives him a credit store card for Selfridges. He reflects on what a relief this is but is then shocked by the fact that there is a credit limit of fifty pounds. I said that he deals with the painful reality of losing his father and me by rewriting a mad story of himself and his mother living a state of perpetual bliss which he can use to avoid doing any real work at all. However, he is aware of what a desert this makes of his life and that it is limited. He responded later in the session by telling me that he had told his wife that he had made a will so that no one would get their hands on his trust fund if he died, including her. He had been surprised when she cried. I said to him that, rather than understand this problem in himself, he makes out that it is other people who are interested in free-loading on him. He uses his belief that he is taking care of others as a way of avoiding getting on with his own life, recreating his time with his mother when, for a brief time, she might have been dependent on him. His wife then has to tolerate having his dependency needs being pushed into her whilst he has none at all. I believe this is further evidence of Mr D being able to become aware of what he does rather than act it out.

The dream as a bridge in this, between acting out and thinking, is extremely important. I believe that as a result of him now being able to hear my communications about his material he is becoming much more aware of his own destructiveness. In a recent Friday session he presented material that was clearly about the painful separation on the weekend. He dreamt that he was going away with me but that I give him a false address. He runs down to the station to see me leaving with my wife and he realises it is him that is being left behind. I said that it was painful for him when, like the false father, I leave him. He feels that if things could be different I would take him with me. I felt that there was a much healthier awareness of the importance of his analysis and the beginning of the awareness of an Oedipal couple. On Monday he reported a terrifying nightmare. It was about death: 'My mother is in the dream; she is dying of cancer. I have a child and I am trying to take care of it. My fear is that he is dying too. I take some of my mother's medicine and give it to the child.' I told him that during the break he was so furious with me for leaving him that he kills off his analysis. He then discovers that not only is his analysis dying but so is the life that he has started here with me. The following weeks were dominated by his fears of dying, and his feelings of dependency on both me and his wife intensified, as did his fear that we would drop him when he is most vulnerable. At this time there was little evidence of his cross-dressing. Perhaps it could have just gone deeper and be more secret, like the rubber sheet, just becoming more compliant and dressing himself up in my theories. I have to say that I don't think so. His fear of disintegrating, as his need for me developed, was palpable in the sessions. I feel that his wife was freed up to go and have analysis herself. She was no longer only a projection bucket into whom he could bury his split-off self. He also allowed himself to continue at work. As he was pretty low down the ladder it meant that he had to experience real dependency in a rather lowly job.

In a final dream I think he gives me a real demonstration of psychotic anxieties of the fears and of his awareness of his dependency on me. Over the weekend he dreams he is sitting on top of a monument but it changes suddenly to a terrifying black industrial chimney that slowly collapses. Someone passes him a rope and he manages to climb out. I said that on the weekend he climbs on top of his analysis but becomes frightened of being stuck inside something that is dead and is collapsing about him – the dead body of the triumphed-over mother. He is then relieved by the return of his analysis on Monday because it and I are still alive.

There could, of course, be many ways of interpreting this material but I believe at this point he is probably more aware of what he does to his objects: the taking over of their good qualities and evacuation of what is felt to be bad in him into them. I think there was a real relief and a hope that someone could save him from this. I think this came about due to the analysis helping Mr D feel that I am able to bear the hatred he projects into me long enough for these elements to be explored and contained effectively. His need to evacuate into an object that is less able to understand him has shifted to one who hopefully is better able to understand his communications and put them back to him in a digestible form. I feel an important part of this work is the capacity of the analyst to bear the projections that are evacuated long enough so that the patient can discover through experience whether the analyst corresponds to them or not. They can then be interpreted to the patient, who through the use of other forms of communication such as dreams, can begin to symbolise rather than act them out. The inevitable attack and destruction of the other can then be avoided and something more creative hopefully allowed to develop.

The patients I have described were looking in different ways for someone who could help them cope. However, any help is attacked so that any object reality is destroyed. They then have no access to an object who has capability; this obviates envy because it's their reality that triumphs, although leaving them in an impoverished world.

Although they come for help, the overriding wish to begin with is to convert the analyst or therapist to support them in their delusions to collude with their projections into their objects. The investigation as to the accuracy of their perceptions is extremely important. All patients saw life as two extremes: complete coping and omnipotence on the one hand, and a disintegrating void on the other. A mother that can partially cope, mourn, bear some reasonable anxiety and build a relationship with them is absent or not accessible to the patient. Thus I have hopefully demonstrated it is the analysis of who the analyst is that is vitally important. Patients seem helped enormously by a willingness of the analyst to be experienced as the recipient of their projections. This counteracts the early failure of containment that prevented proper introjection to take place and, consequently, they live in a world of projective identification. It is only through this process that any genuine appreciation and love of the object is able to develop.

Further reading

Melanie Klein Today (1988) Vol. 1: *Mainly Theory*.
Melanie Klein Today (1988) Vol. 2: *Mainly Practice*.
New Library of Psychoanalysis 8 (ed. E. Bott Spillius), London: Routledge.

References

Bion, W. (1967a) *Attacks on Linking*, London: Karnac Books.
Bion, W. (1967b) Notes on Memory and Desire, *Melanie Klein Today*, vol. 2, pp. 266–275.
Bollas, C. (1991) *Cracking Up*, London: Karnac Books.
Brenman, E. (1988) Creativity and narrow mindedness, in E. Spillius (Ed.), *Melanie Klein Today*, Vols 1 & 2, London: Routledge.
Glasser, M. (1989) Some aspects of the role of aggression in the perversions, in I. Rosen (Ed.), *Sexual Deviation*, Oxford: Oxford Medical Publications, pp. 278–305.
Hinshelwood, R.D. (1989) *Dictionary of Kleinian Thought*, London: Free Association Books.
Rey, H. (1989) *Universals of Psychoanalysis*, London: Karnac Books.
Searles, H. (1963) Patients Who Drive their Therapists Crazy, in *Collected Papers on Schizophrenia*, London: Hogarth Press/Institute of Psychoanalysis.
Segal, H. (1950) Some aspects of the analysis of a schizophrenic, *International Journal of Psychoanalysis*, 31: 268–278. Also in *Melanie Klein Today*, Vol. 2 (above).
Segal, H. (2000) Interview on British Psychoanalytical Society Website.
Steiner, J. (1992) *Psychic Retreats*, London: Routledge.

Chapter 9

Misanthropy and the broken mirror of narcissism

Hatred in the narcissistic personality

David Mann

> It fills me with depression – reduces me to utter despair to see men living as they do. I meet with nothing but base flattery, injustice, selfishness, treachery, villainy everywhere. I can bear it no longer. It infuriates me. I mean to fling my gauntlet in the face of the whole human race! . . . I hate all mankind, some because they are wicked and perverse, others because they tolerate wickedness – because they don't show the unrelenting detestation that virtue owes to vice.
>
> Moliére, *The Misanthrope*, Act One

The occasional state of temporarily hating everybody or permanently hating a section of the population is so common we could probably consider both to be within the 'ordinary' range of human feelings. Indeed, recent research (Hess 2000) suggests that the average person usually has at least three others he or she hates at any one time. We might say that our love, if not for humanity as a whole, extends at least to some sections of the population or individuals and that this keeps any global hatred in perspective: we recognise exceptions and distinctions; there is a recognition of difference between those we love and hate. We could say that, in this ordinary way, love offsets hatred. Misanthropy is a psychological state distinct from this in which mankind in general is permanently hated. Derived from the Greek, *misos* for hatred and *anthropos* for man, misanthropy is a pathological position whereby all people are hated: love is conspicuous by its absence.

To the best of my knowledge, misanthropy has not attracted much previous attention in the psychoanalytic literature. In this chapter I will begin by first describing some of the general features of misanthropy and its relationship to narcissism. This will be followed by some clinical examples, which lead to further elaboration in the discussion section.

I am going to make a case to describe the misanthropic mind. In misanthropy the hatred of mankind extends to the self; there are no exceptions so the misanthrope can only hate himself as well. However, a distinction is usually to be made between self and other. The misanthrope considers he or she has an insight into the human condition, knows the truth that others are blind to, and, therefore, is placed in a position different from the rest of humanity. In that respect he or she is special. This is the essence of the narcissistic component of misanthropy. My title is an attempt to grasp this feature of total hatred. If Narcissus is held spellbound by his own reflection which maintains the state of total self-love, the misanthrope, too, is no less spellbound by his image, but in his case the mirror is cracked or broken and what is reflected is fractured, distorted and disfigured. What is mesmerising is not beauty but a mutilation. For Narcissus, all the world is ugly and hated compared to his own beautiful reflection; for the misanthrope ugliness is all there is except for his knowledge of the truth.

To the misanthrope, humanity is hated for its ordinariness. Kernberg (1974) draws attention to how the narcissistic personality experiences others as dishonest, unreliable, empty and valueless. Such criticisms are the stock vocabulary of the misanthrope's tirade against humanity. In particular, as I will discuss in the clinical section, the most common terms for humanity are scatological: the world is 'crap', people are 'just full of shit', and so on. The whole of the human race is despised for its collective animal behaviour and functions. The very ordinariness of humanity is experienced as gross acts of violence against the narcissistic self. Small acts of lack of consideration are exaggerated and given inflated levels of importance in the psyche. Human achievements in art, science, law, culture or civilisation are either ignored or denigrated as false disguises to the true brutality underneath. All virtues are considered insincere, concealing the iniquities inside.   .

At the heart of this hatred are instinctual, animal and bodily characteristics. All behaviours and psychologies associated with aggression, sex, eating, defecation, disease, ageing and other bodily functions are hated and resented. The phrase 'I hate your guts!' succinctly highlights the body-based nature of this hatred. The misanthropic ideal would be a disembodied mind, free from the body and bodily desire and necessity. Misanthropes are inclined to experience others as 'crap' or 'shit', or the world as a sewer – thereby identifying humanity as nothing more than a defecatory function or product. Humanity is not seen as a beast with a brain but just as a beast. Curiously, the beastly nature of the animal kingdom is denied. Offset with the hatred of humanity is an idealisation of nature, a non-human world free from the polluting and corrupting influence of people. The animal nature of animals is acceptable precisely because it is not filtered through the prism of human desires. Essentially what is hated is all human desire and need for others. It follows that the ultimate ideal is of a peopleless world where the misanthrope can live in harmony by himself or herself, alone with nature. Love, if it exists anywhere, resides only in the non-human environment. But 'love' is the wrong term here: strictly speaking it is more a question of non-hate, nature is not loved but idealised because of the absence of hateful human pollution. Nature is idealised more because it is free from sin rather than as a haven of goodness. It is more defined by what it is not rather than what it is: a definition by absence rather than presence. In fact, nature plays only a minor role in the misanthropic psyche as his or her preoccupations are with the attachment to hate.

This narcissistic fantasy is also the source of the deepest narcissistic wounds: the misanthrope hates people and wishes to do away with them, yet at the same time is forced into confronting the limits of his or her own destructive desire: humanity can be destroyed only in fantasy. The misanthrope stands powerless, like King Lear cursing into an indifferent storm, a storm which pays no attention to his or her hate. Kernberg describes the deepest layer of the narcissistic relationship with external objects as the source of the misanthrope's pathological defences:

> It is the image of a hungry, enraged, empty self, full of impotent anger at being frustrated, and fearful of a world which seems as hateful and revengeful as the patient himself.
>
> (Kernberg 1974: 219)

Despite the misanthrope's destructive desires, humanity continues to survive. Winnicott (1971) has described how the infant needs to be able to destroy the parent in fantasy while at the same time needing the parent to survive the annihilatory hate: this will help the infant get a sense of the limits of his or her destructive fantasy and also confirms that whatever the wish the object (parent) can still survive. With the misanthrope, a different process operates: the survival of the object does not put the fantasy into a realistic perspective. On the contrary, the rage is intensified through frustration and impotence; the object's survival is experienced as a narcissistic wound which is further fuel to the hatred.

Generally, the narcissistic dilemma is that the person wishes to be free from the need for others; ideally, the narcissist would like to be entirely self-sufficient. The problem from the point of view of the narcissistic fantasy is that such an individual is highly dependent on others. This need for others, especially the need to be at the centre of the other's desire, is what grieves narcissistic personalities, faced as they continually are with the obvious and mortifying proof that they are not the most important person in the world.

This process of dependence and hatred of the dependence on others is found in misanthropic thinking and perpetuates the misanthrope's loathing of mankind. He or she sees him or herself as different from all the rest, in fantasy wishing the population to die, yet is confronted with the failure of the wish which is both mortifying and wounding. Both Kohut (1966) and Ledermann (1987) emphasise the narcissist's inability to love others. I consider this is partly an attempt to define narcissism by what is lacking rather than by what is present. Narcissistic personalities are not really indifferent to others, even if they protest they care about nobody. In fact, that is part of the narcissistic problem: they can never be free of an attachment of sorts to others. However, in the absence of love, the nature of this attachment is hateful. We can define narcissism as an absence of love for objects, but it is probably more accurate to say that it is rather a surfeit of hate that overwhelms and floods all the relationships. The narcissistic attachment to others is usually manifested through the passionate ties of hatefulness. In a manner of speaking, the popular lay assumption that narcissism is about excessive self-love is misleading. The narcissistic personality type no more loves him or herself than anybody else. Narcissism is more accurately described as a pathological disorder of hate. This goes some way to explaining why a previously idealised object can so suddenly flip over and be denigrated. The denigration, inspired by hate, is always present underneath the idealisation.

The misanthrope is a particularly extreme form of the narcissistic hateful attachment to the object. Hate binds the misanthrope to humanity in general and everybody in particular, including the self that is despised for its impotence and bodily functions shared with everybody else. The narcissist's body unites him or her with everybody else and therefore denies his or her separateness and unique specialness. Nor can the misanthrope seek sanctuary as a hermit. They remain persecuted not only by the knowledge that humanity exists all around them but also because they are persecuted from within, the hatred turning against the self for all that it holds in common with everybody else and for the failure to reap the benefits of their annihilatory fantasies. There is no love anywhere – neither inside for the self nor for others outside. The hatred is maintained by being caught in a self-perpetuating circuit of hating humanity for its animal ordinariness (that is to say, the presence of human desire), seeing the self as different and special because the misanthrope 'knows' the truth but yet the misanthrope's body and the need for recognition as special can only lead to self-hate because their body unites them and their specialness is not recognised by others. This narcissistic wound fuels the hate so the cycle continues: humanity is hated afresh with renewed vigour, only resulting in renewed narcissistic wounds.

Hatred is readily discernible in all narcissistic personalities. However, it is unclear to me at this stage whether such a domination by hate is an essential feature of all narcissistic personalities. While awaiting evidence to the contrary I would assume all misanthropes are narcissistic personalities but not all narcissistic personalities are necessarily misanthropes.

We can think of extreme narcissistic hate as a defence against unbearable loss, abandonment or disconnection from others. Though striving for separateness and disconnection, the narcissist's grandiosity results in a proliferation of connections to others where, in fact, none ordinarily exist.

Hatred thus unites and binds the narcissist to every available object no matter how inconsequential it is in reality. This is a passionate connection which defends against separateness. The absence of connection is experienced as unbearable discontinuity of being. There is no capacity to be alone in Winnicott's (1958) terms. Separateness would equal annihilation, a fall into an abyss, an emptiness, a wilderness, a solitary confinement of infinite magnitude. Hatred, by expanding connections, maintains a relationship to the entire human race.

Developmentally the world that is hated is that of the mother. Possibly because the mother was too frustrating or unavailable or projectively identifying her own unconscious hatred into the baby, the infant is left bitterly disillusioned in the goodness of life. Instead there is a retreat into an anal universe (Chasseguet-Smirgel 1984; Mann 1997a: 162–79) where all differences are intolerable. Hatred is thus both an attempt to control the mother and compel her into satisfying the infant, and also allows the infant to avoid the painful feelings of disconnection and abandonment. Ultimately such hatred is a defence against narcissistic wounding.

If we consider narcissism as a disorder of inordinate and excessive hate, or as the domination of hate in the psyche, we can examine the myth of Narcissus afresh. Narcissus was exceptionally beautiful but heartlessly rejected his lovers. It must have been lust rather than love his lovers felt as there was nothing about his personality that was appealing, 'for he had a stubborn pride in his own beauty' (Graves 1955: 286): clearly a handsome but odious brat! His relations to others are hateful and sadistic: Echo is scorned, and his most insistent lover, Ameinias, is given a sword by Narcissus to kill himself with. Ameinias commits suicide with the sword but invokes the gods to avenge his death. The god Artemis hears the plea and exacts vengeance by causing Narcissus to fall in love with himself. When Narcissus kills himself it is with hateful despair and grief that he cannot keep his reflected image. Hate is thus more prominent than love throughout the myth. The myth might also shed some light on the origins of pathological narcissism. I have refrained from entering the debate about whether narcissism is a primary or secondary phenomenon resulting from parental failure. Such abstract discussions will always be inconclusive despite eloquent theories. The myth seems to suggest a mixture of constitutional factors, primary narcissism, since Narcissus is born exceptionally beautiful (suggesting constitutional factors and therefore primary processes), but also parental intervention: trouble befalls Narcissus once the god Artemis (parent figure) intervenes (suggesting secondary processes). This suggests to me that narcissistic personality disorders are a mixture of constitutional factors that may or may not become problematic, depending on parental intervention. With less than good enough parenting the infant's narcissistic disposition may suffer the severe wounds that lead to the difficulties of the narcissistic personality.

In ordinary circumstances hatred is not totally self-consuming. Indeed hate may have many developmental advantages. Gabbard (1993) sees hate as helping to maintain a separate sense of self experienced from the disappointments in the other. The ambivalence in Oedipal renunciation means all subsequent relationships must have a degree of hatred. Therefore hate is developmentally inevitable as the child's demands will clash with those of the parents. Ordinarily, objects of our hate remain split off or isolated from other areas of our life so it does not corrupt all our relationships. Of course, a hated object can become so all-consuming that it does disturb the everyday flow of life. While this may sometimes lead to a hatred of the world, more often it leads to a sense of the hated object having so much omnipotent power and influence that even the good things become overwhelmed. Strictly speaking this is not misanthropy because the hated object becomes omniscient and, though pervasive, is seen as polluting. This requires that there are other objects that were not polluted in the first place. In other words, the whole world may be turned bad but was not seen as all bad to start with. There were good things, love for want of a better word, that have not been able to tolerate the power of the bad and the hated; hatred defeats love because it is stronger, not because there is no love in opposition to hate. The misanthrope's problem is that there is nothing in opposition to hate which can attempt to modify or balance its fantastical power.

Freud initially saw hate as an expression of aggression, a different ego function to love. He considered that, for the infant, the external world and what is hated are one and the same, only as the object becomes a source of pleasure does it become loved. He observed: 'The ego hates, abhors and pursues with intent to destroy all objects which are a source of unpleasurable feeling for it . . . not until the genital organisation does love become the opposite of hate' (1915: 138). After the introduction of the structural theory Freud associated hate with the death instinct.

Both Ferenczi (1926) and Suttie (1935) take the view that the infant is essentially born good and that hate is introduced via negative experience from the principal carers. Balint (1952) saw hate arising from a mixture of infantile object love: hating the unloving object and defending against object need through hate

Other writers have seen positive aspects to hate. For example, Kernberg (1993) has seen hate as a core affect 'which contributes to the formation of the aggressive drive'. Elsewhere Kernberg (1995) describes how hate requires sufficient ego development to allow differentiation between self and object representations. Unlike Freud, he recognised lesser degrees of hate that do not necessarily wish to destroy the object – for example, a wish to humiliate or make the object suffer.

Blum (1997) points out that the turning away from the purely destructive aims of hate requires the capacity for self and object love. Therefore it requires ego capacity to differentiate self from other. Aggression can then be tamed and neutralised, and this is less likely to result in severe and persistent hate. Hate is developmentally normal and can be used as a motivating force. A 'healthy hate' is normal to hate our enemies or those that torment others. He also notes that hate is readily elicited by narcissistic injury and easily intensified through identification with hated or hating objects. It would be of interest to explore whether hate is always an aspect of narcissism or whether hate exists independently of narcissistic issues. Freud's (1918, 1921) comment on hate arising from the 'narcissism of minor differences' (I would merely say there is plenty of hate arising from large differences, too) seems to suggest that hate is generally associated with some narcissistic wound.

Hatred, then, has a place, alongside love, as part of the ordinary experiences of passion. Generally, hate serves positive narcissistic functions contributing to the individual's capacity to make distinctions between what is good and bad for the self and those we love. It is also worth reminding ourselves that, as Kohut (1966) demonstrates, narcissism is not necessarily pathological but contains positive functions in normal psychological development. Normal narcissism gives us a healthy enjoyment of our own activities and successes and has an adaptive value regarding dealing with disappointment and anger at our own shortcomings and failures. Kohut suggests that healthy narcissism is an essential ingredient in all creative activity. The narcissistic personality seems to get none of the benefits from normal hate or normal narcissism. The problem for the misanthrope is that hate becomes attached to the narcissistic component of the personality and, through grandiosity, takes on a greater significance. In the absence of any capacity to love or the ability to be indifferent, the hate has no restrictions or boundaries and thus becomes the sole source of relationship to self and others. The misanthrope does not experience relationships as creative. Despite what they might externally achieve, which is usually a superficial appearance of goodness or love, their underlying unconscious relationship is one of hateful destructiveness.

It is quite clear from the description so far that the narcissistic personality obtains none of the positive advantages and benefits in psychological functioning associated with healthy narcissosm hate. Rather, their hate is too consuming and too inclusive. It disables their functioning so all relationships become hateful – not only with those with the external world but also internally. They can feel special, different from the rest, even superior to all humanity, but their sense of uniqueness is not about possessing or giving something life enhancing to others; rather, their grandiose uniqueness keeps them isolated from others: the hate results from the terrible disappointments, and the rage this induces makes contact with others or themselves so painful.

What I have been trying to describe in the misanthrope's mind is the pathological pervasiveness of hate that dominates the total psyche in the absence of, and without the mitigating influence of, love. This pathological hate is in a different relationship to the psyche than that we would usually encounter with ordinary hate. By this I mean that ordinary hate has its place in the psyche alongside other affects and passions: one feeling, albeit a particularly powerful one, among many. The ordinary mind contains a plurality of competing passions of differing, but usually unequal, strengths. For the misanthrope, there is no plurality, rather a totalitarian dictatorship of hate. In this narcissistic pathological hate there is nothing else.

In a world of total hate how can something good, like love, exist? This is the crux of the therapeutic problem posed when the misanthrope seeks psychotherapy.

Clinical material

The two patients I will describe are both men, Jonathan and Clive. I saw them both at the same institution. Though they started at different times, for several years their therapy was concurrent. The work with both men finished simultaneously when I left the organisation.

Jonathan came seeking psychotherapy for his long-standing depression. He had a history of alcohol and stimulant abuse, though when I began seeing him he had used neither for four years. He had given up alcohol after waking one morning and not recognising the woman in bed next to him; he was deeply shocked when he eventually realised she was the woman he had been living with for ten years. During the period of his intoxicated lifestyle he led a violent life. At one point he was considered for inclusion in an armed robbery, but, upon reflection, the violent gang he was associated with dropped him as he was too unstable and unpredictable. His own description of that part of his life was: 'I was an animal in the 1980s, a thug.' Though he was no longer violent he could still be verbally abusive, his favourite phrase being: 'Why don't you eat shit and die?!' A projection of himself as full of shit. He was a aware that a lot of people were frightened of him.

He made his misanthropy clear from our first session where he defined one of his therapeutic goals as, 'It would help if I could just hate people without them knowing it. My hate of people drips off me: they know it in seconds.' This was followed by instant hate about anything I might have to offer. My initial enquiries about his childhood and relationship with his parents brought the retort: 'Don't give me any of that fucking Freudian crap', which I took to mean he wasn't interested in my thoughts. He did say, though, 'I was breast fed on vitriol' but offered no further comment.

Slowly, over the next few months, he did give a picture of his childhood. He thought his past was 'full of shit' but there would be nothing left if he got rid of it; he was now 'just full of crap with my head stuck up my arse'. Father was an alcoholic whose drinking frequently left the family in poverty. He was described as extremely violent to everyone, 'It was blood on the walls kind of violence.' Jonathan also saw another side: his father was a skilled craftsman but his low self-esteem left him too embarrassed by his occupation to want to involve him or pass on his craft. Though his relationship with his dad was bad, he felt he had some understanding and compassion for where his father was coming from. Not so for his mother. She was described in the most vile terms, she would get him and his brother to compete against each other for money. 'Great mothering skills, fucking ragbag shit cunt!' He thought she was attractive on the outside but a 'dirty, smelly bitch otherwise'. He added, 'I can understand why my dad wanted to fuck her, but why did he want to breed with her?!' He thought his mother turned him against all women who he saw as a 'foul, stinking mess but good to fuck now and then'. This was not straightforward misogyny, though, in a way his hate for his mother was projected out by turning the whole world into her. His father was also hated, but perhaps less so than his mother.

His hatred for his parents spilled out onto the rest of the world. He expected people to undermine him; sometimes he felt everybody was better than him or else they were all shit; he hated the world because he hated himself so much. His mother had said she thought he considered himself better than everybody else; he replied he was. He said he would not feel lonely if a nuclear bomb wiped out the human race. He thought people were crap, though when I queried this he conceded there were decent people about. He felt he was like a satanic king, a Midas, except that everything he touched 'turned to shit not gold'. 'I'd make a fucking good dictator', he said after a particularly bad week. He tried to live life mostly as a hermit but because his hatred was for himself and his internalised parents solitary confinement brought limited relief as he remained persecuted by his internal world of objects.

A good deal of his therapy was filled with his disgust at himself and others. He commented that, unlike most people, I did not seem frightened of him. Indeed I was not; in fact, I knew I quite liked him. He was never overtly aggressive with me nor threatening. However much he hated the world he was clearly trying to preserve something better with me. His hatred of therapy would be expressed in other ways: he frequently missed sessions when he felt too bad to leave his house. He was very repetitious in his material, which was often presented in a joky, self-deprecating manner and he frequently said how little he trusted me. At this time I considered my attitude to him to be essentially positive, but I was aware I was becoming to feel increasingly bored in the sessions. I would become alert only when notable new material was mentioned or his colourful use of swearing delivered a memorable phrase. His sessions were filled with long periods of tedium punctuated with bits of material that would suddenly excite my interest. I did not realise the extent of my countertransference until after a summer break when I reviewed the previous year's work by looking over my clinical notes. I noticed that my entries were getting shorter; they often began with the sentence 'Same sort of stuff', followed by a brief elaboration, but one entry described the whole session in a single word, 'Usual'. I was reducing all his sessions to sameness in the same way he treated the human race: dehumanised, devoid of individuality and treated as a faecal mess with no nutritional value. I suddenly recalled his early therapeutic goal of wishing to hate people without them knowing it. In effect, I had been hating him without knowing it, though perhaps he had detected it. I was hating his thoughts because, as he told me in the first session, he hated my Freudian thoughts. His misanthropy was contagious. My boredom had been an expression of my hate for him. I was shocked at this revelation, though I then came to realise that perhaps the situation was not quite so bad. I knew I still had warm and positive feelings for him but, whereas before I assumed that that was all, now I was aware of just how ambivalent I had become with the emergence of more negative hateful feelings. Another possible meaning of this material was that I became his good object. The emptiness and boredom resulting from the evacuation of shit to some other place, leaving a vacancy wanting to be filled by something more replenishing.

Having come to some understanding and acceptance of my own hate left the small matter of trying to do something useful and less destructive with it. I confronted him more about his hateful attacks on the therapy, but whereas I had underestimated my hate I had overestimated his. He said that, apart from occasionally thinking I was 'a smug bastard', which was quite a compliment by his usual standards, he trusted me more than most people as he knew I was trying not to harm him. That genuinely confused his stereotype of people. Over the next few months he had more confusing experiences. He was given a lift by a genuinely nice family who had a disabled child, they had no reason except natural generosity and kindness to do him a favour. He had felt so overwhelmed in their car that he had to get out early. On another occasion he reported spending 10 minutes with his parents that were unexpectedly pleasant and rancour-free. He became more real and trusting in therapy and eventually began to tell me of his sexual abuse as a child from his older brother and sister and later from a paedophile. I had suspected something of the kind but he had rebuffed my initial enquiries during his assessment with 'I wouldn't tell you if I had.' More importantly, his long-standing relationships were becoming less fraught, particularly with his parents, and also with his former partner and child and her new husband. Some positive memories from his childhood, especially his relationship with his grandmother, seemed to suggest that there had been some early goodness that had later been lost in the layers of hate.

As his global hatred of humanity became fractured what emerged in its place was a more confusional state. He still hated the vast majority of the population but a more advanced ambivalence with significant others could be experienced and to some extent tolerated. From his depression emerged guilt at his previous brutal behaviour, especially towards the son of an ex-girl friend and regarding the fact that he had later forced her to abort their child.

What can we say happened in this therapy? Can we say that from the hate emerged a form of love? Love seems like a fairly strong word to use but perhaps no other would do. Jonathan's attachment to others had been filled entirely with hate. Hate was awful, explosive and corrosive but gave him a passionate attachment to others. It was only with hate that he could have any relationships at all. Similarly, in the countertransference, I found I could only reach him by my hate. He would not allow any other feeling to touch him, especially my fondness for him – only hate could form a link or attachment if I was expecting to reach him. But, and this is the point, it was only by really hating him that I could find any way to love him. Bollas (1985) describes a 'loving hate' which we can understand as an attempt to adapt relationships characterised by abuse or neglect. I would like to suggest we can also think about *hating-love*: hating that is really about loving. In hating-love we wish the best for the other precisely because we hate them and want, in effect, to help them be more lovable, perhaps for the selfish reason of wanting them to be lovable so we do not have to feel so bad about them. It seems to me that Jonathan and I established a deep and genuinely passionate relationship. First this was by hate then, once that connection had been made, we could explore other feelings. The therapy had a mutative effect (Strachey 1934; Carpy 1989) on both the analytic participants (Mann 1997a). Mutual insight and understanding were gained when we could reflect upon what we actually felt about each other.

This therapy ended when I left the institution I was working in. I think from the point of view of Jonathan's development that was a premature end. I was confident that, had our work continued, his progress would have been greater. At the end he felt more contained, his relationships were less toxic, less hate-based and more informed with insight and empathy towards others.

By way of a contrast, I would like to give an example of a more destructive encounter with hate in the misanthropic narcissistic personality. Clive was in his forties. He was referred for psychotherapy because of his 'persistent negative attitude' as others described it. When I first got to know him he was a successful manager in a small company; he had a 'comfortable life' with his long-standing partner, had a nice house and, on the exterior, things seemed to be going well. He declared his only vice was an addiction to affairs with the young women with whom his job brought him into contact. He 'had a way' of making young women fall in love with him. He knew this was cheating but felt that, because he was discreet, his partner never knew about it so it barely qualified as a blemish on his character. 'In my way I am nearly perfect!' he declared. He considered he presented a perfectly appropriate front to the rest of the world: everybody who knew him would say he was witty, generous, friendly, helpful and, generally, a nice guy.

Underneath the façade he despised everybody and held the young girls that loved him in contempt. 'I decided when I was young that I didn't like people – and I've stuck with this.' He did not let anybody know what he really thought because he wanted to be liked, approved of and loved. He would never let anybody know what he really thought, which was always entirely bad. He hated humanity for their ignorant stupidity, violence and insincerity. Like Jonathan, his most common descriptions of others were faecal: people were crap and shit, and any number of turns of phrase including these words. People were valueless and led pointless lives. He hated everything about the biological side of people, whether it was their need for sex or the toilet: 'I would like a world where we are just preserved brains', he said, adding: 'I'm not a member of the human race; I'm beyond that.' He hated the people who were taken in by his affable front; this was a further instance of their stupidity. Nobody really had a problem except him. His problem was having to live with the rest of humanity and pretending to be nice. People were not nice but full of ill intent, looking to do bad; everybody was a potential murderer, rapist, criminal or incompetent. The only exception to this was himself. He would like to destroy the human race, even though he continued in his polite ways with everybody. He was beyond the mindless violence of 'the rest of you' as he frequently referred to me and humanity. Unlike the rest of us, he was in possession of the truth, he had the real knowledge about the human condition, about what people were really like: 'I am aware.' This made him special. He wished to be the most wanted person on earth and when he died he would expect the world to stop. He felt so special that his only reason on earth was to be tortured and victimised by the 'mindless bovine herd'. Everybody was out to get him. He could happily see all the human race die: 'The world would be better if I was a dictator. Those who didn't like it would have to step off the world.' His was a world of no exceptions, no distinctions. He once entered a book shop but came out empty handed: he couldn't tell the difference between the books, they must all be the same.

He reported poor relationships with his parents, both of whom he despised. He had a number of early traumas. An elder brother had tried to kill him while he was in his cot and he still carried the physical scars from the encounter; when a toddler the same brother called him across a road leading to him being knocked down. He thought that it had been intentional. He had, therefore, very early experiences of the world as a place out to get him, that people could be bad. Whatever he felt about his brother, he hated his parents more for not protecting him to prevent these disasters. The experience of the parents' lack of care was compounded upon going to school when he found himself for several years in the Special Education class. He said with real, bitter feeling, 'Couldn't my parents tell I wasn't subnormal.' Despite being a high achiever in his working life he was always shadowed by the thought that, at heart, he must be stupid. He had been an anxious child, wet his bed until quite late and sucked his thumb until nine. He thought he was a lot like his dad, especially his negative views: 'I'm just a clone really, just a younger version of him.' He saw himself as somebody who was completely unable to change.

Though he had been referred for psychotherapy because of 'depression and negative thinking' he considered this to be a battle of wills: either I would try to convert him into seeing people as essentially good and wonderful or he would bring me to the truth so I would agree with his view of the world. One of us would become the other's Frankenstein monster. Much of his energy was devoted to thinking about how much I really cared or did not care. His perception of me helter-skeltered back and forth from idealisation to denigration. He thought I could be godlike, unflappable and inscrutable, beyond human need and above people like him. This was a fragile idealisation, since he hoped I was not the kind of man who kept pornography in his briefcase. At other times I was denigrated: just the representative of the herd, uncaring, indifferent to him. In the transference I was often experienced as attacking and malicious like his brother. On other occasions, he thought I was useless and ineffectual like his parents. Sometimes he thought of us as fused together in a narcissistic merger. He visited Paris and walked the route of the Nazi victory parade. He imagined us doing this together, side by side, he as Hitler, me as Hess, 'planning the death of 98 per cent of the world'. It was clear that, in Clive's holocaust vision, few of the master race would be perfect enough to escape the ovens. I queried the 2 per cent that might live. He said it would be just two people, he and I. I said that it was easier for him to imagine us doing something hateful and destructive rather than anything positive or constructive in the therapy.

His misanthropic outlook certainly found a hook inside me as I quickly realised I shared his views about the divisiveness of religion and the futility of war. However, he convinced himself that I was an evangelical believer. On my office wall was a print by Salvador Dali: a surreal image of a mother and baby. I liked it because of the image and the artist. It was though, in fairness, a picture of the Madonna and child. In fact, Clive often found partial truths about me from tiny clues he detected. His observations or deductions were often accurate but his interpretation of their meanings were off the mark. He believed I thought more like him than I cared to admit. He assumed we were very alike, but he could be very wrong: he thought that, like him, I would detest football: it would never have occurred to him that what was actually in my briefcase was not pornography but the Arsenal Football Club Magazine!

The first two years of his therapy I called the mocking phase. Sessions would be filled with his tirades against everybody in general as well as any particular slight he had suffered during the week. Everything would go wrong because he was singled out for misery. For example, he never usually needed to catch trains. On the one day he did it broke down. The train would be fine until he travelled on it. This would be taken as further proof of the conspiracy of the world to grind him down. However, people would not grind him down because he 'knew' what it was all about. These were not paranoid delusions in the psychotic sense. Rather, they were his narcissistic delusions of grandeur that made him the most special person on the earth, albeit with a uniqueness for persecution instead of talent. He always tried to focus the sessions on the obscenity of humanity outside the room. His tone and manner discussing these was a deeply mocking condescension towards all and sundry, especially me. Sometimes he was quite funny, but the humour was not just black but bitter: it elevated nobody and impaled us both on heartless, lonely anguish. He would round on any interpretation about what was happening between us: he could scoff at the fact he was scoffing at me. Sometimes he was so extreme I found I wanted to laugh but could not because the session was really more tragic than comic. But it was so extreme it was a fine line of difference between the two. I was sceptical about whether the therapy was having any sort of impact, but Clive was always punctual, never missed a session and we both seemed to find the sessions were an interesting joust even if they led nowhere.

This first phase of therapy came to an end when Clive's job required him to work in another city during the week. He was therefore unable to attend our sessions for six months. When he returned, his life had taken a dramatic turn for the worse: he was to be made redundant from his job; he had discovered that his partner was having an affair; and the young woman he had been having an affair with, and whom he felt he loved, had decided to end it with him. These collective catastrophes brought a massive deterioration in his mental state. Each was a deep narcissistic wound, but together they catapulted him into a self-destructive depression that stoked the misanthropic fires to the heights of concentration camp chimneys. This second phase of his therapy was almost devoid of the mocking triumph of our former sessions. Instead, I was aware that for both of us the sessions would be overshadowed by feelings of gloom. He became what I have heard GPs call 'a heart-sink patient': your heart sinks as they enter the room. In my case, it was more an uneasy turning in my guts. At times, I felt I kept a good analytic attitude. I at least had an idea of what was happening even if all my attempts to make the situation more therapeutic amounted to little. I still had the desire to keep talking, exploring and interpreting: as long as the analytic process was afloat there was hope of something positive replacing the hate. At other times, I became very pessimistic about the therapy and what we were doing. He would proclaim the therapy to be useless, and in my most gloomy periods I inwardly agreed. He was entirely pessimistic and I found my optimism could slowly seep away. For him the therapy became just another instance of persecution and torture. I was like all the others. From his point of view I was trying to harm him by getting him to lower his barriers, feel pain and hurt.

He was the only patient to whom I fully expressed my anger. On one occasion he began by slowly unwrapping then reading a newspaper with the view of illustrating this week's iniquities of humanity. I lost my temper, called him a 'thug' for his mindless assaults and destruction on the thera-peutic effort. To this day, I do not know if I was acting out or justifiably making a stand for the therapeutic process. He was certainly shocked and could no longer maintain an idealised image of me as someone beyond ordinary passions, a brain behind glass without a visceral body. This made me fully aware of my hate.

There were discernible changes in the second phase of therapy that clearly demonstrated that the therapeutic process was being internalised. Previously, he had only truly felt safe away from people in his own home: at home, he could be encapsulated from the world. Now, during my holiday breaks, he reported even this was infiltrated. His pipes had burst; he felt his human persecutors were entering his sanctuary. I understood this to indicate that my literal absence left him bereft of any goodness to fend off the hate within his internal world. Now there was nowhere safe. Therapy was being used to contain his hate but could not push back its borders or transform it into anything else. A dream seems to summarise the situation. *He is in a Disney scene, singing and getting applause. Then he is in a warm viscous substance like custard. The waves are rough. He tells them to calm and they do. He then turns into an angel. He flies to the highest mountain to get to Heaven. Heaven's gates are IKEA catalogues. He then fell from the mountain back into the viscous custard. Now there are jagged edges and shapes that hurt him. He feels abandoned and engulfed. He then awoke with these feelings.* This dream was full of his narcissistic grandiosity: 'calming the waves', turning into an angel, elevation to Heaven. But he felt crushed by the ordinariness (IKEA catalogues) and falls back into the same viscous substance that had turned from warm and benign to painful and malignant.

When I announced that I was leaving the institution and the therapy would end he triumphantly saw this as a justification that he had been right to keep his walls up in therapy and not trust me, and that I was unreliable and had let him down 'just like all the rest'. He proclaimed that he had won and beaten me, but my departure was experienced as another narcissistic wound: his psychological state deteriorated and he felt he was having a breakdown. With the prospect of losing me he felt his grasp on any goodness he might have loosening: he would have nothing to keep the hate at bay.

Then, in the final session, he re-established his mental grip and used a grandiose narcissistic fantasy to suture the narcissistic wound. He announced he must be the greatest psychotherapy failure of all time. He thought I had tried to be god-like but he was more powerful. The world had matched the greatest psychotherapist with the greatest patient – and I had lost. He added that I should write up his case and the whole psychotherapy profession would be puzzled by him as the 'greatest enigma'. It seems to me he was dealing with the trauma of my departure by incorporating me into his grandiose fantasy and in so doing was able to keep a link with me and both suture the wound and dismiss the loss. He really could not bear to let either of us or our work together to be simply ordinary.

At various times Clive left me questioning if the therapy was worthless or ineffective. I also wonder if, in even having such a thought, this was me standing back trying to evaluate the good and the bad or if his narcissism was contagious? Was his hate so corrosive that it contaminated my ability to think clearly? Did I end up acting out or reproducing enactments from his brother's brutality and parental lack of awareness? In other words, did I just end up adopting his universal hate that dominated the complete picture of the therapy? This leads me to a narcissistic thought of my own: was the therapeutic failure (if that was what it was) essentially my fault? If I had handled the countertransference better, as I did with Jonathan, would the therapy have been better? His wish to be my most difficult patient resonated with my narcissism: because he made me feel so useless, thus narcissistically wounding me. As such I did consider him my most difficult patient. Such a thought, whether right or wrong, places me in a narcissistic omnipotent position. The literature about narcissistic personalities indicates that such countertransference questioning is common when working with this patient population. The nature of hate is infectious so will draw the therapist in. Regardless of my actual therapeutic achievements or limitations, the hate makes it difficult to value the work and may contribute to the observation that narcissistic personalities are not suitable for psychotherapy.

I think the difference between the two therapies was partly about countertransference use and partly about the particular pathologies of the two patients. Though Clive had been able to function successfully for many years in a way that Jonathan could not, I think he was nevertheless more severely psychically damaged. If I had not worked through something in the countertransference hate Jonathan would not have progressed, but he was constitutionally able to utilise the advantage of my adaptation. I am more doubtful about whether Clive could have used me whatever I might have done in the countertransference.

Discussion

It is the erotic that makes connections between people. As Freud puts it: 'Eros, which holds together everything in the world' (1921: 90). Eros forms links, creates bonds. Hate has more in common with Eros than Thanatos, it is part of the connecting principle rather than an aspect of disconnection and inertia. In that sense, hate can be thought of as libidinised aggression. We may say narcissism in general and pathological hate in misanthropy in particular can be conceived of as a self-preservative, though defensive, part of the life instinct, Eros. Though hate and destructiveness share much in common this should not automatically lead us to assume the operation of a death instinct, despite any manifest similarities. As I understand Thanatos, the death instinct, it is a drive towards disconnection, severance and complete and utter separation; in essence, a drive to achieve an inert, non-relational state, free from emotional attachments: the subject is effectively dead and therefore has no relationship to the object. Hatred may include a wish for death (to murder self or other) but in itself it is a form of connection. Hatred binds us to the object: it is Eros with poisoned arrows. That is to say, as a passion it brings us into a relationship with the other (whether internal or external). Though hatred can be destructive and desires severance both the means and the end are relational. Via the conduit of emotional attachment it establishes a connection between the self and the hated object. We might describe hate as a perverse Eros. Stoller (1975) makes us aware that perversion is the erotic form of hatred; we might say hatred is the destructive (or perverse) form of love. A statement like this needs instant clarification: all I mean to imply here is that love and hate are united by their capacity to form links. Desires, whether loving or hateful, bind us in relationships. Desires, whether cold or hot, are neither inert nor dead: they have a vitality. To have no desire is to break the connections that bind, to be severed from the relational: to be dead. To be dead is to have no desire, no connection. It is distinct from the wish to kill or be killed, both of which are highly object related.

Why connect to object with hate rather than with love? There is a simplistic equation that would link love with pleasure and hate with unpleasure. Clearly this takes no account of psychical complexity. Because of the potential loss or rejection love can contain extreme unpleasure. Likewise hate can lead to pleasurable aggression on a continuum from 'having the last word' through to perverse sadism. In a good enough world (with the origins in relation to the erotic pre-Oedipal and erotic Oedipal (Mann 1997a and b) parents) love perhaps ought to be the dominant emotion in ambivalence. However, many individuals, because of a mixture of constitutional and relational factors, have a less than good enough environment. I think it is under these conditions we see the psyche come under the domination of hate in ambivalence. Misanthropy in the narcissistic personality is an extreme form of this domination by hate where ambivalence is not tolerated and love is crushed. Love is obliterated precisely to avoid vulnerability to the object of desire.

Hate, like love or the erotic (Mann 1989, 1994, 1997a, 1999, 2001), draws the patient and therapist into a passionate connection. With such a passionate connection we know they are inside us and we are inside them, thus the emotional distance of indifference is hardly in existence. But hate, as distinct from love and the erotic, has a peculiar fixity: as Blum (1997) notes, love can often turn into hate but rarely do we see hate turn into love. If I can paraphrase William Congreve's famous quote from 'The Mourning Bride': 'Heaven has no rage like love to hatred turned', we might also say Hell hardly needs to worry about hate to loving turned. This is the problem posed by hate disorders, including the narcissistic personality, for when the personality is saturated by a dominion of hate it poses great therapeutic difficulties. How can therapy enable something good to exist in a psychological universe where hateful destructiveness prevails? Gabbard (1996) describes various technical approaches to 'malignant transference hate'. Though he does not use the classification, the patients he describes exhibit profound narcissistic personalities. His description that these patients bring a 'malignant transference' to the therapy epitomises the therapeutic problem with these patients. Blum advocates a calm distance from hate. I consider this a commendable but a somewhat unrealistic idea: the nature of hate is that it forms a connection regardless of the distance. There is a great danger in the therapist trying to keep too great a distance that would leave unconscious hate in the countertransference difficult to register.

It is primarily through loving relationships both as a child and adult that most people find opportunities for psychological growth. Yet love also implies helplessness. Freud (1930: 82) writes: 'We are never so defenceless against suffering as when we love; never so hopelessly unhappy as when we have lost our loved object or its love.' Hatred goes some way to maintaining the relationship to the loved object but seeks to control or punish it for the loss of love. Hate thereby keeps a connection, but more at a distance minimising helplessness. The narcissistic personality and the extreme form of misanthropy I have described establish their relationships via the conduit of hate. In that respect, they are not yet ready to receive the therapist's love. The only connection that will initially establish a genuine relationship is with the therapist's hate. I think this might be the patient group that Winnicott (1947) refers to when he states that some patients actively seek our hate. Hate is a difficult feeling for therapists and goes against not only our attempts at neutrality but also our inner convictions that, both as professionals and as individuals, we are trying to do our best for the patient. Winnicott's concept of 'objective hate' has been seriously challenged (Etchegoyen 1991; Blum 1997) so I would doubt that many therapists, including Winnicott himself, can really hate anybody objectively. By its nature hate is a subjective experience. What is perhaps a bit more feasible is the therapist's willingness to come to terms with the extent of their hate and to be prepared to hate the patient with a view to doing as little harm as possible and hopefully even some good. In so doing, it would be hoped that this kind of hating is new for the patient and gradually has a mutative effect on the misanthrope's internal world. I think of this as a hating-love. The therapist is not restraining his or her hate, which might be the only way the patient can establish a relationship, rather what is restrained is the therapist's desire to act destructively with the hate. Hartmann *et al.* (1949) and Anna Freud (1972) have also indicated that destructiveness in hate may only be tamed by self and object love. Being less destructive, the therapist might then be in a better position to begin doing something more constructive and, more creative, perhaps finding some love, something lovable in the patient, maybe even about his or her own hatefulness.

A hating-love might not be so bad. With this in mind I think of two instances of hating-love. The first is the fictional account of Goethe's *Faust* where Mephistopheles does good:

'Say at last – who art thou?'
 'That Power I serve
Which wills forever evil
Yet does forever good.'

The other example is the Truth and Reconciliation Tribunal in South Africa after apartheid where the hatred of racial division was processed by trying to understand rather than just blame. It would seem from this discussion that the patient needs to know that the therapist can hate as well as love them. In some instances, the therapist's capacity to contain the hate in a loving way allows hatred to be modified and mollified; hatred can be transformed into something less than totally destructive.

Both Jonathan and Clive felt that their lives amounted to little because they had not had children. In the case of Jonathan, there was a daughter with a former partner but he suspected her fidelity and, therefore, he thought there were doubts about his paternal role. It seemed to me that whatever the truth about his ex-partner, Jonathan was not able to think of himself as a father because of psychological factors that did not allow him to imagine himself as creative or procreative. Undoubtedly this was also linked to his primal scene phantasies. Both the examples I have given are men because the issues I wanted to address were so clear with them. I can also think of two women patients with narcissistic personalities who were misanthropes. Both had children but neither felt themselves to be worth while, and both felt their relationship to their children was not good. To consider oneself creative has little to do with actually conceiving children but is more concerned with feeling the self is capable of a 'supremely creative act' (Money-Kyrle 1968), which is very unlikely in a psyche filled with hate. See also Mann (1997a: 138–61) where I give an extended discussion about creativity and the primal scene. That is the misanthrope's dilemma. They cannot get out of the hating universe without the aid of another, a dependency which, in itself, is wounding and hateful. Yet, with the therapist's hating-love there is an opportunity if not for love then at least a different, less toxic, kind of hate.

I read Moliére's comic masterpiece *The Misanthrope* to gain more insight into this condition, particularly in my work with Clive. The play, written in 1666, seemed to be about my patient. Indeed, I found the similarities between the attitude of Alceste (the misanthrope) and what Clive said to be so striking that some of the latter's lines could have been almost verbatim quotes from Moliére. For example, those concerning narcissistic grandiosity, hatred, the misanthrope's lack of personal responsibility, the self-destructive willingness to suffer defeat in order to maintain a moral superiority, the wish for a hermitage, the pollutive effect of any failing destroying all virtue, human insincerity, and so on. The factor of comedy was also shared: the extremity of the views of Alceste, Clive and Jonathan often blurred the boundary between comedy and tragedy.

I am not familiar with Moliére's complete *oeuvre* but *The Misanthrope* seems different from a number of his other plays in that the last act is left in open-ended suspense. The drama of the play does not resolve in the usual manner of an artistic creation. There is no theatrical resolution rounding off the story and tidying up the loose ends. Alceste wants to retreat into a rustic solitude away from the human race. His love, Célimène, refuses such a life of isolation. They argue, split up and leave the stage separately, the misanthrope determined to find his remote sanctuary. The last lines are spoken by their friends who wonder if they can do anything to persuade him to give up his foolish plan. The audience is left to wondering whether Alceste and his love Célimène will ever reunite. I find this ambiguous, uncertainty is like an echo or reflection of the therapeutic work with narcissistic personalities in which a positive therapeutic outcome is so uncertain. An effective outcome relies on the misanthrope's ability to experience something other than hate, and this also requires the therapist to be able to experience the patient's as well as his or her own hate in a more creative, less destructive manner. This presents the narcissistic patient with a potential for working through issues, although it remains uncertain as to whether he or she will be able to utilise the opportunity. Perhaps, in the tradition of Moliére, it is appropriate to conclude these thoughts about misanthropy on such a note of uncertainty.

References

Balint, M. (1952) On love and hate, *International Journal of Psycho-Analysis*, 33: 355–62.

Blum, H. P. (1997) Clinical and developmental dimensions of hate, *Journal of the American Psychoanalytic Association*, 45: 359–75.

Bollas, C. (1985) Loving hate, *Annual of Psychoanalysis*, 12/13: 221–37.

Carpy, D. V. (1989) Tolerating the countertransference: a mutative process, *International Journal of Psycho-Analysis*, 70: 287–94.

Chasseguet-Smirgel, J. (1984) *Creativity and Perversion*, London: Free Association Books, 1985.

Etchegoyen, R. H. (1991) *The Fundamentals of Psychoanalytic Technique*, London: Karnac.

Ferenczi, S. (1926) *Final Contributions to the Problem and Methods of Psychoanalysis*, New York: Brunner/Mazel.

Freud, A. (1972) Comments on aggression, *International Journal of Psycho-Analysis*, 53: 163–71.

Freud, S. (1915) Instincts and their vicissitudes, in *Standard Edition* 14: 117–40.

—— (1918) The taboo of virginity. Contribution to the psychology of love, in *Standard Edition* 11: 191–208.

—— (1921) Group psychology and the analysis of the ego, in *Standard Edition* 18: 65–143.

—— (1930) Civilisation and its discontents, in *Standard Edition* 21: 57–145.

Gabbard, G. O. (1993) On hate in love relationships: the narcissism of minor differences revisited, *Psychoanalytic Quarterly*, 62: 229–38.

—— (1996) *Love and Hate in the Analytic Setting*, Northvale, N.J.: Jason Aronson.

Goethe, J. W. (1986) *Faust*, Harmondsworth: Penguin Classics.

Graves, R. (1955) *The Greek Myths*, Harmondsworth: Penguin Books, 1986.

Hartmann, H., Kris, E. and Loewenstein, R. (1949) Notes on the theory of aggression, *Psychoanalytic Study of the Child*, 3/4: 9–36.

Hess, J. (2000) quoted in 'I hate your guts – in a subtle way', *The Guardian*, 10 May, p. 4.

Kernberg, O. (1974) Factors in the psychoanalytic treatment of narcissistic personalities, in A. Morrison (1986) *Essential Papers on Narcissism*, New York and London: New York University Press.

—— (1993) The psychopathology of hatred, in R. Glick and S. Roose (eds) *Rage, Power and Aggression*, New Haven, Conn.,: Yale University Press.

—— (1995) Hatred as a core affect of aggression, in S. Akhtar and S. Kramer (eds) *The Birth of Hatred*, Northvale, N.J.: Jason Aronson.

Kohut, H. (1966) Forms and transformations of narcissism, in A. Morrison (1986) *Essential Papers on Narcissism*, New York and London: New York University Press.

Ledermann, R. (1987) Narcissistic disorder: a Jungian view of its aetiology and treatment, *British Journal of Psychotherapy*, 3 (4): 359–69.

Mann, D. (1989) Incest: the father and the male therapist, *British Journal of Psychotherapy*, 6: 143–53.

—— (1994) The psychotherapist's erotic subjectivity, *British Journal of Psychotherapy*, 10 (3): 344–54.

—— (1997a) *Psychotherapy: An Erotic Relationship – Transference and Countertransference Passion*, London: Routledge.

—— (1997b) Masturbation and Painting, in K. Killick and J. Schaverien (eds), *Art, Psychotherapy and Psychosis*, London: Routledge.

—— (ed.) (1999) *Erotic Transference and Countertransference: Clinical Practice in Psychotherapy*, London: Routledge.

—— (2001) Erotics and ethics: the passionate dilemmas of the therapeutic couple, in

L. Murdin and F. P. Barns (eds) *Values and Ethics in the Practice of Psychotherapy and Counselling*, Cambridge: Cambridge University Press.

Moliére (1959) *The Misanthrope and Other Plays*, Harmondsworth: Penguin Books.

Money-Kyrle, R. (1968) Cognitive development, in *The Collected Papers of Roger Money-Kyrle*, Strath Tay, Perthshire: Clunie Press, 1978.

Stoller, R. (1975) *Perversion: The Erotic Form of Hatred*, London: Maresfield Library, 1986.

Strachey, J. (1934) The nature of the therapeutic action of psychoanalysis, *International Journal of Psycho-Analysis*, 15: 127–59.

Suttie, I. D. (1935) *The Origins of Love and Hate*, London: Free Association Books, 1988.

Winnicott, D. W. (1947) Hate in the countertransference, in *Through Paediatrics to Psychoanalysis*, London: Hogarth Press, 1987.

—— (1958) The capacity to be alone, in *The Maturational Processes and the Facilitating Environment*, London: The Hogarth Press, 1987.

—— (1971) The use of the object and relating through identifications, in *Playing and Reality*, Harmondsworth: Penguin Books, 1985.

Chapter 10

The mother's hatred and the ugly child

Francesco Bisagni

Introduction: envy revisited

The original Kleinian theory carries the good–evil dichotomy to the extreme: the problem of guilt, seen as a consequence of innate destructiveness, tends to develop deeply expiatory features within and without the analytic situation. The core of the healing process tends to be equalised to the reparation of the damages carried to the object. As the 'good object' is actually seen in a position of ideal goodness, the Kleinian perspective has often underestimated the offences coming from the object and therefore the vital and defensive meaning of hatred.[1]

But the Kleinian notion of *primary envy* is itself theoretically highly controversial. Firstly, it is well known that what makes the Kleinian concept of primary envy quite uncomfortable – among other things – is its being rooted in the Freudian notion of *death instinct* which in its pure form is conceived of as a drive towards a supposed inorganic, amorphous steady state. Any form of overt destructiveness would thus result from an operation set by life instincts to deflect the death instinct, to put it out of the self and, as it were, get rid of it. In this sense primary envy, wouldn't be primal at all, being the result of the fusion of primal instincts.

From a purely epistemological standpoint primary envy represents a cornerstone in the evolution of psychoanalysis: in fact what we call primary envy is the representative of an evil, destructive a priori component of human nature, in itself independent from frustration or from other negative influences coming from the environment. The environment is of course capable of enhancing or modulating this form of primal destructiveness, which none the less is supposed to exist on its own.

It's like recognising the dark side of God – a topic which has been uncomfortable to many. Similarly to St Augustine, who tried to solve the problem by stating that Evil was the *non-being*, psychoanalysis has tried to link destructiveness to frustration, and to say that an appropriate 'loving' attitude on the part of the object – the attitude analyst is supposed to provide – may repair or mitigate it.[2]

Things are not that easy, however, as we all know. Even with the more sophisticated model set by Bion,[3] where the role of the object is definitely much more relevant, the reverie and the object's alpha function are not always that powerful. The mitigation of destructiveness substantially remains an unsolved problem. Radical destructiveness continues to survive in the individual, like a hidden Auschwitz.

If we deal with the problem of a primal, destructive attack upon the sources of life we inevitably enter the territory of subjects that cannot be demonstrated or explained, neither scientifically nor philosophically. What we just know for sure is that evil, as the philosopher Paul Ricoeur says, is a challenge to thinking, it provokes us to think more, and to think differently, forcing us to overcome the Aristotelian principle of non-contradiction that made the Western world the domain of science and technology.[4]

Evil is something that is already there – as the dark side of God. Even God needs to challenge Abraham and Job, and everybody, to be sure that the Man is with him. God needs to be sure, God would lose all his *good* features if there were no Man to recognise them. When asking to be freed from evil the Man helps God to be God.

In my everyday practice, which is after all what I will be writing about, I have no difficulties (so to speak) in postulating a primary destructiveness, assuming that primary envy could be one way, among others, to name it. The philosophical idea of a kind of ontological evil, the notion of a sort of anti-vital component, is something that I usually like to keep in my mind, as I think it helps me in working through destructiveness and keeping hope alive. I would also say that an a priori destructive component, a destructive self, can be postulated and comes into play after intrauterine life[5] as an essential element within the complex and multi-determined relational interaction.

The complexity of object relations

Considering my personal experience, it is quite clear that on a clinical level things are always quite complicated and that philosophic principles only help to a certain extent, as do psychoanalytic models.

As far as I understand, the work of Wilfred Bion[6] marked a divide in the evolution of the Kleinian approach to mental functioning, with plenty of theoretical and technical innovations. The importance of the external object in metabolising so called beta elements projected by the baby is definitely recognised, as well as the implications of this metabolic function of the object in the developing of thinking, dreaming, memory and other complex mental activities.

Primary envy, on the part of the baby, is recognised by Bion as one of the main factors that may impair alpha function by making the object insufficient on the basis of projection. On the other hand the real unavailability on the part of the object to accept and metabolise projections is undoubtedly of paramount importance. This may be due to various emotional factors, such as depression, recent traumas or any situation that may cause a narcissistic withdrawal of the mother. When referring to a child whose projections are not accepted Bion says that this child, exposed to the experience of an impermeable and emotion-rejecting object, receives back its projected elements in the shape of what he calls *nameless dread* and will internalise a rejecting object which will become the nucleus of every anti-mental activity in the child's future development.

Further research has shown how unprocessed psychic elements in the caretakers may affect the child through projective identification. If the parent is for any reason unable to work through certain conglomerates of psychic experience belonging to his/her personal history, he/she will be forced to evacuate them into the child. The child's mind will be the receptacle of the parent's unprocessed nuclei, which will work in its mind as foreign bodies (Williams, 1997).[7] Their effect on the recipient may be devastating unless they are recognised as such and worked through with sensitiveness and technical skill. The terms 'receptacle' and 'foreign body' are intentionally used as opposites to the terms 'container' and 'contained', along with their physiological meanings.

To go back to the problem of how to face the more radical manifestations of primal destructiveness on a clinical level, such as attacks on linking, attacks on the nutritional object relation and so on, we have to ask ourselves if such destructiveness comes out of the self or out of an internal object, and more specifically out of foreign bodies.

In this light the actual history of a person becomes particularly important, as Herbert Rosenfeld (1987) stated in his last book *Impasse and Interpretation*, and in particular the quality of the patient's primal relations with the actual caretakers. This evaluation turns out to be quite difficult, because it is not just a matter of an anamnestic search in a medical sense; rather, it is a approach to the history of the patient that may come out of a continuous distinction between screen memories, projections and introjections gradually clarified within the ongoing working through of the transference and countertransference interactions.

Furthermore, unless a good internal object provided for by the analyst over the years is settled, and unless the foreign bodies are recognised as such and, as it were, sent back to their original owner, we cannot address primal destructiveness as part of the self that the person may take responsibility of, within what we call a depressive position. Actually the depressive position is a matter of ethics, having to do with the acknowledgement of one's own good and evil disposition to the object. This includes the ability to distinguish between what belongs to myself and what belongs to the other, which means the recognition of subjectivity and intersubjectivity in a wide sense. As the analyst's projective identifications are experienced as foreign bodies – with devastating effects on the patients – an appropriate working through of the countertransference is an issue of vital importance in this process.

In this context the problem of the transgenerational transmission of psychic elements becomes relevant. In some cases, as the one I will be describing later on, psychic nuclei are apparently transmitted through different generations. Sometimes they seem to remain dormant for years within a member of the group, then they erupt and become apparent in another member before becoming dormant again for a while, waiting to reappear somewhere else in a kind of endless poisonous movement. This movement in some way creates a kind of culture of the family group that interacts in a very complex way with the more general cultural features of the outer world. The feedback is usually articulated and difficult to detach, at times seemingly working in favour of a general compensation and maintenance of a pathological but pseudo-normal equilibrium, at times with more disruptive effects in the direction of a psychotic breakdown. The case I will discuss may be descriptive of the transmission of a psychotic conglomerate apparently built up around an unprocessed violent envious element, through three generations within a family. The role of cultural elements seem to be quite important in the general evolution of this family group.

Who is crazy?

I would like to introduce the material, giving some details regarding the family group. The greater part of these details came out of the analytic work with my patient, who I will call Lucy, who was in her late thirties when she started her analysis with me. Some other details are taken from a few notes provided by a colleague who had Lucy's elder child in treatment – an eleven-year-old boy affected by a congenital disease that impairs physical growth and bone development.

Lucy's mother apparently had a psychotic breakdown during her adolescence, with dissociation and delusional phenomena. Though well compensated later on she remained fragile and prone to persecutory moods. Very religious and conventional, she seemed obsessed by social respectability. She gave birth to Lucy and her twin sister Mary, and after only one year to Joan, her younger child.

Lucy's father, a very wealthy professional man, was reported to be highly paranoid. During the cold war era he built an anti-nuclear bunker under his house, full of food and survival equipment, together with thousands of gallons of fuel. When this was discovered by the authorities it became evident that in case of an explosion some hundreds of people could have died in the surrounding area. This man was quite obsessed by the idea of losing money; he was quite violent, easily losing his temper and becoming at times overtly abusive towards his wife and children.

The husband of Lucy, who had been himself in analysis for a number of years, was highly narcissistic and depressed, at times clearly in competition with his children to gain a kind of sexualised maternal attention from his wife, at times revengefully withdrawn in a state of silent rage. Very intellectual and cultivated, he had some sort of over-close involvement of some psychoanalytic groups, and – being very rich – he disregarded his official job and devoted himself in a very omnipotent way in social activities for the minorities. His own father committed suicide at the age of 80, when Lucy was already seven years into her analysis with me, by a gunshot in his mouth. He left a message saying he could not tolerate becoming old and dependent on somebody's help.

Lucy reported a seemingly delusional episode that occurred in her late adolescence which is symbolically relevant, apart from the intensity of the psychotic breakdown itself. Watching herself in the mirror she felt terrified and said: '*I've got something small and monstrous in my body.*' This episode came out as a terrifying memory years later when she gave birth to her first child Paul, who had the congenital disease I mentioned before. I have no evidence, but I always suspected a further psychotic breakdown after this first pregnancy.

She had two more children after Paul. A couple of years after her third child's birth she moved to a foreign country where she stayed for one year. Paul, aged eight at that time, was operated on for elongation of his legs, suffering this extremely painful treatment for months and months. Lucy and Paul were isolated in an institution where they could hardly find enough food for themselves, living in a continuous state of anxiety and pain. All this to gain a couple of inches. Lucy reported her experience in that country as terrifying, continuously on the border of depersonalisation.

Paul, the disabled child, had been in psychotherapy for a few months when Lucy was referred to me by his therapist. What was supposed to be a supportive work turned out to be a four times per week analysis which lasted nine years. At the beginning of her analysis Lucy showed intense difficulties in her capacity for thinking and looked hypomanic. Having to deal with her was like having to hug a piece of ice which had a sharp, cutting surface.

Less than one year after Lucy started her work with me her child, Paul, had a severe psychotic breakdown that required heavy medication. He presented with hallucinations, delusional phenomena and suicidal fantasies. He was twelve at that time. He then remained in treatment for years, requiring pharmacological support for a long time.

It's relevant to notice that when Paul started to get better, Lucy had herself a psychotic episode, with manic excitement and some sort of depersonalisation which required medication for a couple of weeks.

The second child, Henry, was referred for psychotherapy when he was eleven but had an extremely phobic reaction to the therapist so that the treatment could not be started. The third child, Marc, was described as apparently able to function more adequately due to his being 'indifferent' to the family events and quite 'self-sufficient' since his early childhood – two different ways of defending oneself from any possible contact with danger-ous, explosive psychic contents.

The coffin–womb, or the reversal of the container

Lucy conveyed some interesting fantasies, through which she wanted to express – among other things – her feeling neglected by me in the trans-ference. She said she had always known that nobody would have suspected that her mother's pregnancy was a twin pregnancy; instead everyone expected a boy, and only one – a firstborn son. After the not very welcome surprise of the first girl there came the second one, from a pregnancy nobody had suspected. Lucy said she was discovered by chance. It would have been easy not to have discovered her presence; she could have died in her mother's womb and in some way been reabsorbed by her body. This expressed in a very concrete way a sense of not being contained in the maternal mind, not only in terms of a deficit in what we call alpha function but also of an absolute experience of being unwanted. On the basis of my counter-transference – particularly my subtle difficulty in welcoming Lucy in my mind, together with a sense of coldness and harshness in the emotional atmosphere – I am quite sure that nobody felt joy when Lucy was born; rather the family took her as a foreign body – possibly as a good receptacle for everybody's undigested mental element as a kind of group mental dustbin. For a long time I used to have an association that came to my mind every now and then, mostly when the analytic relationship showed difficulties. This association came from my studies in gynaecology, when I was a medical student. What came to my mind was a pathological situation where the 'second twin' does not develop and remains within the other child's body as a bizarre conglomerate of nails, teeth and bones – tissues that calcify and constitute a sort of hard, *stone object/stone monstrous baby* that may remain unrecognised for years inside the first twin's body. It was an interesting image of mine that describes the problem of the foreign bodies and, at the same time, of the self-as-a-foreign body. The problem of Lucy's rejecting her mother's milk for a few months after birth and the occurrence of bulimic attacks over the years (including when Lucy was already in analysis) may be related to what I have just described. As I said before, working through my countertransference turned out to be terribly import-ant. The simple fact that I had powerful images like the one I mentioned – images of such a concrete quality – indicates how I was myself at risk of evacuating my own undigested elements into my patients. In analogy with the family functioning this could have occurred as a result of Lucy's projective identification, acting as a stimulus to my possible evacuation.

Whose hatred is it? (the sharp sound of envy)

In order to go deeper into the clinical material I would like to discuss a dream which seems to be quite important in the context I am trying to describe: '*two children ask their mother to give them some water, because they are very thirsty. The mother gives them two glasses, but they are full of broken pieces of sharp glass.*' The dream represents, we may say in general terms, a mother–child relationship overloaded with dangerous, cutting elements; this is the opposite of nutritious and healthy good milk. But the question – which has deep technical implications – is: is it that the glass is projectively put into the mother's breast by the children and therefore given back to them (re-introjection) as a poisonous nutrient? Or is it that the mother gets rid of her own undigested bits of mind, which are possibly her own foreign bodies coming from other generations, and puts them into the weaker side of the system which is (as usually happens) the children? The former would be rooted in the classical Kleinian view, based on the concept of projection and re-introjection which puts the starting point of the cycle of destructiveness in the child's mind. Technically this would result in a style of interpreting that implies – from the very beginning of the treatment – the responsibility of the patient's self in attacking the nutritional function of the object in the transference. I have to say that I was maybe a bit too much influenced by this model at that time, a model which, for me, has turned out to be definitely unsatisfactory over time. But let us go back to the dream and its context, assuming that the latter hypothesis is the right one.

The main way I could recognise the 'glass-bits-of-mind' was the quality of the voice. The voice, emitted or listened to by my patient was often perceived as cutting, at times felt as concretely damaging: I would say that envy in this patient is, first of all, a non-transforming voice; it is sound that hurts and then becomes unusable milk, the word unavoidably the enemy. I remember Lucy's mouth fixed in a sort of icy, hard, cutting smile, I remember her red lipstick that resembled blood, but most of all I remember the tone of her voice that – beyond the content of words – had the same effect as the scratching of fingernails on a blackboard. Projective identification was indeed very powerful: I remember my own voice becoming hard and cutting, and I often felt a physical sense of tension in my throat, mostly when I wanted to underline some positive element in the transference. I realised that this tension in my throat was something that I was aware of, but none the less it remained powerfully beyond my will, and in some way resistant to my alpha function. Though I was quite sure that this voice of mine was not the expression of some sort of evacuation of my own undigested mental bits, Lucy responded to it with a kind of short-circuit reaction, becoming even harsher, triumphant and manic, which described her anxiety of having lost me as a good object and of having in some way made me a member of her family.

Whose voice was that? I think it was the cutting, harsh voice of a deadly bizarre object, included in the mental system of my patient, that tended to migrate from one person to another, like a rejected child who has no home, no place to rest and to be taken care of. Its origin lies far away in space and time; it's a parentless object so it may become anybody's object. The acoustic component of words was very often attacked, in a kind of destructive transformation of the quality of the sound as a proto-emotion transforming container. I use the term 'container' in the sense conceived of by Bion, as well as the notion of proto-emotion. Following this model, we know that in foetal perception, which develops from the fourth month of intrauterine life, noises which have their own rhythm and the ones which have a beginning–end rhythm (like the mother's voice) can be differentiated from each other and from chaotic and totally amorphous sounds. We hypothesise[8] that rhythmic sounds can convey a proto-experience of separateness, an alternating of full and empty. This can be seen as a proto-experience of the relationship with the present–absent object mediated by the sound in both quantitative and qualitative terms. In fact the emotional quality of the sound, and in particular the mother's voice, is a proto-experience of the goodness or badness of the object.

This becomes even more relevant during the first phases of post-natal development when the tone of the mother's voice is what expresses the degree of atunement, the prerequisite of any capacity for reverie at its most essential level, the availability to the basic joy and welcoming of the newborn in the mental space. The cutting voice in Lucy, and its effect in myself, may be traced back firstly to her experience of being unwanted and not thought of and, most of all, to her being the receptacle of all undigested maternal psychic elements which were themselves multi-determined. The role of the disabled child – with the problem of the impossibility to grow – may be regarded as a kind of reinforcement of the experience of non-mentalisation in a very complex interplay of evacuative projections.

As a matter of fact I had better results with Lucy when I started to give more value to her dramatic experiences as a receptacle, which allowed her to partly work through her intense sense of persecution, her guilty feelings, and to develop some kind of sweetness and compassion towards her children. When the baby-Lucy could experience in the analytic relationship a right to existence, and a feeling of warmth and of being wanted, the adult-Lucy learned how to hold her children in her mind as human beings that might be loved and helped to grow.

Conclusions

The problem of evil lies beyond reductionism. No objective causes can be identified. Phantasies can only be grasped on the manifold paths of human interactions, and meaningful connections may just be traced on the basis of subjectivity.

In a way, evil in modern times is theoretically a homeless child. Clinically it is our companion.

I have tried to show how my patient's mind had been homeless. Somebody's hatred was parentless in that family and migrated from body to body, stopping at times in the body of someone's parentless mind.

The attacks on the communication operated by Lucy showed a level that went far beyond the sophisticated levels of verbal representations, which were none the less quite evident. Sounds of death before life.

An intense working through of my countertransference, together with a theoretical review of the classical Kleinian model of the mind in the light of the work of Wilfred Bion, proved to be necessary to me to gain a better understanding of my patients' states of mind. Some contributions of those who work in fields other than psychoanalysis were of great help. As usual.

Love and the right to life had to be invented.

Some parents eventually came on the scene.

Notes

1 See the valuable contribution on the problem of evil from a psychoanalytic standpoint by de Masi (2000).
2 Theologists could help us in developing a deeper understanding of the problem. See for instance the paper by Paolo De Benedetti (2000), an italian Professor of Judaism.
3 Bion was the most creative follower of Melanie Klein's thinking, in some respects changing the Kleinian model and technique in a radical way.
4 See Ricoeur (1993).
5 Interesting though controversial contributions on this issue may be found in Alessandra Piontelli's (1992) work on foetal life. Piontelli shows how the level of vitality in foetuses varies considerably. In particular when studying the twins through ultrasound scanning we can observe remarkable differences between the two in their capacity for reacting to stimuli, aggressiveness and so on, given the same psycho-physical environment. These same features can be further observed after birth in the first stages of character development. In general this method of infant observation provides us with innumerable observations regarding the degree of availability of the baby towards the object's response.
6 See Bion (1962).
7 Williams (1997).
8 The work of Suzanne Maiello (1995) on the sound object is fascinating. Starting from the experience with autistic and deeply disturbed patients, Maiello tries an exploration of the proto-experience of the object in intrauterine life.

References

Bion, W.R. (1962) *Learning from Experience*, London: Heinemann.
De Benedetti, P. (2000) Ma liberaci dal Male, in *Il Male*, Milano: Raffaello Cortina.

De Masi, F. (2000) Il fascino del Male nella Mente: dal Male alla Malattia, in *Il Male*, Milano: Raffaello Cortina.

Piontelli, A. (1992) *From Fetus to Child. An Observational and Psychoanalytic Study*, London: Routledge.

Maiello, S. (1995) The sound-object: a hypothesis about prenatal auditory experience and memory, *The Journal of Child Psychotherapy* 21(1), 23–41.

Ricoeur, P. (1993) *Il Male. Una sfida alla filosofia e alla teologia*, Brescia: Morcelliana.

Rosenfeld, H. (1987) *Impasse and Interpretation*, London and New York: Tavistock Publications.

Williams, G. (1997) Reflections on some dynamics of eating disorders: 'no entry' defences and foreign bodies, *The International Journal of Psychoanalysis* 78(5), 927–42.

Chapter 11

Love and hate in the therapeutic encounter

Jackie Gerrard

> Psychoanalysis is in essence a cure through love.
>
> (Freud, in a letter to Jung)

In 1996, my paper 'Love in the time of psychotherapy' explored the importance of love in the therapeutic encounter – positing that for a successful outcome in therapy a patient needed to engender loving feelings in the therapist. An assumption was that hate was part of the primitive, archaic feelings but was not present in the feelings of mature or civilised love. The paper omitted to take account of the significance of the therapist's hate as a valid, indeed vital, ingredient of the capacity to love. It is clear that there is more to say about this than that 'sadism and hate are secondary phenomena – consequences of inevitable frustrations' (Gerrard 1996: 166).

This chapter is an endeavour to bring hate into the arena of love in its totality. I shall say what I mean by love and hate, review some of the literature on hate and its relationship to love, and then give some clinical vignettes which will demonstrate various situations where counter-transference hate, if successfully overcome, can enable both transference and counter-transference love to emerge. I shall also try to explore some of the similarities and differences between primary and secondary love and hate.

By love I mean 'extreme tenderness', as described in the earlier paper (Gerrard 1996). This was influenced by Suttie's work, defining love as originating in the pre-Oedipal, emotional and fondling relationship with the mother (not based on libido and sexual desire). The concept of love took into account qualities such as 'patience, endurance, humour, kindness and courage' (Coltart 1992: 118–19), containment and reverie (Bion) and tenderness and affection (Suttie).

The two kinds of love that I posited were 'archaic and civilised, infantile and mature, primary and secondary' (Gerrard 1996: 167), the first accompanied by enmeshment and (usually) ruthlessness, the second more separate and reality based. I concluded that certain patients could engender love through 'genuineness, a wish for connectedness and a capacity for work and play' (ibid.: 172), and some clinical vignettes demonstrated how the presence or absence of the therapist's love affected the outcome of therapy. By hate, I mean an intense dislike, a feeling of enmity and rejection and a wish to hurt or even destroy the other. However, when thinking of primary and secondary states, my use of the word 'hate' corresponds with my thinking on love. The primary state is where there is no clear delineation between love and hate, or between self and other – both involving an intense and ruthless relatedness to the (m)other.

The secondary hatred that I posit in this chapter has within it the wish to relate so that while the object is being attacked, hurt, destroyed it is involved deeply and intensely with the subject. What differentiates it from primary aggression/hate (or ruthless love), is a greater awareness of separation of self and other (a relatively late stage of development) and the resulting intentionality of the wish to hurt. Thus, in my view, whilst I am hating you I am wanting to have an effect on you – I need you to be involved with me and affected by me.

My use of the term 'primary hate' could perhaps be more clearly defined by using Winnicott's 'primary aggression'. Winnicott, in fact, sees hate as a later development – the neonate does not feel hatred, he feels greed and ruthless love. Winnicott helps to differentiate these early primary states that I am describing. Based on Freud's erotic and aggressive components, he links the aggressive with ruthlessness and the erotic with the 'sensuous co-existence' of baby in an unintegrated state with mother (1950).

Primary aggression is seen to be hateful, cruel and destructive – but only incidentally; that is, not intentionally. The infant is not yet separate enough from the mother to know of his ruthlessness. It is his aggression that allows for the not-me experiences to develop and is 'only brought into being by active opposition, or (later) persecution' (Winnicott 1950: 217).

It is in the sphere of the object relationship, and at a secondary stage of development, that I see anger as most clearly distinguishable from hate. I accept the *Oxford Dictionary* definition of anger as 'extreme displeasure', which does not necessarily imply the wish or need for connectedness. When I feel angry with you, I may want you to know this or I may not. I may want to blot you out, or again, I may not. My anger may lead to hatred, but is not, of itself, hatred. My anger separates me from you, my hatred and my love connect us.

This formulation has been helped by Bollas (1987) who takes issue with Freud's original thinking, whereby hate is allied with the death instinct and love is placed amongst the life instincts. Bollas offers us the term 'loving hate' – 'a situation where an individual preserves a relationship by sustaining a passionate negative cathexis of it' (1987: 118). Bollas places a valuable emphasis on the preservation of a relationship that can only be felt to exist where love would seem to be unavailable. This is particularly notable in schizoid personalities where love is considered dangerous.

Winnicott (1947) writes of the hate of mother for baby and of analyst for patient, and stresses the importance of finding a way to acknowledge this with a patient prior to the ending of an analysis. This is in the area of secondary hate. In a later paper, Winnicott states clearly that he sees aggression as 'part of the primitive expression of love' (1950: 205), and writes of infants in the state of pre-concern where ruthlessness includes attacks on the mother's body – these are felt to be acts of love (primary aggression/ruthless love).

Continuing in the area of the primary, Alice Balint (1949) delineates the concept of archaic love. She describes this stage as one where reality sense has not yet developed and the infant demands absolute unselfishness from the mother, whilst the mother feels her child to be 'not the external world', but instead a part of herself. Alice Balint and Winnicott would seem to be in agreement that this type of archaic or ruthless love, which has an excessively ruthless basis, contains destruction in fantasy. Thus Winnicott's statement 'While I am loving you I am all the time destroying you in (unconscious) fantasy' (1971: 105).

In this area too, Freud, in *Totem and Taboo*, wrote about ruthless relationships – for example, those obtaining between sons and their 'violent primal father' (1950: 142). Loewald (1979) took up this theme of 'parricide' and stressed the necessity of it in symbolic form for a successful negotiation of the Oedipus complex.

I wish to stress that these primitive fantasies are necessary to healthy development, in order for normal growth into later relationships with their differentiated emotions of love and hate. This is beautifully described by Winnicott in 'The use of an object' (1971). Susan Norrington (1996) in her unpublished paper on hate in the countertransference claims, in agreement with Winnicott, that 'it is only through the recognition of intensely felt hate, that we can come to love and feel concern for the object who has survived our hate through his own resources rather than being magically restored through omnipotence'.

Norrington has differentiated anger from hate – anger as connecting and binding, and hate as separating. It is in this area that I have found it helpful to think about primary and secondary states of being. In a primary state (pre-ruth) ruthless attacks on the mother's body – hardly differentiated from the infant's own self and body – involve a 'mix-up' of love and hate – alternating states indiscernibly separate from each other. Vital to both these experiences of love and hate is an intense primitive relatedness to the other. In a more differentiated state, hate and love are more separately felt and experienced. It is here that I would be in agreement with Bollas, as opposed to Norrington, in terms of hate serving as a means of connecting whilst I would see anger as separating. In this secondary form of relationship, hate is much more clearly discernible from love, but nevertheless is also felt as part of an intense relatedness. It is often said that the opposite of love is indifference, rather than hate. My stance is that whilst I am hating you, I am all the time relating to you. When I am angry with you, I want to cut you off and blot you out.

It is this secondary state of hate that Winnicott (1947) refers to when discussing objective or justified hate which has to be reached before patient (and analyst) can reach objective love.

Like Bollas, Gottlieb stresses that hate contains 'the wish to know, and be known by, another' (1994: 18). She makes an important distinction between 'objective' hatred and hatred resulting from the projection into the therapist of a hating internal object. This may be a distinction that is important to make, but when in the presence of an attacking, contemptuous, destructive borderline patient it can be a Herculean task to do so. If love and hate can be recognised and experienced separately (as opposed to the 'mix-up' in primitive states), the 'loving hate' of which Bollas writes can eventually give rise to a freedom, without danger, for the expression of love in a less repressed form. 'Hate emerges not as a result of the destruction of internal objects, but as a defence against emptiness. Indeed, it represents an effort to emerge from this vacuum into object relating' (Bollas 1987: 130). Hence hate, either in its primary or secondary form (Bollas is describing the latter), with its associated striving to relate, may often be a forerunner to love.

Gabbard (1991) concluded that the goal of termination is not to eradicate hate, but to temper it with love – having introduced us to his paper with a quotation from Samuel Butler: 'It does not matter much what a man hates as long as he hates something.'

In discussing technique, Carpy (1989) and Slochower (1991) have both advocated allowing elements of the counter-transference hate to emerge in a modified way with the patient, Carpy through what he calls 'partial acting out' and Slochower through 'the extremely firm, absolutely non-intrusive, and sometimes *mildly* annoyed analytic stance' (1991: 713; my italics). In other words, both analysts believe in the importance of letting patients know they have made an *impact*, which conveys a living relationship but one where the hate is survivable by the analyst. Coltart too, in her papers 'What does it mean: "Love is not enough"?' (1992) and 'Slouching towards Bethlehem' (1986), stresses the importance to the analytic work of letting patients know the impact they have on the therapist. In both papers the analyst's expression of hatred conveyed the depth of the feelings towards the patient, and the expression of intense hatred paved the way for the loving relationship to develop – one where the capacity for work and play was restored.

Prodgers endeavoured to 'lift the lid off some of the shame that still abounds in respect of our hate in the countertransference' (1991: 153). He suggested that for many therapists there is a blindspot towards their hate which, if not uncovered, could cause an impasse in the work. Coltart seemed to have worked well with hers!

Clinical vignettes

I saw Mr A three times weekly, and was warned early on of the likely sabotage of his therapy. He introduced me to what he called 'the enemy within', which was part of an internalised, parental, scornful and contemptuous object. Month after month he attacked his therapy passively by an increased opting-out from life and work, and more actively by constantly saying that it was only a matter of time before he left and that nothing would change unless there was a magic wand.

Mr A was a patient compulsively tied to his bad object (Armstrong-Perlman 1991), and the hatred he could feel towards her was often projected into me as I began to feel like little Mr A tormented by a chronically hopeless, discontented and persecutory mother-figure. In one session, overwhelmed by my own sense of impotence and hatred, I suggested to him that he seemed to be needing me to feel with him the hopelessness and hatred he felt as a young child – that nothing he could say or do would make an impact. (My inner experience was of being tortured and tormented.) This intervention led, for a while, to his renewed faith in me. When he felt more connected, he offered me a 'gift' – he told me that his partner felt he had changed significantly for the better at home. In my temporarily renewed sense of not being entirely useless and rubbished, I could re-find some warm and loving feelings for Mr A and, it would seem, he for me. Slochower emphasises the need, if the holding environment is to work with certain borderline patients, for the analyst to hold 'their ruthlessness and rage and also analytic self blame' (1991: 716). One might argue that in my intervention I had temporarily stopped holding these. That may be so. One might also argue, however, that it was necessary for us both to be reminded briefly that loving feelings could be experienced among all the hatred.

However, Mr A was not to remain in therapy. He felt that I had damaged his protective disguise when some of his more affectionate and attached feelings had gradually emerged. He increased his anti-depressant medication and returned to his life-strangling, self-destructive behaviour. This was underpinned by his belief that, if he mourned and separated from his dead internal object, he would have betrayed her. So our analytic work was abandoned and, instead, he let me go and held on to the status quo. Sadly, therefore, Mr A, a patient with whom I could find fluctuating feelings of both love and hate, left therapy before there was any true working-through of these deeply felt affects.

Another patient, Mr B, sabotaged his therapy finally by not paying me, allowing his cheques to bounce. There had been prior warning of this several months earlier when the first cheque bounced. I had been unable to make any real contact with this highly narcissistic young man who kept me firmly at bay, through his dilemma of should he marry Miss X or Miss Y. Each session, a new drama emerged – enraged with one of his women and drawn to the other – whilst I felt like a helpless bystander or member of an audience watching the players on his stage. As with Mr A I felt belittled and useless, as I know he too had often felt in childhood. He seemed to be desperate both to connect and to make sure he did not connect with me (the schizoid dilemma: Guntrip 1977). The unconscious way Mr B found to make contact with me was through various stories about his work with children. I found in him a deep empathy and compassion for children, and through this he aroused my love. But, in any personal way, connecting through love was too dangerous and would leave him too vulnerable, so he involved me through hate, excluding, obliterating, denigrating by non-payment. This ensured we remained in an intense relationship – apparently disconnected and yet, as I felt it in my counter-transference, deeply connected. However, this was another patient who, although I could reach moments of love and tenderness, and moments of hatred, sabotaged the therapy before he could work through his feelings and reach a degree of insight.

By contrast, my work with Mrs C was better able to illustrate the movement in the therapist between love and hate and the beginnings of a situation where counter-transference feelings of love begin to emerge and can take firmer hold. Mrs C was a depressed, deeply schizoid patient apparently unable truly to love her significant objects – husband, children and her therapist. The transference relationship she developed was of a distant polite cooperativeness, depressed and with little evidence of lively play and imagination, or indeed of much involvement or dependency. Separations seemed not to be significant or to have an impact. (Mrs C was a patient who had experienced several traumatic deaths in her young adult life, and who as a child had spent an extended period away from her family in hospital.) Over time, however, it became increasingly noticeable that she cut off emotionally prior to a break. It seemed that the system had just shut down to deal with the circumstances!

As I noticed these barely perceptible responses to breaks, Mrs C gradually became increasingly negative towards me – sometimes through her complaints about the awful objects in my room, sometimes through her statements about what a waste of her time this therapy was; such a chore to come. I found that I became more drawn to her through thinking about her in between sessions, worrying about what I had said or might say in order to create more connection between us. I started to feel from time to time that I hated her and was thus able to understand how her depression and isolation was her way of avoiding her hatred of the objects who had deserted her – either physically or emotionally. She was a patient who, in the terms of my previous paper (Gerrard 1996), had not elicited my tender feelings or my capacity to offer her the opportunity to experience herself as lovable. In fact, she often presented, in the way Freud (1917) describes in 'Mourning and melancholia', a total and utter self-loathing – the rage, hatred and disappointment towards her objects having been turned back onto herself.

Later, Mrs C was able to recognise her own destructiveness and hatred. She expressed this with tears about the love she had withheld from a now dead parent. In the session she was in touch with herself as a vengeful and withholding person and also with the despair that reparation could not be made because the parent had died. As she sobbed uncontrollably about this irretrievable situation, I found myself with deeply tender and loving feelings towards her. She was unfreezing and thus owning her feelings. Subsequently, she began to talk of a hatred, both towards her dead objects for dying and towards her live objects for growing up and growing away from her – apparently rendering her useless and spurning her love. I was therefore beginning to understand that, certainly in part, the hatred I felt towards my patient was hers towards her objects for being ungrateful for the love she was bestowing upon them and for deserting her. At these moments of understanding, my hatred dissolved and my love blossomed. Mrs C was owning her feelings and was showing courage at doing so. This allowed for some potential space and I felt connected to her as she expressed her thoughts, fantasies and memories. We had moved from a state of emptiness and occasional 'loving hate' (in a desperate struggle to ward off the emptiness) and begun to reach an area where love could emerge.

Mrs D was a patient who I saw for some years. She came for therapy because she was so filled with hatred towards her children that frequently she could not stop herself from physical violence towards them. Her early life had been deprived, both in terms of actual poverty and emotionally; she was one in a family of many children whose father had deserted, and the mother seemed not to have had the emotional capacity to relate to Mrs D. Thus, she had no solidly good internal object. She was also handicapped by great envy, both of her own children and of other women. This envy certainly extended to myself and there were frequent attacks on me and on the therapy, mostly in the form of 'forgetting' to come to sessions, but also in covert remarks about my religion and my 'stupid rules'. There was a subtle blotting me out by a fixed conviction that, while therapy was a treatment that she needed, I as a person barely existed in her mind as someone to whom she might relate. There appeared to be a total lack of curiosity about me, and no acknowledgement that we had a relationship as two people who might matter for each other, or indeed miss each other at break times.

She attacked me in a much less florid way than some borderline patients; nevertheless for a while I feared and dreaded our sessions, and actually became somewhat paranoid, anticipating attacks and concocting self-defensive arguments about why I had done or said such and such. Nevertheless, over time I must have done a good enough 'holding' job, particularly in the area Slochower mentions – the area of analytic self-blame – as slowly Mrs D became more able to use the analytic space. She brought occasional dreams and wanted to understand much more of her own paranoid reactions in the world out there. I gradually became an important and helpful object to her, and as the hatred (in both of us) slowly turned to love and gratitude (in both of us) Mrs D made a most significant statement. She told me that her therapy with me had radically changed her attitude towards her children and allowed her to love them realistically, so that she felt she had been able to change the impoverishment and disturbance in the line of children in her family. As I became able to love her, with her increased ability to use me and the analytic space, she came to love herself and her children – the hatred of both slowly evaporating and giving way to the love. This, of course, does not mean that moments of hate were not still experienced in the relationship between us. When I raised the fee, she reacted with a flash of fury and a dismissive and denigratory comment, which gave rise to an equally furious response in me and I recalled one of Winnicott's reasons why the mother might hate the baby – 'he is ruthless, treats her as scum, an unpaid servant, a slave' (1947: 201).

Finally, a therapist had a patient, Mrs E, whose mother had been somewhat idealised and had died just prior to the onset of therapy. The patient seemed unconsciously to have sought therapy to work through the hate she had always felt towards her mother. Mrs E felt that insecurity and disappointment had clouded their relationship. This had not been verbalised whilst her mother was alive. For a considerable time the patient kept up a sustained attack on her therapist – she was contemptuous, dismissive, hostile and very critical. The therapist managed an admirably receptive stance – able to consider carefully the origins of the patient's almost unrelenting attacks, and resist from any semblance of retaliation. From time to time she would comment on her patient's hatred and the patient could join her, so that they could reflect together and some analytic work could be done. It was at moments when the patient could sob about the horrible person she really was, could feel true remorse for the perceived destructiveness she had invoked and the possible hurts she had caused, that the therapist could feel tender and loving towards her. At these moments the ruthlessness had moved into a secondary stage.

Winnicott aptly described what happened here:

> in certain stages of certain analyses the analyst's hate is actually sought by the patient, and what is then needed is hate that is objective. If the patient seeks objective or justified hate he must be able to reach it, else he cannot feel he can reach objective love.
>
> (Winnicott 1947: 199)

In these clinical vignettes, would the patients' reactions be seen as objective hatred or as a projection of the hatred into the mother/therapist? This is a real dilemma when trying to understand objective hatred and its distinction, as suggested by Gottlieb. Maybe both processes can occur at the same time. In the case of patients like Mr A, Mr B and to a lesser extent Mrs D and Mrs E, dominated by internal hating and/or denigrating objects which lead them to behave in a hateful way towards their therapist, the therapist's hating response to her patient may be something that is both 'objective' because of the way she has been treated, and introjective because of what has been projected into her.

The more helpful differentiation may be the one between primary and secondary states of hating. A primary state of hating is virtually indistinguishable from a primary state of loving. I hate you therefore I love you is the same as I love you therefore I hate you. It is in the area of primary process thinking. By contrast, a secondary state of hating is clearly separate from loving at the moment at which it is felt. When I hate Mrs D, or when Mrs C rejects me or hates herself, love is not available in the transaction. It can exist beforehand, it can occur again within moments afterwards, but the two feelings are separate. Similarly, when Bollas gives us 'loving hate' he is clear that it is the hate that unites the two subjects – for the ultimate purpose of love, certainly, but one feeling is clearly in the ascendant at the time of the experience.

Love is then incomplete without hate (and vice versa). They are bound up together in a kind of 'mix-up' in primary states or in the shadows in the case of secondary states. The task for the therapist is to try to reach the love, but inevitably, at some point in the work, it has to be reached through the experiencing of hate, else it may be something other than love – liking, sentimentality, kindness, compassion, pity, etc. Patients must engender love in the therapist if they are to know that they are truly lovable. To have generated this love without the hatred having been rather intensely felt on both sides, may be a hollow achievement.

How many times have we ourselves felt, and heard from our patients, 'If they knew what I was *really* like, they wouldn't love me, employ me, associate with me.' If I, a therapist, know that I have hated my patients, and if I also know that my therapist has hated me when I was a patient (how could she not, since I behaved disgracefully and hatefully towards her for this very purpose?), then any resulting love cannot but have more solid foundations and be trusted more readily to endure, to be real, to be true.

There is a fluidity of movement in therapy, whereby love can rapidly turn to hate, then hate becomes resolved and love prevails. Sometimes the more primary states obtain where all seems to be a 'mix-up'. So the patient who can one day, or at any one time, feel remorse, love and a readiness to work and reflect, can at other moments hate with intense passion. If all goes well, however, in time hate will be somewhat understood and overcome, though hopefully not dispensed with, and love will be more readily available. Our therapeutic aim must be for patients and their therapists to reach a point where they are free to love – both themselves and one another.

References

Armstrong-Perlman, E. (1991) The allure of the bad object, *Free Associations*, Part 3, No. 23, 343–356.

Balint, A. (1949) Love for the mother and mother-love, *International Journal of Psycho-Analysis*, 30, 251–259.

Bollas, C. (1987) Loving hate, in *The Shadow of the Object*, London: Free Association Books.

Carpy, D. (1989) Tolerating the countertransference: a mutative process, *International Journal of Psycho-Analysis*, 70, 287–294.

Coltart, N. (1986) Slouching towards Bethlehem, in *Slouching towards Bethlehem*, London: Free Assocation Books, 1992.

Coltart, N. (1992) What does it mean: 'Love in not enough'?, in *Slouching towards Bethlehem*, London: Free Assocation Books.

Freud, S. (1917) Mourning and melancholia, in *Standard Edition* 14, London: Hogarth Press.

Freud, S. (1950) *Totem and Taboo*, London: Routledge & Kegan Paul Ltd.

Gabbard, G. (1991) Technical approaches to transference hate in the analysis of borderline patients, *International Journal of Psycho-Analysis*, 72, 625–637.

Gerrard, J. (1996) Love in the time of psychotherapy, *British Journal of Psychotherapy*, 13(2), 163–173.

Gottlieb, S. (1994) Hateful relationships, *British Journal of Psychotherapy*, 11(1), 8–19.

Guntrip, H. (1977) *Schizoid Phenomena, Object Relations and the Self*, London: Hogarth Press.

Loewald, H. (1979) The waning of the Oedipus complex, in *Papers on Psychoanalysis*, New Haven, Conn.: Yale University Press.

Norrington, S. (1996) Hate in the countertransference, Unpublished paper, given to London Centre for Psychotherapy.

Prodgers, A. (1991) On hating the patient, *British Journal of Psychotherapy*, 8(2), 144–153.

Slochower, J. (1991) Variations in the analytic holding environment, *International Journal of Psycho-Analysis*, 72, 709–718.

Winnicott, D. (1947) Hate in the countertransference, in *Through Paediatrics to Psychoanalysis*, London: Hogarth Press, 1978.

Winnicott, D. (1950) Aggression in relation to emotional development, in *Through Paediatrics to Psychoanalysis*, London: Hogarth Press, 1978.

Winnicott, D. (1971) The use of an object, in *Playing and Reality*, London: Penguin Books, 1974.

Chapter 12

'When love begins to play a role, there are only disputes and hatred'

Confusion and limits in the treatment of a narcissistic patient

Ingrid Pohl

Analysis can be described as a relationship between two persons in which one person (the analyst) helps the other person (the patient) to face up to the reality of his needs and his dependency and to come to terms with the difficult and complex feelings involved. This situation is comparable to the relationship between a mother and her baby, and in many cases the transference via various stages of emotional experience leads to the patient extending his ability to better understand and integrate his own internal emotions, and thus to feel better prepared for the internal and external onslaughts. To the extent that this experience in the analysis is felt to be a good experience, because it leads to further development and growth of the patient's personality, feelings of gratitude towards the analyst are able to set in. It is possible to achieve this good experience with outside help from someone who has contributed towards remedying an initial deficiency situation that could not have been remedied by the patient's own efforts, just as the baby cannot remedy its own primal deficiency situation by its own efforts. The baby is at the mercy of overwhelming anxieties and needs, and only the mother – and later the analyst in the analytical relationship – is able to take appropriate measures to create a state of well-being, peace, satisfaction, dryness, etc., or of understanding. The repeated experience of these conversions from torturous deficiency situations into feelings of satisfaction and well-being generally leads to the establishment of an external as well as internal object, which is felt to be good and which can grant security in dealings with the world. This internal and external object, as the precipitation of good experiences, can only remain good, however, if there is something in the baby/patient that can tolerate and acknowledge that it was the external object which provided what was good and helpful. From a satisfying, alternating succession of projections and introjections, a feeling of gratitude and love can develop in time between the two persons (mother–baby/analyst–patient).

With patients suffering from a serious narcissistic defence we come across a contradictory situation in the therapies: although the patients are looking for treatment, they cannot understand our analytical services as something good. Instead they respond to our interpretations with scorn, contempt, rage, forgetfulness, etc., and it is hardly possible to create a real development towards more emotional liveliness.

What makes patients inexorably suppress their emotional life and that of their objects and maintain the status quo at all costs? Something seems to prevent them from allowing their loving feelings to show through; instead they seem to pursue the analyst as well as other important people in their lives – often in hate – as if they could only see the one side of the coin. If you agree with Rey (1994: 229) that the fact that the patient comes to therapy constitutes an unconscious desire to restore objects attacked in hate, then you can understand seeking therapy as a form of search for love. But there seems to be a serious impediment to carrying through these loving feelings – which become apparent in the process of reparation – because the same forces that guided the infantile development in a specific self-destructive direction take effect with equal weight in the analysis as a reproduction of the unconscious desire for a 'lack of relationship'.

One of the difficulties in narcissistic patient therapies lies in the fact that the patients have an inadequately clear notion of a 'good' object, and equally of their own 'good' feelings; their concept of good seems to form a confusion of good and bad notions or, on the other hand, good and bad parts are separated from each other in such an extreme way that it is not possible to experience ambivalence towards one object. When Winnicott (1965) says, 'Everything is interpreted in relation to the love and ambivalence of the individual', in the case of narcissistic patients, ambivalence and the ability to love – or fore-forms of love – seem to surface only as a result of the analysis, if at all. Reparation presupposes the desire to have good internal and external objects and to care for the well-being of these objects, so that they can be retained as good objects. The conscious desire for this only develops from the mutual experiencing of many emotional storms and crises in which the analyst proves to be someone that can take up and hold the confused and catastrophic feelings of the patient, and in which a notion of a good object surfaces in the patient – an object into which the patient can direct more loving feelings and begin to feel responsible for keeping it, in the sense of a depressive feeling.

The development towards the primary differentiation between clearly good and clearly bad experiences and – connected with that – the differentiation between clearly good and clearly bad objects is obviously disturbed. Britton (1993: 102) stresses that this also leads to disturbances 'relating to all other differentiations like, for example, between the primitive motherly and fatherly part objects' and consequently to a 'propensity to fusion and confusion'. The permanent formation of 'combined objects' destroys sense and significance and leads to thought disturbances; it rigorously forces arbitrary splitting in order to preserve values and meanings, above all 'in order to maintain the notion of good and keep it separate from the bad notion'. Without a good internal object, one's own self seems to be threatened with annihilation, because the destructive emotions are experienced as overpowering. Therefore, keeping the idea of good is a life-preserving splitting process.

In my opinion, the consequence of the congenital primary deficient ability to distinguish between good and bad experiences is that a lived experience is not represented in the quality of good or bad but in a combined form which, like the figure of the parents as a combined object, seems to attack the individual in a threatening way. In the analysis, the patient develops a fear of, and retreat from, lively contact because he is full of mistrust and cannot distinguish whether what appears to be good might not also at the same time prove to be bad, and vice versa. For this experience, Britton suggested the following working hypothesis: good milk in a bad breast or bad milk in a good breast. It reminds me of a patient who – like Britton's patient – merely wanted to listen to my voice in the sessions and was satisfied if it felt calm, like a soft cushion or like music enveloping him. He could not and would not register the content of my words because he was full of anxiety and mistrust and was afraid of being cheated, of being deceived by me, which corresponded to his deception and insecurity about his own feelings. My voice could have represented the good breast, which gave him solace and reassurance, and my interpretations the bad milk, which in its function of 'putting meaning into him' was rejected. This division splits a normally uniform experience of satisfaction into two experiences in order to categorise the confusing and frightening 'combined object' into unambiguous characteristics and to restore orientation.

Theoretically, this condition of primary deficient ability to differentiate between moral experience qualities is to be separated from the situation in which an object at first – no matter how fleetingly – is experienced as a good object, but immediately transforms into a bad object as a result of intense envy. Hinshelwood (1991: 171) writes, 'Envy is a phantasy of forced entry (by projective methods) and destructive attacks on the *good* object, just because of its goodness.' The destruction therefore does not take place out of ambivalence and frustration but in order to 'create a hostile relationship to a good object – and not to the evil and feared pursuer'. Through its envious attacks, the baby leaves behind inside it a 'good object turned bad', which can no longer be distinguished from 'bad objects, from which it has to save itself', and thus it is incapable of 'putting its experiences into . . . order'. When the envy is too intense, it can lead to a state of confused experience in just the same way as with a congenital primary lack of ability to differentiate between good and bad. Clinically, it will be hard – if possible at all – to differentiate between a congenital limitation of the ability to discriminate between good and bad qualities and an inability resulting from projective mingling of good and bad. In my opinion, however, there is a way of differentiating in the countertransference. When the concept of a clearly good experience is missing, a permanent intensive feeling of hopelessness and resignation spreads in the analyst as to whether the experiences in the analysis can ever become available for the patient in a process of transformation, and whether more stable desires for an object can develop from rudimentary fore-forms of love. If, through envious attacks, the experience that is primarily felt to be good – and with it the object that relates to it – is blurred, then the phenomenon of negative therapeutic reaction, which includes a preceding clearly good experience on the part of the analyst and the patient, seems to play a decisive role in the analytical process. The idea of a life-preserving good object is there, but through permanent attacks it also appears to have taken on a mixed quality that gives cause for retreat. The countertransference is dominated by an atmosphere of annoyance and devaluation.

The defence against envy also leads to confusion and disorientation. Omnipotent forms of projective identification are directed against experiences of separation and dependency, resulting in a mingling of subject and object. In omnipotent fantasies, an omnipotent self is created – and also omnipotent objects which are always present, and therefore are felt to be superior to the real objects and the real analyst because they appear to make possible a state that is free from anxiety and tension. At the same time, the patient's own libidinous impulses which are directed at the objects are denied and a state of 'non-relationship' established. The whole situation is denied, as Segal (1997) says, by removing the libidinous need for a satisfying object as well as the awareness of this need and the object that satisfies this need. The vacuum is filled with an omnipotent fantasy that the patient is the source of all life, not only in respect of his own self but also in respect of the objects, which do not seem to have any independent existence apart from that projectively attributed to them.

When in the primary mingling of instincts the destructive powers prevail, which is generally assumed in seriously narcissistic patients, this results in confusion because the life-sustaining object is hated and is 'to a certain extent destroyed by mistake' (Hinshelwood 1991). Desires for satisfaction by the good breast are awakened, but at the same time even stronger desires are awakened to attack the need-satisfying object and to want to dispose of it in hate. In his work *Analysis Terminable and Interminable* (1937), Freud reflected on why some analyses take such a long time and concluded that there was 'no stronger impression of the resistance during analytical work than that of a force that uses all means to defend itself against recovery and actually wants to hold on to illness and suffering'. He equated this force with the aggressive and destructive instinct that was deduced from the death instinct and thought that in the 'rejection of femininity' in both sexes he had found the ultimate reason – 'the bedrock' – where psychoanalytic work comes to an end. Klein (1957) saw in this rejection of femininity the work of intensive feelings of envy, which she also related to the death instinct, and whose intensity was decisive in determining the chances of change. Rosenfeld (1971) saw the effects of the death instinct in destructive narcissism, in which the impulses to destroy are idealised and in which not only the patient's own libidinous side is suppressed but also libidinous object relationships are disabled. Feldman (2000) reached the opinion that the satisfaction of the death and destruction instinct is not in the destruction of the object but in the fact that the object is precisely not dead or destroyed; it is kept in a state of permanent lifelessness. He says the main aim 'is not to destroy life completely but to take the life out'. The patient feels a conscious pleasure and satisfaction in attacking and distorting the creative work of the analyst and also his own thinking. These attacks are not solely of a defensive nature but contain feelings of triumph and omnipotent power over the objects, which are kept in a very tortured state; they are related to perverse mechanisms, which accordingly can be frequently observed in narcissistic patients.

In some seriously disturbed patients one finds an accumulation of the above-mentioned defence mechanisms, which all work in the same direction and lead to negation and destruction between good and evil, love and hate. Good and bad qualities cannot be sufficiently distinguished from each other and are internalised as a mixed experience, which results in the inability to evaluate both internal states and impulses as well as external events, and this leads to a state of great insecurity and anxiety – even panic – in the company of other people. This combined experience quality which is reflected in the patient is projected into the analyst in the transference so that the analyst – because of his/her identity with mixed good–evil qualities – can no longer be evaluated by the patient. From the patient's view, he is being approached by something unknown that has unfathomable, confusing and often enough evil intentions. The 'evil' intention consists in an interpretation which attacks the patient's defence system; it mingles with the 'good' intention of letting something become experienceable in order to set a development in motion. The patient cannot distinguish the good intention from the bad, and his reaction to this 'mingled phenomenon' is extreme rejection and retreat because he cannot think about it. For both the analyst and the patient, the treatment is a common search for the 'offspring' which could contain the idea of good, which are hidden in the objects and feelings of the patient in a defective, tangled and mingled form and from which – via transformation processes – perhaps the ability towards forms of love can be developed.

The rejective attitude of the patient leads, in the countertransference, to considerable problems, which show the analyst his limitations. As not only the patient but also the analyst brings his own damaged internal objects into the analysis session in order to restore them, a stagnation at status quo level questions his ability for reparation and leaves him open to anxieties that he might not be able to counteract his destructive impulses because his loving powers are inadequate.

When speaking of the congenital ability or disability of the self, thera-peutic pessimism should not spread. But the question is how, under the circumstances of a serious narcissistic defence, anything can change at all, if all the loving emotional qualities are felt to be deceptive and threatening and are only intended to seduce the patient to open his inner doors so that his ideas can be destroyed. Freud, Klein and others rightly stress the power of the destructive arsenal of instincts as a limiting factor to analytical treatment. Whether a therapeutic process and, as a result, psychological growth have taken place can often only be judged at the end of an analysis. At the beginning of treatment involving a patient who is as disturbed as the one I am going to introduce below, the results are completely open, and working together is a risk. Accordingly, Rey's statement gains significance when he underlines that

> it is at that level of representation that psychotherapy takes place, a vital place to influence by environment the future development of the psyche. That is why we must take and give full importance to the phantasies of the patients, to know how they have gone astray. They tell us what to do, how to treat and do reparation.
>
> (Rey 1994: 73)

Clinical report

In the following report from the analysis of an approximately 27-year-old patient I would like to show, on the basis of clinical material, the beginning of a way of moving out of his destructive narcissistic omnipotence towards the awareness of an analyst who became important for him and set in motion something like a wish for loving, albeit only for short moments and in a very rudimentary form.

His life comprises three areas: (1) the analysis, (2) his life at home and with his partner, (3) his work. He has no friends and does not seem to miss them; he does not miss anybody, which sometimes takes on autistic characteristics.

In the early phases of the analysis the patient spent his free time drinking alcohol, masturbating, looking at prostitutes and pornographic literature, etc. This has gradually lessened and seems almost completely to have been replaced by an excessive interest in literature, which he fetches in stacks from the library and whose content appears to be connected to the current analysis situation. He counters any attempt on my part to connect his obsessive concern for literature with our sessions with scornful rejection or with the categorical statement: 'I have said all there is to say on the subject – there is nothing more to say.' In time I began to get the impression that he was tearing up the literature he had, in a kind of frenzy, and piecing it together again, sometimes in a bizarre way. And more and more frequently

I experienced in the sessions that by misunderstanding and distorting my interpretations in a similar way, he made me speechless and there was a danger of him driving the analysis into a dead-end situation. In these cases he reminded me of the infant described by E. O'Shaugnessy, an infant that lies under a tree all day, without making a sound, and stares at the leaves in a hallucinatory state of self-sufficiency. That is how the patient stared at the torn-up texts, in which his feelings and needs lay in pieces, and he was free of the hunger for a breast/an analyst/friends. He played out his need for 'no analyst' as a re-enactment of a traumatic situation in his early infancy in which, at the age of one and a half years, he had to be admitted to hospital because of unaccountable vomiting after the birth of his brother. When, after four weeks in which he had no contact with his parents, he came home, he did not recognise his parents any more; he effectively no longer had any need for them. At the age of four he had to put up with a total of three younger siblings, all of whom – just like his parents – played practically no role, however, in the course of the analysis. He seemed to have no family.

He was all the more completely fulfilled with notions of a colleague at work, B, for whom he had developed a delusional infatuation at the beginning of treatment and with whom he was permanently preoccupied, while I became an observer of his delusionally excited interpretations. With this delusional love he had created an omnipresent object which was able constantly to satisfy his desire to have somebody, so that in external reality he did not have to feel this need. I gained the impression that he had survived the *infantile* separation situation by means of delusional notions which could house both his 'good' and his 'hateful' feelings, and that this omnipotent solution became the model for his frequently recurring delusional infatuations in later years. It was not until much later that he gave hints from his preoccupation with literature as to what was probably his central unconscious fantasy: for him and me to become a wedding couple as a result of the analysis. The relevant literature goes back to the Veronica myth, which is related by the Greek poet Kallimachos and which centres around the description of the wedding night of the king and the queen. On the morning after the wedding night, both show traces of the night before, in which love and violence mingled. The king had cut the queen's hair, perhaps to make her less attractive while he was away. When the patient was sixteen, he had fallen in love with a Veronica – probably delusionally – but she had a boyfriend, who died some years later, probably from kidney failure. Just under nine months ago, in a holiday break, he resumed his previous excessive search for all available literature on the subject, and since then his thoughts have revolved around this again and again.

When his infatuation with his colleague, B, slowly declined, and with it his perverse fantasies, which were based on equally omnipotently created objects, he again and again moved in the above-mentioned bizarre world in which he took texts out of context and stuck them together arbitrarily to suit his own needs. He now only occasionally talked about his reading expeditions, in order carefully to avoid being confronted with the reality which he saw represented in *my* view of his text processing or in *my* interpretations, because that could have questioned his system and raised the danger of subsequent fragmentation or impending depression. Just like in a dream he recounted:

He was walking with a group of people in a town, which only consisted of façades, however. Behind these façades there was a beach and a deep-black sea. He walked along the beach with a woman. He climbed up onto a bridge; it was not clear whether the bridge spanned the water. It was high time to return. A man sat naked on the ground; he was talking and demonstrating how many languages he could speak. The patient looked at his penis. The man noticed this and said it was not at issue.

At this stage I would merely like to point out how the patient uses narcissistic means to repel his impending depression.

The patient had settled into his narcissistic omnipotent world and conveyed through his extreme passivity in the sessions how useless I was for him. In the countertransference I felt like his evacuated infantile part: left alone, as I had no sufficiently co-operative counterpart in the patient and because he had shut me out of his thoughts; he left me without orientation; his absolutely controlled speech did not allow me to obtain any hints as to his state or to develop any moderately accurate fantasies. His words came out briefly and sharply, like blows or knife cuts which were often very hurtful and degrading. His predominantly concrete way of thinking hid a permanent danger of misunderstandings, which forced me to be extremely cautious and held me in constant fear of choosing the wrong words – a fear that paralysed me over long stretches. His rigid transference allowed the patient to be seemingly free of anxiety when he was with me, while I felt terrorised by the permanent fear of the analysis being broken off. When the patient arrived, I gave him a scrutinising – almost penetrating – look in order to find out something about his mood in the minute facial movements or gestures. But he made himself impenetrable and inaccessible, and remained that way most of the time. For him I was someone who he viewed with extreme mistrust and who probably had evil intentions towards him. From his point of view, this idea seemed to be justified, but it repeatedly made me wonder whether I would have enough loving power in this treatment to create and maintain a counterpoise to the destructive impulses. Over long stretches I felt very miserable and was genuinely glad and relieved when he sometimes had a trace of friendliness on his face, which I did not want to run the risk of losing so quickly. I was trapped in his grip and was incapable of moving freely with my thoughts. Sessions in which there was a touch more contact were followed by even longer silence, which was at once an attack on reflection and experiencing as well as a result of it.

After two years a slight change became apparent in the sessions which were held before a two-week holiday break and which followed a period that offered somewhat more frequent opportunities to have moments of contact and interchange. He had not felt well over the weekend, and there was a long silence, which I interpreted to him as being a fear of speaking because he was afraid I could think he might have wished to have an analysis session at the weekend, but that if he felt such a wish it would only make him feel worse. Thereupon he conceded, 'It would probably have been good to have had an analysis session at the weekend.' He was able to admit to a feeling of having missed the analyst now that, with my interpretation, I had for a brief moment reached him in his libidinous strivings. His old defence set in all the more strongly, and for the rest of the session he was buoyed up and euphoric at the idea that he could be the winner of an international essay competition. Thus he manically and omnipotently denied the significance of the weekend break, which unconsciously implied a repetition of his hospitalisation as a child, and he saw himself as the winner when he abolished his parents/ analyst and replaced them with omnipotently created objects which are always present and can never be missed. However, he considered me the winner when I thought that he had wished for the analysis session.

Having come into contact with more loving feelings towards me, he was able in the ensuing sessions to observe himself and to impart something of his insight into his exciting, lustful, destructive infuriation with me. As a consequence, this also led him to perceive something of the hurt his attacks inflicted upon me and to approach – short-term – a feeling with a more depressive hue.

His perception of hurting me did not, however, lead to feelings of remorse or concern, but seemed to transform his guilt feelings into pursuing elements, against which he defended himself with great fury; and with this fury he had in his hands an effective means of preventing further inter- pretations from getting into him. His incapacity for reparation threw him – on the threshold to depressive feelings – back again into the paranoid– schizoid state and perpetuated the catastrophic inner world full of damaged objects. The destruction of his perception of his destructive impulses allowed him to continue his unhindered hate of all that was libidinous between us, from which he took out the life.

The last session before the weekend

Shortly before the session was due to begin, there was a funny episode with my cat, and I had to make an effort to get the laugh on my face under control before the doorbell rang. I didn't quite succeed.

PATIENT: *He began by saying that yesterday and today he had again and again been in a boisterous mood; otherwise he felt shattered and burned out. Then he was silent.*

ANALYST: *(That was one of his remarks, with which he announced that the session would be futile; he didn't make any move, either, to add any further explanation. I tried to get to grips with my feeling of resignation) and said that this seemed to mean that the part that wanted to examine and know what had just happened was no longer inside him; it was now in me, and he felt empty.*

PATIENT: *He said, 'I got the impression when I came in that you were quite exhausted. If you still feel like exploring, so be it. [This was extremely derisive. He paused briefly.] When I find you looking so exasperated, I can't help thinking of my mother and what it was like with her.' He went on to describe a mother who had always wept a lot and who had given lots of beatings. When she couldn't give any more beatings, she had wept because she felt that she was not getting the right support from the father. She had felt left alone and had withdrawn into the bathroom. Time after time the patient had found her there. In such cases he had felt some pity for her.*

ANALYST: *I said, 'When I seem to you to be so tired [he corrected me: shattered], you feel pity for me because you think I don't feel well, perhaps as bad as your mother. But something surfaces in you that becomes ironic or angry when I don't seem to be strong enough to take your blows. Perhaps you ask yourself whether I might not be quite exhausted with your pleasure in playing the "saying no" game.'*

PATIENT: *He said, 'I don't just want to romp about [the day before yesterday he had been able to perceive the "romping" part in him]. Everything I do apparently converges on the fact that I beat my mother, not the other way round, and that I project it rather transparently.' After a bit of to-ing and fro-ing about who beats who, he ended the session with the remark, 'In my mother's case, the solution to the conflict would have been to have fewer children.'*

Comment: The patient could not help but notice my cheerful face when we met. I think that in split seconds his seemingly not quite stable manic defence broke down; he seemed to feel shattered and broken by the happy expression on my face. These signs of cheerfulness let him know immediately that I had a source of happiness which was not him but somebody else; expressed in the imagery of the Veronica myth: the visible signs of the king's and queen's night of love-making were like blows, which he countered immediately by saying: 'You are quite exhausted and shattered.' With this sentence he made visible how he damaged me: when he pressed his denial into me with massive force, I was seized by its paralysing venom; I was only in a position to describe my condition but no longer capable of describing what happened in the session; he had paralysed my thinking, my peace, my containing function. With his denial he had taken away my cheerfulness and made me into a shattered object, exhausted by his attacks. At the beginning he immediately denied the intolerable perception that I was obviously in a different state than he was; that is, that I came from other relationships, that I led an existence which was independent of him and which apparently did me good. It can be assumed that, with the denial of my being separate from him, he was able to avoid above all painful feelings of being excluded, not knowing, being helpless, going to hospital, falling into the deep-black sea. He created an immediate identity between his idea and his perception of me; a third possibility was negated. In doing so he closed up a space for possible experiences, of which he did not know how he would be able to bear and digest them, other than in the usual fashion. He replaced the sudden impression of having a cheerful analyst in front of him with a version of me that fitted me into his omnipotent thinking, and the effect on me was so successful that I at once forgot my happiness and did not get it back again in the session but, instead, remained completely wrapped up with the patient. In a powerful way he had made me into the depressive mother/analyst who he could now save from her depression. He did away with the entire introductory scene by means of negative hallucination and replaced it with his version of us: an analyst/ mother – neglected by her husband (the source of well-being) and therefore depressive – who he can save with his love, a very greedy, possessive love. With his omnipotent, manic deliverance/reparation fantasy he succeeded in both him and me losing sight of the fact that he was the originator of my sorrow, and in this way he seemed to escape the paranoid fear of my taking revenge for his attack. All I could say was that I was at least willing to investigate what happened, but his denial of my internal references (the sources of my laughter and cheerfulness) had the effect that in the session I did indeed remain cut off from them.

Monday session

Half of the time passed in absolutely motionless silence, in which he seemed to be in me with his senses and synchronised my slightest movements with short, almost unnoticeable movements of his own. By listening very closely he seemed to crawl into me in order to control me.

Finally he told me – reluctantly – that at the weekend he had first drunk a glass of wine with his partner, A; later he had emptied the bottle alone. Then everything had gone haywire inside him, and nothing but sexual desires and fantasies had flushed up inside him; for example, desires to look at prostitutes in cars or to constantly occupy himself with his colleague, B (to whom he had developed a manic infatuation at the beginning of the analysis). He had continually masturbated. Finally he had started to read and had come across a

*woman who reminded him of me. Thereupon the pressure had eased off
somewhat. He had kept telling himself that he would manage on his own but
did not want to lose his self-control again like that.*

Comment: Before the backdrop of the desolate weekend and his breakdown, the patient tried at the beginning of the session to take possession of
me through projective identification and to find in me a safe place again.

Under the influence of alcohol his earlier defence strategies had an easier
time gaining ground and putting him in a rather disarranged state. When he
drank a glass of wine with his partner, A, warmer feelings obviously sur-
faced in him, perhaps even the wish for a lasting relationship, which he had
hitherto categorically rejected. I know from similar situations, especially on
the main feast days, how difficult it is for him to tolerate a cosy
atmosphere; for example, he once bought a terribly puny Christmas tree, so
A sent him away with it again and Christmas was ruined. He understands
coming together in a cosy atmosphere as if A denied all that is negative
with a glass of wine and as if she wanted to eradicate all the difficult things
in the relationship. That is why a good feeling appears treacherous and
cannot be differentiated from a bad feeling. He said at a later date: 'When
love begins to play a role, there are only disputes and hatred.' Love and
hate mingle inside him to form a combined figure, which exerts terror and
attacks with all means his unconscious yearnings for a place where he is in
good hands. He feels compelled to deny such yearnings, and the fact that
they are missing seems to give him just as much security from pursuing and
depressive feelings as his insistence on having bad feelings. He had felt
closer to his partner, A, over a glass of wine, and I believe also closer to me
the week before with his wish for an analysis session. The perception of a
concrete, real trace of something third (the actual cat situation, and in a
general sense: peer group, psychoanalytic reference system, etc.) on my face
in the last session before the weekend seemed to materialise his fear of such
a combined figure, which at the same time represented the Oedipal couple
with their pursuing qualities.

Tuesday session

*He enlarged on which literary figure he had connected me with: with Hypathia
of Alexandria, the philosopher and mathematician who was killed by the
Christians because she was a heathen. He had thought to himself that that
was the reason why he had become calmer on Sunday, because the story was
so murderous and brutal. Hypathia had given lectures; he particularly liked
her interpretation of Plato, which he had copied from her a year ago. He had
not been able to find the book any more. And without any further explanation
he added, and he formulated this in a somewhat affected way, 'You [analyst]
were charged by me with value.'*

ANALYST: *I said he was letting me know that he appreciated my 'interpretations' of the last sessions, and they obviously had a value for him and were a good experience with me. He had come to the sessions and had tried, together with me, to communicate on the interpretations (= finding meaning); in some way or other there had been a somewhat closer feeling with me. But then came the weekend break and I had withdrawn into another world, of which he was not a part; the good feeling had been lost and then all he could do was hate me and get excited – and at the same time calm himself – at the thought that I was being tortured and finally killed.*

PATIENT: *After a while: that sounded strange to him when I said he would like to kill me, although he did see the point. In his exciting thoughts there had been a lot of sex and violence, and with a very determined voice he added, 'But that didn't have anything to do with you.'*

Comment: With this last decisive remark, 'that didn't have anything to do with you', the patient split his destructive emotions away from his loving emotions towards me. It seemed to me that, in splitting between good milk and bad breast (the analyst's interpretations and the analyst's person), he was trying to maintain the idea of something good in order to avoid further fragmentation. Good and bad experiences with one and the same person – an analyst who had been able to give valuable interpretations and an analyst who was not there – had come together, were immediately fragmented and got the patient into a confused state, which served to defend him from depressive contents. The various female figures of the weekend contained the fragmented parts of me, to which he related with different fantasies. I assume that the aspect of Hypathia or the analyst which was helpful was the one that was not sexualised, not perverted, not delusively distorted or murderously attacked; that is, was not a mixed element: that was the aspect of me that could give interpretations, that was independent of him with thoughts of my own. That is why this part had been able to keep its value and take on the function of a third object, which again pulled him out of the highly excited and violence-ridden relationships to the other fragments.

Through manifold splitting, the patient again established his narcissistic retreat position, in which he now had the feeling I wanted to pull him into the mad world, 'sink my hooks into him' as he once put it.

The patient nevertheless seemed to have kept something of a good, non-pursuing figure in him, which some time later expressed itself in a wish that was completely unusual for him: when saying goodbye to his girlfriend, he wanted a 'proper' kiss instead of just a cheek held out to him, a cheek that – to cap it all – was covered with makeup. Also the request he made, under great strain and suffering, to have a replacement session seemed to give very cautious expression to his wish for 'more' analyst; that is, he began now and again to tolerate object-related wishes.

Summary

I have tried to describe some of the moments in the analysis of an extremely narcissistically withdrawn patient, moments in which he experienced himself somewhat more separated from his analyst and in which she took on an importance for him. As a consequence of his perception that he could hurt the analyst, depressively shaded feelings did surface, but his overwhelmingly pursuing guilt feelings prevented any possibility of reparation and threw him back into omnipotent defence forms which promised him protection from his destructive super-ego. This dynamic manifested itself, on the basis of his conscious and unconscious fantasies in the sessions, in transference/countertransference events and their complications.

In his breakdown he could not maintain a relationship to an analyst who was valuable on the one hand but, on the other hand, was not there over the weekend; that is, she did not represent a whole object with a sense-endowing potency. When the two categories 'good/valuable' and 'bad/absent' met, they broke into many fragments. He made contact with the part he felt to be good by splitting off all other qualities housed in the remaining fragments and, for a moment, succeeded in giving the idea of something good, without other elements mixed into it, a life-supporting function, in the sense that it saved him from further psychotic disintegration.

The patient's sentence, 'When *love* begins to play a role, there are only disputes and hatred', is manifestly exemplified in the course of the sessions. The ways in which the patient experiences and thinks move along the paranoid–schizoid organisational level described by Klein and show love in its respective fore-form as a delusive, greedy, possessive, manic, perverse (etc.) impulse. More creative and more fulfilling aspects of love are, in the transference–countertransference experience, at first only localised in the analyst, who again and again tries to newly generate her loving feelings, free of vengeance, in the form of patience, reliability, wanting to understand and who does not have to sink into disputes and hatred: therefore, in contrast to the patient, it is possible for her to muster up greater tolerance for feelings of doubt, persecution and ignorance, but also to show sympathy and love. Her inward reference to something third outside the treatment situation can help her to maintain a gestalt of what has developed within the session between her and the patient. However, over long stretches this proves to be very difficult, because being filled with projected aggressive contents during the sessions greatly hinders the necessary differentiation in the countertransference between one's own destructive aspects, those of the patient and the communicative elements – a differentiation which is often only possible after the session. The confusing feelings and the mixed-up elements projected into the analyst experience within her a transformation that places at the patient's disposal a more tolerant version of his feelings, with which he can identify. Thus a basis can be formed for a process of transformation in the patient which opens up to him the prospect of emotional and cognitive growth.

References

Britton, R. (1993) Fundamentalismus und Idolbildung, in J. Gutwinski-Jeggle and J.M. Rotmann, *Die klugen Sinne pflegend*, Tübingen: edition diskord.

Feldman, M. (2000) Some views on the manifestation of the death instinct in clinical work, *International Journal of Psycho-Analysis*, 81.

Freud, S. (1937) *Analysis Terminable and Interminable*. German edition: *Gesammelte Werke Vol. XVL*, Frankfurt: S. Fischer.

Hinshelwood, R.D. (1991) *A Dictionary of Kleinian Thought*, London: Free Association Books.

Klein, M. (1957) *Envy and Gratitude*. German edition: *Gesammelte Schfriften Vol. III*, Stuttgart: Frommann-Holzberg.

Rey, H. (1994) *Universals of Psychoanalysis in the treatment of Psychotic and Borderline States*, London: Free Association Books.

Rosenfeld, H. (1971) A clinical approach to the psychoanalytic theory of the life and death instincts: an investigation into the aggressive aspects of narcissism, *International Journal of Psycho-Analysis*, 52.

Segal, H. (1997) On the clinical usefulness of the concept of the death instinct, in *Psychoanalysis, Literature and War*, London: Routledge.

Winnicott, D.W. (1965) *The Maturational Processes and the Facilitating Environment*, London: Hogarth Press.

Chapter 13

No one to hold the baby

The traumatised individual's incapacity to love

Daphne Lambert

A few patients in my practice have caused me to think about the kind of defences that repeatedly smash up their capacity to become more conscious. This leaves them cut off from their ability to love. I want to explore the structure of these defences in their dual aspects. Firstly, how the purpose of them seems to be to protect the fragile early ego/self from unendurable psychic pain; secondly, the way in which these interventions cause splitting and dissociation within the psyche. The effect of these sadistic attacks is to stimulate repeatedly a re-enactment of the original trauma, and to cut the beleaguered evolving ego off from meaningful relationships. Any sign that the patient shows of connecting to any feelings of love or hate activates an immediate internal sadistic smash up of the patient's psyche.

The definition of 'trauma' that I will use is any experience that has caused an infant or young child unendurable psychic pain and anxiety. Thus, I understand the meaning of trauma to be that it overwhelms the usual defensive measures which Freud described as 'the defensive shield against stimuli' (Freud, 1920: 27). For instance, if something touches upon a complex in the patient they disappear, implode; or, alternatively, erupt into violent primitive rages which preclude any possibility of thinking about the cause of the disturbance. By complex I mean a repressed part of the self within the psyche which functions autonomously without connection with consciousness.

Trauma varies from an acute and shattering experience to more cumulative traumas of unmet dependency needs that accumulate to the point where they become the 'unthinkable' x–y–z (Winnicott, 1963: 90). Acute anxiety is a secondary symptom which precludes the possibility of thinking about what is going on. This could reflect fears of disintegration and unnameable dread associated with threats to the cohesion of the core self based upon an inability to trust or love another person. Thus, dissociative mind psyche defences can severely interfere with an individual's capacity to sort out what feels good or bad as well as what to love and hate. Wilfred Bion postulated that the sadistic superego perversely attacks not only the infant's ego but all linking processes in the mind which would allow the child to experience a coherent self: that is to say, a self that can discriminate.

Bion states in his book, *Learning from Experience*:

> to learn from experience alpha-function must operate on the awareness of the emotional experience; alpha elements are produced from the impressions of the experience, these are thus made storable and available for dream thoughts and for unconscious waking thinking. A child having the emotional experience called learning to walk is able by virtue of alpha function to store this experience. Thoughts that have originally to be conscious become unconscious and so the child can do all the thinking needed for walking without any longer being conscious of it. Alpha-function is needed for conscious thinking and reasoning and for the relegation of thinking to the unconscious when it is necessary to disencumber consciousness of the burden of thought by learning a skill.
>
> (Bion, 1962: 8)

He goes on to state:

> that if there are only beta-elements which cannot be made unconscious there can be no repression, suppression, or learning. This can create the impression that the patient is incapable of discrimination. He cannot be unaware of any single sensory stimulus: yet such hypersensitivity is not contact with reality.
>
> (ibid.)

Continuing:

> Attacks on alpha-function, stimulated by hate and envy, destroy the possibility of the patient's conscious contact either with himself or another as live objects – this state contrasts with animism in that the live objects are endowed with the qualities of death.
>
> (ibid.)

The psychological defence of dissociation allows external life to continue, albeit at great internal cost. Patients who have experienced acute trauma or cumulative trauma at an early point in their lives tend to have a split-off part that lives in a fantasy world. The purpose of living in a time warp seems to be to create a protective shield for the traumatised part of the psyche. The effect this has is to make it impossible to process feelings and to benefit from meaningful close relationships. They are, according to Winnicott, in the grip of the false self and have become 'do it yourself' personalities unable to trust or love either themselves or another person. The blotted out, but not forgotten trauma continues to haunt their inner world in the form of nameless dread. Bion understands this state as being locked in an inner world saturated by beta-elements. These feeling-toned complexes stem, in my view, from the archetypes and can act autonomously within the psyche as critical voices, frightening bullies, thugs, monsters, or, in the case of very early trauma, global catastrophes. The energy fed by dissociation and driven by hate seems to stem from a very primitive level of aggression which evolves out of an absence of any capacity to make connection with a loving relationship.

For Jung 'affect is the central organising principle of psychic life' because it links together the different compounds of the mind by giving each of them a feeling tone. If early traumatic experiences are accompanied by a strong affect, all the associated perceptual and mental elements of that experience will accumulate around this affect, thereby forming a 'feeling toned complex' (Jung, 1907: para. 82).

By 'archetypal', I refer to the inherited part of the psyche, structuring patterns of psychological performance linked to instinct, a hypothetical entity irrepresentable in itself and evident only through its manifestations. Complexes are unconscious and therefore take on archetypal dimensions. Since an archetype encompasses both love and hate, regression carries with it the hope of a reworking of the original 'feeling toned complex'.

Jung writes:

> A traumatic complex brings about dissociation of the psyche. The complex is not under the control of the will and for this reason it possesses the quality of psychic autonomy. This autonomy consists in its power to manifest itself independently of the will and even in direct opposition to conscious tendencies; It forces itself tyrannically upon the conscious mind. The explosion of affect is a complete invasion of the individual, it pounces upon him like an enemy or a wild animal.
>
> (Jung, 1928: paras 226–7)

Donald Kalsched's (1996) book has helped my understanding of how these processes work and I have drawn upon his ideas for this chapter. Later on I shall be giving some dreams from work with patients that demonstrate the unconscious defensive complexes that the psyche has set up at a very early point in their lives. Their purpose seems to have been to protect the fragile early ego/self from unendurable pain, but for the patient their inner world seems to be experienced as a living death. They have become prisoners of their own merciless and murderous defences which cut them off from any possibility of loving connection with another.

Patients with a split-off part feel in constant danger, which causes them to live anxious, and often diminished and fragmented lives. This was illustrated in the dream of a patient who had not felt emotionally held from the beginning of his life. During an analytic session he had picked up a difference in my mood. I think I may have been a bit preoccupied over the preceding session where the patient had been very angry. He assumed that I was angry with him, which was his constant fear. This was not talked about or even thought about consciously, but was turned into a smash up of the analysis as well as himself. It included an attack upon his own neediness, which resulted in agonising feelings of shame. After he left the session he had a brief idea never to return to analysis. His horror at the dream that followed this session brought him back. I had been left in the dark over what he had been feeling. I shall call the patient Mr B. I want to concentrate upon the dream and try to make sense of it within the theoretical framework of this chapter. The dream took place the night before my patient was due to return after the weekend break that followed the incident. I am grateful to him for agreeing to the use of his dream and for his collaboration with this part of the chapter, which we worked on together.

B borrowed my beige mini from outside my house. He was driving down a motorway in it. He realised that a huge aeroplane was going to land on the road behind the mini. His terror was about the idea that the aeroplane could crush the mini. He threw himself out of the beige car into the ditch. The beige mini went on driving autonomously without a driver. Later on he arrived at the police station to claim his lost car, only to find that the car had crashed on the spot where the 'accident' had happened. But it had acquired colour and turned into a white and blue mini. It was a complete write-off – smashed to pieces. The beige mini had disappeared down the road without a driver. He realised, to his horror that the car he had borrowed was not my car but my uncle's, a man with a short fuse, so he was filled with guilt and anxiety about my survival of my uncle's rage.

This dream reveals the violent internal trauma that is constantly being re-enacted within this patient's internal world. In the dream, the beige mini could represent a neutral space – that is, my beige consulting room, the analytic container. Within this space the patient had become able to recover previously unavailable feelings of neediness, accompanied by terror and dread about his neediness. He was constantly fearful of my anger, which carried a projection of his own unconscious anger. B and I have, in this long analysis, been trying to create a language to describe mindless panics that sweep over him and annihilate him. He was able to tell me, with long hesitations, that his feelings must not be felt or looked at or shared with another person. So I am left in the dark as well. B has always used the couch to hide himself and be invisible. When he picked up my slight preoccupation with the previous patient, he projected his murderous rage into me via projective identification. The huge black aeroplane in the dream seemed to represent the archetypal rage from the self that had swept over him. It also represented memories of his father angrily looming over him in his cot and terrifying him. B and I came to realise that this internal catastrophe is constantly being replayed within his psyche as well as in his analytic sessions and represents his hatred of me because he needs me so much. It also reveals how this murderous rage is repeatedly smashing up his fragile ego. Thus the beige mini continues on its way empty without a driver, the destroyed thinking space of the analysis. The blue mini seems to represent the smashed-up feelings. This leaves the child part of the psyche – that is, feelings that must not be felt – thrown in the ditch. The rage that the diabolos/protector turns onto him when he experiences a feeling is to tell him that it is all his fault – he is useless – he should never have been born. The police station seems to reflect the cold dissociated place that the patient has been catapulted into. He is without the containment of a caring ego-building analytic space ('I will leave the analysis') which leaves him totally alone. The defence rules, feeding him with more negative poisonous thoughts, the basis of which are that he should trust no one. This space has autistic features since there are no people in his internal world, except himself as a helpless child and his caretaker/abusers as a terrifying internal presence. In this state loving feelings cannot become metabolised and rendered meaningful because linkages between different parts of B's psyche have been violently smashed up.

Kalsched describes the state where there are no words for feelings most graphically:

> This process might be imagined as analogous to the circuit-breaker in a house. If too much electricity comes in, ie: more than the wires of the house can carry without burning up, then the circuit blows and the connection to the outside world is annihilated. But in the psyche the process is more complicated because there are two sources of energy – both the outside world and the inner world, the unconscious. So when the psychological circuit-breaker trips, it shuts off both, the person must be defended against dangerous stimulation from the outside world, but also from those needs and longings which arise from deep within.

> (Kalsched, 1996: 23)

The feeling aspect of the patient's psyche has been dumping in a time warp, ditched in a transitional zone, an autistic state where neither imagination or living in external reality is available. B becomes totally unavailable. I feel confused, helpless and full of anxiety. More recently I have begun to feel increasingly angry and frustrated.

However, the fact that Mr B is beginning to dream seems to me to be hopeful. Bion's formulation of the emergence of the alpha-function, where dreams become available, is helpful. My hope is that an endurable transitional space is becoming a possibility. Within this space imaginative activity connected to good and bad experiences, as well as loving and hating feelings within the analysis, could begin to be worked through and gradually replace the lonely and sterile world of inflation and autistic deadness.

Leopold Stein introduced the idea of archetypal defences of the self in 1967. He proposed the idea that the extreme negativity and self-destructiveness of some patients who are primitively defended might be seen as an attack by the primal self upon parts of the ego that it has mistaken for foreign invaders. This creates a repetition compulsion which gets nowhere. Stein points out that

> proper immunological response depends on the ability of the body's immune system to accurately recognise not-self elements and then attack and kill them. In defences of the Self, parts of the personality are mistaken as not-self elements and attacked leading to self destruction in a kind of auto-immune disease.
>
> (Stein, 1967: 97–111)

For Kalshed the idea that the response of the body's immune system to net-self elements is like an Aids of the psyche could reflect Stein's point of view, bearing in mind that Aids is an acquired immune deficiency syndrome. Bion's understanding of these defences – that is, an inability to convert beta-elements into alpha-elements, which precludes the possibility of making a loving connection with another person – seems to be highly relevant.

Michael Fordham (1974) extensively explored damage to the early self in his seminal paper 'Defences of the self'. He considered that an infant had defences before ego development, which he observed through his work with infantile autism, where catastrophic impingements of negative psychic stimuli were defended against by autistic encapsulation and total withdrawal, even on the first days of an infant's life. This could, in his view, completely cut the baby off from any capacity to form a loving relationship with another.

Fordham noticed that – for a baby that is exposed to pathological stimuli – a persistent over-reaction of the defence system may start to take place (attacks on not-self objects) and

> may become compounded with parts of the self by projective identification, so that a sort of auto-immune reaction sets in; this in particular would account for the persistence of the defence after the noxious stimulus has been withdrawn. [When this happens] . . . little or no inner world can develop; the self integrate becomes rigid, all later development based upon maturational pressures result not in deintegration but disintegration and the predominance of defence systems

leads to the accumulation of violence and hostility which is split off from any loving communication with the object that may take place.

(Fordham, 1974: 91)

For Fordham the core self cannot be destroyed. The problem lies with the amount of primitive hate that has been activated within the psyche that precludes any loving connection with another. This can cause the patient to test out his relationship with the analyst to the utmost. For Fordham there is a hope that working with this primitive hate in the transference could lead to transformation and an increased capacity to trust. This then leads to internal change and releases new capacity for love and feelings of aliveness in the patient.

In my work with B it has become clear that part of the self has been encapsulated in a time warp which has led to constant repetition of his unconscious feelings of violent unconscious hate that then turns on him in the form of self-hate. Recently he realised that because he often feels *so awful* it does not necessarily mean that he should masochistically perceive himself as *an awful person*. This revelation has begun to make a difference to the way he perceives himself in his internal world.

A patient I shall call F was full of sadism, masochism and hatred. She tried to repeat these dynamics in her relationships and later within the analysis. Her internal fantasy was of an idealised world of fusion and oneness with a mother who was not separate. This has eventually led the patient and myself, during a long analysis, towards the painful understanding that this fantasy is a defensive manoeuvre driven by hate, to protect her from the realisation that her mother had not been able to act as a container for her baby feelings. She managed to plug herself into her mother's internal world and anticipate her every need, which meant that she substituted her mother's needy baby for her own baby needs. F is an intelligent and intuitive person. She is sensitive to people's changes of mood, which can set off states of panic and terror in her because her internal defences preclude any possibility of twoness.

My countertransference was very uncomfortable since I found myself shaking with rage in her presence. The force of these feelings was driven by projective identification, that is, putting into me feelings she was not able to feel. An important part of analytic work with borderline patients is for the analyst to be able to digest and process within their own body the emotions that the patient is unable to feel. It is necessary to be the vessel, the alchemical container the patient had not originally had in infancy.

F has gradually come to realise that she will never be able to make the analysis fit her fantasy of blissful union with an idealised mother in the concrete way that she has always longed for. To give up this fantasy of fusion has been a shattering blow for her. The loss of control she experienced following this realisation catapulted F into violent eruptions of primitive rage within the analysis, leading to a psychotic episode which took her into hospital. These rages, previously unconscious, had been directed onto herself in the form of self-harm as well as the smashing up of her vulnerable ego/self baby. This was her 'self-care system's' way of avoiding the unendurable reality of not having had a maternal container for her feelings of love and hate. She came to realise that the wiping out of the analysis during these rages, wiped out her fragile ego again and again and was constantly replicating the original trauma. This is where Kalshed has been helpful at unpicking the elements of the primitive global hate which emanates from the core self. F realised that a move towards a productive breakdown of the self-care system by experiencing pain within the analytic space, where she was not alone, was marginally preferable. She also began to discover that she could work through painful early memories of loss and increasingly stay with painful feelings without being plunged into a catastrophic hard, empty autistic space where her defences had previously thrown her. For this complex, anything that threatened the cohesion of the self was experienced as a catastrophe and was rejected by the self-care system. To borrow Stein's (1967) analogy, the immune system had not been wired up correctly for any sort of separateness. By the time F left the analysis she had become capable of gratitude, as well as becoming more able to feel love and compassion for her own internal needy child.

What is the psyche trying to achieve? It would be possible to say that an internal agency stemming from the self brings the patient into analysis. The unconscious defences then set about repeatedly throwing the analyst and patient back to the original problem. In the case of F, since any degree of separateness was equated with catastrophe, the complex had repeatedly taken her back to the original complaint; namely, that she had suffered massive impingement of a noxious kind when she was born. This had introduced F to separateness in a traumatic way, causing a massive split with autistic features. In our work together she and I have realised that her mother had left her to cry for long periods as she followed the techniques of the child guru of the time, Truby King. It is also clear that her mother had suffered from severe depression all her life.

The constant repetition over fifteen years offered the detective in the analyst time to think about and process what the self was trying to bring into consciousness. Thus, the repetition compulsion (Freud, 1926) was continuously playing out the original trauma of abandonment in all its ramifications. It was also testing out the analyst's capacity to survive while making sure that the analysis made haste slowly. The problem in this analysis seemed to be how to contain my despair and keep alive the prospect of the patient ever being able to move into life. It gradually emerged that my task was to process within my countertransferences F's mother's depression. I found that I had to wrestle with feelings of violent rage with F, as well as hopelessness and despair over my inability to love her. The question that I constantly asked myself was: are these constant regressions malign or do they have a therapeutic purpose? I believe that in this case the repetition compulsion served an important purpose which was needed to protect the patient's sanity.

I shall call the next patient Kate. For the purposes of this chapter I want to concentrate upon Kate's self-care system and the difficulties that she and I faced in attempting to penetrate it in a way that she could find half-way endurable.

When Kate was born, her advent did not have the effect upon her mother that the family had hoped for. She did not create a miracle and make her mother better. Kate lived with her father, mother and sister in primitive conditions in a cottage in her paternal grandparents' garden. It was an extremely noxious environment, with a very young mother depressed and crying while her father exploded into frightened rages. Kate's mother was severely depressed, in and out of mental hospital where she had shock treatment. Kate often went with her. Her mother had received some kind of psychotherapy which she had found helpful. For a long time I thought Kate had been sexually abused by her father. But she and I have now come to understand in the course of our story-making that her father's angry shouting went up her vagina, and was experienced by her as a rape. The psychic atmosphere was exacerbated by the fact that both her parents smoked heavily.

Kate has recovered three important memories from her past, where she gave up hope and died. The first was when she fell down the steps of the cottage at two years of age and was knocked out. The family noticed that she did not cry when she came round. The second event occurred when she was on the school bus at five years of age. Coming home, she fell down the steps of the bus hit her head and again did not cry. Her grandmother asked her if she was all right. She knew that she was dead but could not find any words. The third event was when she was about six years old. She went into town with her sister and an aunt who was about fifteen years old and an unpleasant and sadistic individual. They walked about town for what seemed hours. She didn't know how to survive it. The sister and aunt, as was their wont, mocked her for her slowness. She did not complain. When they got to the bus, all she could think of was that she could sit down at last. The aunt said, 'Where's your money then.' She had no money and was immediately overwhelmed with shame. There was no money to pay for her bus fare, so they had to walk home. She remembered turning into a zombie, all alone and without hope – dead.

In the words of Samuels *et al.* (1986), for Jungians 'The Self represents an archetypal image of an individual's fullest potential and the unity of the personality as a whole. The self as a unifying principle within the human psyche occupies the central position of authority in relation to psycho-logical life and, therefore the destiny of the individual.' It was the self that came to Kate's rescue, creating a fantasy world that she could retreat into. In this world she had a friend: she talked to Jesus. This was a secret perfect world that no one else knew about. When she was about two years old she went on holiday to her aunt and uncle who lived near the sea. She was malnourished and in a bad way. We think that her mother had been admitted to hospital. There were other visits to these relations when her mother went into hospital again. Eventually, when she was seven years old she went on yet another holiday and stayed ten years. Her mother never went home again as she was no longer wanted by the family. Kate wondered what she had done to be sent away like her mother.

I want to concentrate upon Kate's internal world, which contains a lost autistic child without a mother. Second, there is a fantasy world where she is secretly a beautiful princess. Third, there is the defence of the 'self-care system' that is in control of the dynamics of her internal world. Its aim has been to protect her from consciousness and reality. In her dreams, critical motorbike thugs in black leathers repeatedly smash up any connection to her vulnerability and neediness. The force of the attacks seems to be driven by violent murderous hate. The care plan devised for her by the internal saviour/diabolos was: 'You can live in a fantasy world where nothing can touch you and be a princess, but it is our secret and, by the way, the lost autistic child must stay in limbo. Any attempt to get her out will be severely punished.' Kalshed has helped to metabolise these abusers in the analysis in a way that Kate found helpful. But Kate did ask for help when she came into analysis.

The task of the useless analyst, replicating the useless parents, seems to have been to rescue this child from her internal thugs. This led to violent attacks of contempt and scorn upon the analysis. 'See how you can survive our attacks upon this useless analyst. Let's see what stuff you are made of. Let's see if you are reliable. See if you can survive this load of shit.' There was no place for love or emotional connection in this violent, hating internal world. Love could only be imagined as a wonderful idealised split-off fantasy where she could have spiritual love affairs with pop stars and her doctor, who for the purpose of this chapter I will call JC since he was perceived by her as her saviour. My problem was that I kept falling asleep, which I think reflected how much of Kate was not emotionally present in the room. I got into a lot of trouble over my neglect.

Kate came into analysis via her doctor, who thought that analysis could help her. He had recognised that she was very ill. The result was that the ill part of her felt seen for the first time and she fell in love with him. I call the object of her love 'JC' since in no way did Kate see him as a real person. She was convinced that he reciprocated her feelings. This love was, she told me, adult, sexual, and perfect, nothing to do with my rubbish about her lost child. This love was not to be touched or analysed because it would undermine the perfection of the relationship.

In the analysis the split was manifested as an idealised fantasy love affair between a beautiful woman and a perfect man; a secret – except that I knew about it. I was useless, continually subjected to critical attacks over my inability to see an invisible, beautiful, silent, wordless and perfect woman who was in the room but would have nothing to do with me. My job was to chip away at the coal face and internally process the pain of her feelings of uselessness, which the patient projected into me via projective identification. Provided I stuck to my role as the useless analyst I could be tolerated. I got kicked about as she had been. The fantasised love affair between her and JC, who seemed to be an idealised internal father, became more difficult to sustain as she revealed to him the wonderful love affair that they were having and how it was not a fantasy. JC understandably became more and more worried about his position as a potential abuser, while I became increasingly concerned that if Kate's fantasy was dismantled prematurely she would go psychotic. This, I think, was her unconscious fear as well. There were times when I felt flooded by the psychotic emotions in the room, which had the effect of blowing my mind to pieces. I came to realise that this was how she felt inside. I concentrated on recovering and reconstructing previously sealed off memories of her early life so that she and I could begin to build a coherent story of her life. It was a slow and painful process. I often felt as if I was literally cleaning up her bottom and processing the faeces and urine that she attacked me with.

At the same time, Kate's disillusionment with JC gathered momentum. Kate surprised me about two years into the analysis by telling me that the relationship between her and JC was interfering with the analysis. Nevertheless I was still useless and a lost cause. She went through a prolonged period of mourning his loss, which took about two years. This phase of the analysis contained a working through of the ramifications of the repetition compulsion (Freud, 1926). She went back many times to try to convince JC that they really had been lovers and had had perfect intercourse. During these professional interviews JC tended to withdraw emotionally, which she found incomprehensible and most painful. I was not able to touch upon the delusional nature of this relationship because I was immediately turned by her defences into an envious critical thug. It seems to me that the number of times that I have been able to use interpretations throughout the long analysis has been minimal. This has sometimes had the effect of breaking up my capacity to think, which made me feel rather crazy since it was not possible to return and interpret Kate's delusional fantasies about JC. She insisted she wasn't mad, but that I was. Bearing in mind that her mother had been psychotic this makes sense as a working through of her original introjection of a crazy mother. My countertransference of accepting the role of the mad mother made it possible for me to process unbearable feelings through my body which Kate's mother would not have been able to do. I also needed to humanise within my reverie the power of Kate's unconscious hate towards her mother for her neglect and abandonment of her when she was a baby. What I think has mattered most has been that I became just about able to maintain a consistent and stable environment, which made it possible for Kate to process the discoveries that she was continually making for herself at her own pace and gradually to own her own mind. In a way it seems to me that it has been a self-analysis. Do I mean that this analysis is conducted by the self? It often felt like that.

Dream A. *Kate is up in a First World War Zeppelin with JC. They are partying and celebrating coming down to earth. The Zeppelin lands and Kate is in a hostel or brothel. Daff is preparing her to sleep with her husband, but Kate is four months' pregnant and wearing a broderie-anglais nightgown, a wedding dress. Now she is naked. She is afraid that she will lose the baby, which is JC's baby. She enters the loo crying; the floor is cold. She has lost the baby. Now she has to get on with her life. She feels desolate.*

I think that this dream speaks for itself. In October 1996 Kate said goodbye to JC. At the time of the dream it would have been four months. It seems that she began to give up her fantasy world at this point. This was a very worrying time in the analysis.

Dream B. [I will call her husband Jack] *Kate is at her husband's place of work. A mutilated fox is trying to make friends. There is also a mutilated pig in a loo. Then she is walking in Cornwall with Jack. They find a funeral stone with figures of children on it. It is a child's grave. The weather turns grey and it gets darker. As she stands with Jack, by the grave, feeling sad, she starts to float upwards. She is calling Jack to get her down. But she is too far up and finds herself cradled in God's arms. God had pulled her up to heaven.* [She woke up and wondered if she was dead and realised that she really wanted to live. She went back to sleep and dreamed] *Back at Jack's workplace. Two children, a boy and a girl, are rubbishing gay people.* [Feelings] *Gay people are stupid, ugly and useless.* Kate said that they could be people who are intelligent, articulate and attractive. [This seemed to be an accurate description of herself] *After this she seems to have fallen out of the sky into a toy box, a Loobie Loo rag doll with a voice, crying.*

I am left speechless. I eventually say that it sounds as if her looby loo rag doll was finding her voice at last. Kate had often looked like a rag doll while lying on the couch – flat, empty and limp without substance.

Looking back now at Dream B I can understand that the mutilated fox and pig represent the analyst. I can now understand how mutilated and kicked about I felt and how sadistically I was treated by her internal thugs.

It is worth noting that the patient's husband was subjected to the same sort of contempt. The reconnection with God the Father, as opposed to Jesus, could be understood as an agency from the self that represents the possibility of unconditional parental love. After this encounter Kate had the strength to stand up to her internal thugs. She seemed to be speaking up for tolerance and the respecting of difference. However, she continued to tell me that she could not love me and that in some way I was deeply flawed. I understand this to mean that she still had difficulty in balancing her love and her hate for me. More recently I have been able to process my anger with her and become able to agree with her disappointment in me without rancour. There can even be jokes about my imperfections. The feeling tone of these exchanges is less sadistic. I cannot be her mother, so I am useless.

The first patient, B, who dreamed about the car crash had little sense of having any primary needs of his own. In times of stress he retreated into an autistic space where he became an abandoned baby all alone, while living in a secret grandiose fantasy world. The reverse side of this was that he experienced himself as a shit baby that should never have been born.

The second patient, F, discovered in her analysis that her autistic ego-baby had been abandoned in a rocky autistic place where 'it felt emotionally dead, empty, abandoned'. She depicted this internal state in her drawings as being trapped in a rocky chasm, which she has come to understand as representing the archetypal stony mother. In the analysis, this baby's feelings of intense rage were projected into me via projective identification and needed to be processed within a human relationship. This involved my processing the murderous rage from the self about the neglect that she felt that she had endured. This rage has helped the patient and myself to reconnect with the abandoned baby. The hope was that this baby might eventually be persuaded to return to the imperfect world of feeling and reality. However, there has been constant regressive pulls that have prevented any improvement in the patient's quality of life. More recently F became able to access her love for me, as well as for her own internal baby, and it became possible to terminate the analysis.

The third patient, Kate, found herself in an analysis where she used me and JC as her internal agents of the self. All the idealised good was invented in JC while all the bad stuff was invested in the analysis. The dreams seem to show that the self represented by God had decided that it was time for this patient to come down to earth and live in the good/bad world of reality. Recent events connected with a bereavement, as well as a conscious wish to come back into the world and try out new experiences, have caused her to relive the original loss of her mother and the intense pain that had previously been somatised. I do not think that she could have sustained this level of grief without the underpinning of a long analysis, and I feel more hopeful that her psyche could be moving her towards life.

In this chapter I have wanted to demonstrate that when an early moving relationship between a mother and her baby has not been established, defensive measures are set in motion by the agency of the self whose aim is to protect the vulnerable evolving ego/self from catastrophic pain. The negative side of defences of the self are that a part of the self becomes split off and unavailable to consciousness, forming a complex. This means that a damaged part of the ego/self has been incorporated into a defensive system that resists any attempt to grow and move towards greater consciousness. Thus any efforts that the weakened ego makes to move towards a loving relationship with another are constantly subjected to internal smash ups filled with hate, replicating repetitions of the original failures that took place within the patient's inner world. In my experience with these three patients I found that my task was to develop a capacity within myself to experience their hate and to gradually become able to process their internal murderous feelings rather in the way that a mother, under normal circumstances, holds a screaming baby through states of deintegration. In this case, because of the original failure in maternal bonding, these states carried with them fearful memories of disintegration and madness. There had been no one to hold the baby. Therefore for the analyst there is the extra task of processing primitive feelings connected with a defensive system erected to protect a small baby in danger of psychic disintegration. The violent rage that results from this failure, in my view, needs to be transformed within the analyst's psyche. It was necessary for me through my understanding of each patient's story, to process their feelings of primitive hate and the attack upon love that resulted before I could begin to be able to experience feelings of love towards them.

All three of these patients had suffered from severe deprivation of love at an early point in their lives and were possessed by feelings of hate which violently attacked life itself. At the other end of the spectrum they all in their different ways suffered from feelings of worthlessness and acute low esteem, coupled with suicidal thoughts. Yet all three shared in common the overwhelming hope that analysis could help them to seek out and recover their own capacity to love. The enormous energy from the self has propelled them, in their different ways, into a very long analysis and sustained them through long years of painful work. I am grateful for their generosity and co-operation over this chapter.

References

Bion, W. (1962) *Learning from Experience*, London: Karnac Books.

Bion, W. (1967) 'Attacks on Linking', in *Second Thoughts*, New York: Jason Aronson, 1977.

Fordham, M. (1974) 'Defences of the Self', *Journal of Analytical Psychology*, 19(2).

Fordham, M. (1976) *Autistic States of Mind*, London: Routledge.

Freud, S. (1920) 'Beyond the Pleasure Principle', in *Standard Edition* 18, London: Hogarth Press.

Freud, S. (1926) 'Inhibitions, Symptoms and Anxiety', in *Standard Edition* 20, London: Hogarth Press.

Jung, C.G. (1907) 'The Psychogenesis of Mental Illness', in *Collected Works* 3, London: Routledge & Kegan Paul, 1960.

Jung, C.G. (1928) 'The Therapeutic Value of Abreaction', in *Collected Works* 16, London: Routledge & Kegan Paul.

Kalsched, D. (1996) *The Inner World of Trauma*, London: Routledge.

Samuels, A., Shorter, B. and Plaut, F. (1986) *A Critical Dictionary of Jungian Analysis*, London: Routledge.

Stein, L. (1967) 'Introducing Not-Self', *Journal of Analytical Psychology*, 19(2).

Winnicott, D.W. (1963) 'Fear of Breakdown', in C. Winnicott, R. Shepherd and M. Davis (eds) *Psychoanalytic Explorations*, Cambridge, MA: Harvard University Press, 1989.

Chapter 14

The love/hate couple in the primal scene

The problem of dyads and triads in relationship therapy

Martin Stanton

Do love and hate contain the fundamental forms of our impulsive and interactive *relationship* to the world, so that with love we affirm and add to our world and with hate we deny and subtract from it? Are love and hate in this sense the most basic of our drives?

Since Freud, the whole issue of the function and status of such drives has been fraught and controversial. A major reason for this has been a conceptual confusion between instincts and drives: a subtle and complex distinction intimated by Freud between instinct (*Instinkt*) as a primary body-sourced impulse (such as self-preservation and the continuation of the species) and the drive (*Trieb*), which derives on the whole from instinctual bases, but elaborates itself independently from them. For Freud, sexuality provides the main category of drives because it is based in some fundamental biological way in the instinct to continue the species, but develops very different orientations through a specific psychological elaboration of the instincts incorporated in the erotic. In Freudian terminology, the erotic therefore 'leans on' (*Anlehnung*) the instinctual impulsion to continue the species but produces different psychological strategies to maximise the pleasure and minimise the displeasure – which is where in some basic way love and hate face up to each other as opposite game plans. The question still remains open whether love and hate are instincts – with love as the life-force and hate as death – or whether they are drives, in which case they are inextricably enmeshed in the erotic, and need to be approached differently as 'leaning on' instincts, and branching off in different directions through the psychological input of the drives.

Freud attributes the presence of this open question to the borderline character of the concept of the drive. He tells us that 'The concept of the drive . . . lies on the frontier between the mental and the physical' (Freud, 1905: 168). The drive process may originate in body stimulus but their actual aim varies according to 'the demand made on the mind for work' (ibid.), so, for example, the body stimulus involved in sexual excitation may construct and inhabit different erogenous zones following the different psychic process that shapes the drive. Amongst other things, this helps him explain why and how hetero-erotic and homo-erotic drives follow different erogenous elaborations even though they both originate hypothetically in a single organic stimulus.

The problems – and the open-ended nature – of the Freudian model arise with issues of the reality status of the drives. The elaboration process of the original stimulus introduces the possibility of a purely psychic form of reality which is functionally distinct from the organic level of instinct. In this scenario, reality is inevitably bifurcated between instinct and drive – and this bifurcation in turn raises a whole series of basic epistemological questions about how to determine the reality status of any given psychic production: for example, how to distinguish fantasy as a purely psycho-logical form from some hypothetical primary instinctual or physical reality. A central issue here is whether it is possible for anyone to extricate themselves from the drive process in which fantasy plays a formative and elaborative role. And if thought were nominated as the main vehicle of this extrication, then it would have to constitute through its own process a third reality beyond the original bifurcated reality of the drive – a transcendent process intimately linked to the status and function of interpretation.

The relationship of the thought process to the drive process has gener-ated a fraught and continuing debate within psychoanalysis. It is parti-cularly striking how the variant contemporary protagonist positions in this debate have chosen to view the thought process as replicating in some essential way the form of a primary instinct. Much has been made, for example, of the replication of sexual and intellectual intercourse. Thought here works on the tension between the body-sourced stimulus and the drive elaboration of it, which mirroring the original bifurcation follows two forms: the male thought which penetrates and enters the erogenous body-site of the drive, and unlocks the various associative chains that bind the drive to its erotic 'aim' (see Derrida, 2000); and the female thought which absorbs the tensions engendered by the bifurcation of drive and instinct reality, and implodes its binary logic to produce diffuse clusters of 'mean-ing' interconnecting various erogenous sites (see Irigaray, 1985).

In contrast, others have observed a form of primary replication between the digestion of food and thought: Bion's notion, for example, that the psyche 'operates on the principle that evacuation of a bad breast is synonymous with obtaining sustenance from a good breast' (Bion, 1967: 112), so that the process of thinking evacuates the psyche of accumulations of bad objects. In this model, the mother receives these bad objects through projective identification. Her capacity to accept them, then respond thera-peutically (re-digest them), and then feed them back in a form that the infant can tolerate form the basis of thought communication. If the mother fails to provide this re-digestion and feed back of the tolerable food for thought, the internal objects of the child become stripped of goodness: 'The internal object *starves* its host of all understanding that is made available' (ibid.: 115; my italics).

Despite the privileging of different source instincts for thought, psycho-analytic approaches do share common assumptions about the dynamic process of thinking. First of all, there is the common assumption that thinking negotiates communication between the inner and outer world. In object relations in general, for example, thoughts produce a *relationship* to the world, in which emotions or affects orientate thought towards *objects* along the lines of basic *drives*, and enable the construction of a directional and differential space in our *experience* of the world. In this way, distinctions can be made between pleasure in love and pain in hate; which in turn enables further distinctions between the inner source of the drive to love and hate, and the outer 'object' to which it is aimed. It can then supposedly be determined both whether the drive has a *real* object or a *fantasy* one, depending on whether it has an intrapsychic aim (like self-gratification), or an interpsychic aim (such as the production of pleasure or pain in others).

Secondly, there is a common assumption about the *form* of the thought process: thought follows either a projective trajectory or an introjective one (though there is important dispute over which takes priority). This not only enables a to-and-fro dynamic between inner and outer world, but also introduces a binary structure to the thought process itself. So thought progresses through the proliferation of dyads: the inner/outer dyad is endlessly reproduced in other dyads ranging from male/female to child/adult and mother/father; or from pleasure/pain to good/evil and love/hate. The basic assumption in all these cases is that you can only think about these things in couples.

Let us turn now specifically to the love/hate couple. Freud's seminal discussion of love and hate in 'Instincts and their Vicissitudes' (Freud, 1915: *SE* 14) provided four fundamental propositions for subsequent elaboration and debate. First, the proposition that love and hate furnish a unique and crucial example of the transformation of a psychic drive into its opposite, in so far as 'it is particularly common to find both these directed simultaneously towards the same object' (ibid.: 133). In this context, love and hate both mark out the entire feeling-range of drives, and also install a directional current between them which generates a whole spectrum of emotional ambivalence. Secondly, Freud proposes that within the very psychic production of this emotional range, hate is an older object relation than love:

It [hate] derives from the narcissistic ego's primordial repudiation of the external world with its outpouring of stimuli. As an expression of the reaction of unpleasure evoked by objects, it always remains in an intimate relation with the self-preservative instincts ('Trieben ["drives"] der Icherhaltung'); so that sexual and ego-instincts [Ichtriebe und Sexualtriebe] can readily develop an antithesis which repeats that of love and hate.

(ibid.: 139)

In this dynamic, hate both operates a primary reactive response to the external world and enables its affective integration into psychic function.

Thirdly, following on from this, Freud proposes that the love and hate drives only occur at a later stage in psychic development when the ego is able to negotiate 'whole' objects, by which he means whole persons as opposed to component drives orientated towards the breast, food or the faeces:

> We might at a pinch say of a drive (Trieb) that it 'loves' the objects towards which it strives for purposes of satisfaction; but to say that a drive (Trieb) 'hates' an object strikes us as odd. Thus we become aware that the attitudes (Beziehungen ['relations']) of love and hate cannot be made use of for the relations of *drives* (Triebe), but are reserved for the relations of the *total ego* to objects.

(ibid.: 137; italics in original)

In this sense, Freud talks of 'object love' or 'object choice' only when whole objects/persons are involved (see Laplanche and Pontalis, 1980: 301). This proposition has become particularly controversial because it implies that love and hate involve the integration of the total ego, so are absent from earlier infantile psychic life, and also from more dissociative or psychotic states. Winnicott notably took up this aspect of Freud's proposition, suggesting both that 'there is a theoretical earlier stage in which whatever the infant does that hurts is not done in hate', and that there is a primal relational disparity between the mother and infant in this respect (as the mother can hate and the child cannot) (Winnicott, 1987: 201).

Finally, Freud proposes that love and hate are not a simple antinomy – a creative couple of opposites that promote the subjective emotional integration of reality – but rather that their opposition has a tripartite form, and that 'loving' adds two additional oppositional levels to the original love/hate one: namely, loving/being loved, which negotiates being active or passive in relationship (which he sees as central to the development of narcissism); and loving/hating, taken together as an antinomy, form another separate opposition to unconcern or indifference (Freud, 1915: 133). Following the previous proposition, Freud emphasises that love and hate in this way enable 'our mental life as a whole . . . [to be] . . . governed by *three polarities*, the antitheses subject (ego) – object (external world), pleasure–unpleasure, and active–passive' (ibid.). For Freud, this final position was observational and scientific in the sense that the subject/ego acquired the capacity to think independently about what the original couple were doing and were all about. Misleadingly perhaps, Freud called this the 'primal scene' – the scene in which an infant 'observes' (which includes the 'whole object' sense of 'being able to think about') her/his parental couple's communicative and sexual intercourse. The problem is that this scene rarely emerges in the observational and generative sense that Freud intimates, precisely because any objective (whole object-related) sense of communicative intercourse in the observation is inevitably undermined by fantasy (which may well include the observation that the primal scene never in fact took place).

So why does Freud introduce a third into the love/hate couple? He needs a third to form a new dyad – copulators/observers – from the original one (mother/father copulating). But the position of the observer in this second dyad is compromised by the contradictory associations of 'knowledge' embedded within it, notably the presence of indifference (as separating the love/hate couple), and the quality of observing the object in its entirety (as supposedly in scientific observation). Both these associations fail dramatically to concord with the position of the child as observer in the primal scene. In fact, a child is hardly likely either to 'know' what the scene is about (particularly what the couple's drives are about or 'aim' to achieve), and indifference is not the first, exclusive or predominant emotional response that springs to mind.

This point precisely led Ferenczi to criticise Freud's introduction of thought and objectivity as third elements of the primal scene:

> The child is not the scientist who wants to know where children come from; it is interested, of course, in this question as it is interested in astronomy, but it is much more desirous of having the admission from parents and educators that the genital organ has a libidinal function, and as long as this is not admitted by the parents, no explanation is satisfactory for the child.
>
> (Ferenczi, 1955: 70)

The thrust of Ferenczi's polemic – apart from inverting the standard perspective of this scene by foregrounding the adult's view of the child – is to privilege the erotic over the instinctual, and to separate the experience of this scene from the position of objective or indifferent observer. Furthermore, Ferenczi proposes replacing the love/hate couple with more enmeshed (*Verwirrt*) and complex interactive and interpersonal forms of psychic process, notably the languages of tenderness and passion (*Die Sprache der Zärtlichkeit und der Leidenschaft*). The language of tenderness involves the pre-Oedipal, pre-linguistic psychic process of the child; whereas the language of passion involves Oedipal triangular space and is 'policed' by the formal and regulatory properties of language and thought. For

Ferenczi, the crucial feature of these two languages, or experiential registers, is that they are not readily inter-translatable – even though they obviously enmesh and intertwine in everyday life. Above all, the love/hate couple is absent from the primary language of tenderness. The love/hate couple only emerges in the primal scene as a result of the adult input of passion:

> it is the *guilt feelings* that make the love-object of both loving *and* hating i.e. of *ambivalent* emotions, while the infantile tenderness lacks as yet this schism. It is hatred that traumatically surprises and frightens the child while being loved by an adult, that changes him from a spontaneously and innocent playing being into a guilty love-automaton imitating the adult anxiously, self-effacingly. Their own guilt feelings and hatred felt towards the seductive child partner fashion the love relation of the adults into a frightening struggle (primal scene) for the child. For the adult, this ends in the moment of orgasm, while infantile sexuality – in the absence of the 'struggle of the sexes' – remains at the level of forepleasure and knows only gratifications in the sense of 'saturation' and not the feelings of annihilation of orgasm.
>
> (ibid.: 167)

What in fact Ferenczi discovers in the love/hate dyad is the disruptive presence of the observer – including all the self-monitoring issues raised by 'objectivity' like 'what's really going on here?' or 'what's the *point*?' Such thoughts may well disorientate or even annihilate the primary saturation of tenderness – thoughts which challengingly transform orgasm into a thought process rather than one primarily based in body sources.

Ferenczi's crucial innovation here was to intimate a notion of functional gaps in communication between couples which actually occur in communicative exchange as a result of a structural mismatch between a primary sensorial (body-sourced) level of psychic drive and a secondary thought level. These gaps occur in interpersonal exchange, so are dynamically formed in the communicative progression (such as gaps in the flow of conversation), and consequently involve performance issues (such as who is speaking or looking at whom to what effect) – hence the singular appropriateness of referring the primal *scene* to all communicative exchanges between two or more protagonists. In this context, Ferenczi implies that the separate intrapsychic input of the individuals involved may provoke different dynamic forms of communicative gap within the group. These gaps cannot be approached simply through analysis of each of the individual's psychic process, but demand a group perspective in which individual positions enmesh rather than inter-translate. Individuals will take in bits from the communications of others and psychically process them to different effect and then reintroduce them into the communicative exchange. What gets absorbed or lost depends not on the formal exchange of thoughts but on the group transference dynamic where primary process elements intrude and dislocate the performance.

This implies a radical revision of both the supposed coupling function of thought and of the nature and function of transference. First, the Oedipalisation of the primal scene – and its introduction of the third observer as constitutive of the primal couple – needs to be replaced by more complex and dynamic forms of group interpersonal process. The space in this primal scene is not fundamentally triangulated, but open-ended and punctuated by vortexes in the communicative flow. Similarly the progression of thought is inadequately conceptualised as a two-way psychological process from inner to outer world which is constructed around the (intercourse of the) primal couple; but thought process needs rather to be seen as a series of *effects* generated within a communicative process. I have explored elsewhere two such forms of effect: the *bezoaric effect*,[1] which articulates the psychic process of trauma; and the *caddis effect*,[2] which articulates the psychic process of primary defences (Stanton, 1997: 69ff.). In the bezoaric effect, the various sensorially based unconscious elements of traumatic experience shift, realign and transform through communicative exchanges in therapy. In the caddis effect, pre-formed chunks of primary sensorial material cluster to form unconscious defences in communicative exchange in therapy.

Another site for fundamental re-conceptualisation is the transference. Clear dynamic restrictions are imposed by the notion of two autonomous transferences projectively lined up opposite each other in any communicative exchange – with the analyst claiming privileged access to observer status through interpretative use of projective identification. What this misses is the complex dynamics of the interactive space between communicators in which various projective and introjective processes enmesh, as well as occupy simultaneous separate and common ground. There is a shared group unconscious process here which needs to be acknowledged. For example, to view a Freudian slip (parapraxis) in a conversation as solely symptomatic of the speaker's transference – and only interpretable on that level – necessarily obscures the open-ended group interactive context in which 'mishearing' might connect to another protagonist's unresolved issues intimated by prior communicative exchanges. The slip may well indeed enmesh in group condensations and displacements, such as when conversations continue to discuss something (a person, animal, object, film, etc.), which is mutually wrongly identified – so ricochets in various displaced and condensed directions – but continues for some time to make 'sense'.

The crucial issue here is the shared space in the middle of the communication. Rather than viewing this as a one-way track in two directions (or three, if you include the observer), it is more productive to locate all the unconscious processes in the middle of the communicative exchange, and to look at their form and function (such as displacement and condensation) in these terms rather than as simple psychic derivatives of one party to the exchange. How then to conceptualise such a shared space? If we extend into this communicative group context Freud's metaphoric term 'leaning on/anaclisis' (*Anlehnung*) – in which two protagonists might push something in the middle in different directions – a range of other options emerge: first of all the notion of interactive *filtering*, in which various primary unprocessed psychic material might pass through, but be condensed or displaced by the other, or left unprocessed, and even in any case bounced back; secondly, the notion of *stalling* (see Lacan, 1991; Lagache, 1993), where the actual interactive pressure from mutual introjective/ projective transference processes closes down the communicative flow; and thirdly, the notion of the *vortex*, where some 'thing' is emptied or sucked out of the communication.

All these options involve to varying degrees the opacity or viscosity of the transference. The opacity or viscosity is generated by the unconscious unassimilated elements in the shared space of the transference. Laplanche's couplet of the 'embossed' transference (*transfert en plein*) and the 'hollowed out' transference (*transfert en creux*) opens up important new dimensions in this area (Laplanche, 1999: 214ff.). The 'embossed transference' articulates the intrusive pervasion (or *intromission*) of unconscious unprocessed material from one side to the other of the communication, which immediately forecloses further interpretative work. A good illustration of this might be a mother's outburst of anger towards her child, which the child fails to understand or process but which obtrudes into the child's own psychic processes. The child's subsequent image production might then become 'embossed' by the mother's anger, in the sense that introjected unprocessed elements of this anger will disrupt and distort in specific ways the child's thinking (see Scarfone, 1994). At the other pole of the couplet, the 'hollowed out' transference is provoked by the absence of any immediate intrusion of emotional input, which foregrounds a different connective response of intrigue, and the wish to explore further things that appear both enigmatic and denying. Within this binary framework, two specific scenes emerge: the incandescent or enigmatic image, which threatens, or even succeeds to possess you and take you over; then the hallucinatory scene which challenges you to add things to rearrange dissonance, or unresolved equations, which has provoked endless thought about what's enigmatic or missing in (a) thought.

In summary, these speculations suggest a small and contained site for the love/hate couple in the group-transference process: transference-love and transference-hate occur only at the integrative thought-pole of the communicative process, and are provoked by whole persons in their socially identifiable bifurcated positions (such as mother/father, adult/child, etc.) (Laplanche, 1987: 242ff.). But underlying this love/hate couple is a primary sensorially based level of transference whose effects are fundamentally dissociative. This level is not founded on couplings, but on the transference effects (such as the bezoaric and caddis effects) of dissociative communicative transitions (provoked by the processes of filtering, stalling, and the vortex).

How then might love and hate be variously framed in the transference dynamics of clinical work? Superficially, they are obviously framed dyadically, in so far as the analyst/patient transference is assumed to be modelled on the parent/child one, and its dimensional space is calibrated around the poles of love (positive transference) and hate (negative transference). The love/hate couple set out the relational limits of the original couple(s) of analyst/patient, parent/infant. To add a third observer position to this original *copula* effectively closes off the dyadic communicative intercourse through an observation (by a third) of their relationship. The relationship therefore not only becomes the third equal partner in a new triad but this triad also closes down the open-endedness of the flow of the original communicative intercourse with an interpretation. The interpretation of their relationship (on a scale somewhere between love and hate) integrates the original communicative copulation into something that can be known, assessed and processed, as opposed to simply being registered on a sensorial level. The crucial factor in the triad is therefore knowledge, based on the supposed independence of the observer. The knowledge of the observer – displayed above all through interpretation – effectively closes (down) the creative free-play of the intercourse of the original couple.

There are three basic reasons why the couple offers a particularly appropriate context in which to explore the love/hate drives. First, in the Western tradition, couples tend to describe their relationship in terms of the love/hate spectrum: typically, couples come into therapy because they have significant reasons to question the love between them, or even come to hate each other in various ways. In this context, relationship therapy attempts to unpack the dynamics of these various love/hate feelings between the couple in terms of the transferences operative both between the couple themselves, and between the couple and the therapist(s). Secondly, the couple as the 'patient' in therapy inevitably reactivate the triangulation of the primal scene: the therapist(s) directly observe the intercourse between the couple (which provides the main focus of the therapy). In this way, the couple in therapy compacts or pulverises the transference – a factor frequently cited in arguments against the very use-value of relationship therapy. It is important to note here that to describe this pulverisation or compacting of transference as 'splitting' simply recuperates the assumed primal dyad, as opposed to exploring more complex and dissociative transference forms. Thirdly, the addition to the therapeutic dyad, which in theory could be either the partner or the therapist, implies some later secondary process added to a more primal one: the couple, for example, were engaged in their intercourse prior to the arrival of the observer(s) – how could they (any side of the communicative exchange) ever know about this, in the sense of link up to all the sides and enclose the exchange in some knowledge of the relationship as it supposedly operates? The practical question here is why add at all?: why not stay with the classic therapeutic dyad?

To reduce the couple to two individuals in their separate analyst/patient relationship would necessarily obscure important group dynamic features of the foursome in couple therapy sessions. First of all the reflective process in which the co-therapist couple reflect in conscious or unconscious ways features of the therapeutic couple's relationship (Mattinson, 1975); for example, strong tension or disagreement (hate) or strong concordance or bonding (love) between the co-therapists may mimic and form along the transference lines between the therapeutic couple.

Secondly, to argue for two separate dyadic transferences inevitably closes down the potential group transference space between the four participants into either a dialogual (individual transference) or triangular form (based on the Oedipal intrusion of the parental couple). In contrast, the fourth position in the couple therapy group actually opens up the communicative space in important ways: the fourth position consolidates a potential observer space of various couple interactions – for example, one co-therapist can observe the effect of the other co-therapist's interaction with the couple; the fourth position also renders complex the place of 'knowledge' in the therapeutic exchange – for example, the couple cannot compete for the approval of a 'knowing' therapist when there are two therapists present who may well disagree.

I propose at this point to provide a brief clinical illustration of how the more thought-out (whole object or person) communications of love/hate between a couple are subtended by both the reflective process with the co-therapist couple, and by more primary sensorial forms of transference process (which engender the bezoaric and caddis effects). The case involved was a couple who for their independent professional reasons lived for half the year in separate countries, but scheduled an annual set time together in their flat in London. The wife had informed her husband on the telephone that she no longer loved him. He was both 'gutted' by this information, and refused to believe it, as he felt still loved by her and in love with her. They had had long 'amicable' conversations about the situation in which he failed to make 'any sense at all' of her feelings other than that they were part of her 'mid-life crisis' (a view she rejected as 'hateful'). They decided therefore to seek relationship therapy in London to try and find some 'common ground' on what might have happened. They entered this on the agreement it would be time-limited, as inevitably they were both scheduled to leave London in three months. They were referred to me and my co-therapist because we were known to specialise in time-limited relationship therapy. In fact, my co-therapist was herself due to return home to her husband and family in Latin America in five months, so the three-month format fitted well within her professional and personal schedule.

The couple both rigorously kept their contributions to the initial sessions to their different views of their love for each other – which she insistently and repeatedly declared dead, and he insistently and repeatedly declared alive, though 'not at the present kicking'. They both turned up immaculately dressed, as if going to some business or formal occasion, and both remained very calm, collected and 'professional' with each other, as if they were engaged in some debate with us to declare one or other of them objectively accurate about their descriptions of shared events and previously presumed 'common ground' in their relationship. We – the co-therapist couple – both tried independently on various occasions to point to their respective inability to understand, empathise or believe the other, so we increasingly felt together in our feelings of irritation and being stuck. In our review after the sessions, we started humorously to refer to them as the 'couple from hell', and came to realise that we were both provocatively reflecting (in counter-transference) strong negative – or hate – feelings towards them. These negative feelings bonded us together in sessions, and gave us a sense of sharing some basic response to the couple's inability to relate to the other's elaborate feelings about love.

After the fourth weekly session they both started to ask independently if we might reschedule the time of sessions for 'professional' reasons – to which we, the co-therapist couple, replied independently that such changes were not possible for our 'professional' reasons, namely, the therapeutic contract discussed in the beginning which set out the agreed terms on which we would meet, and also legitimately miss sessions. We both asked them how 'professional reasons' could lead them separately, for independent reasons, to abandon this contract, and give up this time-for-them-with-us together, to which we had all agreed? Here again, we – the co-therapist couple – felt very together in our resistance to changes in the scheduling of sessions, but felt differently and disproportionately concerned about how to manage their blatant disregard for any mutual sense of agenda. I felt more inclined to give more time to unpacking why this couple might want to hijack any mutual agenda – and my co-therapist felt a keen need to confront the issue of disregard of agreed grounds for our work together. We (my co-therapist and I) had quite a heated exchange about it – particularly about our own relationship as co-therapists (in which I was staying in London, so had all the time in the world, and my co-therapist was leaving, and so for her our common shared professional time was running out). After some discussion we came to realise that our own heated exchange was in important ways a reflection of their lack of common ground and failure to understand each other in sessions.

The priority they both gave to their respective professional agendas imposed unacknowledged limits on what they could hear, see and take in. They both maintained an unruffled tolerant air, and talked to each other and us as if we were missing some basic logic which they were patiently trying to lay out for us. This shared attitude separated them in a quite formal way: they would allot each other a space to talk, and hand over to each other as if they were chairing a discussion. This was also reflected in their overall general timetable, in which their 'home' in London was scheduled in between two independent professional spaces. They shared a common notion that they could defer any conflict or lack of understanding between them to some later time at 'home' – although this sense of home served simply to empty the emotional charge of differences operative between them when they were apart, rather than to evoke some 'knowledge' of shared common ground. This helps explain the poignancy of his feeling 'gutted' when she cited the incidents at 'home' where he had put work before sharing time with her. Following their shared logic, work could only formally exist before or after 'home', so, paradoxically, there was no room to negotiate some shared space or common ground for work in their 'home'.

This paradox was variously reflected in the co-therapists' sense of shared space in the sessions. On one level we both felt they allotted us together some empty formal function as a couple without actually engaging with our relationship to each other. We both found ourselves emphasising the different things we had independently said, as we felt they reduced everything to couple statements. They even disregarded our irritation with each other in sessions when they tried to renegotiate the schedule of the therapy – which served to heighten our sense of our own emotional conflict in contrast to their shared cold logic. On one occasion when my co-therapist had brusquely interrupted me to state categorically that there could be absolutely no negotiation over times of sessions, he simply commented to her in a disaffected way that he had just realised that she was not wearing her wedding ring. She had never actually worn a wedding ring, but an opal ring which she was still wearing. In our discussion of this, it emerged that he had assumed we were married, but seemed disinterested in pursuing what the ring might say about the co-therapist relationship. In contrast, he declared himself 'gutted' again when his wife pointed out that he had in fact failed to notice that she had taken off her wedding ring prior to coming to the session.

In short, the reflection process here formed around a separately organised couple transference, which in important ways obscured and/or foreclosed the individual transference dynamic. This couple transference formed around the particular dynamic in which this couple negotiated their relational space, notably the paradoxes surrounding the (lack of) space or time for their independent work in their home. It is significant in this context that they both felt compelled to negotiate this in terms of love, which followed an exclusive logic for both of them which both placed it outside their everyday life and was denied access to any shared emotional space. The reflective space in the co-therapists' couple transference consequently and responsively formed in the hate pole of the dyad. The co-therapists were united in irritation and frustration at the absence of shared space in the unconscious collusion of the couple's logic, but were equally denied any other space than a formal vacuous one which reinforced the specific time limitations of their professional relationship.

To illustrate the more primary sensorial forms of the transference which subtend the reflective process, I propose now to explore the time, place and function of a dream in this therapy. The night after the ring incident in the therapy, the wife had the following dream, which she raises in the next session:

I am in a queue in a theme park – I think it is Eurodisney in Paris – but it looks very small and compact, and has high wooden fences all round. I am with a very young boy of about six, and I am holding his hand. I am suddenly struck that he looks very like you Martin [i.e. me]. *You are looking around, completely disinterested, and I am afraid you are going to run off. I look around though, and am reassured that there is not very far you could go. I am very anxious too that the ride we are queuing for might scare you, but you seem quite calm about it all. I am then actually on my own in the carriage in the ride we were both waiting for. The carriage is a cross between a roller-coaster and a helicopter – it floats, hovers around, then plunges up and down. There are two drivers in front. One is Bruce Willis, who seems very confident and relaxed and turns round to smile at me; and the other is you again Martin, only you are older, actually older than you are now, and you are staring ahead and looking very anxious indeed. Bruce and I look out in front and see you, Chloe* [my co-therapist] *waving frantically and happily at us to greet us, and we wave back, but then suddenly the carriage swerves out of control. Martin struggles at some steering wheel* [which I have not seen before] *to get the carriage back on track, but then I see that Bruce is tugging in the other direction at another wheel, and that he actually wants to crash into you Chloe, and kill you. I shriek and scream and jump on his back to try and distract him, but we crash into you. There is then a blue sky above me and calm. I see a crunched-up block of metal in front of me like the way cars are crunched up in scrap yards. I see there are different coloured tubes sticking out, like exhaust pipes, and they are a dark and burned colour in the midst of this shiny crunched aluminium. I feel reassured and even happy that there is no one in this crunched mass, but do not know how I know this.*

First of all, following my previous speculations, this dream was not approached by the co-therapist couple as a route to understanding the wife's position (in the marriage and therapy), but rather as a site for group exploration through free association of what might be happening between us all. In this context, we did not immediately invite the wife to free-associate around the details of the dream. First, we asked the husband for his response, and he curtly replied that he 'hadn't got a clue' what it might mean, implying that her very introduction of the dream might be some strategy to upstage him ('professionally') in the therapy. It was all part of her 'mid-life crisis'. He initially found it very hard to accept her dream as common ground. Following this preliminary transference stalling, Chloe (my co-therapist) and I set out briefly to explore our own communicative exchange as a co-therapist couple around our own first reactions to the dream. My own first reaction was to ask the group how they felt about me shifting in the dream between an indifferent child to an older 'goodie' trying to avoid a murderous turn of events. And Chloe's first reaction was to ask the group why she might be the main person that Bruce wanted to kill.

The wife felt dispossessed by all this, and claimed (more or less unconsciously) centre stage with a central revelation. First, that she had visited Paris whilst a student and had had an affair with an American student there. She had become pregnant by him, and returned home to inform her lover (and future husband). Her lover was 'gutted' by this revelation. She felt and explained to him that she would not have become involved in this affair if he had told her he loved her prior to her leaving on the student-exchange visit. He felt 'guilty and inadequate', and offered to adopt the child, but she decided to terminate the pregnancy without discussing it with him. In retrospect, they both felt literally 'gutted' by this, but resolved independently never to discuss it again together – that is, until it figured associatively in the dream in this way. Henceforth there was this empty 'gutted' space between them that was associated with love, but remained impossible to negotiate until the option to renegotiate or reconfigure it reflectively through the co-therapist couple re-emerged in therapy.

In this context, Chloe wondered associatively in the session why she was substituted in the second half of the dream for both me and a six-year old boy, and why, in this function she had to be killed off. In our post-session discussion we also explored ways in which this might reflect our own anxieties about the end of our own professional couple relationship. Was I in some specific configured and reflective sense avoiding termination in the same way? The bezoaric process here variously attempts to negotiate the trauma of termination through the absence of love – literally perceived as 'gutted'. In the reflective process there can be no love between a professional couple – their lack of love leaves them 'gutted'.

The caddis – or defensive sides – of the bezoaric process here were associatively explored in the therapy through the figure of Bruce Willis. Bruce Willis occupied considerable time and space in the sessions, first of all because he was American (like the wife's student-lover) – so inevitably became provocative in various political ways to our multi-national-cultural small couple-group – and also because he is/has been variously cast in various heroic/salvation roles in contemporary film culture. In the dream, this role seemed suddenly inverted towards an aggressive mission to destroy Chloe – in short, a polar shift from love to hate. In our long associative exploration of this, we actually got stuck in endless discussion of various scenes from Bruce Willis films which we could mutually recall (though not necessarily agree in detail). Then, post-agreement (that is, following some sense of a negotiated knowledge-space), we moved on to look at how these scenes might help us identify and work with areas of resonance, and to move on from our stuck-state.

We talked first of all about *Armageddon* – which they had both seen independently but talked about on the phone – a film in which Bruce Willis 'saves' the world from an asteroid attack, though is left in an inverted paradoxical sense sustaining and 'preserving' his daughter's past sexual relationship (an observed event – or *copula*) with her secret lover (though the father knows but formally disavows this perspective all along until the tragic and traumatic finale). But then our therapeutic group moved on to discuss *The Sixth Sense*, which all of us had seen – but our couple had seen it in London last time they were 'home' – but never discussed together before the therapy session. In this film, Bruce Willis – a celebrated (child) psychologist – is shot by an ex-patient, but continues to treat a damaged child in a one-parent family. Willis (Malcolm Crowe in the film) is about to make love to his wife when she realises there is an intruder, who proceeds to shoot him. Through our independent re-view of the film, we all came (for obvious group-observer transference reasons) to focus on a crucial scene in the film where Willis/Crowe returns 'home' to his wife to tell her he loves her. In this scene, she is asleep, turns over, and a wedding ring falls off – which to his surprise he discovers is his. At this point, he begins to realise that he is/has been actually dead, and is/has been resuscitating through the child–patient relationship some extrasensory perceptual sense of his love for his wife, and his formal connection to her as his wife. The child–patient relationship subtends this marriage, as it is both a professional relationship that ends murderously (despite love), and the source of knowledge about life and death (the central dyad that negotiates 'termination' in every relational sense for them).

It is neither important here to go into the rich and complex associative detail of this dream nor to come to some closure or interpretative conclusion. It is more valuable in this context to appreciate how the couple–group–therapeutic dynamic senses in (or introjects) 'primal scenes' in Bruce Willis films in an attempt to find 'common ground', which part-fails, leaving some (unconscious) part to be reprocessed. The caddis effect here employs some preformed cultural product (Bruce Willis) as a defence against loss of love, but the bezoaric effect then proceeds to unpack and de-digest the details of the caddis defence work to gain some 'knowledge' of the damage already done. This is encapsulated in the dream-work in the shift within the crunched-up block of metal to the awareness of the different coloured tubes sticking out from it.

In conclusion, I would like to suggest that love and hate as a dyadic relationship carry all sorts of third-party risk – not least the potential trauma of becoming an observer, or, even worse, the speculative promotion through an Oedipal gamble (which triangulates the situation) of an inner-child-based prediction of the outcome of parental intercourse, whereby one side of the couple is inevitably killed off by someone or something unknown (or unconscious). In this primal scene, various forms of termi-nation might well become favoured fantasy sites, but never actually form into real practical options for coupled-up punters. Love and hate in this primal scene promote a later, deferred, more complex, whole, sophisticated and often unacceptable resolution to the problem of accepting a third: a resolution that founders on the more diffuse, pulverised, and disconnected body-sourced sensations any incognisant infant bestows on its parental carers, or their co-therapist-couple reflectors. In *The Sixth Sense*, the child, Haley Joel Osment/Cole Sear asks Bruce Willis/Malcolm Crowe the central question: 'How can you help me if you don't believe me?' In such cases, in asking the question, the child (between the couple) must inevitably feel (s)he is right against the adult(s)' common perception. Bruce Willis/Malcolm Crowe actually reaffirms the exclusivity of the parental couple by telling his wife that there is no room for another in their love dyad: 'You were never second ever . . . I love you.' No such 'wise baby' demanded belief or intruded as an observer in our co-therapist couple-space (see Ferenczi, 1955: 135–136). In her/his place, there was an absence which silenced the intercourse. Neither of them could bear to allow space between them for the child aborted long ago.

Notes

1 The bezoaric effect is an analogy based on the production of the bezoar stone, the calculus that develops from the progressive regurgitations of camels, antelopes and llama.
2 The caddis effect is an analogy based on the caddis insect's elaborate construction of spectacular cases for defence purposes (see Duprat, 2000).

Bibliography

Balint, M. and Balint, E. (1961) *Therapeutic Techniques in Medicine*, London: Tavistock.
—— (1968) *The Basic Fault*, London: Routledge.
Bion, W.R. (1962) *Learning from Experience*, London: Heinemann.

Bion, W.R. (1967) *Second Thoughts*, London: Heinemann.

—— (1970) *Attention and Interpretation*, London: Tavistock.

Britton, R. (1989) 'The Missing Link: Parental Sexuality in the Oedipus Complex', in R. Britton, M. Feldman, E. O'Shaughnessy (eds) *The Oedipus Complex Today: Clinical implications*, London: Karnac.

Deleuze, G. and Guattari, F. (1972) *L'Anti-Oedipe*, Paris: Editions du Minuit.

Derrida, J. (2000) *Dissemination*, London: Athlone Press.

Duprat, H. (2000) *The Wonderful Caddis Worm: Sculptural Work in Collaboration with Trichoptera*, Boston: Leonardo/MIT Press.

Ferenczi, S. (1955) *Final Contributions to the Problems and Methods of Psychoanalysis*, London: Maresfield.

Fisher, J. (1999) *The Uninvited Guest: Emerging from Narcissism Towards Marriage*, London: Karnac.

Freud, S. (1905) 'Three essays on the theory of sexuality', *Standard Edition of the Complete Psychological Works of Sigmund Freud, Volume 7*, London: Hogarth Press, 1953.

—— (1915) 'Instincts and their vicissitudes', *Standard Edition of the Complete Psychological Works of Sigmund Freud, Volume 14*, London: Hogarth Press, 1957.

Irigaray, L. (1985) *Speculum of the Other Woman*, Ithaca, N.Y.: Cornell University Press.

Lacan, J. (1991) *Le Seminaire Livre 8: Le Transfert*, Paris: Seuil.

Lagache, D. (1993) 'Some Aspects of Transference', in *The Work of Daniel Lagache: Selected Writings*, London: Karnac.

Laplanche, J. (1976) *Life and Death in Psychoanalysis*, Baltimore and London: Johns Hopkins University Press.

—— (1987) *Problematiques 5 – Le Baquet – Transcendance du Transfert*, Paris: Presses Universitaires de France.

—— (1999) *Essays on Otherness*, London: Routledge.

Laplanche, J. and Pontalis, J.-B. (1980) *The Language of Psychoanalysis*, London: Hogarth.

Mattinson, J. (1975) *The Reflection Process in Casework Supervision*, London: TIMS.

Meltzer, D. (1995) 'Donald Meltzer in Discussion with James Fisher', in S. Ruszczynski and J. Fisher (eds) *Intimacy and Intrusiveness in the Couple*, London: Karnac.

Ruszczynski, S. (1993) 'The Theory and Practice of the Tavistock Institute of Marital Studies', in S. Ruszcyznski (ed.) *Psychotherapy With Couples*, London: Karnac.

—— (1998) 'The "Marital Triangle": Towards "Triangular Space" in the Intimate Couple Relationship', *Psychoanalytic Psychotherapy*, 12.

Scarfone, D. (1994) 'Ma Mere, ce n'est pas elle', in *Colloque International de Psychanalyse*, Paris: Presses Universitaires de France.

Searles, H. (1955) 'The Informational Value of the Supervisor's Emotional Experience', in *Collected Papers on Schizophrenia and Related Subjects*, London: Hogarth.

Stanton, M. (1997) *Out of Order: Clinical Work and Unconscious Process*, London: Rebus.

Winnicott, D.W. (1987) *Through Paediatrics to Psychoanalysis*, London: Hogarth.

Chapter 15

Love and hate

A fusion of opposites – a window to the soul

Paola Valerio

> The little girl was sitting right against her mother, and now she put up her hand to tug her elbow down, to get her attention.
>
> 'Oh leave me alone,' snapped the mother, in a voice so irritable and full of dislike it was hard to believe this was the same voice she used to love the baby. And now she used this voice again, rich full, and sexual, and she kissed the baby's neck with an open mouth. 'Darling, darling, darling' murmured the mother. 'Little Ned, my darling Ned'. And then removing her mouth from the baby's neck for this purpose, she snapped at her daughter. 'I told you, stop it. Stop bothering me, don't crowd me like that'. And she went on loving the baby as if the child did not exist.
>
> . . . The child sat frozen . . . looking sombrely in front of her – looking in fact at Sarah, at the dull old woman there on the bench . . .
>
> Sarah was silently telling the child, 'Hold on, hold on. Quite soon a door will slam shut inside of you because what you are feeling is unendurable. The door will stand there shut all your life: if you are lucky it will never open, and you'll not ever know about the landscape you inhabited for how long? But child time is not adult time. You are living in an eternity of loneliness and grief, and it is truly a hell because the point of hell is that there is no hope. You don't know that the door will slam shut, you believe that this is what life is and must be: you will always be disliked, and you will have to watch her love that little creature you love so much because you think if you love what she loves, she will love you. But one day you will know that it doesn't matter what you do and how hard you try, it is no use. And at that moment the door will slam and you will be free.
>
> (Doris Lessing *Love Again*)[1]

Sarah, the central character in Lessing's novel, witnesses a painful scene. It is one which will resonate with many psychotherapists whose patients describe their childhood experiences. But, what happens when, perhaps as a result of therapy, the door is opened; what rage and hatred may be ushered into the consulting room? This extract from the novel brought one particular female patient to mind. I will discuss how I managed the fact that I found her particularly loathsome. She was open in telling me how she was 'always disliked'. What working with this patient highlighted was the question of how open psychotherapists should be in turn, in connection with disliking or even hating a patient, and how can the therapist do this in support of the patient's individuation process and not as a clearing of the emotional decks?

In this chapter, I will describe work with patients where strong countertransference feelings, ranging from irritation to actual repulsion and hatred of patients, were judiciously disclosed and worked with in the consulting room. Hate is more commonly written about in relation to work with severely disturbed or borderline patients, but in my experience it is a more frequent occurrence than is usually acknowledged in work with all patients, if the analyst is open to it. Of course we feel uncomfortable if we hate our patients, particularly if they are paying us, but also because there are very real issues about whether or not we need to like our patients in order to be able to work with them. A still common view is, as Suttie stated it in 1935:

> From our own practical point of view the necessarily subconscious and involuntary nature of love has this significance, that if we do not like a patient we are hopelessly handicapped in treating him. No amount of technical skill, theoretical knowledge or conscientiousness will atone for the absence of a sympathetic understanding and the capacity to put oneself in the patient's place.
>
> (Suttie [1935] 1988)

The question is whether dislike of the patient is necessarily a handicap or could sometimes be an opportunity. At the very least, the therapist has to examine whether or not her dislike mirrors aspects of herself that she cannot bear. If this process of self-reflection does not occur then the patient may suffer as a result of the therapist's limitations.

But there is more to hating one's client than its stimulation of introspection. There may be some positive therapeutic value in it. While this chapter is primarily written from a clinical viewpoint, I was struck when reviewing the literature that despite some illuminating papers by female therapists on the importance of acknowledging loving feelings towards one's patients (Benayah and Stern 1994; Gerrard 1996), there is little on the therapeutic value of acknowledging and working with hateful feelings. There is a growing literature about the erotic countertransference in connection with female therapists (Wrye and Welles 1994; Schaverien 1995; Valerio-Smith 1997). Perhaps it still runs counter to traditional social and cultural conventions for female therapists to slip out of their nurturing maternal robe and admit to aggressive enactments with patients. John Beebe (1998) addresses a more general issue that may also be relevant in this context. Perhaps there is a tendency amongst Jungians to overemphasis analysis as a 'cure through love', an idealisation of the analytic relationship or the idea of individuation at the expense of an analysis of simply put, 'disagreeable character'. He writes:

> we are told by our critics that we fail our patients in their work on character because we have to be their friends – because, that is, we emphasise loving connections at the expense of objective scrutiny of their faults . . . Nowhere are our limitations said to be more evident than in our handling of patients with significant drawbacks of character.
>
> (Beebe 1998: 55)

A note on countertransference

As much of the clinical material involves discussion of my counter-transference responses, I would like to discuss briefly my understanding of countertransference. Few would regard the existence of a therapist's emotional response to her patient in the clinical setting as a hindrance to the work. On the contrary, a therapist's countertransference response is considered a rich and crucially useful source of information. Nor is it expected that a therapist will be immediately conscious of her counter-transference responses. Yet as Renik (1993) points out, a common view is that 'an analyst's *awareness* of his countertransference is an asset that contributes to analytic work, while *expression* of his countertransference in action is a liability that limits analytic work' (my italics). However, while we have little difficulty regarding transference enactment as a necessary prelude to transference awareness for a patient, it seems we find it hard to countenance that the same might sometimes be true for the therapist in connection with her countertransference. Let's begin from the starting point that analytic work unfolds in a process of mutually active embroilment between patient and analyst. From a Jungian perspective, therapy is a dialectical, reciprocal interaction in which two psychic systems enter together in what has been characterised as a chemical or alchemical reaction. Not only does the patient 'infect' the analyst but either party may be transformed by the interaction. (A full review of the many different post-Jungian approaches to countertransference is discussed in Sedgwick's (1994) very honest and elucidating book.) However one thinks about it, countertransference is by nature 'personal'. Perhaps with experience one becomes free to acknowledge and experience feelings of all sorts, including hatred for one's patients. At best we strive to remember the agreed-upon purpose of the partnership which is to further the patient's self-awareness. The analyst, in so far as she is in control of her self-revelations, has to hold this distinction in mind.

Clinical material

Ann

Ann is a 34-year-old accountant. She came to see me following an unsatisfactory assessment at a local NHS clinic. Her version of this contact was
that she had gone there for some career advice and they had focused on her
lesbian relationship and recommended that she should have five-times-a-
week psychoanalysis in order 'to cure her of her lesbianism'. She is a tall,
fair-skinned and slim woman with a very voluptuous figure, oestrogen
oozing out of her pores. As she cycles everywhere she always arrives for
sessions in very clingy and tight fitting lycra. Yet, I found her strangely
unattractive and masculine when I first saw her and I felt pretty sure that
this was not a conventional reaction to her lesbianism. She is the youngest
child from a very conventional and wealthy farming family. Her father was
always out on the land and her mother ran the home. She decries her
mother as a cold, bitter and narrow-minded character; her three older
brothers are also depicted as conventional and materialistic. Her mother
did not want a fourth child and told Ann that she had almost had an
abortion. For the first nine months of therapy, Ann, who came three times
a week, would lie mutely on my couch. It was almost as if she had no
personality, and she seemed to have no idea of what to do or say. I tried to
stay connected to her, recognising that she was an intelligent, competent
woman and that she was probably finding the limitations of the therapeutic
situation very difficult. However, I felt increasingly bored, and wondered if
I could stand the silence much longer. I felt that I was sitting beside a
corpse.

For many months I too had little to say and felt little in the way of
introspection. I found myself surreptitiously sneaking a look at the clock.
Recognising that it would be too sadistic to leave her in silence, session
after session, I started to ask questions. In reply, she would tell me what
seemed to me to be mundane stories about what she had for dinner or
things about her colleagues at work. Eventually I asked her if she had any
dreams. This seemed to me at the time to be a real mistake. She had lots of
them! Bitty, disjointed dreams, mostly about her schooldays. She had been
sent off to boarding school at eleven and rarely saw her parents after this
time, despite the fact that her school was only a few miles away from the
family home. Her recounting of these bits of dreams became a cold, emo-
tionless exercise. I felt as tortured as she must have felt in her schooldays –
so near (dreams) yet so far away (told without emotion). I was being pulled
into a coffin with her and, by now, I was able to admit to myself that I
really wanted to get rid of her.

What I did not realise at the time was that I had become the mother and
she the child, as presented in the opening extract from Lessing's novel, and

she simply could not capture my interest. Eventually, after another session in which she would recount her bits of dreams, toss down her dream book and wait for me to tell her what they meant, she stood up to leave and turned to me saying 'Well that was a waste of time wasn't it?' It was on the tip of my tongue to say 'Yes, yes', but her departure was too sudden. I felt she left with the velocity of a high-speed bullet and was stunned into silence. The following day (as I experienced it genuinely), I felt unwell. I telephoned and cancelled, noting my relief as I did so, adding that I would see her for her next session in two days. When she arrived she looked drawn. She burst into tears. She didn't have any friends and I was just the same as everyone else. I couldn't stand her either. Now I had a dilemma. Should I lie and say that it was all her fantasy that I had rejected her; that I had simply been ill? Or was this the moment to do something with these intolerable countertransference feelings? What she said was true, I was fed up. She was young; she was rich and therefore didn't need to work. What did she have to moan about? Frankly, if I was honest with myself I was a little envious of her. I had felt used by her, rather like a family servant. She had often commented on how much I charged, and checked her watch at the end of sessions; letting me know whether or not I had ended the session exactly on time or deprived her of a few minutes, according to her calculation of things. As she looked at me waiting for a response, I knew that she deserved at least some genuine feeling from me. It was the only way to climb out of the grave and try to get some life into this soulless relationship. A brief extract from this session follows this interaction.

PATIENT: [crying not looking at me . . . continues] *I've been thinking about how to kill myself but wouldn't want May* [her partner] *to find me so I couldn't do it at home. At least I could leave everything to her.*

THERAPIST: *I understand how you might feel that I couldn't stand you and that I cancelled yesterday in order to avoid you. I have come to realise that, despite the long periods of silence between us, I felt that somehow it was important that I did not give you the impression that I wanted to abort you as your mother had.*

PATIENT: [Suddenly looks at me directly for the first time]

THERAPIST: *But yes, I have been feeling fed up with you and frankly, I think that without realising it I wanted a day off. I feel as if you think that because you are paying me you can just come here and let me do all the work. It's as if you are in many ways behaving like your mother when she paid to have you taken care of. You're paying me therefore I have to deliver the goods. A bit like getting you the A grades at a good school.*

This interpretation was given in a restrained way, especially when I recall my feelings of hatred. But it was also genuine and not delivered in an artificially detached way. I was drawing attention to the real stalemate in our relationship, thus acknowledging the reality of her perceptions, but also linked this to her underlying expectation of cure without participation from her. Although simple enough, I think that this was extremely important and resulted in a real shift in the therapy. In the following year she entered a period of intense anger with her family, especially her mother. She left her lesbian relationship, recognising that it had been a defensive choice. Though probably bisexual, she had reached the conclusion that she was more sexually attracted to men. As far as I experienced it, silent sessions became a rare occurrence and I no longer dread them. I have also begun to notice what a good-looking woman she is and am bemused by my earlier feelings of her as physically repulsive which – I don't think I am being defensive in repeating – did not seem due to homophobic processes in me. Recently she informed me that she feels more attractive these days, somehow different, and feels good about the way she looks.

Bill

Another short example highlights an inappropriate enactment of hateful countertransference feelings. In this case the patient was an intelligent and successful barrister. He had a materially privileged, but emotionally fairly barren, childhood. His father was described as a bully and his mother as cold. He entered therapy with rigid intellectual defences and was full of unconscious rage. However, he was also a creative man, an excellent father to his own child, and had been involved in the growth movement in the 1970s and therefore he had a lot of psychological insight. I had been seeing him for almost a year and felt that we had done a lot of useful work. Following his initial assessment he had written a long letter questioning the actions of the male assessor.

As the individual therapy approached an end, Bill became very depressed. He started to take medication. He started to interrogate me about our work. He wanted to know exactly what my diagnosis was. What would happen, he asked, if he ended up in court as a result of the marital break-up? Would his treatment in the clinic result in him being denied access to his daughter? What would I say about him in a court report? Now, although I thought that phantasies of persecution were in play, I said to him that I did understand his concern about the hypothetical court scenario. I also reassured him that I did not have any concerns about him as a parent based upon his need to seek therapy. I continued the struggle to get him to recognise the need to focus on our relationship and his feelings of anger and abandonment as we approached the ending of therapy. He became relentless. He would not or could not let go of the court issue. He was almost screaming at me in one particular session. Although able to understand the reality base of his anxiety, I became filled with almost uncontrollable rage and dislike for the man, which I recognised as a form of projective identification whereby I was caught up by the patient's unconscious communication of this disavowed affect.

Kernberg (1975) was one of the first analysts to write about communication by borderline patients and the primitive affects that are routinely communicated via the mechanism of projective identification. While this helps us in the understanding of such affects, there are still fewer examples of how we avoid reacting as a result of these strong feelings, if indeed we really can. To return to my patient, he had now left me in a pot of simmering stew, and dealt his final blow. 'Well,' he said, removing a letter from his briefcase, 'I have taken the liberty of writing to Dr S. [who had originally assessed him] asking him for a full explanation of my treatment. Here's a copy for you.'

I had in fact anticipated this response after his earlier letter complaining about my colleague, and had already spoken to Dr S. But by now I had had it with this man. I turned to him and said 'Yes, well I told Dr S. that you would probably be writing to him.' He dissolved in his chair and looked truly deflated. But I, in turn, had a strange response; I did not feel triumphant. I knew that I had failed to contain his hatred and rage. The next day Dr S and I received a letter in which he wrote about how much he valued the therapy. How he 'had every confidence in me as a therapist, and how he would have gone on to see me privately if he could'. He stressed 'that he was not complaining about me'. When I next saw him I apologised for my outburst. I had been indiscreet and I had undermined him, as I felt he had tried to do to me. I added, however, that there was a danger that we would finish this contract without dealing with his feelings of loss and anger and that I felt that I was being forced to carry these unconscious feelings for him. He seemed to respond to my genuine apology, in which I acknowledged my indiscretion. In the last month he has remembered that his mother had told him that she had had a miscarriage before he was born. He began to understand why he had felt both abandoned by her and extremely angry with her. It seems that he was the son who, in his dead sibling's shadow, had never matched up to parental expectations, while in my indiscretion I had unconsciously identified with his mother and enacted her hatred with him – perhaps for being alive whilst her other son had not survived. In this respect, with both Bill and Ann, I was caught up in feelings of hatred for the child, rather like the mother in the Lessing quote.

The woman's part

POSTHUMOUS: Could I find out
The woman's part in me – for there's no motion
That tends to vice in man, but I affirm
It is the woman's part: be it lying, note it,
The woman's; flattering, hers; deceiving, hers;

> Lust and rank thoughts, hers, hers; revenges, hers;
> Ambitions, covetings, change of prides, disdain,
> Nice longing, slanders, mutability,
> All faults that may be nam'd, nay, that hell knows,
> Why, hers, in part or all; but rather, all;
> For even to vice
> They are not constant, but are changing still . . .
>
> (Shakespeare, *Cymbeline*, Act II, Scene 5)

Posthumus, has been taken in by an Italian trickster, and believing in his wife's apparent betrayal, he flies into a raging tirade against all women. Like Hamlet and Troilus before him, he wants to rip out 'the women's part' in him because it is vicious, it is deceitful. While re-enacting the cultural stereotype, the disavowed feminine or negative 'anima' is both projected out into others and colours all of such a man's subsequent interactions with women.

In this final section I would like to focus on two young male patients. Both men came into therapy with a highly idealised view of their mothers. Subsequent work suggested that there had been a fair amount of ambivalent behaviour from their mothers, which was also of a highly seductive nature. Both mothers combined over-protective with caustic treatment of their sons. In both cases the father was absent or belittled by the mother. To continue in Shakespearean vein, the father is thus more akin to Hamlet's Ghost, perhaps to a certain extent a super-ego figure, but more importantly a kind of hallucination, an archetypal figure – all skeleton and no flesh – which helped to prevent the son from being engulfed or completely taken in by the mother. Both men, who are intelligent and highly articulate, learned to fight back against their abuse with oral aggression, with words, sarcasm and gestures. This is a pattern that I have often found in male patients with overbearing mothers. It is almost as if they struggle to find their masculine power but instead fight back as 'women', in the grip, as I have suggested above, of a negative anima sort of possession. I am also minded of a kind of infantile even impotent line of attack whereby, like Hamlet, they say to themselves: 'I will speak daggers but use none.' Yet inevitably they become tortured by their impotence. Both men are in their thirties, dark and conventionally attractive. Sean is an osteopath and Gary is an artist. Both were born with rare medical conditions, giving their mothers an opportunity, or at least a legitimate reason, to over-protect them. Sean has a rare eye condition resulting in progressive blindness. Gary has an acute pancreatic disorder, resulting in progressive weakness. Both men have endured numerous medical interventions. A significant factor in Sean's case is that he is a non-identical twin. Sean describes his twin, Lou, as the robust healthy and athletic one. The impression I have formed is of a shared ego that somehow became split at birth so that all of the masculine identity was carried by Lou, who identifies with the largely absent alcoholic Greek father, while Sean carried all the feminine, identifying with the mother. A cruel joke at school, according to Sean, was to compare the twins and suggest to my patient Sean 'that he must have been the after-birth'. There is a specific literature on problems of identification in twins, and I will not focus on these issues here (see Athanassiou 1986; Fisher 1986).

Gary complained that he 'was a 30-year-old virgin' at the start of his therapy. He would repeatedly get into relationships with women who would become abusive. They would be unfaithful, appearing to sleep with every-one but him, including other women. His father was described as a very wealthy but mean, punishing, and intimidating man who ran the family like a large company. His childhood put me in mind of a Dickens novel, full of tortured childhood abuse and unjust punishment. The mother would frequently run away and disappear for a few hours at a time, leaving Gary and his brother alone. He was caught in a double bind of needing to care for his mother and protect her, but also of being abandoned by her when she failed to protect him. I often wondered if the illness, which he developed at around the age of eight, was the only way of getting her to take care of him. But despite his obvious charms, Gary was surprisingly boring. Each week was a long soliloquy about the corruption of the system, and of how women hated men and were out to get them all. My interpretations, however mild, failed to shift his perspective one inch. I would often sit in sessions and, as the months went by, find myself drifting off into my own world, abandoning him like his mother had but also indirectly expressing my contempt for him as he 'rambled on'. I began to lose my capacity to reflect, mirroring his limited self-reflective capacity. Eventually, I began to feel like a toilet into which he would evacuate his loathsome parts. When not silently withdrawing from him, I settled into another pattern: I became very cerebral and challenging of his views. I realised I wanted to appear cleverer or wiser than him, perhaps reflecting my own insecurity in the light of his apparent brilliance. Or was I mirroring his lack of self-esteem? He described his ideal physical type to me as young, mid-twenties, slender and blonde. In my countertransference I felt disregarded as a woman, as I am neither mid-twenties nor blonde. After a recent holiday in which my hair was lightened by the hot sun, my fantasies became more explicit and defensive: did he think I was trying to mould myself to him to be his type? I wanted to put him down, to make it clear I did not find him attractive. In this way I reflected his narcissistic vulnerabilities. I realised that my dislike of him was a response to his apparent rejection of me and in this respect I was caught up in an avoidance of looking at our relationship. Eventually I tried to address this issue with him. If all women were so hateful, so loathsome, what about his previous female therapist and me? He appeared to value us, but were we man-haters? Could he be avoiding reflecting on us, on our relationship, with all this camouflage about abusive women? 'Perhaps', I said, 'you are afraid of me, of therapeutic intimacy, of being truly known by someone'. This resulted in stunned silence 'I never think about you', he replied. However, I felt that on some level he acknowledged my words. While I, in turn, glimpsed the possibility of a connection.

Gabbard (1996) refers to Bollas, who coined the term 'loving hate' to describe a situation where an individual preserves a relationship by sustaining a passionate negative cathexis of it. Hate is a substitute for love, but may conceal a longing for love and acceptance. From the patient's point of view, being hated may be preferable to being abandoned. He cautions against premature interpretations of the patient's hateful and envious feelings. Envy of course often lies behind such contempt and denigration of others, as compulsively expressed by Gary. Gabbard reminds us of our need to contain such feelings for the patient while also acknowledging that there will be some countertransference enactment (as I have described above in relation to Gary). Gabbard feels it is important to tolerate being a bad object for the patient. He feels that only in this way can a patient's hate be tinged with love. With Gary it has become clear that this is an impossible feat in one year of weekly analytical therapy.

In returning to Sean, the partially sighted twin referred to above, I realised that in order to understand the emotional impact of severe visual impairment requires for me, as a sighted person, an imaginative leap into a world that I can never understand. On the other hand I came to realise that I was also handicapped by fear of overemphasising blindness in the external world and not allowing myself to acknowledge the way in which Sean produced a kind of 'blurred vision in the transference'. This 'blinded' me psychologically to the ways in which I was being manipulated into aligning with his victim stance and, through guilt, was not owning up to the fact that I did not feel sympathetic towards him. In fact, I disliked him. If I was honest I found him suspicious and even repulsive at first. Because of his eye condition he would often arrive in ill-fitting or mismatched clothes that were stained. He would frequently make a mess of my consulting room. Once he walked straight in with his shoes covered in dog faeces. But I never felt like cleaning up after him; more often I just felt frustrated and disgusted. How could I have this response to someone who could not help it? I was faced with my own shallowness and vanity.

A breakthrough occurred after a few months in an extremely bizarre fashion. I was at that time working in my conservatory at the back of my house which has a side entrance. Shortly after the start of one particular session with Sean, three policemen suddenly burst into the consulting room demanding to know who we were. While it became an amusing tale, at the time it was fairly frightening. It seemed that a neighbour had reported Sean to the police as a suspicious character, ironically chiming with my fantasy of there being something a little shifty about him. Of course, I recognised that this was partly a result of his shortsightedness. He did not carry a white stick and as a result he would walk over-carefully in a rehearsed fashion. But there was more to it.

He brings the following dream to therapy; it was his initial dream. *His girlfriend is lying on my couch having their baby, and he is sitting in my chair, when the devil appears.* His association to the devil reflects the extreme good/evil split in his mind occasioned by a strong Catholic upbringing. The psychodynamic ancestry of Satan is an archetypal shadow personification who once sat on the right hand of God; the figure of an archangel lies in the projective identification of human envy. God, who is absolute and therefore unable to have a defect such as envy, must be split (divided) into a good and a bad part. But the devil is said not to have a reflective capacity, and so it was with Sean. He complains that people do not believe in his goodness. They accuse him of being disingenuous, suspicious. I am beginning to think that the difficulty he has in reflecting upon himself is connected with feelings that his mother did not mirror him. He was seen as an extension of her needs and a useful barrier to a full relationship with Sean's father. I suspect that his more destructive emotions weren't acknowledged. He grew up with the illusion of omnipotence, of kinship, of getting mother away from his twin and his father. My countertransference response is to feel sorry for his twin Lou. The fact that he is sitting in my chair also reflects the continual power struggle between us, his image of being the 'doc' in his family and his resentment at not getting my seat (symbolically the family throne), of not achieving kinship with me. He has to denigrate what he cannot get; for example, pointing out as a matter of professional etiquette that the chair I am sitting on will damage my back. Therapy becomes incestuous as he tries to twin me with him as he did his mother. When he feels psychologically impotent and angry in his relationship with his girlfriend he asks her for anal sex, which she refuses him. When he feels attacked by me, he fantasises about having anal sex with me. While this contains elements of core-complex relating (Glasser 1986), I am struck by the psychological presentation of doing things from behind in a suspicious or underhand sort of way.

I tried to address the shadow elements in his dream. Yet, somehow, I feel that it is I who am sadistically exposing him. Just before the break, he informs me that he is 'obsessed' with me. He sees my face everywhere. It is ruining his relationship with his girlfriend. He says that he doesn't want to dump on me and ruin my holiday as he knows that I won't have anyone to talk to about this. Yet the comment, like the sexual fantasy of attack from behind, is timed to do exactly that. I pick up on this hypocrisy and he admits to it. I make him feel powerless, he responds. I realise that I am the intrusive mother he is obsessed with. His wounded child part is felt in his navel area. It tortures him to imagine it being touched. He often holds this area in a protective way in therapy. Significantly, his feeling about this part of his body also corresponds to the idea in Japanese Buddhist philosophy of the *hara*, which is located in this area.

In therapy the opportunity of being mirrored exists perhaps for the first time, but it also involves exposing this vulnerable easily shamed part. As we explore this together he begins to remember, slowly and painfully, that his mother used him, used his blindness when he was small. For example she used to send him on errands to get money from relatives. The 'poor little blind boy' – who could refuse him? She also used him to shoplift. They would go into a shop together and she would dress him up in new clothes and then send him out of the shop. As we explored these events more he let go of his previously idealised view of his mother, and his rage became great. He was able to leave his mother's house and move in with his girlfriend. He bought some powerful spectacles, which enabled him to see a great deal more; as if changes in the inner world of seeing were being paralleled in the external world. He bought a drill to use as a symbol of his emerging masculinity. Strangely, as he began to let go of his mother and her hold over him and own his own masculine power, I began to see him in a different light. I found myself blushing a little when he flirted with me. In one session he asked if he could touch me, which I understood on one level as an expression of his incestuous feelings. But on another level, I realised that for a blind child touch must be so much more a way of learning about the world. In place of my earlier feelings of repulsion, although we do not touch, I found myself imagining what it would be like to be touched by him, even massaged by him. My images of him ranging from a 'dirty little boy' to an 'old woman' shift, I began to see him as an attractive, potent man.

Conclusion

Where intimate relations are concerned there is no passionate love without a tinge of hate, or hate without a thread of love. When love and hate are treated as mutually exclusive the tendency is to idealise the one and demonise the other. As Winnicott (1949) noted (rather radically for his time), the mother hates her infant from the word go, for all sorts of good reasons. Primitive feelings of love and hate are inevitably stirred up in this analytic vessel. I am struck by how often psychological shifts are followed by apparent changes in physical appearance. Patients whom I considered loathsome or even repellent become attractive to me. It is almost as if in working through feelings of hate we become aware of their intimate relationships with love, of their polarity. Perhaps we are offered a window to the self, or even soul, of the other behind the hateful persona. Or do we need to acknowledge hateful feelings in ourselves as well as our patients in order to love them truly? The irony is, as Romeo laments, that:

Here's much to do with hate, but more with love.
Why then, Oh brawling love. Oh loving hate.
O anything of nothing first create;
O heavy lightness, Serious vanity,
Misshapen chaos of well-seeming forms,
Feather of lead, bright smoke, cold fire, sick health
Still-waking sleep, that is not what it is!
This love feel I, that feel no love in this,
Dost thou not laugh?

(Shakespeare, *Romeo and Juliet*, Act I, Scene 1)

Note

1 The author and publishers wish to thank HarperCollins Publishers for kind permission to reprint the extract from Doris Lessing's *Love Again*.

References

Athanassiou, C. (1986) A study of the vicissitudes of identification in twins, *International Journal of Psycho-Analysis* 67, 329–334.

Beebe, J. (1998) Towards a Jungian analysis of character, in Ann Casement (ed.) *Post-Jungians Today*, London: Routledge.

Benayah, C. and Stern, M. (1994) Transference–countertransference. Realising a love by not actualising it, *International Journal of Psychiatry and Related Sciences* 31(2), 94–105.

Fisher, S. (1986) The metaphor of twinship in personality development, *British Journal of Psychotherapy* 2(4), 271–278.

Gabbard, G. (1996) *Love and Hate in the Analytic Setting*, Northvale, N.J.: Jason Aronson Inc.

Gerrard, J. (1996) Love in the time of psychotherapy, *British Journal of Psychotherapy* 13(2), 163–173.

Glasser, M. (1986) Identification and its vicissitudes as observed in the perversions, *International Journal of Psycho-Analysis* 67(9), 9–17.

Kernberg, O. (1975) *Borderline Conditions and Pathological Narcissism*, New York: Jason Aronson.

Renik, O. *et al.* (1993) Countertransference enactment and the psychoanalytic process, in Horowitz *et al.* (eds) *Psychic Structure and Psychic Change*, Madison, Conn.: International University Press, pp. 135–158.

Sedgwick, D. (1994) *The Wounded Healer. Countertransference from a Jungian Perspective*, London and New York: Routledge.

Schaverien, J. (1995) *Desire and the Female Therapist*, London and New York: Routledge.

Suttie, D. ([1935] 1988) *The Origins of Love and Hate*, London: Free Association Books.

Valerio-Smith, P. (1997) Secret friends: borderline symptomatology and posttraumatic stress disorder in a case of reported sexual abuse, *British Journal of Psychotherapy* 14(1), 18–32.

Winnicott, D.W. (1949) Hate in the counter-transference, *International Journal of Psycho-Analysis* 30, 69–74.

Wrye, H.K. and Welles, J.K. (1994) *The Narration of Desire*, London: The Analytic Press.

Chapter 16

Following in the footsteps of Ferenczi, Balint and Winnicott

Love and hate in a setting open to body- and action-related interventions

Peter Geißler

In this chapter I would like to shed light on a field of psychoanalysis which has become increasingly important in the German-speaking countries in the past ten years. It was not least due to the influence of modern baby and infant research that a discussion long considered taboo in analysts' circles was resumed: engagement with the technique-related experiments of Ferenczi and the object-relations theorists Balint and Winnicott. A small but growing number of psychoanalysts are again opening the analytical approach to experience-activating and body-related techniques, daring to break new ground in psychoanalysis. In Germany it is mainly the Freiburg-based psychoanalyst and body psychotherapist Tilmann Moser who has made a name for himself in the field.

This tendency comes as no surprise: after all, and for various reasons, psychoanalysis is in a serious crisis, at least in the German-speaking countries. New types of developmental psychology force practitioners of psychoanalysis to examine, and at times to revise, familiar theoretical concepts to avoid a widening gap between the 'reconstructed' and the 'observed' baby. Babies turn out to have a large number of innate abilities which they actively use to shape early baby–parent interaction. The growing importance of interactive processes, and the way they are reflected in representations, has increasingly drawn attention to interactions in the therapeutic and psychoanalytical process. Given the resulting concept of interactive transference, it seems justified to re-think the possibility of introducing concrete interaction into a notion of transference and counter-transference. Today, we have a much better understanding of counter-transference than in Ferenczi's days, so we can base our ventures into new experiments and variations on much sounder foundations.

Thus, it comes as no surprise that the Second Vienna Symposium on Psychoanalysis and Body, which the editor of this book was also invited to as a speaker, was held in September 2000. Traditionally, the Vienna Symposium is a forum for open discussions and controversial statements about these new developments in psychoanalysis. Among others, the list of participants at the last symposium included David Mann, Joseph Lichtenberg,

Tilmann Moser, Günter Heisterkamp, Jörg Scharff, Gisela Worm and Hansjörg Pfannschmidt. This chapter ties in with the discussions in Vienna.

Early object-relations theorists

Early on, analysts started to consider the classic setting of psychoanalysis as not effective enough for some of our patients, either denying too much or unsuited for other reasons. Even during Freud's era, pioneers such as Wilhelm Reich and Sandor Ferenczi pondered over the problem, but their models of theory and treatment technique raised much scepticism, which eventually led to their exclusion from the psychoanalysts' community. I would like to present a very brief overview of the criticism and attempts at innovation dating back to those days.

Ferenczi (1939), who considered the classic setting of psychoanalysis as strict, denying and even potentially re-traumatising, was one of the first pioneers and object-relations theorist. He strongly advocated a motherly principle of indulgence, even pampering, *vis-à-vis* his patients, some of whom suffered from serious personality disorders; he wanted to enable his patients to have a certain degree of need fulfilment, a reparative new experience, which was the reason why his attitude towards the patient's regression – considered more of a detour than a road to success by Freud – was highly indulgent. Thus he arrived at entirely new conclusions concerning technique while the failure of many of his experiments was due to the fact that the concept of counter-transference was in its infancy at the time. He wanted to give as much love as possible to his patients but had no suitable instruments to cope with their destructive hate and the way they acted full of hatred. At that time it was not possible to allow for such hatred in the shape of fantasies in counter-transference, and to return it to the patient as interpretations. Instead, Ferenczi let himself in for mutual analysis, which resulted in hopeless entanglement.

Balint tried to find a compromise between the attitudes of Freud and Ferenczi, since he was against an exaggerated position of neutrality and abstinence but never went to the same extremes as his teacher Ferenczi. His concept of 'primary love' and his view of the baby, revolutionary in his day and age, anticipated insights which seem to be fully confirmed by modern baby and infant research. When engaging with regressing and 'fundamentally deranged' patients, he made it clear, notwithstanding the dubiousness of technique-related guidelines, that there are certain do's and don'ts an analyst must observe. For example, when dealing with fundamentally deranged patients, he/she is not allowed to act in a denying way but should grant them 'satisfaction for the purpose of recognition', which, in certain circumstances and within limits, might include physical touch. At the same time, the analyst is forbidden to satisfy the wishes of patients suffering from 'malignant regression', i.e. patients who insist on the satisfaction of drives.

Thus, Balint drew a distinction between the patient's primary needs for love/being loved on the one hand and the satisfaction of drives on the other; the latter would be understood as needs at a level of defence today. Concurrently, his statements about the mutuality of behaviour and influence in the analytical situation prepared the ground for a modern notion of interactional transference (Balint, 1973).

Winnicott, too, recommended that the distance required in the treatment of neurotic patients should be given up for psychotic patients and borderline cases, and that patients be given the leeway they need for regression. For him, it was more important than interpretation to give these patients the right atmosphere, loving, motherly warmth, as an analyst. In *Through Paediatrics to Psycho-Analysis* (1976), he wrote something to the effect that the couch, the warmth and comfort could be a symbol of a mother's love for a neurotic analysand, while it would be more appropriate to say that these things were the physical expression of the analyst's love for a psychotic patient. The couch would be the analyst's lap or womb, and the warmth of the surroundings would be the bodily warmth of the analyst. However, Winnicott also said that in spite of all the motherly attitude the tremendous hatred and destructiveness of these patients should not be overlooked. In counter-transference the analyst's hatred should not only be allowed to come out as intensely as possible in the analyst's own fantasies, it should also be included in the interpretation given to the patient in a well-dosed and tactful manner so that he/she becomes aware of the extent of hatred and destructiveness. Another important notion developed by Winnicott was the psychoanalytical situation as a potential space or 'playground'.

Condensed physical–sensual experience: the psychoanalytical situation as a potential space

Winnicott's concept of the psychoanalytical situation as a potential space or 'playground' was taken up by Hansjöpg Pfannschmidt, a psychoanalyst and former bioenergeticist at the Second Vienna Symposium (2000), which focused on sexuality. The title of his paper given at the symposium was 'Die Auswirkungen der Leib-Seele-Phantasie auf Erotik und Sexualität'. Pfannschmidt referred to Winnicott when he said that for any ability to develop a space is required where these abilities can be discovered and mastered in a playful way:

> By playfully using this space, the child gradually develops its own internal space, a feel for its own body, the world and potential relations ... For example, a little girl may wish to possess the father, and having his child, and she may experience this in her imagination as long as it is clear that the father must not depend on the affection of his daughter in his erotic-sexual identity, i.e. as long as he is able to provide, together

with his partner, the need-free space for the desire of his daughter that is fantasised and experienced physically.

(Pfannschmidt, 2001)

To further this space for feelings of love and desire in an optimal way, Pfannschmidt believes that it is required to advance the development of all senses of the patient while not touching him/her physically 'since physical touch is a massive manipulation of the patient's imaginative space, in such a way that his/her physical fantasies cannot unfold freely and undisturbedly any longer'. Or, to say it in even more pointed words:

My claim is that the physical experience of sexuality and thus corporeality itself is only enabled when erotic touch is not physically performed in analysis. Conversely, a reduction in experiencing sexuality and eroticism reduces corporeality. If we allow for corporeality in analysis, we will very quickly feel that this type of abstinence is not renunciation; on the contrary, it is a very specific kind of satisfaction.

(ibid.)

The experience made possible in this intermediary state is thus highly corporeal and sensual but not an experience in the sense of the satisfaction of drives:

This kind of pleasurable experience of eroticism and sexuality in the intermediary space of sexuality does not correspond to the satisfaction of drives in the genital-physical sense but an initiation successful in itself as a whole but also transcending its boundaries as a whole and pointing to the adult and independent sexual identity of the individual.

(ibid.)

Pfannschmidt underscores that erotic and sexual issues can be dealt with in transference just like other issues; he considers the specific difficulties arising from it as 'perceiving that one has touched the other with one's own erotic–sexual feelings and having received an emotional response that can be felt physically', a process which also applies to the therapist. In other words, if the analyst wants to be able to respond to the loving and erotic–sexual needs of the patient in an affective-physical way he/she has to allow him/herself to get involved. He/she must be able to have an erotic–therapeutic relation with the patient. He/she must let him/herself in for the process with all his/her feelings; from this angle, a neutral and abstinent attitude would have to be seen as counter-transference resistance on the part of the therapist. This act of letting oneself in for the relation does not call the division of functions between therapist and patient into question; on the contrary, this assignment of roles is actually required (cf. also Ware, 2001).

The therapist's involvement in the psychoanalytical process applies not only to erotic–sexual experiences but to all feelings developing between patient and therapist – including feelings of hatred. In this context hatred is to be understood as the defence of love, and the patient fears these loving emotions because they led to serious traumata in his/her early experiences. If the analyst tries gradually to approach the loving feelings of the patient, it will not be uncommon for him/her to be exposed to the patient's caustic mockery. When interpreting the restaging of the traumatising situation, the analyst can feel the patient's original fear very clearly: he/she is deeply humiliated in the understanding approach to the patient, and thus the beloved person, in transference. An analyst understanding this situation, overcoming his/her own fears and really allowing him/herself to be drawn into the setting built together with the patient, will create the prerequisite for the development of a 'loving relationship' between analyst and analysand – without any physical touch.

However, transference love is no longer a one-way street and the analyst cannot simply hide behind interpretations any longer: the patient will feel that he/she is a person with emotions of love and hate, with fears and erotic feelings of his/her own. For this reason, we need a different type of transference that is more appropriate for this interaction.

Excursus: modern baby and infant research

At least implicitly, offences and early traumata play an important role in the psychoanalytical view of the way in which the structure of the human psyche is formed; in this context, the term 'high-tension learning' is used. However, modern baby and infant research has emphasised that we must also pay attention to atmospherical elements and learning processes ('low-tension learning') and that entirely unspectacular experiences, repeated thousands of times in the everyday life of babies and infants, are represented mentally – as experiences of interaction or 'rigs' (representations of interactions that have been generalised), as Daniel Stern (1992) calls them.

Such contemporary research is gaining importance, causing us to rethink constructs of psychoanalysis, such as the psychoanalytical theory of affects. Without wishing to go into detail here (I would rather refer to the overview in Dornes, 1992) I believe it is important to underline that the psychoanalytical view of undifferentiated affects in babies, and the dependence of affective development on ego growth, seems one-sided from the perspective of new currents in developmental psychology. In view of the evident perceptivity of babies, which has been proven in experiments, the inability of the baby to perceive the self as separate from objects, as we find it in Mahler's symbiosis theory and in other theories from Spitz to Jacobson and Kernberg, has at least to be reconsidered. Thus, it has meanwhile become very likely that infants are able to perceive seven categories of affects in their first year: interest, surprise, disgust, joy, annoyance, sadness and fear. Apparently, these affects are part of the innate abilities human beings are equipped with. Moreover, babies perceive time and intensity in a very accurate way so that they are most probably able to grasp affects of different degrees and as 'contours of vitality' (Stern, 1998). They are able to differentiate between slowly building and explosive anger. Vital dimensions of human beings and events are thus taken in, and a range of feelings and sensations rich in nuances is experienced and represented mentally.

The extraordinary significance of early interactive processes and their mental representation compel us also to rethink and re-evaluate interaction in the therapeutic setting in the form of concrete and physical interaction in the psychoanalytic space. This interaction takes place at all times in non-verbal dialogues of actions. The psychoanalytic space is no longer a language space only – it is also a space of action, or playground.

The notion of interactional transference

The traditional psychoanalytic notion of transference assumes that transference is first and foremost a projection of internal conflicts and object fantasies of the patient onto the therapist and results from the fact that the therapist gradually identifies and interprets the fantasies of the patient through an attitude of neutrality and abstinence. From this perspective, transference is a 'one-way street'.

Just as babies and their parents continuously exchange affective-physical signals from the moment the child is born, the psychoanalytic relation is increasingly seen as a circular process of exchange and negotiation based on reciprocal and complementary responses from the respective other party. Today, we recognise to a growing extent that we as analysts/therapists with our own subjectivity are directly involved in this process of exchange. The non-verbal dialogue of actions always takes place even though the couch setting prevents any visual exchange. The reduction of non-verbal exchange at the visual level, which gives the patient less control over the process of exchange, may be justified in certain cases, but many of our patients make up for the lack of eye contact caused by the setting by more auditory attention; in the course of the analytical process they have a keener ear for subtle noises coming from the analyst. Hence, it is *impossible* not to communicate, not to act. Object-relations theorists such as Ferenczi, Balint, Winnicott and others have always said this, and from the angle of new currents in developmental psychology there are many arguments supporting this opinion and this view of human beings.

Hence, the notion of transference that I consider adequate is a concept assuming that there is a readiness to interact on both sides – on the part of the patient as well as the analyst – and that the readiness of the therapist to act is a significant element in the scene established together. At the Second Vienna Symposium Bettighofer emphatically advocated such a notion of transference. An interactional notion of transference

> claims that both of us personally contribute to the way in which transference is shaped. Apart from the usual projects, basic situations of the patient are staged. And these also contain the contributions I have made as a therapist . . . Projections are not the only things concerned, in fact, real interaction takes place . . . neutrality and abstinence no longer mean that I am e.g., not allowed to touch but that I have to be aware of my motivation for touching and that I have to keep an eye on what this could mean for the scene. Against this backdrop, it is quite possible to use a variety of methods. The point is then no longer what speaks in favour or against this method but the question will be: what is it that I stage with the patient if I work with him/her the way I am working now?

Such an interactional notion of transference is the prerequisite for the analyst letting him/herself in for the process a little more unreservedly and allowing him/her to become involved to a certain extent. From my own experience as a patient and therapist I would now argue that this involvement into the shared interaction makes the psychoanalytical atmosphere more open, more lively and also more enjoyable so that it has a positive impact on the affective experience of the patient. When patients notice that I, as a therapist, act in an unconstrained way, that I show my personality the way it is and do not hide behind utterances reflecting detachment, they are also able to let themselves in for the therapeutic process in a more direct way, overcome their anxieties and sense of shame, and allow for loving feelings and hatred to happen with more intensity. ·

Setting and experiential space

The therapeutic relation is a space emerging in the framework of a psychoanalytical process and it is shaped by contributions of patient and therapist alike even though their positions are different. Certain modalities of the setting favour certain experiences with oneself and with others to a greater or lesser extent. Even though there is no compelling reason why the setting and the patient's experience should be connected, we can safely assume that a certain connection exists between the two (Scharff, 1998: 45).

Having made my own experiences as an analysand, I am in a position to comment on this. After having dropped out of psychoanalysis in a couch setting after one year, I did five years of body-energetic analysis according to Lowen which created the emotional prerequisites enabling me to approach deep emotional experiences and being touched by love and hate in a way I had not experienced for decades. My third therapy, seven years of psychoanalysis, eventually made it possible for me to profit from the analysis because I had acquired the ability to open myself to emotions.

I would like to describe the difference in affective experience in terms of a caricature: whereas I mourned in the analytical setting, I frequently cried like a little child in the course of body-related therapy. Whereas I felt the physical tension of subdued anger in the analytical setting, I had the opportunity occasionally to express that anger through my whole body, which not only meant short-term relief but also gave me the comforting certainty that I was even able to cope with extremely heavy affective loads. Work with affects in body-related therapy is based on an immediacy of experiences that can hardly be achieved in a purely verbal setting. To my mind, this immediacy of experiences is not only linked with an opening of all sensory channels, as described by Pfannschmidt, but also with the physical-motor innervations one experiences in the course of physical contact or in motion.

Let me summarise the benefits and risks of body-related approaches and their impact on affective experience:

1   Body-related work gives much more immediate access to affects than would be the case in a purely verbal setting. Of course, this comes with certain risks, e.g. the possibility of shifting defences of the patient, manipulated transference by instructions for body exercises, and the risk of a positive correction of experiences while negative developments in transference are overlooked. Moreover, the more directing body-related approach does not foster the patient's fantasy space quite as much as the psychoanalytical setting. Even though the approach is different, the result is the same as in psychoanalysis: traumatic positions of the patient gradually rise to the surface and can be worked through.

2   In the patient–therapist relation, while working 'in transference', the affects experienced by the patient are more intense and dense; they also have a different quality, different 'states of aggregation' (Moser, 1989a). Love and hate can be felt more strongly than in a purely verbal therapy space; they are quasi-embodied. The opening of all sensory channels leads the way towards a comprehensive experience of emotions and body while also occasionally requiring concrete physical interaction with the therapist, which may but does not necessarily have to include physical touch.

3   This method broadens the range of indications of patients with whom we can work in psychoanalysis, so as to e.g. include patients with 'traumatic affects': as a defence against their dangerous affects, which they fear might break out like an explosion, thus flooding their ego, they use a high degree of verbal and intellectual detachment which may

even border on a state of unreality. It is practically impossible or very difficult to approach such patients verbally, the psychoanalytical process often stalls whereas more direct access to their affects – always taking into consideration their anxieties and resistance – would be advantageous because the analyst is 'on site' then. However, there is a risk of the self being flooded when doing body work 'in transference' so that occasionally one might better switch to scenic interventions (e.g. role play) that are easy on oneself.

4   By fostering body perception – in affects such as love and hate, but not only these – a 'body space' getting ever more differentiated gradually emerges in the patient. Thus Freud's idea that the I is primarily physical in nature (Freud, 1923) continues to be valid. In times such as our post-modern age that is hostile to the body, increasingly turning to virtual contacts as a substitute for real ones, a time of alienation from corporeality and sensuality, when the feeling of being part of nature is lost, it seems to me that a body-friendly basic attitude is an indispensable corrective in psychoanalytical therapy.

Description of a case

The following description of a case (Scharff, 1998: 46ff.) shows exemplarily how body-related work – in the present case it is an intervention by touch – can be introduced into a psychoanalytical situation in a discerning manner, and what kind of impact such an intervention has on the way in which the patient experiences her affects. In this context, the term 'psychoanalytical situation' is used as a heading for situations 'where the methodical use of transference and resistance makes it possible for a psychoanalytical process to develop' (ibid.: 45).

> In my practice, the . . . patient . . . a borderline case with autistic traits, is in an experiential space which also includes the possibility of a staging interaction. She suffers from a severe organic visual disorder but primarily sought treatment for feelings of vacuity and depressions. Earlier, analysis had come to a standstill for a long time, and even now, the relation between the patient and myself was characterised by rigidity, mask-like stiffness and ritualisation. We changed the setting from her lying down to sitting face to face. This patient also talked about dreams she was unable to finish because she woke up in a panic. For example, she is afraid of being submerged in water even though a swimming instructor is close by and tells her what to do. Or she dreams that she is a little girl in a children's home and I tell her all of a sudden that the treatment is over. In her dream, she falls silent and holds on to a spoon before she wakes up. I will say more about the background of

her disorder below and also explain why I eventually suggested a staging interaction to the patient in one session: I said that we could just wait and see what happens when she lies down on the couch and I sit beside her and perhaps put my hand on her shoulder for some time if she wants me to. When we really did that in the following session, the room fell totally silent and like a little child, the patient seemed to feel in good care in my presence for long, almost timeless moments, even though she was not entirely free from anxiety. Finally, we exchanged a few words. When I withdrew my hand after announcing that I would do so, the patient recoiled as if she was experiencing something very dreadful. We sat face to face for a while and spoke about what was experienced.

(Scharff, 1998: 53)

In contrast to conventional body-related therapies (bioenergetics, biodynamics, Hakomi, Radix, Reichian therapy, etc.) the guiding principle of all interventions – including those at the level of body and actions – is the dynamic of transference and counter-transference. In spite of all differences, this guiding principle, as well as work with internal, unconscious ideas, so-called representations, is shared by all analytical approaches. This also applies to processes which deliberately include times of (inter)action by gestures or movements, with or without touching. In terms of structure, such actions should be considered 'testing actions', an 'intended model scene expressed in movements' (Scharff, 1998: 47). Usually, the analyst's intervention takes as its point of departure a certain aspect of the relation which spontaneously develops between patient and therapist while they are speaking. In view of this, the method is not rooted in the body but in the relation, while attention to bodily (i.e. non-verbal) dialogue processes plays a major role. Relations are always also articulated at this basal non-verbal level forming the communicative backdrop without which the transmission of verbal messages would not make sense. The communicative backdrop ensures a fine-tuning of closeness and distance that is negotiated unconsciously, and a specific atmospheric colouring of the therapeutic situation that it usually easy to feel and difficult to express in words. If we consider the quantity of information exchanged, the backdrop accounts for some 80 per cent of communication on the whole (Fivaz-Depeursinge, 1998). It is also present, but hard to articulate, in purely verbal settings because the exchange of information does not so much take place in the realm of declarative knowledge but of implied procedural knowledge. Settings which include body perception and occasional opportunities for body experiences by action and touch facilitate the conscious perception of implied procedural processes because of their closeness to body and action. In the present case, the setting helped the patient out of the deadlock she had found herself in when undergoing verbal analysis.

The biographical background of the case

Over time, the following description of the patient's early relationship to her mother emerged through reconstruction, elements from transference and counter-transference, dreams and biographical details: the patient's mother had apparently had little tolerance for insecurity, anxiety or dissension *vis-à-vis* her baby:

> She did not let herself in for the venture to turn the child into her baby by trying to empathise but entrenched herself behind a wall of regulations derived from her own mother about how she and the baby would have to behave. The baby's vivacity was a threat to the mother so that the actual unconscious motivation behind all her actions was to keep the baby quiet before she actually let herself in for any internal engagement with the child. Breast-feeding and feeding was thus tantamount to taking all vivacity away from the child, a way of putting it off and thus preventing herself from becoming involved with it. However, this mode of behaviour was not at work all the time, there were moments when the mother briefly engaged with the child but then broke their togetherness off again. In response to this experience, the patient withdrew to an autistic-contagious position (Ogden, 1989). Premature sham autonomy in the presence of a relationship characterised by clinging and psychic non-separation from the object, permanent hypervigilance, almost delusional omnipotent control over everything, those were the characteristics of their relationship. The patient felt deep-rooted anxiety and aversion to any affective movement and real affective experience because she feared a traumatic slip of the mechanisms regulating her affects in case the experience suddenly stopped. Her relation to the object was characterised by a deep-seated ambitendency, the object was at the same time good and bad, seducing and repudiating ... This was exactly the configuration of the relation in which treatment had been stuck for a long time. The patient was neither able to leave nor was she able to develop something new with me as she stayed on.
>
> (Scharff, 1998: 53)

Details of the intervention by touch

The first thing to do is work with the anxieties and resistance which the patient starts to feel when the analyst offers to touch her; after all, her resistance must not be overruled. Once the analyst has suggested to the patient to try a clearly delineated intervention by touch, advance work on the scene will start in the patient's fantasies, before the interaction actually takes place. This also happened with the patient in the case described above. 'She is afraid that she will lose her footing, to fall, to surrender, and also to become too heavy for me' (Scharff, 1998: 53).

The analyst does not urge the patient, leaving options for the suggested intervention open – this can be compared to offering an interpretation which the patient may accept or reject. 'When the patient lay down on the couch on her side the next day, I remained seated on my chair first and then sat down beside her after some time of asking questions and co-ordinating' (ibid.).

When the patient lies down and before the analyst places his hand on her shoulder, both pay attention to the atmosphere that materialises and the non-verbal quality of the emergent relation:

> She is lying there silently, her hand at her mouth, and I experience from a different angle close up what she told me earlier: on the couch, she would sometimes feel like a little child, or actually was a child. As she does not move and her face is slightly flushed, I presume that she is still not entirely free from anxiety and tension. However, at the same time a surprising feeling of calmness is conveyed.
>
> (ibid.: 53)

After the patient has adjusted to the new situation triggered off by less of a distance between herself and her analyst, he says 'after a while . . . I could also imagine putting my hand on her shoulder the way we had discussed. Eventually, the patient asks me to do that' (ibid.: 53–54).

At the level of a non-verbal exchange of signals, the patient's response to the act of touching is directly perceivable for the analyst, and the non-verbal dialogue in the form of bodily signals and messages guides the complete interaction when this technique is applied: 'The state of peaceful arrival is reinforced, perfect calm sets in. I can also feel this in the changing tonus as the patient accepts my hand. It is only the slightly flushed face that seems to signal some continuing tension' (ibid.: 54).

The end of the intervention actually causes a drastic change in the affective state of the patient:

> When, some time before the end of the session, I announced that I had to lift my hand, the patient responded by convulsively recoiling and withdrawing, dissociating and disconnecting herself in an embittered way. I commented on the change and said that this would perhaps be like retreating from unbearable pain caused by the change in our relation due to the separation. Then the patient sat down on her chair again and we continued to talk for a while.
>
> (ibid.)

Experiencing affects

Scharff continues:

> When the patient arrived the next day she had obviously changed, she was lively, full of interest in the session. She told me she was astonished on what one could experience on the couch – *I* had always said that but now *she* knew, too, and she would be curious about what would lie ahead. While she had been lying on the couch yesterday, she had felt like a small child, all delighted and she had totally lost her sense of time. However, it had been absolutely horrible when I 'suddenly' announced that I would have to take my hand away. For a brief moment she had realised that something in her was crying out: 'If it hurts so much when you leave, I don't want anything from you anymore.' What preoccupied her most was that she had the feeling the whole thing had not been true and real when she rose from the couch.
>
> (ibid.)

The affects triggered off in the patient – probably a combination of love and hate – are very intense and assume a different 'state of aggregation':

> Even though the patient's affects take on a traumatic quality, especially as I lift my hand from her shoulder – and we were both surprised at the intensity of what was happening – the affective process also has certain characteristics of a testing action as it is grounded in a sequence that had been discussed and agreed earlier.
>
> (ibid.: 55)

The scenic work 'in transference' may have affectively flooded the boundaries of the patient's ego briefly, not sustainably. 'At best, the creation of a scene with the mediating structure of a planned "third element" furthers optimal distance and optimal proximity in the therapeutic situation' (ibid.). Without the mediating structure, the therapeutic situation would be too close and too immediate, and the boundaries of the patient's ego would be flooded sustainably, which would be tantamount to a re-traumatising experience. A sufficient degree of the analyst's own experience and long-term supervision in body-related work 'in transference' gives the analyst a feel for the rhythm, dosage and tact that is not only required for verbal interpretations but also for the technique of using physical interventions.

In the present case, the patient's response shows that the intervention by touch had a releasing effect: 'Previously [in the couch setting] my patient's experience was always characterised by a simultaneity of "no distance" in the sense of naked traumatic immediacy, and "absolute distance" in the sense of affective negation' (ibid.). It was only possible for the patient to find a way out of the deadlock when she made the concrete physical experience. 'Via the line linking the doctor at the bedside, the mother at her child's bed, the soothing-accompanying presence of an early part-object' a sensual-gestural relation comes to bear, taking up pre-verbal communicative moments and giving the patient 'support . . . at a concrete-symbolic level.' Such 'closeness' – at least in respect of the spatial configuration, with the analyst entering the protected area around the patient – does not usually exist in psychoanalysis, with the exception of Winnicott (Little, 1985), or 'it is not used methodically' (Scharff, 1998: 56).

Why is it that this experience was so important for the patient, and why was she unable to make such an experience in the classic psychoanalytic setting? For Scharff, the reason for the impact of the concrete intervention by touch lies in a specific quality of regression:

> Here, the result is that the patient feels like a little child, her sense of time changes and for a few moments she feels safe even though the experience is not clearly positive throughout. The patient also reached early somato-psychic states in the classic setting on earlier occasions but it happened in the context of a negative object configuration which she/we were unable to correct for the time being: she felt totally abandoned, isolated, and I was perceived as inaccessible, as if behind glass. *The ambitendency[1] of simultaneous seduction and repudiation, so deeply engrained in the patient's experience, is now taken at least one step towards an understanding of successive stages in time.* This is due to my offering discernible shapes of events in the fields of positive and negative object experience alike, including the sensomotor level and thus also the feedback loops of physical experience, e.g. sitting very close to her, linked with the warmth and slight pressure of my hand on the one hand, and then severing the connection and leaving on the other. The patient will later on undermine these shapes fantasmatically by anticipating the ending at the beginning and in the end believing that she never started in the first place – but the shape of the process experienced haptically will be something that cannot be pushed aside permanently, primarily because it is at the same time the object of our attention.

(Scharff, 1998: 56)

Scharff concludes with a comparison between the verbal-analytical setting and a setting open to body-related interventions:

> Some patients . . . may use parameters of the classic setting, such as the regularity of sessions and the surrounding environment, the act of lying on the couch, the analyst's voice, to name but a few possibilities, to make sure of precisely that quality. Other patients do not succeed

in doing so for a long time or even not at all due to their specific traumata.

(ibid.)

Thus it seems 'that certain patients are only able to face their anxieties of impending doom to the full if a concrete environment is available to affirm the bodily ego senso-motorically so that an oscillating motion between support and catastrophic experience can emerge' (ibid.).

Conclusion

The patient's affective experience is in the centre of the therapeutic process of change. Without affective engagement of patient *and* therapist alike, the therapeutic effects obtained will be unsatisfactory. Without a 'fire that needs to be burning' in the therapeutic process, changes will remain superficial or stuck at an intellectual level. Love and hate are thus indispensable ingredients of any psychotherapeutic treatment.

Due to its very discerning approach to transference and counter-transference, which has meanwhile started to put an emphasis on inter-action, the psychoanalytical process offers a methodological framework in which impulses of love and hate can be given free rein and worked through *in* transference. In many cases, it is helpful to allow the space of imagi-nation to unfold so that affects such as love and hate can be felt in their full intensity. The more senses are allowed to be involved, the more intense and ultimately beneficial will the development of the therapeutic process be. In certain circumstances, it will not be enough to open up the patient's imagination; additional interventions will be required, including the dimen-sion of acting through transference and counter-transference. After all, modern baby research makes it clear that the development of all affects, including the stages leading up to love and hate, starts very early on; initially, it is strictly and closely linked with sensomotor experiences. Some patients only will feel that the therapeutic process touches them sufficiently when they can directly tie in with that level of sensomotor experience.

In some patients, certain specific characteristics of the psychoanalytical setting cause them to see the setting in itself as identical with a central injury of theirs. This may lead to a therapeutic stalemate which will be very hard to break. It is especially the simultaneity of highly contrary tendencies such as seduction and renunciation, as well as love and hate, that may lead into a quandary where there is no more leeway.

In such cases of regression to what is usually a very early traumatic position, the use of modes of sensory perception corresponding to develop-ment (Heisterkamp, 1993), i.e. concrete body-related interaction such as conveying physical support, is often a useful way to break the stalemate. A 'concrete-symbolic' level (Moser, 1989b) comes to bear through a sensory-gestural relation which thus introduces pre-verbal communication into the psychoanalytical setting to a greater extent than is usually the case, eventually setting the ball rolling again. This way, the direct physical experience of emotions within clearly structured therapeutic sequences may give the feelings of anger and love – originally experienced as something dangerous by the patient due to their simultaneity – a chronological order, turning them into defined sequences of interactions or processes of tactile experience, and making the patient's ego more flexible again.

Hence, working in an open psychoanalytical setting would be specially indicated in patients with traumatic affects. It is not a setting where emotions are acted out blindly. The space of action and the body is systematically incorporated in the analytical process while keeping an eye on transference, counter-transference and resistance.

Moreover, experience-oriented, body-related intervention techniques are meaningful as they complement the classic analytical repertory of interventions due to the fact that they counteract the physical and emotional alienation many patients suffer from in our post-modern days. Love and hate can be experienced in a very elementary way, near-physically, when the analytical setting is open to body-related interventions. Patient and analyst will again get a feel for the early experiential world often buried deep down in an adult, a feel for the different experience of time, wholeness and force linked with it, and for a feeling of power that is rooted in the body – an experiential world which in all of us forms the primary rock which all experience is grounded in.

Acknowledgement

This chapter is printed with the support of the Federal Ministry of Education, Science and Culture in Vienna.

Note

1 'Ambitendency' denotes a state of ambivalence, including the aspect of action (i.e. contrary physical impulses).

Bibliography

Balint, M. (1973) *Therapeutische Aspekte der Regression*, Hamburg: Rohwolt.
Dornes, M. (1992) Der Kompetent Säugling. Die Präverbale Entwicklung des Menschen, Frankfurt: Fischer.
Ferenczi, S. (1939) *Bausteine der Psychoanalyse. Arbeiten aus den Jahren 1908–1933*, Bern: Huber.
Fivaz-Depeursinge, E. (1998) Gestische und mimische Interaktion in der primären Dreiecksbeziehung. Therapeutische Implikationen, in P. Geißler and K. Rückert (eds) *Psychoanalyse und Körper* (*Psychosozial*, issue 74), Giessen, pp. 33–43.

Freud, S. (1923) *Das Ich und das Es, GWXIII, S*, 237–289, Frankfurt: Fischer.

Heisterkamp, G. (1993) *Heilsame Berührungen: Praxis leibfundierter analytischer Psychotherapie*, Munich: Pfeiffer.

Krutzenbichler, H.S. and Essers, H. (1991) *Muss denn Liebe Sünde sein?*, Freiburg i.Br: Kore.

Little, M. (1985) Winnicott working in areas where psychotic anxieties predominate, in *Free Association* 3, 9–42.

Moser, T. (1989a) *Körpertherapeutische Phantasien. Psychoanalytische Fallgeschichten neu betrachtet*, Frankfurt: Suhrkamp.

Moser, T. (1989b) Psychoanalyse und Körper, in H.V. Werthmann (ed.) *Unbewußte Phantasien*, Munich: Pfeiffer, pp. 301–318.

Ogden, T.H. (1989) On the concept of an autistic-contiguous position, *International Journal of Psycho-Analysis* 70: 127–139.

Pfannschmidt, H. (1997) Der Körper der Übertragungsliebe, in K. Höhfeld and A.-M. Schlösser (eds) *Psychoanalyse der Liebe*, Giessen: Psychosozial.

Pfannschmidt, H. (1998) Der 'Gebrauch der Lüste' in der Analysestunde, *Forum der Psychoanalyse* 14, 364–384.

Pfannschmidt, H. (2001) Die Auswirkungen der Leib-Seele-Phantasie auf Erotik und Sexualität, Paper given at the Second Vienna Symposium on Psychoanalysis and Body, September 2000 in P. Geißler (ed.) *Über den Körper zur Sexualität finden*, Geißler: Psychosozial..

Scharff, J. (1998) Der 'Erfahrungsraum' der Psychoanalyse und der 'Erfahrungsraum' bei inszenierender Interaktion: ein erster Vergleich, in P. Geißler and K. Rückert (eds) *Psychoanalyse und Körper* (*Psychosozial*, issue 74), Giessen, pp. 45–58.

Stern, D. (1998) 'Now-moments', implizites Wissen und Vitalitätskonturen als neue Basis für psychotherapeutische Modellbildungen, in S. Trautmann-Voigt and B. Voigt (eds) *Bewegung ins Unbewusste. Beiträge zur Säuglingsforschung und analytischen Körperpsychotherapie*, Frankfurt am Main: Brandes & Apsel, pp. 82–96.

Stern, D. (1992) Die Lebenserfahrung des Säuglings, Stuttgart: Klett Cotta.

Ware, R. (2001) Gebrauch der Lüste/Befreiung des Eros. Erotisierte und 'zölibatäre' Gegenübertragungen, in P. Geißler (ed.) *Über den Körper zur Sexualität finden*. Collection of papers held at the Second Vienna Symposium on Psychoanalysis and Body, Giessen, Psychosozial.

Winnicott, D.W. (1973) *Vom Spiel zur Kreativität* [*Playing and Reality*], Stuttgart: Klett.

Winnicott, D.W. (1976) *Von der Kinderheilkunde zur Psychoanalyse* [*Through Paediatrics to Psycho-Analysis*], Munich: Kindler.

Worm, G. (1998) Zum Umgang mit Übertragung in einer analytischen Körperpsychotherapie, in P. Geißler (ed.) *Analytische Körperpsychotherapie in der Praxis*, Munich: Pfeiffer bei Klett-Cotta, pp. 69–82.

Chapter 17

Love, hate and violation

Richard Mizen

Introduction

In this chapter I wish to consider patients for whom the experience of the passionate affects of love or hate is apparently to be avoided at all costs. Such patients seem to ignore the present emotional and even the concrete realities of relationships and are unable to conceptualise or be consciously aware of the presence or operation of affective elements in their lives. The impression is created that they are divesting themselves of their own experience. Cognitive and intellectual capacities are also impaired, in contrast to an infinite capacity for rationalisation and intellectualisation.

In due course it may become clear that the patient is actively avoiding circumstances likely to evoke feelings of love or hate. Alternatively relationships and events will be interpreted in an idiosyncratic manner, which casts them in a persecutory light. It will be noticed, however, that the persecution takes a form which leaves the patient feeling essentially passive, if not paralysed, and at the mercy of other people's passions or the storms of life. Only over time will analytic work reveal that their passions are eschewed because they are experienced as violent, and especially as taking the form of intrusion or violation. Furthermore such intrusions or violations are felt to be closely linked with the threat of imminent annihilation. These threats may be conceived to be of a psychological kind for example, mental breakdown or quite concretely as a threat to physical survival, like war or natural disaster.

The apparent lack of affect will also be manifest within the transference and, in consequence, analysts may be presented with considerable problems of technique. For long periods these patients seem unable to make use of analytic work or the analyst's interventions but rather settle into what may have the makings of an interminable, addictive and parasitic dependency. On analytic investigation, the apparent static quality of this situation is belied by the fluidity of the underlying processes of mentation and in particular the operation of defences at varying levels of psychic functioning. Initially Oedipal material may suggest the operation of ego defences;

however, interpretation of these alone is likely to prove ineffectual. Further analysis is likely to reveal the dominance of the patient's reinterpretation of the analyst's comments in the light of underlying, unconscious phantasies or preconceptions, of a pre-Oedipal kind. This has the effect of neutralising the analyst as a mutative agent and ensuring that the basic structure of the patient's defences remains intact, in particular a phantasy of 'ideal' feeding or following further regression, a defensive phantasy of fusion, between mother and baby. Michael Fordham has described these defences, as 'defences of the self' (1996).

In analysis, it may be surprising when it is found that these patients are extremely antipathetic to the development of passionate feelings, as the reason they often give for wanting analysis is their perceived lack of capacity for feelings of love (and rather less often hate). Commonly, instead, they feel that their lives are dominated by anxiety, usually of a more or less persecutory kind, felt to be of uncertain origin, and often by an overwhelming sense of grievance. Despite the ostensible absence of strong affects, fear of breakdown or emotional outburst may be close to consciousness.

None the less the analyst may be aware of the presence of passionate affects, as a consequence of the patient's emotional impact on him or her, through the patient's description of passionate elements in distorted or projected form or, alternatively, in an awareness of 'absences' or lacunae in the patient's mental life.

The presentation by patients of 'absence' is particularly misleading in that an impression of homogeneity is created in the face of heterogeneous mental processes. I hope to show that it is important that the particular nature of the experience, which is being voided at any particular moment in the analysis, is addressed. This is with particular reference to the severity of psychopathology, but also for the purposes of treatment and technique. In my view, for analysis to be effective, it is critical that the analyst's interventions are syntonic with the character of the current anxieties and concomitant defences operating at any particular time.

Clinically, presentation of an 'absence' in some patients at one particular moment may be due to the operation of relatively well-developed defences of the late Oedipal constellation. In other people or the same patient at another moment it may be related to defences of a more primitive kind (pre-Oedipal in Freud's terms, early Oedipal in Klein's).[1] This may be further complicated by the presentation of the pre-Oedipal within a late Oedipal arena.

This makes for a complex clinical picture in which the successive levels of psychological functioning may be collapsed, and disparate emotional realities may have the appearance of being the same. An example of this, which I will consider in more detail below (p. 295), is the superficial similarity in presentation as a consequence of repression on the one hand

and of projective identification on the other, further complicated in some patients by their movement between these as modes of defensive organisation.

The analyst's ability to discern and interpret these distinctions is crucial, clinically. Failure to do so may, on the one hand lead to an interminable pseudo-analysis, reliant on death, illness, or some external factor to stop it. Alternatively collusion between analyst and patient, which ignores the most pressing aspects of the patient's psychopathology, may develop. In the former case the sense of being helplessly at the mercy of the external world will prevail. This may be consistent with Winnicott's concept of the 'false self' (Winnicott 1968) but is more likely to be related to the formation of split-off, 'cystic', areas in the patient's mind. In the latter case whilst superficially this may effect a better adaptation to the world, at a deeper level the underlying atmosphere of hopelessness and despair is reinforced.

I will proceed by giving two illustrations of the ways in which this phenomenon is manifest according to the nature of the underlying anxieties. I will put this simply – too simply of course – as a matter of whether the anxiety relates to the fear of being hurt, therefore Oedipal and related to castration anxiety, or pre-Oedipal and related to anxieties about annihilation.

A previously withdrawn and socially isolated woman was admitted to a mental hospital having hit the man and woman who lived next door to her. The reason she gave for the assault was that they were sending 'electrical waves' through her bedroom wall in order to interfere with her body. Talking to her it became clear that what had happened was that she had heard the couple having sexual intercourse through the party wall between their houses. The woman's description of her body sensations seemed to indicate that she had become sexually excited. She had, however, experienced her own sexual excitement as both alien and a violation – an assault – to which she had responded 'in kind'.

In the second example a woman found herself sexually excited by a man she met, having previously considered herself to be lacking a capacity for sexual feelings. Her response was to vilify the man on the basis that *he* had ruined her sense of equanimity and self-containment.

It may be seen that in essence the experiences of these two women are similar; but there are also important differences. The first woman felt that her sexual sensations were an attack upon her by concrete, alien elements to the extent of threatening her survival. For the second woman, her sexual feelings were experienced as an intrusion by alien elements, the harbinger of emotional hurt. The defences employed (and undermined) will be seen to be of projective identification in the first case and repression in the second. An important distinction is that in repression it is the contents of the mind that are subject to splitting, whilst in projective identification it is the mind itself which is subject to splitting (i.e. the structure of the mind). Repression presupposes the establishment and continuing existence of a structured mind (so-called horizontal splitting), whilst projective identification presupposes the lack or destruction of a structured mind or part of a structured mind ('vertical' splitting). In my experience these phenomena are often conflated.

In both cases it is the pain associated with depressive anxieties that threatens. The link to a primal scene inherent in sexual sensations and their concomitant images, and experiences of love and hate, arouses the reality of Oedipal exclusion. Feelings of love or hate are experienced both as links between objects and as links to objects. In these cases the experience of love and hate in relation to the objects are felt to be precursors of mental pain. Severing the links – denying the love or the hate – is intended to set aside the pain. The difference between the cases, however, is in the significance that the Oedipal situation holds. For the first woman, it contains a sense of a violent assault upon the mother/infant relationship (which is to be evacuated by means of the violent assault on the parental figures). For the second woman, being faced with the internal reality of the primal scene has the significance of an intrusive, narcissistic blow, against which her sexual feelings have been repressed as a means of severing a mental link between the experience of desire and its possible frustration and pain. In the first case, the link that is broken is of the kind described by Bion (1987) in terms of a destruction of a part of the mind. It is the primal scene itself that is destroyed, along with the sensory apparatus that perceives it. In the second the link is of a different order. The mind is intact, but the contents repressed so that they are unavailable in a direct way, but will be apparent in dreams, thoughts or other symbolic forms (Freud 1966; Bion 1977). A blind eye is turned. In both cases what is defended against is the emergence of the experience of loss and the defensive arrangements are tenaciously held on to, even if the significance of the loss is different. Likewise, in the transference the defence will be against an appreciation of the nature of the analytic dyad (and of the primal scene), with concomitant technical problems for analysis. As noted, patients are likely to be highly ambivalent about any change taking place both internally and in the analytic relationship, although the resistance to change will vary considerably, both quantitatively and qualitatively.

A further layer of complexity is that, of course, most patients do not fit into a discrete category but rather demonstrate aspects of both. Some degree of both elements is very likely to be found in all people. There may, however, be considerable differences in terms of the distribution of the defences along an 'integrated–neurotic–psychotic' continuum, and I wish to give particular attention to patients showing fluid movement along this line. This seems to be particularly characteristic of patients for whom the experience of passionate feelings is of violation or intrusion. Notable, however, is the way in which the various levels of functioning can be maintained, without a permanent movement into one or the other. This seems to be achieved by means of complex patterns of splitting, which allow for movement between different defensive positions according to the nature of the current presenting threat, both during the period of infant development and in the contemporary situation.

One consequence of the disruption of links in such patients is their apparent passivity and difficulty in remembering or thinking logically (Freud 1984; Bion 1987). An atmosphere of overriding urgency or crisis can develop. This may take the form of the analyst becoming aware of a sense of the concrete circumstances of the patient's life intruding upon, or even violating, the integrity of the analysis. If undetected it may be easy for the analyst to become seduced by the patient producing pressing, even dangerous situations in their external life that appear to need urgent attention if injury or loss is to be avoided. The patient may appear to be oblivious to the consequences of their actions, even though similar situations may have repeatedly occurred during the analysis. The patient seems to be unable to learn from their experience and appears unable to link the steps that have led to the crisis or loss. These situations may be assaultative, intrusive or violating and can be genuinely dangerous or likely to lead to 'unnecessary' and painful loss.

The fundamental, unconscious purpose of producing such persecutory situations is likely to be the production of a sense of violation or intrusion in the analyst. If the analyst seeks to avoid the sense of violation or intrusion by means of action (in Bion's terms) they will be successfully prevented by the patient from investigating the psychological circumstances that produced the original sense of violation in the patient. The analyst attending to the matter of the underlying problem is likely to be met by the patient asserting that the analyst does not understand, is unempathic, callous, mad, and so on. Essentially, however, these may be considered as pressures upon the analyst to abandon an analytic attitude and to establish an addictive dependency based on a collusive, illusory sense of safety from mental pain.

During the early years of an analysis a patient, Rose, claimed that she had no capacity for having her own ideas or thoughts. She contended that any ideas that she possessed were in reality other people's ideas adopted by her. In the same way she said that she lacked passionate feeling so that her life felt to her to have little or no purpose or direction. In a short time this became constellated in the transference so that the contents of her mind were held by her to be a consequence of my having put them there. Any suggestion that she had her own ideas or feelings of love or hate was firmly rejected on the basis that she lacked the capacity for them. Amongst many similar statements was one to the effect that 'my brains are scrambled eggs'.

This development in the transference was signalled at the outset when, after her initial consultation, she wrote to say that she had thought better of analysis and did not wish to proceed. I had anticipated as much but responded by writing to say, in a rather general way, that she might be afraid of continuing because she feared what she might discover about herself. This prompted her to return, but it soon became clear that this return was as though it was on the basis of her having been urged by me to do so. This was in contrast to the pressing feelings of despair and neediness that had led her to seek an analysis in the first place.

The main tenor of sessions was to do with the ways in which she had to struggle to manage a barrage of demands made on her. She felt that she was incapable of meeting these but had none the less to attempt to do so in order to defer a final, inarticulate catastrophe. An almost overwhelming sense of despair and hopelessness prevailed, of a 'worked to death' kind. All interventions by me were felt to be inadequate to the task of containing, processing or understanding the factors contributing to Rose's sense of chronic anxiety, which was partly expressed as insomnia. This attitude also pertained in relation to her three children, whom she felt to be either constitutionally impaired in their capacity to learn or irreparably damaged by the circumstances of their births. As such they too were condemned to an unsuccessful struggle to meet the demands of relentless teachers and the like. Success was to be brief respite periods of managing to meet some demand or other, but the more usual circumstance was failure to fulfil other people's insatiable demands.

My interventions were interpreted in the light of this, as demands, exhortations, threats, instructions, advice or, alternatively, as evidence of my incapacity to bear reality and thus a delusional retreat into 'thought'. Comment about Rose's descriptions of her world was inferred by her to be an attempt to get her to be different or to distort the unbearable reality of tortured existence. This took very subtle forms; for example, the patient contending that I was operating upon the basis of a system in which I was prohibited from trying to control patients. None the less I felt compelled to do so, albeit in a covert fashion, by means of hints and innuendo in order to avoid the prohibition. On other occasions Rose considered that I operated on the basis of an illusory system, which was intended to substitute masturbatory fantasy for unbearable reality. At times I was excused on the ostensible grounds that this was undertaken for 'benign' reasons. At others she was afraid that I was the devil incarnate, and that the plausibility that she sometimes felt my comments to have as a trick to ensure her fall, damnation and eventually her entry into hell.

Two aspects of Rose's biographical details are relevant here. Rose's mother had several other children and considered herself to be devoted to them and to the many grandchildren that in time were born. Birth and the production of children were, in the culture of the family, its very *raison d'être*. A particular aspect of this, which was highly valued, was the capacity to breast feed, ostensibly on the grounds that this was what was best for the children's physical and emotional growth. As an infant, Rose was alone amongst her siblings in being unable to breast feed. It was unclear if she had rejected the breast or whether her mother had been in some way unable to produce milk, or a combination of these. After a few weeks of attempting to breast feed, Rose's mother gave up. Rose's notion was that her mother had become demoralised by the difficulties, and her husband had taken her on an extended holiday abroad without the infant. Rose was passed to another carer, who even after mother's return continued to care for her a good deal of the time. Another child was conceived during the holiday and within a year mother was able to breast feed 'successfully' once more. In her life, Rose considered this to be a tragic failure, which had marked her out as different and inferior. Associated with this Rose considered her own breasts to be inadequate, both less attractive and less functional than her sisters' whom she considered had larger and better breasts. Fertility problems had meant that Rose and her husband were unable to have children and eventually they had adopted three. Rose commented that ironically these children felt more hers than any babies biologically her own. In this circumstance, she would have felt that her mother would have appropriated them. As adoptees mother had less invested in them.

The other biographical facts concerned the patient's father. Throughout Rose's childhood he had displayed his genitals to the children, ostensibly as a demonstration of liberal and unfettered relationships within the culture of the family. He also insisted that his daughters swim naked in rivers into their late adolescence. During Rose's latency period he had often touched Rose's and her younger sister's vaginas in a masturbatory fashion and had also got them to masturbate him during shared baths under the guise of 'washing'. Penetration did not take place, but father's penile erections placed his actions firmly in the sexual sphere. An elder sister had been sent home from school for masturbating and had apparently refused to comply with father's sexualised behaviour.

Associated with these matters was a family story, ostensibly amusing and with the currency of a family myth. This concerned father's father who insisted, when Rose's father was a boy, that he often walk through a gaggle of geese, despite the boy's terror that his penis would be pecked off. Rose associated this with a time when her son developed a phobia about chickens after a cockerel attacked him. Also with a childhood memory of being teased by her parents about being sent to a sausage factory passed on journeys to school and a fantasy about castrating her husband, when she saw him naked, praying at the side of their bed.

In trying to understand the experience of patients such as Rose a pronounced difficulty is the fluidity of their mental states, as they move between different modes of mental functioning not only between sessions but also, importantly, from moment to moment within them. Of course such a state of affairs is axiomatic, as portrayed in Bion's statement that 'Winnicott says that the patient *needs* to regress: Melanie Klein says that they *must not* regress: I say they *are* regressed' (Bion 1992). It is to be emphasised, however, that this fluidity of movement between defensive mental states is particularly marked in patients such as these. Its mercurial quality is itself a defence and adds a further layer of complexity to the other aspects of the defensive arrangements employed, as they move between relatively primitive defences of the self and relatively well-developed ego defences of a more established Oedipal constellation.

Michael Fordham's extension of Jung's theories and their application to infancy concerned itself initially with normal development – the unfolding and personalisation of the innate, the archetypal, especially the self, into childhood. In Fordham's scheme mental life grows out of an initially undifferentiated psychosomatic entity, which he refers to as the 'primary self' (Urban 1992) following on from Jung's concept of an 'original self' (Jung 1927). The most important aspect of this is the infant's experience, which is organised around innate expectation on the one hand and around relationships with external objects on the other. Internal objects, and therefore psychic structures, are created as a consequence of the archetypal – the innate – meeting with experience. Love or hate are feeling qualities that mediate the relationship between the object and the self, although initially they are experienced as inherent qualities belonging to the object. Only later are they felt to belong to the self and, relatively later still, to qualities of relationships. Fordham's concept is similar to Bion's notion of an innate preconception meeting with the preconceived object, leading to the formation of a conception. Fordham noted that he was unable to improve upon Bion's notion of alpha function and where things go well a relationship (usually with the mother at first, but later with other objects, both animate and inanimate) mediates the expectation. In consequence meaning may be derived from the experience, and toxic elements – annihilatory anxiety for example – which are painful to the infant can be kept within bearable limits.

In this way mentation and mental structures develop in their various aspects and levels of sophistication. Fordham refers to these processes as 'deintegration' (of the innate expectation), and 'reintegration' (of the expectation met, modified and personalised). These mechanisms are carefully distinguished from disintegration. The term 'disintegration' in Fordham's model is reserved for those situations in which the anxiety generated by the experience is too great for the infant to bear. In this circumstance the threat is dealt with by means of a destruction of the sensory apparatus (mostly through splitting and projection), so that which is feared cannot be seen (Fordham 1985). Characteristically the fragments of the experience are dimly apprehended as a disaster. This is equivalent to dread (Bion) or psychotic anxiety (Winnicott). This is qualitatively different from the situation in which the deintegrate is reintegrated, with concomitant growth in ego strength or situations were the risk is of emotional hurt, leading to subjection to ego defences such as repression.

In this way Rose's experience can be understood as having its earliest roots in a specific failure in the mother/infant relationship. Both Bion and Fordham emphasis the communicative as opposed to the defensive role of projective identification in the ordinary development of the relationship between mother and infant. Thus primitive or proto-mental elements (beta elements) can be contained by mother in a way that transforms the experience into mental elements and mental structures. Failure of containment on the part of the mother, or an excess of innate aggression in the infant unmet by mother, may lead to the conversion of the projective identificatory processes into evacuatory defensive measures against annihilatory anxiety. Something of this may be inferred both from Rose's material and from her emotional impact upon me. This would appear to be along the lines of excessive (i.e. violent) projective identification by mother into the infant, combined with her inability to accept the infant's (presumably increasingly violent) projective identification, leading to the breakdown of the mother/infant relationship. In part it would be the avoidance of a repetition of this situation that Rose so avidly guarded herself against. Mother's projective identification is experienced as a violent, concrete intrusion into the infant, and the infant's projective identifications (including the re-projection of mother's projective identification) as an evacuation of concrete matter which is unmet. In consequence an overwhelming sense of emptiness, coupled with external menace, prevails. This pernicious combination gives the patient's experience the tone of violation or incipient violation and in defence a tendency to an escalating resort to violent projective identification.

Thus Rose was aware on the one hand of the absent 'good' mother providing an ideal feed to her needy sisters (but not to her) and on the other of a 'bad' phallic father intruding upon her with his pressing, infantile neediness. It should be noted, however, that it is irrelevant whether the affects are destructive or creative, of love or hate or potentially pleasurable or painful. It is the passionate, fierce nature of the affects that is important, so that the destructiveness is brought to bear on the affects regardless of their nature. The destructiveness also compounds the anxiety in a paranoid manner in consequence and a vicious circle of undifferentiated passionate elements is created, which can only be voided. Amongst these elements is crude, undifferentiated, ruthless love, in which the wish to possess and the wish to devour may be confused where not differentiated by the mother. Rose's account suggests that her infant need to feed is felt to be destructive of that upon which she depends, and the conduct of her adult relationships reflects this. This much is to be expected, of course, but in patients such as Rose this situation is complicated by the mother's projection of her own, similar qualities into her baby. In contrast to the 'Lady Bountiful' fantasy of mother is the 'Old Woman Who Lived In A Shoe' reality. The result is a system in which there is difficulty in taking things in, as to do so would explode the myth of 'mother's' self-sufficiency and reveal the essentially anal and evacuatory character of what purports to be a creative or feeding relationship. Should this happen it is feared that mother's depression (and of course Rose's) will lead to collapse and annihilation in the light of the underlying conviction that her food is shit and that she can give birth only to little shits. The failure to take in leads to further impoverishment, which in turn is defended against by projective identification and resort to further, omnipotent Lady Bountiful-type solutions. Further difficulties in taking in arise, potentially *ad infinitum* or until events, disease or death intervenes. The solution that appealed to Rose was embodiment of a mother's Lady Bountiful identity (mother's large, full breasts) but was constantly painfully aware of her inability to meet this (her sense that her own breasts are in some way inadequate).

This situation is overdetermined, however, and reinforced by Rose's defences against her envy of her mother's real creative feeding capacity. The defences are lent substance by the extent to which the mother's real capacities for feeding or creativity are diminished or destroyed, by the exaggeration and denigration contingent on the idealisation, thus 'proving' in Rose's mind her mother's inability to provide or make anything worth while.

I am aware that to this point I have frequently used the words 'love' and to 'hate', and that as they stand these terms lack sufficient precision, clinically. In my view they are useful only as empty concepts available to be filled by clinical experience as it arises, and it is necessary to consider closely the nature of the experience being discussed. What I have in mind here are inferred infant experiences of strong, passionate but poorly differentiated affects of an 'I' and 'not I' kind – that love and hate are at least initially felt to be concrete qualities of an object, its love-fullness or hate-fullness, rather than qualities of a relationship. The distinction between body sensation and psychic experience may be almost entirely absent. The establishment of a 'skin' and therefore of some sense of internal and external spaces will, however, have been achieved. Only as a later development are love and hate felt to be qualities of relationships, and it is the failure to firmly establish this mental development which is an important aspect of the difficulties of patients like Rose. This distinction, if overlooked by the analyst, is likely to lead to impasse. Attention to the patient's experience is critical in order to avoid an intellectualised, adult-centric, defensive collusion in the analytic dyad. In analytic work, clinically it is important to interpret the distinctions between love, which is based upon an apprehension of the whole object and the idealised phantasy based on the exploitation of aspects of objects. Nor is the phantasy to be confused with actual early object relating or the idealisation that results from a good mother and baby experience, which may in due course coalesce into rich and full whole-object relationships.

Similar mechanisms may be seen in the interaction of Rose's defences with her father's projectively identified anxieties. It is to be understood here that her father's phallic qualities are not considered to be masculine. The sexual relationship between father and children can also be seen as the expression of Rose's phantasy about her family which is essentially pre-Oedipal in the sense that only mothers and infants exist. The phantasy includes father being experienced as a kind of 'super' mother, the possessor of a super nipple/penis. In this way he can be disregarded as a threat to the central underlying phantasy of the relationship with a mother (although of course envy is considerably increased) because he *is* a type of mother. At the same time his potential as a 'third' in the Oedipal configuration is negated, along with his potential as a masculine figure, his penis and his testes (the latter's existence being completely disregarded). Rather than father facilitating the progression into the world and effecting a separation from mother, he was experienced as reinforcing maternal dominance. It seems likely that this situation was further compounded by her father's own uncertainty about his masculinity, in turn reinforced by the family phantasy. The projective identificatory aspects of the sexual contact between him and his daughter may be a reflection of his own need to enact a phantasy of a fused relationship with mother in the face of his own catastrophic fears of abandonment and annihilation. The descriptions of the geese, sausages, cockerel and castration seem to support this as expressions both of the wish to possess by devouring, father's penis/nipple, at the same time as his potential to come between mother and baby, and especially produce new babies, is destroyed.

For Rose only the shadow of her father as a real object remained in the background as a place into which a crude criticality or moralising judgement could be located. This is the world of 'should', 'ought' and 'must' (and so on) as opposed to 'need', 'want' or 'desire'. One may wonder whether Rose's father was anxious about being the recipient of his wife and daughters' projections contingent on the masculine role of symbolically embodying separation, and that the concomitant hate, as well as Oedipal love, proved to be overwhelming.

These early developmental difficulties may mean that the impact of pre-Oedipal defences on the individual's experiences of the Oedipal situation may be overriding, so that the establishment of stable whole-object relating may be effectively prevented. One consequence of this is that, whilst the passing of time and increased physical maturity expand the opportunities for the exposure to affective states, there is not a parallel increase in the capacity to manage or process them. It is to be noted, however, that the Oedipal configuration is not destroyed. Only by recourse to splitting may the Oedipal and the pre-Oedipal be kept separate or bypassed, rather than integrated or fail altogether. I believe that it is a consequence of the particular nature of these splitting mechanisms that the fluidity of the overall defensive structure is achieved.

In addition there is a conjunction between the infant's destructiveness and the parent's projective identification into the infant. Thus an actual failure on the part of the parent, coincides with the infant's wish for a failure by the parent in order to escape jealousy and envy. In extreme cases psychotic illness, latent or frank, may result; satisfactory pre-Oedipal development, in the sense of firm establishment of self-structures, coupled with problems in the Oedipal situation, will lead to neurosis. In Rose's case the picture is a much more mixed one, with fluidity in the modes of mental functioning. I use the word 'fluidity' in order to distinguish it from instability.

Clinically the movement is between modes. Thus in a session which had in its early part a good deal of material about impulsive sexual behaviour and distinguishing between explicitly sexual and non-sexual relationships, Rose said anxiously: 'My daughter told me that she would be home by eleven o'clock last night but was not home until after midnight.' I responded: 'You are anxious because there is a muddle in your mind about what are your sexual ideas and what are your daughter's. This makes it difficult for you to know what it is you feel about her staying out late.' Rose replied: 'So you think I should not say anything about it then?'

In this situation the analyst's interpretation is experienced as threatening to precipitate a withdrawal of a projection into her daughter, where her sexual fantasy is safely located. This may lead to a lifting of the repression and the emergence of sexual feelings, which for Rose are a threat in a number of ways. In order to avoid the pain contingent on the emergence of sexual feelings, more primitive defences are employed, so that a part of her mind is evacuated into the analyst – in this case the part that is capable of thinking about sex. In consequence the interpretation is concretised and subverted into an attempt by the analyst to control her.

Rose gave an example of such a situation that emerged during the analysis, when suspicion arose that Rose's father was sexually interested in his granddaughters. The matter was reported to Rose's mother, who curtailed the complaint, with the comment 'Say no more', following which father's behaviour stopped.

This can be thought about in terms of her need to keep a particular type of relationship going. In the transference, this way of relating renders the analyst incapable of having a seminal influence upon her in a way that might lead to her developing a conception. Instead the interaction was transposed so that the intercourse is anal in character (masquerading as feeding), with a central aim of exerting power and control. When anxiety about the nature of this addictive form of dependency makes itself felt, the wish to be fed can be projected into the analyst so that he is felt to demand a need for reassurance. In this way separation is avoided and the defensive phantasy of an ideal breast unified with a feeding baby is preserved. Intercourse, which might lead to a conception, is obliterated along with the possibility of progress in psychic development and the analytic work.

A central problem is the insistence on absolutes and of either/or conceptions of inside or outside. There can be no in and out either sexually or psychically. This can be as concrete as experiencing sexual intercourse – for example, as a series of experiences of being 'inside' side by side with a parallel set of experiences of being 'outside'. With Rose this was given concrete form in the manner of her entry and exit to the consulting room. On arrival she had the capacity to hurl herself from about half way across the room to land horizontal upon the couch in the prone position. On leaving she jack-knifed her body in a way that brought her vertical, to land running, out of the room. This affected me with a sense of being intruded upon on entry and a painful caesura on her departure.

The purpose of this and similar devices is to attempt to exclude anything which might touch on a loving intercourse between the internal parents. Equally, the reality of hateful intercourse is also avoided. In the analytic relationship this was expressed in the denial of relating or activity, which operates on the basis of curiosity or of learning from experience. It should be noted here that in stark contrast to the explicit culture within Rose's family, which idealised babies and motherhood, was a profound hatred of real babies who are real, separate people rather than extensions of the mother's narcissistically invested self. Babies, like ideas, can only be adopted, although in the background was the fear of the 'real' mother returning, filled with vengefulness to reclaim her infants. The potential for mother having her own babies, or the patient realising a conception, is avoided by resorting to 'scrambled eggs'.

The way in which the reality is done away with is of critical importance here, both theoretically and clinically. The 'absence' that is experienced by the analyst may be to do with the operation of repression, or it may be to do with more primitive mechanisms of splitting and projection and, in particular, projective identification. With repression, what is implied is the operation of defences of a more sophisticated kind related to the rendering unconscious of mental elements, which are well established within the psychic structure. Where more primitive it is related to the pre-Oedipal. Thus this relates to the operation of alpha function, by which means proto-mental elements can be transformed into various forms of mental representation, dreams and associations or, alternatively, to its absence in which case the failure of alpha function results in psychic fragmentation. In both cases the objective is to destroy the reality of the loving and hateful qualities in the relationship. It is to be understood that the patient does not lack the capacity for love and hate, only that the patient has created a mental system in which they have, by resort to splitting and projection, divorced themselves from their passionate affects.

In analysis I believe that it is important to follow and interpret the development of these defensive movements within the transference. This may be done by considering the affective impact of the patient upon the analyst in order to discern those elements which are countertransferential and informative of repression or the projective identificatory activity of the patient. In this way the 'missing' affects of love and hate may be recovered within the transference, which at least carries with it the possibility of reintegration in place of splitting and violent projective identification. Failure to do so is likely to lead to an acting out, by the analyst, of the identificatory aspects of the projective identification, and in my experience there is considerable emotional pressure to do this.

Note

1 It is beyond the scope of this chapter to address the issue of the onset of the Oedipus complex. I do not wish to disagree with Klein's contention that the Oedipal elements will be present early in the infant's life, indeed pre-natally, and may be considered to be archetypal or as innate unconscious fantasy. For ease, however, I will use the terms 'pre-Oedipal' and 'Oedipal' to distinguish between mental phenomena related to oral, anal and genital foci for mental functioning, on the one hand, and the procreative relationship between the parents upon the other.

References

Bion, W.R. (1977) *Two Papers: The Grid and the Caesura*, London: Karnac Books.

Bion, W.R. (1987) 'Attacks on Linking', in *Second Thoughts*, London: Karnac Books.

Bion, W.R. (1991) *Cogitations*, London: Karnac Books.

Fordham, M. (1985) 'Abandonment in Infancy', *Chiron* 2(1).

Fordham, M. (1996) 'Defences of the Self', in *Analyst–Patient Interaction*, London: Routledge.

Freud, A. (1966) *The Ego and the Mechanisms of Defence*, London: Hogarth Press.

Freud, S. (1984) 'Repression', in *On Metapsychology, The Theory of Psychoanalysis*, London: Penguin Books.

Jung, C.G. (1927) 'Introduction to Wickes' "Analyse Der Kinderseele"', *Collected Works* 14.

Urban, E. (1992) 'The Primary Self and Related Concepts in Jung, Klein, and Isaacs', *Journal of Analytical Psychology* 37(4).

Winnicott, D.W. (1968) 'Ego distortion in terms of true and false self', in *The Maturational Processes and the Facilitating Environment*, London: Hogarth Press.

Index